# Augmented Reality

Edited by

Soha Maad

**Augmented Reality**

Edited by Soha Maad

**Republished by InTech**

Janeza Trdine 9, 51000 Rijeka, Croatia



**Technical Editor** Teodora Smiljanic

**Cover Designe**r Dino Smrekar

Additional hard copies can be obtained from orders@intechopen.com

Augmented Reality, Edited by Soha Maad
p. cm.
ISBN 978-953-7619-69-5

For EU product safety concerns:
IN TECH d.o.o., Prolaz Marije Krucifikse Kozulić 3, 51000 Rijeka, Croatia,
info@intechopen.com or visit our website at intechopen.com.

# Meet the editor

Dr. Soha Maad obtained her PhD from the University of Warwick in the UK in 2002. She has several years of experience in coordinating, managing, and providing expert advice for research projects in various institutions including Fraunhofer Institute of Media Communication in Germany, INRIA in France, Trinity College in Dublin, Royal College of Surgeons in Ireland, and University College Cork in Ireland. She was involved in various projects funded by the European Union, Science Foundation Ireland, National Center for Scientific Research in France, and Federal Ministry of Education and Research in Germany. She was the recipient of six Enterprise Ireland grants to coordinate and manage European Union projects and is expert member of various EU initiatives. She is also the founder and manager of IGROW EEIG (Integrated Technologies and Services for Sustainable Growth European Economic Interest Grouping) in Ireland.

# Preface

## The Horizon of Virtual and Augmented Reality: The Reality of the Global Digital Age

Virtual Reality (VR) and Augmented Reality (AR) tools and techniques supply virtual environments that have key characteristics in common with our physical environment. Viewing and interacting with 3D objects is closer to reality than abstract mathematical and 2D approaches. Augmented Reality (AR) technology, a more expansive form of VR is emerging as a cutting-edge technology that integrates images of virtual objects into a real world. In that respect Virtual and Augmented reality can potentially serve two objectives: reflecting realism through a closer correspondence with real experience, and extending the power of computer-based technology to better reflect abstract experience

With the growing amount of digital data that can be stored and accessed there is a rising need to harness this data and transform it into an engine capable of developing our view and perception of the world and of boosting the economic activity across domain verticals. Graphs, pie charts and spreadsheet are not anymore the unique medium to convey the world. Advanced interactive patterns of visualization and representations are emerging as a viable alternative with the latest advances in emerging technologies such as AR and VR. The potential and rewards are tremendous:

Social networking and blogging tools such as Facebook, Flickr, Twitter, etc., are creating a wealth of digital data that can be used to create a new culture, the global digital culture. The latter needs to be conveyed using novel approaches that go beyond simple conventional visualization techniques. AR and VR technologies can be leveraged to depict a new reality the "Reality of the Digital Age".

Medical data records are growing alongside a rising need for personalized healthcare. Preventive healthcare, a key initiative for a healthier global society, needs to be promoted using advanced personalized techniques harnessing converged ICT and media and deploying breakthrough advances in AR and VR.

Converged ICT and Media are evolving at a rapid pace and the challenge is to maximize the benefit from deployment and to increase uptake. This opens the door for new advanced computational activities that were previously difficult to realize.

Governance, social cohesion, entrepreneurship, public and private partnership, transparency of government activity and citizen engagement in the policy making process are continuously revolutionized by new means and techniques to store, access, transmit, and represent government, legal, and citizen profile data. This is fostered by new trends in the use of AR and VR technologies.

The urgent economic problem, linked to the financial crisis, challenges current research and technological development. The scale of the fiscal crisis that undermined the credibility of the financial system motivates the consideration of global financial state visibility as a key global challenge that validates research and technological development activities to support the engineering dynamics of automatically adaptable software services along the global financial supply chain. AR and VR technologies promise a great potential in accelerating the shift from mediating the financial state using reports or static models to mediating the financial state using advanced visualization and interaction techniques. This potential could be extrapolated to convey the state of vital economic activities across domain verticals, hence a greater ability to counteract devastating events and crises.

Last but not least, traditional uses of AR and VR in assembly and design, pilot applications of the technology, can be a model to be followed in exploiting the potential of AR and VR in a wealth of other application domains.

Despite the potential and promises of AR and VR technologies, major challenges are still posed: the maturity of the technology, the choice of the medium of delivery, and the supply and demand for this technology.

This book tells a story of a great potential, a continued strength, and penetration of AR and VR technologies in various application domains. It also addresses challenges facing the development of the technology. The chapters of this book are classified under three categories. ***The first category*** considers novel approaches for the development AR and VR technologies. This spans chapters 1, 2, and 3. ***The second category*** considers the penetration of AR and VR technologies in various application domains including healthcare, medicine, assembly, entertainment, etc. This spans chapters 4 and 5 covering the penetration of AR and VR technologies in medical and healthcare applications; chapters 6, 7, 8, and 9 covering the penetration of AR and VR technologies in assembly and industrial applications; and chapters 10 and 11 covering the penetration of AR and VR technologies in entertainment and service oriented applications. ***The third category*** considers the horizon of emerging new potential applications of AR and VR technologies. This spans chapters 12 and 13 covering the potential support of AR and VR technologies for social application domains and activities: finance and social collaboration are considered as typical emerging application models.

The book is targeted at researchers and practitioners in the field of AR and VR and the deployment of the technology in various novel applications. Researchers will find some of the latest thinking in the domain and many examples of the state-of-the-art in advanced visualization and its use across domain verticals. Both researchers who are just beginning in the field and researchers with experience in the domain should find topics of interest. Furthermore, practitioners will find the theory, new techniques, and standards that can increase the uptake of AR and VR technologies and boost related industry supply and demand. Many chapters consider applications and case studies that provide useful information about challenges, pitfalls, and successful approaches in the practical use of AR and VR. The chapters were written in such a way that they are interesting and understandable for both groups. They assume some background knowledge of the domain, but no specialist knowledge is required. It is possible to read each chapter on its own.

The book can be also used as a reference to understand the various related technology challenges, identified by regional Research and Development authorities, within the various research framework programs. The latter are intended to create lead markets in Information and Communication Technologies and to enact regional development plans motivated by initiatives such as the Lisbon strategy and the i2010 initiative.

Many people contributed in different ways to the realization of this book. First of all, we would like to thank the authors. They have put in considerable effort in writing their chapters. We are very grateful to the reviewers and technical editors who contributed valuable efforts and dedicated time to improving the quality of the book. Furthermore, we would like to thank Vedran Kordic, Aleksandar Lazinica, and all members of the Editorial Colleqiums of IN-TECH for giving us the opportunity to start this book in the first place and their support in bringing the book to actual publication.

Editor

**Soha Maad**

*Financial Services Innovation Centre, University College Cork UCC, Cork, Ireland*

# Contents

# 1

# Coordinated and Multiple Data Views in Augmented Reality Environment

Bianchi Serique Meiguins, Aruanda Simões Gonçalves Meiguins, Leandro Hernadez Almeida, Rodrigo Augusto de Moraes Lourenço and Sergio Clayton Vianna Pinheiro
*Universidade Federal do Pará, Centro Universitário do Pará*
*Brazil*

## 1. Introduction

The advances in software and hardware technologies have enabled, in an increasing rate, electronic storage of great amounts of data in several formats and fields of knowledge, such as medicine, engineering, biology, financial market, and many others. A correct and fast analysis of these data is essential to guarantee the differential in competitive marketing or progress in investigative sciences.

Information visualization tools are one of the most used computational resources for a good and fast analysis of data and the associated relationships (Spence, 2001)(Chen, 1999). These tools provide users visual and interactive representations of the data (Card et al, 1999). Currently, the use of multiple views of the data is appreciated in information visualization, for it enables the creation of better-manageable visualizations of the data, i.e., less complex visualizations (Baldonado et al., 2005) (North & Shneiderman, 2000), and improves the perception of the user through diverse perspectives on the data.

It is important to remark that the great concern is the cognitive overload that the user may suffer when manipulating and analyzing the data by using multiple views. In order to reduce this problem, the user interactions that refer to data manipulation must be coordinated among all views, updating their visual representations coherently, improving the user's perception of the data and facilitating the discovery of nontrivial relationships.

The usage of multiple coordinate views brings some current challenges, such as: development of easy interaction mechanisms for coordination, configuration and organization of layouts among views. One of the objectives of the Augmented Reality (AR) as a research area is to provide more natural and intuitive interfaces for the interaction with computational systems (Bimber & Raskar, 2005) (Azuma, 2001).

Moreover, AR enriches the real environment with virtual information. This allows the user to use objects or to collaborate with other people in the real environment while he or she simultaneously visualizes and interacts with virtual information. Finally, AR provides much more natural and ample environments to organize the information that will be visualized when compared to desktop environments. Thus, AR presents alternatives of solutions for the current challenges on multiple coordinate views applied to information visualization. This chapter presents a prototype that implements coordinated multiple views in information visualization for augmented reality environments. The applied information visualization technique was the 3D scatter plot for each data view, and a modified version of ARToolKit (Kato, 2005) has been used for the visualization of the augmented environment. The prototype was developed based on recommendations for a good information visualization tool (Shneiderman, 1996)(Carr, 1999) and multiple coordinated views (Baldonado et al, 2005), with coordinated characteristics of views, configuration, dynamic filters, selection and details on demand. Finally, this paper presents initial usability tests results after the application of some tasks proposed by (Pillat et al. 2005).

## 2. Related work

This section presents some tools that apply multiple coordinated views or augmented reality to different fields in information visualization.

(Maple et al. 2004) uses multiple coordinated views in three-dimensional virtual environments to assist navigation and orientation in these environments.

(Slay et al. 2001) uses augmented reality with the main objective of visualizing a graph information technique. The interface for configuration and generation of view is bidimensional.

(Meiguins et al. 2006) developed a prototype in augmented reality for visualization and interaction of data by using the 3D scatter plot technique.

## 3. Multiple views in information visualization

### 3.1 Information visualization (IV)

Information visualization is an area that studies transformation of abstract data into images that can be visualized and easily understood by human beings (Spence, 2001)(Chen, 1999). Information visualization tools are computational tools that implement data interaction and presentation mechanisms. The tools must offer the user a fast and easy manipulation and visual reorganization of the multidimensional data to assist tasks such as data query or analysis.

According to Carr's work (Carr, 1999), a good visualization tool should present characteristics according to possible user tasks. Among them, some can be remarked: general view, zoom, filter and details on demand.

Systems of multiple views use two or more distinct views to assist the investigation process of a single conceptual entity (Baldonado & Kuchinsky, 2000).

In order to develop information visualization systems with multiple coordinated views, the most frequent recommendations are (Baldonado & Kuchinsky, 2000):

- When there is a diversity of attributes, models, user profiles, abstraction levels;
- When the different views point out correlations or disparities;
- When there is a need to reduce the complexity of the data set, by using simpler multiple views;
- Use multiple views minimally; justify the use of multiple views in relation to the cost for the user and visualization space.

(Pillat et al. 2005) stands out the main possibilities of coordination in multiple views:

- Selection: data items selected in a view are pointed out in other views;
- Filter: to reduce dataset for analysis in all views;
- Color, Transparency and Size: visual characteristics to represent the variation of values of attributes in all views;

- Sort: values of an attribute define the order of the visual representations of the data;
- Label: it determines what content the labels will present for each data item of the views;
- Manipulation of Attributes: it allows the user to add/remove attributes off the data views.

## 4. Augmented reality

Augmented reality is a system that supplements the real world with computer-generated virtual objects, which seem to coexist in the same space and present the following properties (Bimber, 2005)(Azuma et al., 2001):

- It combines real and virtual objects in real environment;
- It executes interactively in real time;
- It lines up real and virtual objects;
- It is applied to all senses of the user.

The augmented environment was based on the ARToolKit library (http://jerry.c-lab.de/jartoolkit), developed by the HIT Lab in C Language and distributed as open source, which allows the programmers to develop applications in AR (Kato et al., 2005).

ARToolKit uses computational view techniques for identification of predefined symbols inserted in the real scene. Once a symbol or a marker is identified, the virtual object is inserted in the real scene in the same position of the identified object. The final scene presented to the user is the visual combination of the real world with virtual objects.

The construction of the objects that are combined with the real world can be made through applications in OpenGL and VRML. There is also an ARToolKit version written in Java (JARToolKit) (Kato et al., 2005) with which JAVA3D can be used (Walsh & Gehringer, 2002).

## 5. Prototype

The prototype uses augmented reality to implement multiple views of 3D scatter plot technique in a coordinated way. The main points of its conception were:

- An environment of easy interaction;
- Work with several database types;
- Implement the 3D scatter plot technique;
- Develop mechanisms of dynamic filters in the augmented environment;
- Develop coordination mechanisms among data views, such as: selection, filters, details on demand;
- Develop auxiliary graphics, such as pie and bar, also coordinated with data views;
- Conception of software architecture that facilitates the inclusion of new information visualization techniques.

### 5.1 Architecture

ARToolKit has three basic modules: Scene Capturer, Augmented Reality (AR) and Augmented Image Generator (Kato et al., 2005). The Scene Capturer module is a set of video routines that captures input frames sent by webcam or any other video device. The Augmented Reality module is responsible for identifying the markers in the scene, tracking the captured markers and associating virtual objects with them. Finally, the Augmented

Image Generator module is responsible for generating the augmented image (real scene and virtual objects), and is a set of graphical routines based on OpenGL and GLUT.
The modifications made in the ARToolKit in order to implement multiple coordinated views can be seen in Figure 1, and are concentrated in the AR module. The creation of several modules was taken into effect in order to help the maintainability, extensibility, efficiency and reutilization of the code (Figure 1).

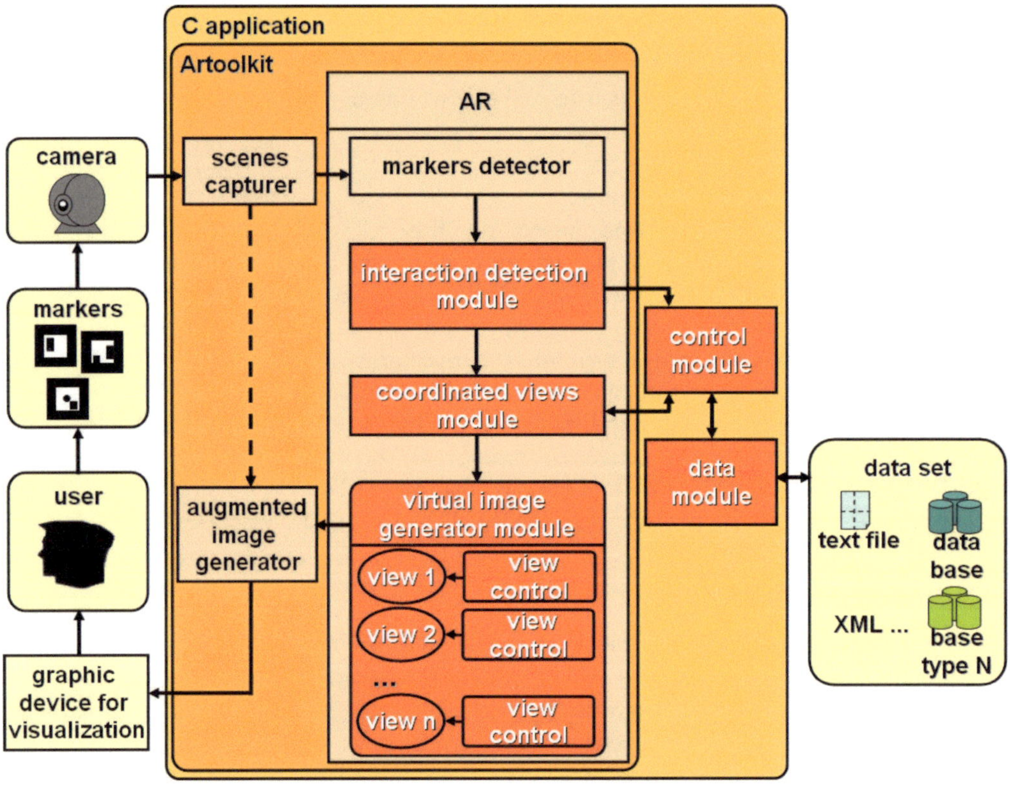


Fig. 1. Summary of the prototype architecture

A brief description of the implemented modules is presented below:

- Identification of Interaction Module identifies the type of interaction with markers performed by the user: insertion, occlusion or leaving the scene. It sends a message either to the control module in order to change the view data, or, when interaction is performed only visually and there is no modification in the visible data set, to the coordinated view module;
- Control Module is responsible for managing the communication between the coordinated view module and the data module, providing transparency when these module exchange messages;
- Data Module is responsible for data access in text files, XML or relational databases;
- Coordinated View Module is responsible for managing what each data view must present, and thus assure coordination among all views;

- Virtual Image Generator Module is responsible for rendering every data view or virtual object in the scene. Therefore, it does not take into consideration how data are stored or manipulated. This module's task is to represent a subset of data by using an information visualization technique.

### 5.2 Augmented interface

The augmented interface is formed by the 3D scatter plot view and other virtual objects, as well as the interaction controls based on markers and real objects. The prototype builds two data views by using the 3D scatter plot technique to represent the elements in a dataset. The main view configurations are axis X, Y and Z, 3D Shape, Color and Size. Figure 2 shows an example of the prototype during its execution, pointing out the simultaneous presence of real and virtual objects.

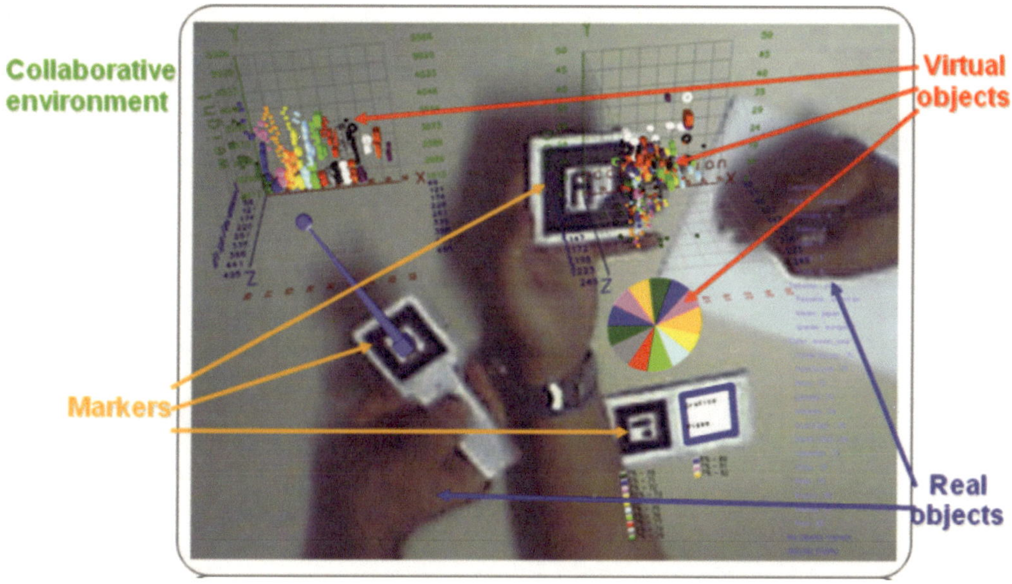


Fig. 2. Example of the prototype in executing mode

Most of the user interaction is directly performed by the occlusion of the markers. The occlusion-based interaction consists of blocking the capture of the marker's symbol by the video device. This may be performed with his or her own hands. It is possible to apply transformations based on translations, rotations and scale in data views or other virtual objects in the scene just by moving or interacting with the markers. The markers are grouped according to their functionality (Figure 3), and can be freely manipulated in the real environment, enabling an infinite array of layouts to visualize the analyzed dataset.

An important characteristic of the prototype is its ability to set a fixed position to any generated virtual object in the scene, as a 3D scatter plot, just by occluding the object's marker (Figure 4). The prototype stores the last register of the transformation matrix in order to place the virtual object in the fixed position in the scene. This is important because it avoids any unintentional interaction of the user with markers.

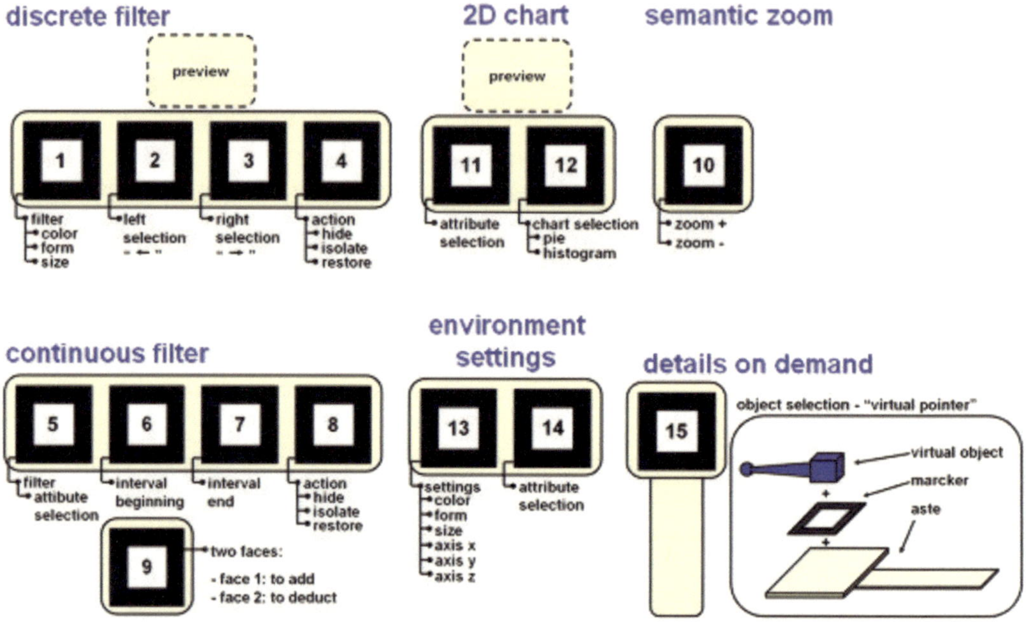


Fig. 3. Markers set according to functionality

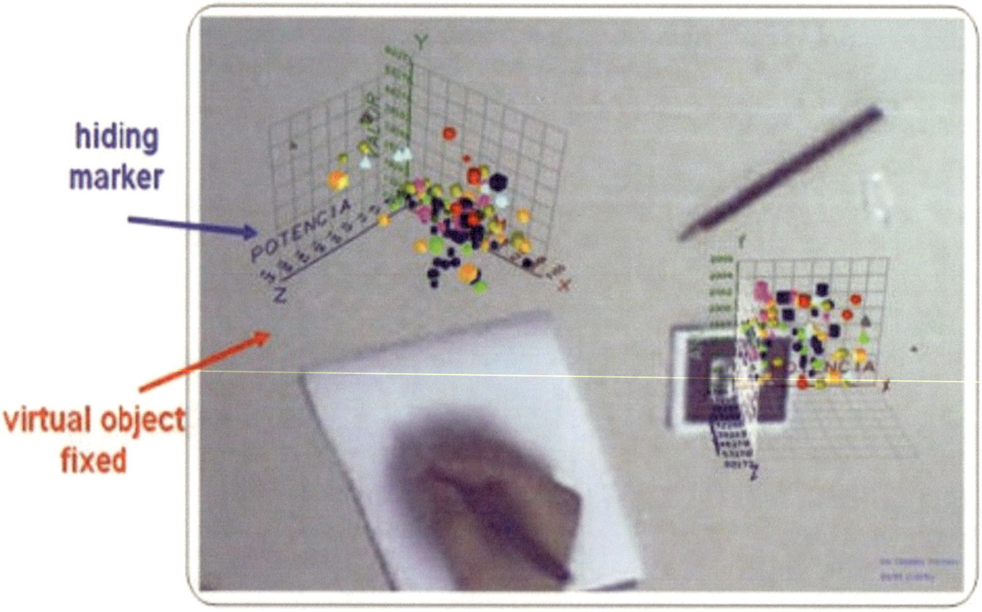


Fig. 4. Virtual object fixed in the scene

### 5.3 Coordinated views

Some of the coordinative characteristics of the prototype should be remarked:

- Data: It uses a single dataset for all views;

- Layout flexibility: the user may analyze or query data with individual or simultaneous views (Figure 4);
- Coordination: It is classified as static, i.e., the coordination between pairs of views is predefined. It may be either strongly coordinated, as color (Figure 2) - once defined, the same color is applied to all views, or loosely coordinated, as semantic zoom or Axis values, which can be used in any data view, but have to be manually configured for each view in the augmented interface.

The coordinated actions are:

- Strongly Coordinated Actions: filters, environment configuration for color, shape and size attributes, and for selection of objects. They affect directly all views, even if they are not present in the scene (unreachable by the video device);
- Loosely Coordinated Actions: axis configuration, semantic zoom (Figure 6) and navigation (translation and rotation). They only affect a view which is present in the scene

### 5.4 Filters

Concepts of dynamic queries have been applied (Shneiderman, 1994) for categorical and continuous values. This type of action allows the user to check databases without needing to use command lines, manipulating only graphic components of interface (Figure 5 and 6).

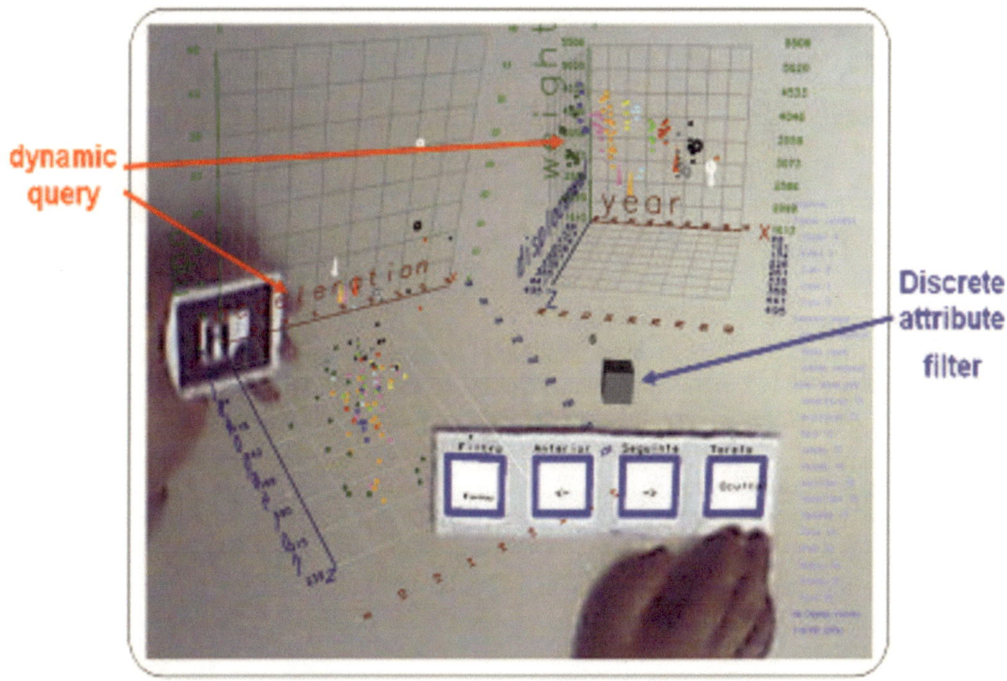


Fig. 5. Augmented representation of the categorical attribute filter

In the prototype, any filter can perform the following actions:

- Hiding: Take off the scene a determined item or data items which have a previously selected characteristic;
- Isolating: Leave only items which have a previously selected characteristic in the scene;
- Restoring: Undo the filtering processes previously performed on data items.

- The categorical attribute filters work on configurable characteristics of a data view, such as: color, shape and size. Figure 5 illustrates the filter control for categorical attributes.
- The continuous attribute filters specify ranges of values to isolate and hide data items from views (Figure6).

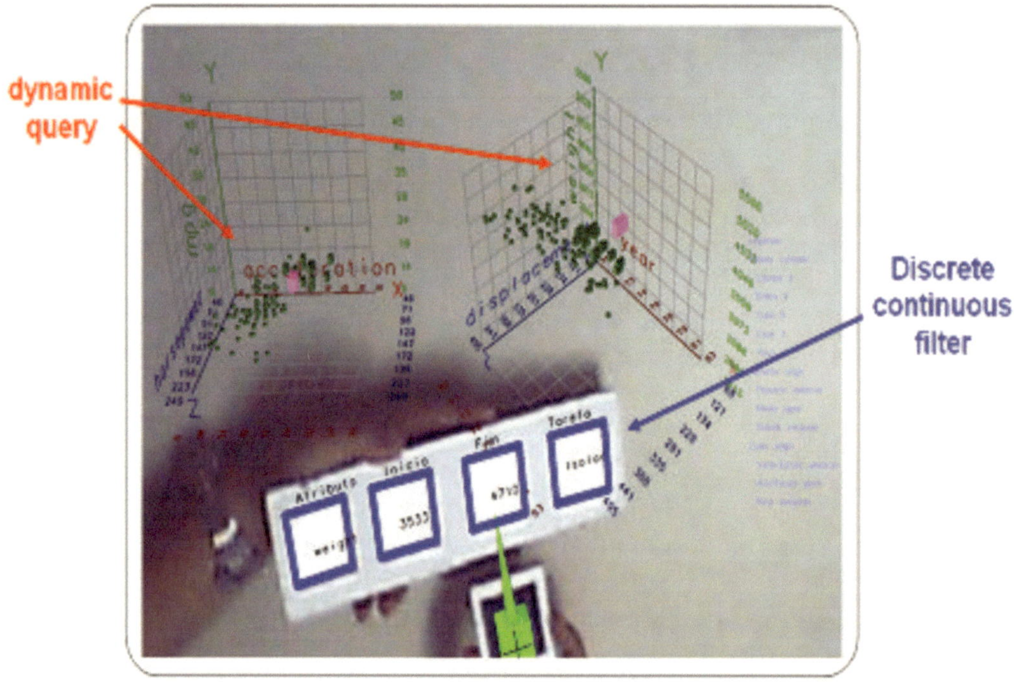


Fig. 6. Augmented representation of the continuous attribute filter.

### 5.5 Semantic zoom and auxiliary chart

Semantic Zoom allows the user to visualize the data space more precisely and with additional details as his or her perspective gets closer to the virtual objects (Figure 7). The zoom marker has two faces, one to zoom in and the other to zoom out.

### 5.6 Environment configuration

The prototype allows the user, though an environment configuration control, to freely change the attributes of X, Y and Z Axes and of Shape, Color and Size for each data view. Figure 8 shows a situation in which the user changes the color and shape configuration to another categorical attribute, and the changes are presented in the multiple coordinated views.

### 5.7 Details on demand and help

A resource called "Virtual Pointer" has been developed to select virtual objects and analyze their hidden information. The selected objects in one view are pointed out in the other view (Figure 9).
This item helps to detail the activities of each marker, in case there is a doubt about its functionality. Its use is simple: while the help marker is visible, all groups of markers present in the scene provide information related to its use mode.

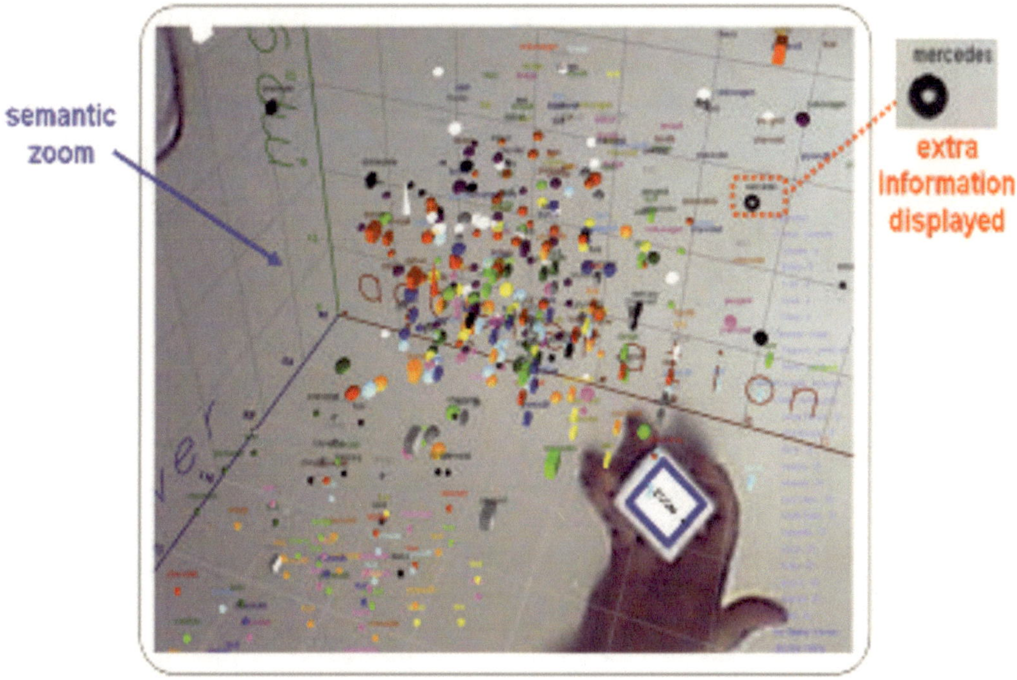


Fig. 7. Example of Semantic Zoom

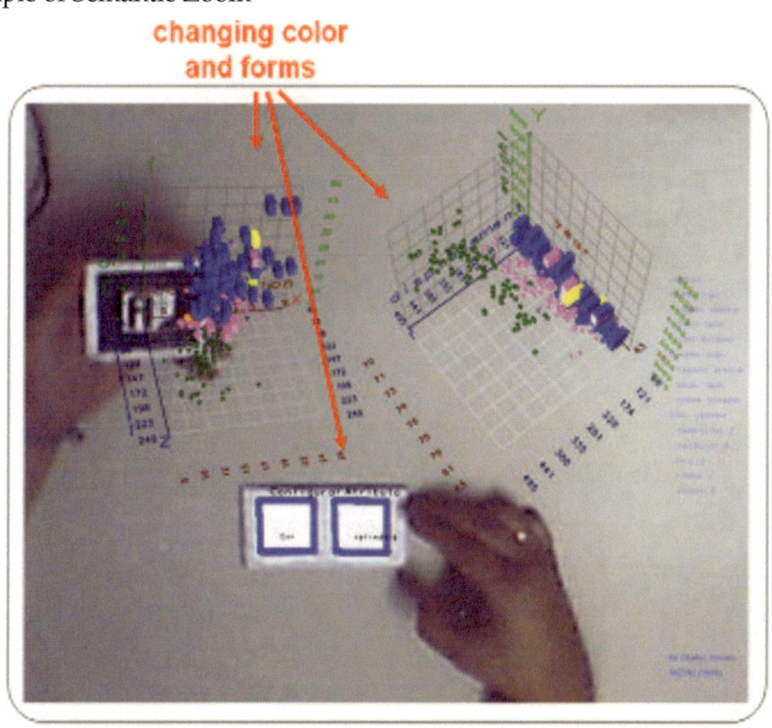


Fig. 8. Changing the color and shape attributes in views

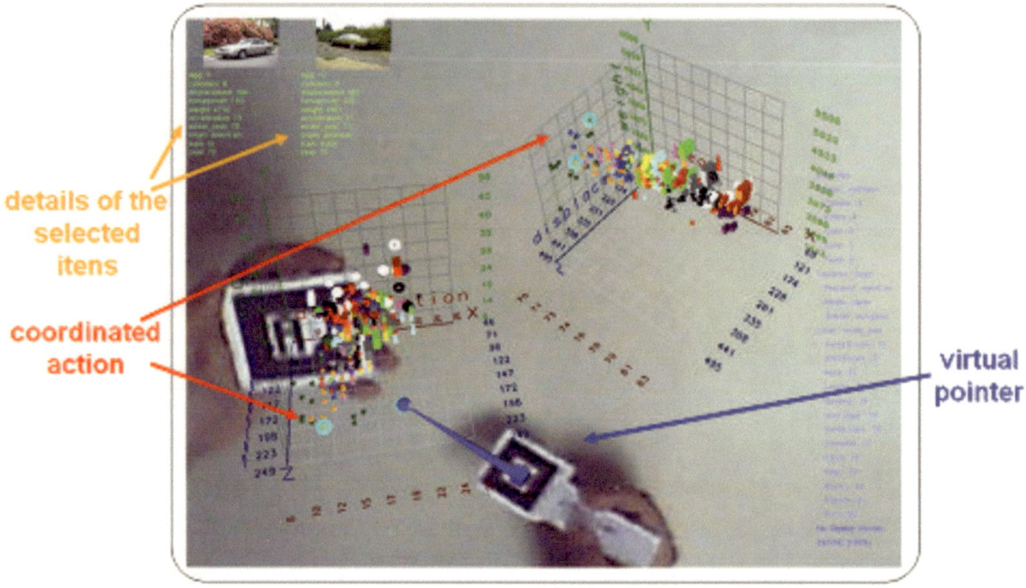


Fig. 9. Selection of items performed in a strongly coordinated way

The prototype presents auxiliary bidimensional pie and bar graphics that provide additional information on the visualized data (Figure 10).

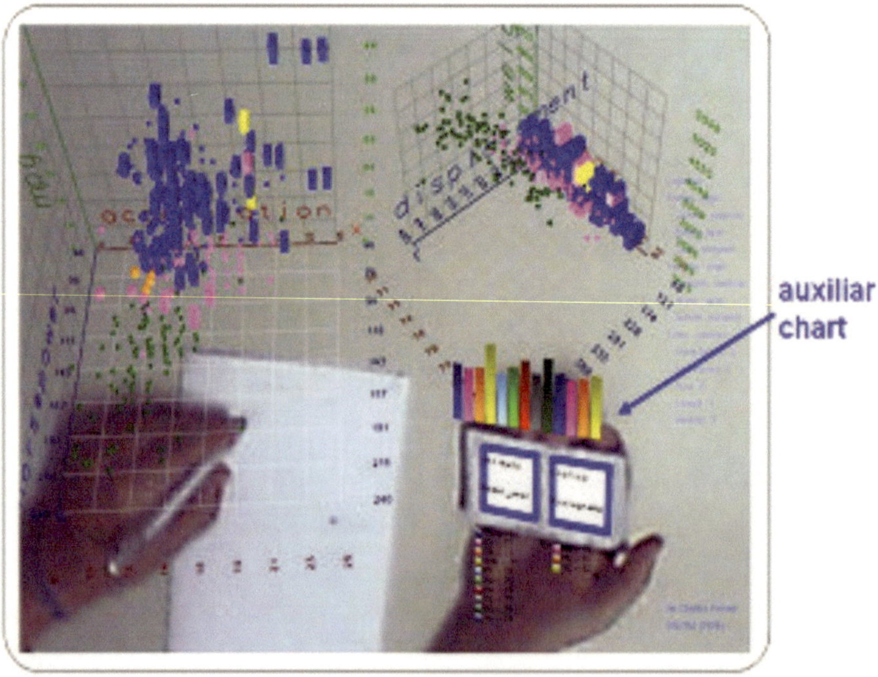


Fig. 10. Example of auxiliary charts (Pie and Bar)

## 6. Usability tests

Usability tests were performed to evaluate the use of information visualization techniques in an augmented reality environment with multiple coordinated views. The users were asked to perform a set of tasks previously defined by (Pillat et al. 2005) that demand different actions such as: view configuration, data correlation, and range specification, among others.

- Task 1: Are the 4-cylinder Japanese cars usually lighter than the 6-cylinder American cars?
- Answer 1: No.
- Task 2: Analyze the data and describe the main characteristics of the American cars;
- Answer 2: Acceleration is between 8 and 22.2, mainly between 11 and 19. Most of the cars have 8 cylinders. Weight is uniformly distributed. MPG values are also uniformly distributed. Horsepower is concentrated between 88 and 155.
- Task 3: What is the tendency of European cars over the years?
- Answer 3: Acceleration between 12.2 and 24.8, and light weight. The horsepower kept stable until 1977 when it rose just to reduce again the next year. There are few 5 or 6-cylinder cars but most of them are 4-cylinder. MPG was between 10 and 31 from 1970 to 1976 and considerably rose since them.

The used dataset contains information about American, Japanese and European cars from 1970 to 1982. (Pillat et al. 2005) There are 8 attributes: 3 categorical and 5 continuous.

After a 20-minute training in augmented environment and interactive markers, task one was used as a practical example in order to build confidence and improve the users skills. The comparative tests were restricted to tasks 2 and 3 that are similar but with increasing level of difficulty. The tests involved 5 users, all 21-32 male with good computer skills. None of the users had previously interacted with augmented reality environments with markers. All users had previous knowledge on information visualization techniques.

Each item of user answers was analyzed. For example, for task 2 what was the answer to attribute1, attribute2, and so on. The accuracy rate is based on the total number of correct answers to each item of each task. Figure 11 and Figure 12 present the results in terms of accuracy rate and task execution time, respectively.

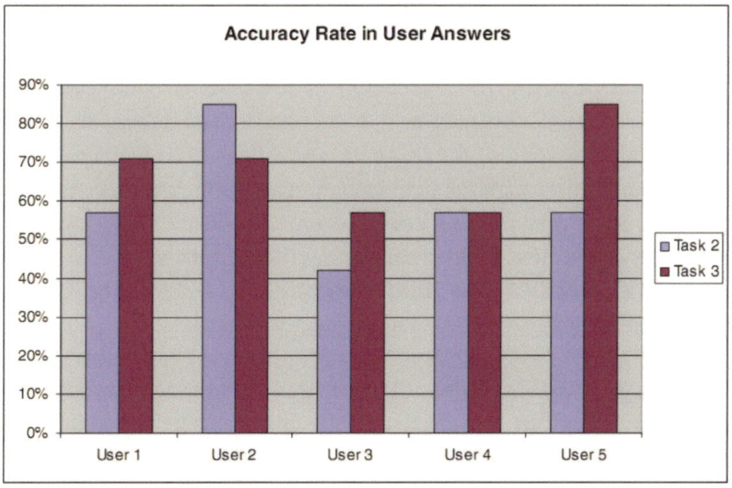


Fig. 11. Accuracy rate in user answers

The accuracy rate plot indicates that 80% of the users had a better or similar accuracy for task 3 that is considered complex (Pillat et al. 2005). All the users spent less time performing task 3 than task 2. So even with a reduced number of tests it is possible to infer that once the user has experience and confidence in the environment he tends to achieve precise and prompt results.

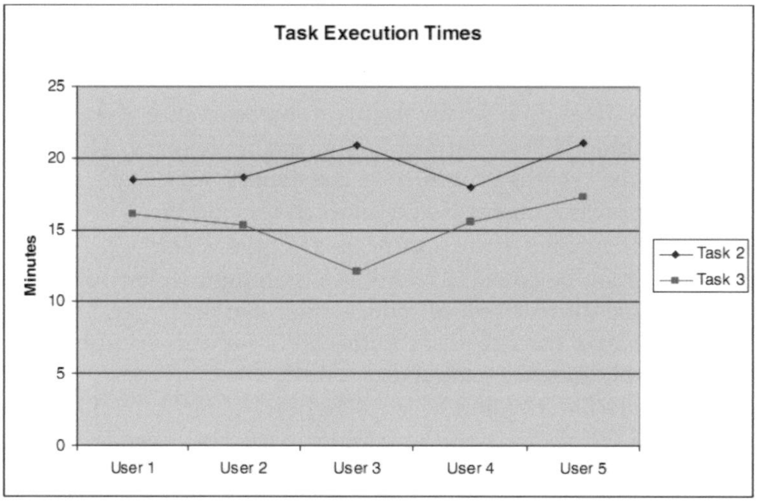


Fig. 12. Task Execution Times

## 7. Final remarks

This chapter presented a prototype that implements multiple coordinate views in augmented reality environments. The main supported views are based on the 3D scatter plot technique. The augmented interface provides coordinated actions control among views, such as dynamic filters for continuous and categorical attributes; details on demand (object selection); environment configuration; auxiliary pie and bar graphics; semantic zoom; and free navigation.

Initial usability tests were performed in order to evaluate the proposed approach to information visualization. During the execution of the tests it was possible to observe the efficient use of the developed controls and the coordinated views to solve the assigned tasks. Usability tests also revealed the high adaptability of the users to the augmented environment. Only one user had major problems performing task one, taking 11 minutes to adapt to the environment and to the marker-based interaction. Other pointed out difficulties were related to the excessive use of markers and video capture or identification problems that made the interface unstable. The following remarks were made by the users on the interview following the tests.

- A first experience in AR environments: users highlighted the main advantages, such as the easy adaptation and learning, the more immersive, free and sometimes fun environment, the freedom to move and manipulate virtual and real objects simultaneously and a larger workspace. As disadvantages the users pointed out the lack of precision of some movements because of marker detection failures; the excessive need to repeat interactions; the excessive use of markers.

- Use of information visualization techniques in AR: the users pointed out the freedom to manipulate data views and the free workspace to work with virtual and real objects, and the collaborative aspect as the main advantages. The main disadvantage was the need for more appropriate equipment like augmented reality glasses that would, according to the users, significantly improve precision and performance.
- The use of a multiple views coordinated environment in AR: the configuration of graphics axis on views and the different information perspectives allowed better and faster data comparisons and analysis.

## 8. References


Azuma, R.; Baillot, Y.; Behringer, R.; Feiner, S.; Julier, S. & Macintyre, B. (2001). Recent advances in augmented reality. *Computer Graphics and Applications*.Vol6, n. 6, November/December, p.34-47.

Baldonado, M. & Kuchinsky, A. (2000). Guidelines for Using Multiple Views in Information Visualization, *Proceedings of AVI 2000*, Palermo, Italy. p. 110-119.

Bimber, O. and Raskar, R. *Spatial Augmented Reality – Merging Real and Virtual Worlds*. A. K. Peters Ltd. Wellesley, Massachusetts 2005.

Card, S., Mackinlay, J., and Shneiderman, B. *Readings in Information Visualization Using Vision to Think*. Morgan Kaufmann. 1999.

Carr, D. (1999). A Guidelines for Designing Information Visualization Applications. *Proceedings of ECUE'99*. Estocolmo, Sweden. December.

Chen, C. & Cserwinski, M. Empirical Evaluation of Information Visualization: An introduction, *Int'l J. Human-Computer Studies*, vol.53 2000. p 631-635.

Chen, C. *Information Visualization and Virtual Environments*. Londres: Springer, 1999. 223 p.

Kato, H.; Billinghurst, M. & Poupyrev, I. (2005) *ARToolKit Manual version 2.33*. url http://www.hitl.washinton.edu/research/shared_space. Access in 11/15/2005

Maple, C.; Manton, R. & Jacobs, H. (2004). The Use of Multiple Co-ordinated Views in Three-dimensional Virtual Environments. *Proceedings of IV04 Information Visualization 2004*. p. 778-784. London United Kingdon.

Meiguins, B.; Carmo, R.; Gonçalves, A.; Godinho, P. & Garcia, M. (2006). Using Augmented Reality for Multidimensional Data Visualization. *Proceedings of IV06 Information Visualization 2006*. p. 529-534. London United Kingdom.

North, C. and Sheneiderman, B. Snap-Together Visualization: A User Interface for Coordinating Visualizations via Relational Schemata. *Proceedings of Advanced visual interfaces International Working Conference* May, 2000. Palermo, Italy.p23-26.

Pillat, R.; Valiati, E. & Freitas, C. (2005). Experimental Study on Evaluation of Multidimensional Information Visualization Techniques. *Proceedings of CLIHC'05*, 2005, Cuernavaca - Mexico. p. 20 - 30.

Shneiderman, B. Dynamic queries for visual information seeking. IEEE Software, vol. 11, n. 6, Novembro, 1994. p.70-77.

Shneiderman, B. The eyes have it: a task by data type taxonomy for information visualizations. Procedings of IEEE Visual Language, 1996. p.336-343.

Slay, H.; Philips, M.; Vernik, R. & Thomas, B. (2001). Interaction Modes for Augmented Reality Visualization. *Proceedings of Australian Symposium on Information Visualisation*, Sydney.

Spence, R. *Information Visualization*. Addison-Wesley. 2001.

Walsh, A. & E., Gehringer, D. (2002). *Java 3D API Jump -Start*. Prentice Hall PTR.

2

# Probeless Illumination Estimation for Outdoor Augmented Reality

Madsen and Lal
*Aalborg University*
*Denmark*

## 1. Introduction

Without doubt Augmented Reality (AR) has the potential to become a truely widespread technology. The mere concept of AR is immensely fascinating for a tremendous range of application areas, from surgery, over equipment maintenance, to more entertaining and educational applications. What drives most of the research in AR is the vision that one day we will be able to create real-time, interactive visual illusions as convincingly as we have become accostumed to seing in large Hollywood productions.

Unfortunately, there are some technical challenges in reaching this goal. Generally, there are three major challenges associated with AR: 1) camera tracking (matching position and orientation of the camera to the coordinate system of the scene), 2) handling occlusions (having sufficient 3D information of the real scene to handle occlusion between real and virtual geometry), and 3) illumination consistency (having sufficient knowledge of the real scene illumination to be able to render virtual objects with scene consistent illumination, including shadows). This chapter addresses the latter of these challenges.

Figure 1 shows how important it is to handle the dynamically changing illumination in outdoor scenarios when aiming at visually credible augmented reality (Jensen, Andersen, & Madsen, 2006). As will become apparent in the review of related work in section 2 the bulk of the work in illumination consistency for AR is based on measuring the illumination using some sort of known illumination calibration object, a probe. Obviously, for operational AR in outdoor scenes, with rapidly changing illumination, the requirement that the illumination be *captured/measured* is prohibitive.

Fig. 1. Three frames from a 3 hour long sequence showing virtual sculpture rendered into scene with consistent illumination.

This chapter describes a technique we have developed which allows for illumination estimation *directly* from the images with no requirement of illumination calibration objects in the scene prior to image acquisition. This enables the approach to function adaptively in the sense that it can automatically adapt to the changing illumination conditions.
The work presented here is based on images of outdoor scenes in daylight conditions captured with a commercially available stereo camera (a Bumblebee XB3 camera from PointGrey Research, Inc.) providing dense 3D and color information of the scene. The AR renderings we show are rendered with non-realtime rendering software, but in section 8 we discuss how the technique can be implemented to operate in real-time. At present we are in fact making such an implementation.

## 2. Overview of related work

The classical approach to achieving illumination consistency for AR is to employ a light probe image, also called an environment map. A light probe is an omni-directional image of the scene, acquired at the location where a virtual object is to be inserted. The light probe image must be acquired in High Dynamic Range (HDR) to capture illumination sources without pixel saturation. This approach was pioneered in (Debevec, 1998) and has later been employed as the basic illumination technique in a multitude of real-time AR research (Barsi et al., 2005); (Franke & Jung, 2008); (Havran et al., 2005); (Kanbara & Yokoya, 2004); (Madsen & Laursen, 2007).
While the approach of using a captured HDR environment map of the scene allows for really realistic illumination interaction between real and virtual scene elements, it is of course totally impractical for an adaptive real-time system to require such environment maps. They must be captured where an augmentation is to be made, and the basic idea cannot be used for scenes with dynamically changing illumination.
Another family of research into AR illumination is centered around manually creating detailed 3D model of the real scene, including the sizes and positions of the light sources, combined with one or more images of the scene. Using inverse rendering techniques virtual objects can then be rendered into views of the scene with consistent illumination. Examples of work in this category include (Boivin & Gagalowitcz, 2001); (Drettakis et al., 1997); (Yu et al., 1999); (Loscos et al., 2000). The amount of manual 3D modelling required by these techniques, combined with the need for multiple views of the scene (for some of the methods), make them unrealistic for general purpose real-time illumination adaptive AR systems.
In addition to the work mentioned above there is a large body of research into using image information directly to estimate the real scene illumination conditions. Some work utilizes the shadows cast by a *known* object to compute the illumination (Sato, Sato, & Ikeuchi, CVPR 1999, 1999); (Sato, Sato, & Ikeuchi, 2001); (Kim & Hong, 2005). The disadvantage with these techniques is that it is necesary to place a known object, e.g., a cube, in the scene, and the techniques are based on an assumption that the known objects casts shadows on some known geometry in the scene, typically a planar surface.
Other work is based on estimating the illumination using shading information from images of glossy spheres in the scene (Hara et al., 2005); (Zhou & Kambhamettu, 2008). Some work combine the information from both shadows and from shading, (Wang & Samaras, 2003). Again, these techniques are impractical in the fact that they require an object in the scene for which perfect geometric information is available.

The final category of related work we mention is quite related to the research presented in this paper in the sense that it also addresses outdoor daylight scenarios. Under the assumption that two different views of a static outdoor daylight scene are available, and assuming that there are shadows from vertical structures in the scene, the camera can be calibrated to the scene and the direction vector to the sun can be estimated, (Cao & Foroosh, 2007); (Cao & Shah, 2005). In that work manual identification of essential object and shadow points is required. Shadows from virtual objects onto real scene surfaces are generated using information extracted from semi-manually detected real shadows, under the assumption that the shadows fall on uniformly colored surfaces.

As seen from the above overview of related work there is a substantial body of research into the problem of achieving illumination consistency in AR. Nevertheless, all of the presented work has some inherent drawbacks in terms of being suitable for an AR system which is to automatically adapt to changing illumination conditions. As described these drawback are things such as a requirement for known objects in the scene, the need to acquire an omni-directional HDR image the scene at the location of a virtual object, or the need for manual 3D scene modelling and/or identification of essential elements in the images, and in most cases an assumption that the scene is static.

In this chapter we present our proposed approach to dealing with these problems. The title of the chapter refers to the fact that our technique does not require placing known probes or calibration objects in the scene. The technique presented here is based on 3D scene information acquired automatically by a commercially available stereo camera, combined with illumination information extracted automatically and directly from shadow information in the input image stream, thus completely obliviating the need for manual input. The approach is suitable for real-time operation, and is based on a sound theoretical model of the problem domain.

## 3. Overview of approach

The input is a video stream of color images of a dynamic outdoor daylight scene. In addition to the color images we have partial 3D information of the scene in the form of a stream of depth maps generated by a stereo camera (Bumblebee XB3 from PointGrey Research, Inc.). A color image and its corresponding 3D scene data is shown in Figure 2.

Fig. 2. Left: color image from video sequence. Right: corresponding 3D scene model.

Our approach is essentially a three-step process. In the first step the combined color and depth data stream is monitored continuously and shadows from dynamic objects are detected. Such dynamic objects can be people walking by, cars driving by, or shadows from tree leaves moving in the wind. In the second step the color information from detected shadows, combined with the depth information from the scene, are combined in an estimation of the real scene illumination. In essence the color and intensity of the sky are estimated, as are the color and intensity of the sun. In more rigorous radiometric terms we estimate the radiances (in three color channels) of the sky and the sun. In the third step, the estimated illumination information, plus the color image and the depth data, are used to render virtual objects into the video sequence.

Fig. 3. Top left: input image containing walking person. Top right: detected dynamic shadow. Bottom: image augmented with virtual objects consistently shaded and casting shadows.

The position of (direction vector to) the sun is computed from additional input information. Given knowledge of the date, the time, the location on Earth (from GPS), the direction of North (from a compass) and the inclination of the camera (from an inertial sensor) the direction vector to the sun can be computed using standard expressions, (Madsen & Nielsen, 2008). Using this extra information is not considered a limitation of the approach as more and more consumer cameras already have such sensors built-in.

## 4. Theoretical framework

The work presented in this chapter builds upon research presented in (Madsen et al., 2009) and (Madsen & Nielsen, 2008). The novelty in this chapter lies in demonstrating how these two previously published techniques can work together to achieve adaptive illumination for AR. The interested reader is referred to these papers for a little more depth on the theoretical framework, but a crucial element in both the shadow detection and the illumination estimation steps outlined in section 3 is a fundamental assumption that the real scene is dominated by diffuse surfaces (brick, asphalt, concrete, etc.). The reflected radiance from a diffuse surface is proportional to the incident irradiance. When taking an image of such a surface the pixel value given by the camera is proportional to the outgoing radiance from the surface at that location. The constant of proportionality depends on things such as lens geometry, shutter time, lens aperture, white balancing, camera ISO setting, etc. In practice the constant of proportionality is unknown and can only be determined through complex radiometric calibration of the camera. Our work is based on relative image measurement where this constant of proportionality cancels out and is immaterial, i.e. can remain unknown.

The pixel value, $P$, corresponding to a point on a diffuse surface can be formulated as:

$$P = c \cdot \rho \cdot E_i \cdot \frac{1}{\pi}$$

Here $c$ is the aforementioned constant of proportionality, $\rho$ is the diffuse albedo of the surface point, and $E_i$ is the incident irradiance at the surface point. All of these variables are color channel dependent, but we just present the expression here as a general cholor channel independent expression.

Given the assumption of an outdoor, daylight scenario, the incident irradiance is the sum of the flux density received from the sky and from the sun. In other words:

$$E_i = E_{sky} + E_{sun}$$

The two-part irradiance, consisting of the irradiance from the sky and from the sun, respectively, is central to our approach. This can be described as follows. Assuming for now that we actually can detect dynamic shadows, i.e. detect when a pixel goes from being illuminated by both the sky and the sun to being illumination only by the sky, then we could divide the pixel values corresponding to the two pixel conditions (shadow, not shadow):

$$\frac{P_{shadow}}{P_{sun}} = \frac{c \cdot \rho \cdot E_{sky}}{c \cdot \rho \cdot (E_{sky} + E_{sun})} = \frac{E_{sky}}{(E_{sky} + E_{sun})}$$

That is, the ratio of pixel value in shadow over the pixel value in sun is indepedent on camera constants and surface albedo, and only depends on the shadow to sun irradiance ratios. Thus the detected dynamic shadows contain essential illumination information that can be used to compute the radiances of the sky and the sun, respectively.

For a given surface point a number of factors determine exactly what amount of irradiance is received from the sky and the sun, respectively. These factors relate to the scene geometry, i.e. the angle between the surface point normal and the direction vector to the sun, and the amount of sky dome visible from the surface point (parts of the sky dome are occluded by scene geometry such as walls). For the sun contribution these elements can be formulated as follows:

$$E_{sun} = (\vec{n} \cdot \vec{s}) \cdot E_{sun}^{\uparrow}$$

The normal vector of the surface is $\vec{n}$, the direction vector to the sun is $\vec{s}$, and $E_{sun}^{\uparrow}$ is the irradiance received from the sun by surface perpendicular to the direction vector to the sun (surface normal pointing straight into the sun). The direction vector to the sun is computed based on GPS and date/time information, as described above, and the normal information per surface point comes from the depth data.
For the sky contribution the geometric factors can be formulated as:

$$E_{sky} = V_{sky} \cdot E_{sky}^{\uparrow}$$

where $E_{sky}^{\uparrow}$ is the irradiance from the sky by a surface point which „can see" the whole sky dome, and $V_{sky}$ is the fraction (range 0 to 1) of the sky dome a given surface point can see (ambient occlusion term). The ambient occlusion term can be computed per surface point from the depth data of the scene.
Our task thus is to estimate the two terms, $E_{sky}^{\uparrow}$ and $E_{sun}^{\uparrow}$, using the detected dynamic shadows, combined with per surface point geometrical information from the depth data. Given that we can estimate these two irradiance contributions we have all the information required to render virtual objects into the scene with proper shadows and shading.

## 5. Detection of shadows

The first step in our approach is to detect pixels that represent shadows cast by objects that are moving in the scene. Dynamic shadow detection based on a combination of color and depth information is presented in detail in (Madsen, Moeslund, Pal, & Balasubramanian, 2009). In this section we give an overview of the technique. First we give a more precise description of the equipment and setup used for the experimental results.

### 5.1 Equipment and setup

We are aiming a constructing a real-time AR setup with a computer monitor mounted on a pole so that a user can rotate the monitor around a vertical and a horizontal axis, essentially being able to aim the monitor in all direction, see Figure 4.

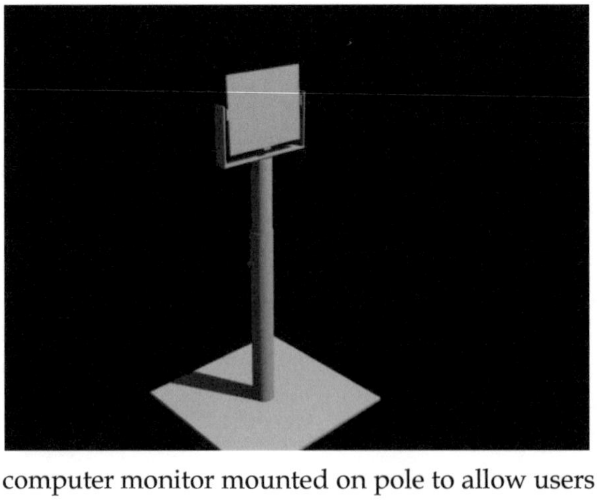

Fig. 4. 3D model of a computer monitor mounted on pole to allow users to aim monitor in various directions.

Behind the monitor a camera will be placed, and the monitor will show the video image from that camera, including augmented virtual objects. For the experiments presented in this chapter we use a static camera.

As described the camera is a commercially available stereo camera, the Bumblebee XB3 from PointGrey Research. This camera provides rectified color images, and the accompanying API enables generation of dense disparity maps, which can be converted into metric depth maps. On an Intel Core Duo 2 2.3 GHz maching with 2 Gbyte memory, 640x480 disparity maps can be generated at 10 frames per second. We operate the disparity generation process in a mode which provides sub-pixel disparities encoded in 16 bit resolution to have as high as possible depth precision. The color images are also in 640x480 pixel resolution. For all images shown in this chapter we have used to rightmost of the two color images supplied by the stereo camera.

We have used Google Maps to look up the earth latitude and longitude of the positions where we have placed the camera for the reported test sequences. The camera is calibrated to a scene based coordinate system using a standard camera calibration process involving a checkerboard pattern. This pattern is visible in the images shown in Figure 2. We orient the pattern such that one of the axes is pointing North (done with a compas).

In the future when we place the stereo camera on the pan-tilt rig shown in Figure 4, we will use angle encoders to determine the pose (viewing direction) of the camera in real-time, and then the orientation only has to be initialized to level and North in an initialization phase, i.e. leveling the camera and pointing it due North and pressing a key on the computer. From then on the system will know the camera pose with very high precision, similar to what we did in (Madsen & Laursen, 2007) for a system which was not adpative to scene illumination, and which used a pre-recorded environment map for real-time shading.

### 5.2 Detection of shadow candidate regions

We employ a conceptually simple approach to detecting pixels that are candidates for representing a point that has come into shadow from being in direct sunlight. Dynamic shadows are traditionally detected in video sequences by employing a trained background model, see (Madsen, Moeslund, Pal, & Balasubramanian, 2009) for a review of the research literature. For our application we consider this approach to be unrealistic since we are aiming at a system which must operate for hours, days, or even more. With the drastic illumination variation that can occur over such a time span, including seasonal changes in the color and amount of vegetation we do not consider a background model as viable.

Instead, we have based our dynamic shadow detection on image differencing. To be able to respond correctly to rapid illumination changes on windy, partly overcast days, we continuously subtract a 0.5 second old frame from the current frame. This is done both on the color image stream, and on the disparity image stream. By thresholding these difference images we get two "change has occurred" triggers, corresponding to a color change and a depth change for any given pixel, Figure 5. In this illustration we have used not a 0.5 second delay for the differencing but a 10 second delay to show changes more clearly. With a 10 second delay the system will not be as responsive to rapid illumination changes, though.

Regions where there is no depth change, but where there is a color change, represent shadow candidate pixels. In the example in Figure 5 the walking person has poured water on to surfaces in the scene, effectively changing the surface albedo at those locations. In this first step these regions qualify as shadow regions, but are discarded in a subsequent step.

Fig. 5. Left: thresholded disparity difference (change in depth). Center: thresholded color difference (change in color). Right: changes classified into moving object (grey) and shadow candidates.

### 5.3 Verification of shadow regions

The shadow candidate pixels detected by the color/depth differencing step are analyzed for how well each pixel conforms to the expected behavior of a pixel coming into shadow in an outdoor daylight scene. Given the combined sky and sun illumination environment, and given the fact that the sky is much more bluish than the sun, shadows undergo a color transformation which can be termed a blue shift. The chromaticity (red and blue channels normalized with the green channel) of a pixel will shift towards blue, when a pixel transitions from being in direct sunlight to being in shadow; this is proven in (Madsen, Moeslund, Pal, & Balasubramanian, 2009).

This can be exploited to filter out those shadow candidates which are not really shadows, such as the water splashes in Fig. 5. This is considered a powerful feature of our approach since we do not have to worry that a sudden rain shower will cause false detections of shadow regions.

We have designed a simple filter which only accepts those shadow candidate pixels which vote for the same blue shift direction in chromaticity space. The accepted shadow pixels are shown in Fig. 6, which clearly demonstrate that water splashes are not detected as shadow pixels.

Fig. 6. Input image and verified dynamic shadow pixels.

## 6. Illumination estimation

Having thus demonstrated how dynamic shadows can be detected in the scenes, time has come to look at how these shadows can be used to estimate the illumination conditions, or more precisely: estimate the radiances (in three color channels) of the sky and the sun, respectively.

### 6.1 Assumptions

The illumination estimation is described in greater detail in (Madsen & Nielsen, 2008). In this chapter we focus a little more on the overall approach, rather than going into detail with the derivation of the expressions. Yet, the process rests on a small number of assumptions that are worth mentioning.

First of all it is assumed that a majority of the surfaces in the scene behave as Lambertian reflectors, i.e. are diffuse and reflect light equally in all directions. In our experience ordinary outdoor man-made environments exhibit such behavior quite well, for example materials such as concrete, brick and asphalt. At normal imaging distances grass areas are also approximately diffuse (when getting too close the individual grass straws can be quite glossy).

Furthermore, as described, it is assumed that the only illuminants are the sky and the sun. Artificial light sources, such as outdoor lamps at night or near-night conditions are not modeled and we cannot at present, with the framework presented here, take their contribution into account. Strong solar reflections from windows in buildings can also present an illumination contribution which is not part of the model. If such reflections are significantly present in the scene, the contribution will be included in the estimate of the irradiance from the sky dome.

We also assume that we have all the information available to use an analytical approach to determining the direction vector to the sun (as described in section 3).

Finally, it is assumed that the camera is white balanced such that if a white/grey surface were placed at a known orientation, for example straight up, in the scene it would actually image as a white-balanced region. Notice that we do not assume such a surface to be *present* in the scene. The estimated illumination (sky and sun radiances) using our proposed approach will be tuned such that a white virtual surface with normal pointing up will render to a white-balanced surface. This way we can operate the camera with automatic white-balancing and thus maintain proper color balances across day long sequences, and across various weather conditions (overcast to bright sunlight).

### 6.2 From detected shadows to estimated illumination model

Section 4 presented the theoretical framework for formulating the relationships between measured pixels values, sun to shadow ratios and the various geometric properties of the scene. Key to the illumination estimation process is per pixel information about normal direction and ambient occlusion term. These are easy to compute from the depth data provided by the stereo camera, see Figure 7. At present we compute per pixel ambient occlusion by using a ray tracer (RADIANCE) to shade the geometry with a sky dome having a radiance of $1/\pi$ [W/(m$^2$ sr)]. With such a radiance any point receiving light from the entire sky dome will receive an irradiance of 1 [W/m$^2$], and a point receiving light from half the dome will receive an irradiance of 0.5 [W/m$^2$], etc.

With this geometrical information, combined with knowledge of the direction vector to the sun, each detected and verified shadow pixel can essentially vote for the two unknown scene illuminants, namely the unknown sky and sun irradiances, $E^{\uparrow}_{sky}$ and $E^{\uparrow}_{sun}$, as described in section 4.

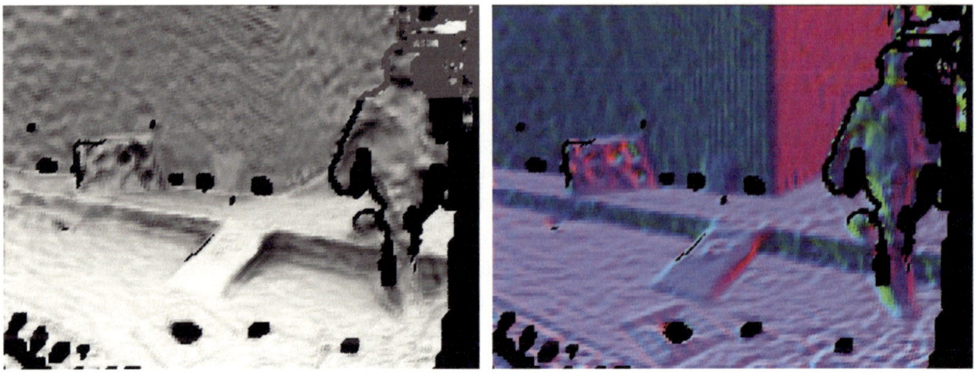

Fig. 7. Left: ambient occlusion coded as grey level in the range from 0 to 1, where darker areas see a smaller fraction of the sky dome. Right: per pixel surface normals shown as a normal map with xyz normal components encoded into offset, normalized rgb values.

In theory a single shadow pixel is enough to provide information about the sky and sun irradiances, but naturally we achieve a much more robust estimate by incorporating all shadow pixel into a voting scheme to find the sky and sun irradiances which have the strongest support in the available data. This way we can also filter out outliers due to any pixels falsely labelled as shadow, and thus we are less sensitive to any violation of the assumption that surfaces are diffuse.

For the frame shown in Figure 7 the approach estimates the radiance of the sky to [0.72 0.79 0.87] (rgb values, respectively) and the sun radiance to [69000 64000 59000]. We convert the estimated irradiances into radiances, since the radiances are more suitable for actual rendering. Radiance is the proper measure of the „brightness" of a light source. We notice a couple of things from these estimated numbers. First of all the color balance of the sky is towards blue as compared to the sun's rgb values. Secondly, there is roughly five orders of magnitude difference between the sky radiance and the sun radiance, which is entirely consistent with what is expected. As a sule of thumb the combined irradiance from the sky is considered to be equal to the irradiance from the sun, but the sun is 5 orders of magnitude smaller than the sky, and therefore 5 orders of magnitude brighter (5 orders of magnitude higher radiance).

## 7. Rendering of augmentations

After the radiances (in all three color channels) of both the sky and the sun have been estimated it is possible to setup the rendering of augmented objects. Available for this process are: the color image of the scene, the 3D model of the scene (the depth map), and the illumination environment.

Specifically, the illumination environment is set up as a hemi-spherical light source (hemi-spherical around the up-vector of the scene), combined with a disc source to act as the sun. The sun disk source has a 0.53 degree diameter, and the direction vector to the disk source is the computed sun position corresponding to the time and place of the image acquisition. The hemi-spherical and the disk light sources are assigned the estimated radiances, respectively.

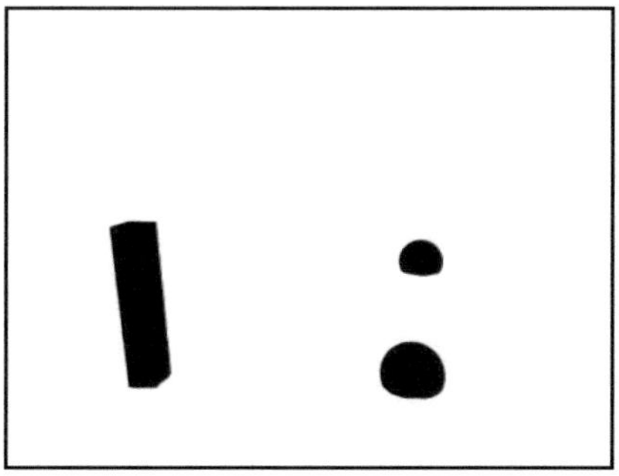

Fig. 8. Binary mask indicating image positions of augmented objects.

For the renderings demonstrated in the chapter we have employed the RADIANCE rendering package. The depth map is imported as a triangle mesh, and augmented objects are modelled as triangle meshes or volume primitives into the same coordinate system as the mesh.

We employ a basic technique similar to the differential rendering approach described in (Debevec, 1998). Roughly speaking this technique focuses on rendering the modelled part of the scene *with* augmentation, and rendering it *without*, finding the difference between these renderings and adding the difference to the original image (hence the name differential rendering).

First, though, the albedos of the real surfaces in the scene are estimated. This is done iteratively as follows: the input image is copied to an new image called the albedo map, and the scene mesh from the depth map is textured with this albedo map. Then the scene is rendered with the estimated illumination environment and the rendered image is divided into the input image, yielding a scale map. This scale map is multiplied with the first version of the albedo map to produce a new albedo map; using this map as mesh texture, the scene is rendered with the estimated illumination again, and the result is divided into the input image. This process is continued until there are no significant changes in the albedo map. Typically, three to four iterations suffice. This process will eliminate all global illumination effects from the albedo map. All subsequent rendering involving the real scene geometry uses this estimated albedo map as texture for the real scene mesh.

Then a binary mask image is rendered to indicate where in the image the augmented object will be projected, see Figure 8. This mask is used to mask out areas in the image resulting from rendering the scene mesh, textured with estimated albedo map, and illuminated with the estimated light. Then the scene mesh, textured with the albedo map, *plus* the augmented objects, are rendered with the same illumination. These two renderings are subtracted, see Figure 9. The shadows cast by the augmented objects will represent negative pixel values in this differential image, which is added to the masked input image to produce the final render, see Figure 3.

The described approach has been applied to multiple frames from a range of different input sequences acquired at different times of day, and under varying weather conditions, and some examples are shown in Figure 10. Since we have an estimated radiance for an entire sky dome (hemi-sphere) we can allow the scene to contain quite glossy objects, which can then reflect the illumination from the sky dome. The color balance of the estimated sky radiances is very consistent with what is expected from looking at the images (which to some extent indicate the sky color even if sky pixels are a close to being saturated). Naturally, with the technique presented here, the entire sky dome will have uniform color, and any illumination effect in the real scene from clouds will sort of be spread across the entire estimated sky. Therefore, if the virtual objects augmented into the scene contains too glossy surfaces, where one would expect to see reflections of clouds (if any in the real scene), the actual sky reflections will be uniformly colored and cloud-less.

Fig. 9. Modelled part of scene rendered with no augmentation and masked with binary mask indicating augmented objects (left), is subtracted from scene rendered with augmented objects (center), yielding a difference image (right).

The depth and color balance of the shadows cast by virtual objects onto real objects will more or less by definition be correct. This is because the whole basis for the estimation of the illumination environment is the chromatic properties of the detected *real* shadows in the scene.

The 3D scene information from the stereo camera naturally also contains information about the dynamic objects in the scene. In the example images presented in this chapter the primary author is present to provide movements generating shadows for detection and illumination estimation. The 3D mesh information concerning him enables various shadow interaction between real and virtual geometry. In Figure 9 it can be seen that the hand of the walking person casts a shadow on the red augmented sphere; in Figure 10 (top) the entire red sphere in the front of the scene is in the shadow cast by him; in the same figure (bottom) the person's lower legs are partially occluded by the virtual pillars inserted into the scene.

## 8. Discussions and future work

The entire shadow detection and illumination estimation can run at interactive frame rates (approx. 8 frames per second) in our present C++ implementation. The rendering process described in section 7 is at present entirely non-real-time since it is based on physically-based ray-tracing. Nevertheless, we have previously demonstrated that albedo estimation as well as rendering augmentations into real scene with complex shadow interaction can be done in real-time, (Madsen & Laursen, 2007). The hemi-spherical sky dome illumination can be replaced with a set of directional lights scattered uniformly across a hemi-sphere, and the sun can be rendered as a single directional light source.

A key element behind the technique presented here is an assumption that the real scene is dominated by surfaces which approximately act as diffuse reflectors (follow Lambert's cosine law). As described we have experienced this to be a fair assumption in typical man-made urban environments. We are presently investigating techniques based on robust statistics to identify areas in the scene, which do not over long sequences concur with the rest of the scene in terms of estimated illumination. Since we get illumination estimation per

Fig. 10. Two different augmented scenes. The small blue fields on the right are the estimated sky colors (the color balance estimated for the sky using the presented technique).

pixel and use voting schemes it is actually possible to label the pixels which do not exhibit a temporal color development which is consistent with the illumination conditions voted for by the majority of the pixels. This will enable us to label and rule-out highly glossy surfaces such as windows, pools of water, and metallic surfaces such as cars.

At present our technique cannot handle the problem of double shadows (cases where a shadow cast by a virtual object falls on top of an already existing shadow in the scene, creating a double shadow). If the 3D data from the stereo camera correctly models the geometry casting the real shadow, the rendering process will ensure that no double shadows are created. For example, the little red sphere in the front of the bottom scene in Figure 10 does not cast a double shadow inside the shadow already cast by the walking person. But, if the shadow caster geometry is not available, e.g. is outside the camera's field-of-view, double shadows can occur. We are developing techniques to deal with this problem based on creating "shadow protection masks" from the detected shadows in the scene. Since we know where the real shadows are we can use these masks to avoid casting extra shadow in them.

## 9. Conclusion

For photo-realistic Augmented Reality it is important to ensure that the augmented objects are rendered with illumination which is consistent with the real scene illumination. Especially the shadows are very important. Related work on illumination consistency for AR all involves a special purpose, known object to be placed in the scene, or requires manual interaction. In this chapter we have presented a novel, completely alternative, technique which does not have these constraints. Using only real-time stereo images as input the proposed technique can estimate the illumination information for an outdoor scene directly from image measurements of natural scenes.

An important additional benefit of the presented approach is that it does not require High Dynamic Range imagery, and the technique allows the system to use automatic gain control (AGC) on the camera, so that the system can operate across very long sequences with proper exposure of the images. In fact the estimated illumination parameters will follow the AGC on the camera so that, if the camera reduces light sensitivity with for example 10%, the estimated illumination is also 10% lower. This means that the rendered virtual objects will appear directly to be subject to the same AGC behaviour and thus match the real scene images perfectly. The same argumentation is valid for automatic camera white-balancing (if present).

With this work we believe we are an important step closer to being able to make Augmented Reality systems that function in real-time, and automatically adapt seamlessly to changes in the illumination conditions in the scene.

## 10. Acknowledgements

This research is funded by the CoSPE (26-04-0171) project under the Danish Research Agency. This support is gratefully acknowledged.

## 11. References

Barsi, A., Szimary-Kalos, L., & Szecsi, L. (2005). Image-based Illumination on the GPU. *Machine Graphics and Vision* , 159 - 169.

Boivin, S., & Gagalowitcz, A. (2001). Image-Based Rendering of Diffuse, Specular and Glossy Surfaces from a Single Image. *Proceedings: SIGGRAPH.* Los Angeles, California.

Cao, X., & Foroosh, H. (2007). Camera Calibration and Light Source Orientation from Solar Shadows. *Computer Vision and Image Understanding* , 60 - 72.

Cao, X., & Shah, M. (2005). Camera Calibration and Light Source Estimation from Images with Shadows. *Proceedings: IEEE Conference on Computer Vision and Pattern Recognition,* (s. 928 - 923).

Debevec, P. (1998). Rendering Synthetic Objects into Real Scenes: Bridging Traditional and Image-based Graphics with Global Illumination and High Dynamic Range Photography. *SIGGRAPH*. Orlando, Florida.

Drettakis, G., Robert, L., & Bougnoux, S. (1997). Interactive Common Illumination for Computer Augmented Reality. *Proceedings: Eurographics*. St. Etienne, France.

Franke, T., & Jung, Y. (2008). Real-Time Mixed Reality with GPU Techniques. *Proceedings: International Conference on Graphics Theory and Applications*. Funchal, Maderia, Portugal.

Hara, K., Nishino, K., & Ikeuchi, K. (2005). Light Source Position and Reflectance Estimation from a Single View withou the Distant Illumination Assumption. *IEEE Transactions on Pattern Analysis and Machine Intelligence* , 493 - 5050.

Havran, V., Smyk, M., Krawczyk, G., Myszkowski, K., & Seidel, H.-P. (2005). Importance Sampling for Video Environment Maps. *Proceedings: Eurographics Symposium on Rendering*, (s. 31 - 42). Konstanz, Germany.

Jensen, T., Andersen, M., & Madsen, C. B. (2006). Real-time Image-Based Lighting for Outdoor Augmented Reality Under Dynamically Changing Illumination Conditions. *Proceedings: International Conference on Graphics Theory and Applications* (pp. 252 - 261). Setubal, Portugal: INSTIC.

Kanbara, M., & Yokoya, N. (2004). Real-Time Estimation of Light Source Environment for Photorealistic Augmented Reality. *Proceedings: International Conference on Pattern Recognition*, (s. 911 - 914). Cambridge, United Kingdom.

Kim, T., & Hong, K.-I. (2005). A Practical Single Image Based Approach for Estimating Illumination Distribution from Shadows. *Proceedings: IEEE International Conference on Computer Vision*, (s. 266 - 271).

Loscos, C., Drettakis, G., & Robert, L. (2000). Interactive Virtual Relighting of Real Scenes. *IEEE Transactions on Visualization and Computer Graphics* , *6* (4), 289 - 305.

Madsen, C. B., & Laursen, R. E. (2007). A Scalable GPU-Based Approch to Shading and Shadowing for Photorealistic Real-Time Augmented Reality. *Proceedings: International Conference on Graphics Theory and Applications*, (pp. 252 - 261). Barcelona, Spain.

Madsen, C. B., & Nielsen, M. (2008). Towards Probe-less Augmented Reality - a Position Paper. *Proceedings: International Conference on Graphics Theory and Applications*, (s. 255 - 261). Funchal, Madeira, Portugal.

Madsen, C. B., Moeslund, T. B., Pal, A., & Balasubramanian, S. (2009). Shadow Detection in Dynamic Scenes Using Dense Stereo and an Outdoor Illumination Model. In R. Koch, & A. Kold (Ed.), *Dynamic 3D Imaging. LNCS 5742*, pp. 110 - 125. Berlin Heidelberg: Springer-Verlag.

Sato, I., Sato, Y., & Ikeuchi, K. (1999). Illumination Estimation from Shadows. *Proceedings: IEEE Conference on Computer Vision and Pattern Recognition*, (s. 306 - 312).

Sato, I., Sato, Y., & Ikeuchi, K. (2001). Stability Issues in Recovering Illumination Distribution from Brightness in Shadows. *Proceedings: IEEE Conference on Computer Vision and Pattern Recognition*, (s. 400 - 407).

Wang, Y., & Samaras, D. (2003). Estimation of Multiple Directional Light Sources for Synthesis of Augmented Reality Images. *Graphical Models* , *65*, 185 - 205.

Yu, Y., Debevec, P., Malik, J., & Hawkins, T. (1999). Inverse Global Illumination: Recovering Reflectance Models of Real Scenes From Photographs. *Proceedings: SIGRRAPH*, (s. 215 - 224). Los Angeles, California.

Zhou, W., & Kambhamettu, C. (2008). A Unified Framework for Scene Illumination Estimation. *Image and Vision Computing* , 415 - 429.

3

# Design of Embedded Augmented Reality Systems

J. Toledo, J. J. Martínez, J. Garrigós, R. Toledo-Moreo and J. M. Ferrández
*Universidad Politécnica de Cartagena*
*Spain*

## 1. Introduction

The great majority of current Augmented Reality (AR) applications are built using general purpose processors as development platforms where the processing tasks are executed in software. However, software execution is not always the best solution for the high intensive requirements of the many processing tasks involved in AR, and it inevitably constrains frame rate and latency, which compromises real time operation, and magnifies size and power consumption, hindering mobility. These limitations make the spread of AR applications more difficult. This is particularly remarkable in the case of mobile real time applications.

To overcome the aforementioned constraints in the design of embedded AR systems, this chapter presents a hardware/software co-design strategy based on Field Programmable Gate Array (FPGA) devices and Electronic System-Level (ESL) description tools as an alternative to the traditional software-based approach. Modern FPGAs feature millions of gates of programmable logic, with dedicated hardware resources and with the widest range of connectivity solutions. FPGA internal structure makes itself perfectly suitable for exploiting parallelism at several levels. Moreover, because of its flexibility, it is possible to implement not only specific algorithms, but also AD/DA interfaces, controllers, and even several microprocessors, what makes it feasible to build more complex and powerful Systems on a Chip (SoC) with improved performance and reduced costs, size and power consumption. FPGA (re)programmability is also a key factor, which provides not just reduced time to market and design flexibility, but also in-the-field upgradability and intellectual property protection. Thanks to these characteristics, FPGAs are giving rise to a new paradigm in computation named Reconfigurable Computing. ESL, on the other hand, is an emerging electronic design methodology that focuses on building models of the entire system with a high-level language such as C, C++, or MATLAB, which are later used by improved electronic design tools to generate an automated and correct-by-construction implementation of the system. ESL codesign tools allow for developers with little or no prior hardware design skills to implement complex systems composed of mixed software and application-specific hardware modules.

The objective of this chapter is to provide a clear vision of the possibilities of FPGA devices and the new development methodologies for embedded AR systems. To do it so, the authors explain the FPGAs key features which make them suitable for the implementation of AR applications. The design flow and tools for hardware description and hardware/software co-design from low to the highest level are described. A survey of the most noteworthy FPGA-based works in image processing, computer vision, computer graphics, multimedia, communications and wearable computing is presented. Finally, the chapter is completed with an example which illustrates the advantages of the FPGA-based approach as platform for developing AR applications: a portable real time system for helping visually impaired people. This system enhances the patient's knowledge of the environment with additional video information using a see-through head mounted display. The description of its main processing cores for video acquisition and processing, for hand recognition, for the user interface, etc. and the evaluation of their performances highlight the advantages of the FPGA-based design and reveal the key topics for the implementation of AR systems.

## 2. On the suitability of reconfigurable hardware for mobile AR applications

After a successful decade of exploration and consolidation of fields and applications, it is time for AR to break the border of the research domain and reach the common people domain. For it, the user needs to feel AR as a part of his own body, not as an external an uncomfortable artefact. Inevitably, this entails ubiquity and mobility. For such a qualitative jump, one of the major challenges that AR has to face is the hardware under applications and the development of new platforms for interaction (Veas & Kruijff, 2008). It is the key to find the optimum solution to the complicated trade-off between quality, speed, power and size. Most AR research published to date relies on the use of general purpose computing hardware to perform computations, render computer graphics and provide video overlay functionality. Systems that rely on general purpose computing hardware are larger in size and consume more power than those which have devices customised for specific tasks. When working in indoor environments, such issues are rarely considered since the systems are not normally required to be mobile, but the challenge of ubiquity and mobility raises a new scenario. In it, doubtlessly, computer processing hardware is one of the research topics where an extra development effort must be done in order to provide a more effective AR experience (Zhou et al, 2008).

Over the last years, several hardware platforms have been introduced to support mobile AR in two different directions: the head-mounted display direction using laptops in backpack systems, and the handheld direction using lightweight portable devices. Both directions share a design feature: the great majority of AR applications consist of software being executed on general purpose processors. However, not all applications can be solved through the use of the traditional software-based approach since it imposes limitations that force the designer to choose between robustness/compactness, power consumption and processing power, what, in last term, difficult the spread of AR.

In spite of their importance, only a minority of papers describing AR mobile systems report on features such as timing performance, frame rates, power consumption, size, weight, etc., which, in the last instance, determine the viability of the AR application. When these data are provided, they show important weak points, like in the case of the ArcheoGuide application described in (Dähne & Kariginannis, 2002), where the incapability of the hardware platform of the system of parallelizing processing tasks causes that authors rule out a gesture recognizer based on interaction due to its interference with the video tracking performance. This is also the case of the video see-through AR system on cellphone described in (Möhring et al, 2004), which hardly can manage four 160×120 12-bit colour frames per second.

Such limitations lead to approaches where the AR device tends to be 'dumb', acting simply as a viewport of the AR application with the largest part of the processing taking place in remote servers. This is the philosophy behind the AR-phone (Assad et al, 2003). In it, the system performance relies on the wireless networking. Without reporting frame rates, the authors admit the convenience of moving some parts of the processing into the user interface module with the aim of avoiding the overload in the communication that ruins the performance. The mobile phone-based AR application for assembly described in (Billinghurst et al, 2008) is also a client/server architecture where the complex processing is executed on a PC. It works with still images instead of video and the virtual model is quite simple, but the data transmission between the phone and the PC over the WLAN rises the time to send and receive an image up to 3.4 seconds. A similar client/server implementation is presented in (Passman & Woodward, 2003) for running AR on a PDA device. It uses a compression algorithm developed by the authors to relieve the communication of the rendering data overhead, but the best case refresh rate hardly reaches two frames per second. Another interesting approach can be found in (Wagner et al, 2005), where the authors present a system architecture for interactive, infrastructure-independent multi-user AR applications which runs on a PDA (personal digital assistance).

Due to these limitations, some applications resign to video processing on behalf of usability. AR on-demand (Riess & Stricker, 2006) presents a practicable solution on low-end handheld devices where images of the real scene are taken only when needed, superposing real-time virtual animations on that single still image. The information is not blended in the field of view of the user, but can be easily watched over the display of a PDA or a head worn display beside the eye. The goal of this approach is to develop a system which does not dominate the user, but offers support when required.

The use of image sensors is probably the most common way to capture the real environment and enhance it with virtual objects, i.e. to create augmented reality. For this reason, it can serve us well to understand the role of FPGAs and custom-made hardware platforms for AR applications. In the cases where designs must be prepared to meet frame rate, image resolution, algorithm performance, power consumption and size requirements, traditional platforms based on desktop computers and their corresponding slight variations based on laptops are unsuitable. Some examples of these works can be found in (Piekarski et al., 2001; Feiner et al, 1997; Hoellerer et al, 1999). Although these works may be interesting for validating their respective systems for their corresponding intended applications, the proposed devices appear to be complex, heavy, expensive and fragile. Developments made in standard microprocessors-based units are not efficient or inconvenient for the purpose of unconstrained mobility. The authors of (Piekarski et al., 2004) noticed this fact, and proposed modifications in backpack designs which aim to improve its size, weight and power consumption. The authors conclude that FPGAs and specialized video overlay units result beneficial to minimize power and to accelerate computation. In (Johnston et al., 2003), the authors point to FPGAs and developments in hardware for embedded systems as the most likely alternative platform for real-time performance of AR devices. Indeed, parallelism and concurrency can be exploited for image processing while keeping power consumption low, bringing a solution to the challenge of embedded image processing.

A good example of exploiting FPGAs with an image sensor can be found in (Matsushita et al, 2003), where a FGPA device controls a fast CMOS image sensor for ID recognition. In (Foxlin & Harrington, 2000), a self-reference head and hand tracker is presented and its applicability in a wearable computer is shown. Smith and colleagues in (Smith et al, 2005)

improved the work presented in (Piekarski et al, 2001) by migrating the proposed hand-tracking algorithm from the laptop to an FPGA. Indeed, this new development allows a further miniaturization of the system and minimizes power consumption. In (Luk et al, 1998; Luk et al., 1999), some good initial examples of the use of reconfigurable computing for AR are shown. In concrete, video mixing, image extraction and object tracking are run on an FPGA-based platform. In this line, our group presented in (Toledo et al, 2005) a fully FPGA based AR application for visual impaired individuals affected by tunnel vision. A Cellular Neural Network extracts the contour information and superimposes it on the patient's view. Finally, the authors of (Guimaraes et al, 2007) present an interesting platform which aims to help developers on the construction of embedded AR applications. The infrastructure is based on FPGA and enables the creation of hardware based AR systems.
This short review is enough to come to the conclusion that mobile AR applications are severely constrained by the up to date usual software-based approach and that many real-time applications require algorithmic speedup that only dedicated hardware can provide. Hardware implementation of algorithms and processing tasks can considerably improve the performance and by the hence the utility/viability of the AR system.

## 3. FPGA characteristics and architectures

The introduction of the Field-Programmable Gate Array (FPGA) devices about 25 years ago gave rise to the reconfigurable computing concept. Early FPGA generations were quite limited in their capacities. Nowadays, the most advanced manufacturing technologies are used to feature devices with millions of gates of programmable logic, with dedicated hardware resources, with the widest range of system connectivity solutions, enabling more complex and powerful systems on a single chip.
Reconfigurable hardware offers a trade-off between the very specialized solution of application specific integrated circuits (ASIC) and the inefficiency of general purpose processor (GPP), combining the desirable high performance of ASICs with the characteristics of system flexibility of GPPs. Like ASICs, it involves hardware implementation and consequently parallelism and high performance. Like GPPs, it provides reconfigurability, and hence, flexibility and rapid prototyping. The key of reconfigurable hardware lies on that the flexibility is provided by the hardware design rather than by software-programmable hardware. With clock frequencies an order of magnitude lower than that of typical microprocessors, FPGAs can provide greater performance when executing real-time video or image processing algorithms as they take advantage of their fine-grained parallelism.
There are several companies that produce diverse flavours of FPGAs: Xilinx, Altera, Atmel, Lattice Semiconductor, Actel, SiliconBlue Technologies, Achronix or QuickLogic are the main competitors. At an architectural level, however, all of them share some common characteristics, which define an FPGA as a regular structure of programmable modules, including three types of resources:

1. Logic Blocks (LB), used to implement small parts of the circuit logical functions.
2. Input/Output Blocks (IOBs) that connect internal resources with the device pins, and usually adapt the electrical characteristics of the signals to interface the output world.
3. Routing channels with programmable Interconnect Blocks (IBs), which allow the connection between LBs or between these and the IOBs.

In an FPGA, both the connection of the wire resources and the functionality of the logic blocks can be programmed by the user. Logic blocks and routing architectures differ from vendor to vendor, but their regular distribution make all of them well suited for highly parallelizable algorithms, composed of bit-level operations that can be distributed in regular structures. Nevertheless, they are ill suited to high precision arithmetic operations, such as large operand multiplication or floating-point calculations. The presence of on-chip memory is also limited, thus many applications require the existence of an external RAM chip. The data transfer increases circuit delays, and increases power consumption and board area.

To overcome these difficulties, researchers and manufacturers proposed new architectures with specific purpose resources and advanced configuration characteristics. Up to Several hundred dedicated MACs (Multiply and Accumulate) modules are included in the larger devices for fast DSP calculations. To increase data storage capabilities, RAM blocks are distributed over the circuit, providing several Mbits of dedicated memory. Recently some devices come with dedicated interface controllers, such as Ethernet MAC, USB or PCI bridges. The list includes also AD/DA converters, PLLs for highly customizable clock generators, or hard-core microprocessors (with much better performance than their soft-core counterparts). As an example, Xilinx's latest Virtex 5 chips include one or two embedded PowerPC™ 405 processors. These 32-bit RISC processors from IBM Corporation are included as hard-cores, making them run at around 450MHz, without decreasing the number of user (LB) resources. Several real-time operating systems (RTOS), included different Linux porting are available for this processor, allowing the designer to centre his efforts in the application-specific parts of the project.

Devices can be classified with respect to their *granularity*, which is a measure of the number of resources that the logic block incorporates. *Fine-grain* devices consist of small cells containing for example a single NAND gate and a latch, or a multiplexer-based function generator and a flip-flop, like Actel IGLOO™ devices. In a medium-grain device, the typical LB consists of two or three function generators (called look-up tables, LUT), each one being able to implement any combinational function from 2 to 6 inputs, and (typically) two flip-flops. A LUT can also be configured as a small memory or as a shift register. The LUT's output can be connected to a flip-flop or routed directly to the cell's port. Finally, the logic block can include logic-specific resources, such as fast carry generators. Xilinx's Spartan and Virtex series are a typical example.

IOBs can be configured as input, output or bidirectional ports. They frequently include on-chip pull-up/down resistors and tri-state buffers. Connectivity is guarantied by supporting main standards, including 3GIO, Infiniband, Gigabit Ethernet, RapidIO, HyperTransport, PCI, Fibre Channel, Flexbus 4, between others. Some chips, like the Virtex 6 family, accommodate several multi-gigabit transceivers to perform serial I/O from 3.125, up to 11Gbps.

Most devices can be programmed by downloading a single-bit stream into the configuration memory. The device's configuration is typically memory-based, using any of the SRAM, EPROM, EEPROM or the most recent flash technologies. Other OTP (one-time programmable) devices use fuse or antifuse technologies (for a detailed description of the different technologies and chip characteristics, the interested reader is referred to companies' web pages).

SRAM devices are the dominant technology nowadays. However, SRAM cells are volatile, meaning that the stored information is lost when power is not applied. These devices require and external "boot", and are typically programmed from a host processor or a non-volatile memory after chip reset. Memory-based FPGAs have the advantage of been re- and in-system programmable. Devices can be soldered directly to the PCB, without using special sockets. If the design changes, there is no need to remove the device from the board, but it can be simply re-programmed in-system, using typically a JTAG interface. On the other hand, the non-volatile EEPROM and flash devices are better protected against unauthorized use and reverse-engineering, because the programming information is not downloaded to the device at power up.

### 3.1 Dynamic reconfiguration

The re- and in-system programmability of the memory based FPGAs has opened a broad area of new application scenarios. The term (Re-) Configurable Computing refers to computers that can modify their hardware circuits during system execution. The key for this new computing paradigm has been the development of new FPGAs with extremely quickly configuration rates. While first devices required several seconds to get programmed, in newer FPGAs the configuration download can be done in about one millisecond, and devices with configuration times of about 100 μs are expected in the next years.
Dynamic reconfiguration can be used in a number of ways. The least demanding technique consists of switching between several different configurations that are prepared beforehand, what enables to perform more computational algorithms than those permitted by the physical hardware resources. This could be seen as the hardware equivalent of quitting one program and running another. When faster programming times are available, reconfiguration can be done in a kind of context swapping: the FPGA reconfigures itself time-sharing the execution of different tasks, making the illusion that it is performing all its functions at once (multi-tasking). An example of this techniques was used in (Villasenor et al., 1996) to build a single-chip video transmission system that reconfigures itself four times per video frame, requiring just a quarter of the hardware needed by an equivalent fixed ASIC.
The most challenging approach to dynamic reconfiguration, and surely the most powerful, involves chips that reconfigure themselves on the fly, as a function of requirements emerged during algorithm execution. In this computing system, if a functional unit is missed, it is recovered from the resources store and placed on the chip, in some cases replacing the space occupied by another not-in-use circuit. The problem here is double: loading the proper configuration *bitstream* in the device and finding an appropriate location for the unit, what gives an idea of the complexity of the task. To support this kind of applications, some commercial devices (VirtexII, Virtex4) are now offering dynamic partial-reconfiguration capabilities. These devices allow reprogramming only part of the configuration memory, in order to update just a selected area of the circuit.
Partial reconfiguration enables the remote upgrade of hardware across a network, by delivering new *bitstreams* and software drivers to the remote hardware. The benefits of this methodology include shortening time to market, because the hardware can be shipped sooner with a subset of the full functionality, and performance/corrections upgrading without the need for returns. This methodology has been proved in the Australian satellite FedSat launched on December 14, 2002, featuring a configurable computer (HPC-I) that enables the satellite to be rewired without having to be retrieved, thus drastically reducing cost and development time (Dawood et al., 2002).
With their re-configurability characteristics and the introduction of new special-purpose resources blocks, FPGAs offer a number of advantages over classical design methodologies based on general purpose processors or even the more specialized Digital Signal Processors (DSP), such as unmatched parallelism, versatility, and short time to market. Moreover, Re-

configurable Computing has been presented as a promising paradigm that will compete against the traditional von Newmann architecture and its parallel enhancements (Hartenstein, 2002), (Hartenstein, 2004). Augmented Reality applications and, particularly, embedded ones, can take huge benefits from these emerging so called config-ware technologies.

## 4. Tools and design flows for reconfigurable hardware

From a historical point of view, the first FPGA design tools where traditional schematic based editors coupled with a physical design software that performed the *place and route* of the architecture-specific components (or primitive cells) in which the circuit is decomposed for a particular FPGA device. Schematic-based tools had however several disadvantages. Firstly, the enormous number of sheets that a large design can consist of made it difficult to handle or update, with changes in one area propagating from sheet to sheet. Secondly, the design methodology proposed by the schematic tools consisted of *structural descriptions* of the circuit; that is, a system was described in base to the entities that composed it. However, in most cases, a system is more naturally described in base to its expected behaviour or *functionality*. The aforementioned limitations are the cause of the wide adoption of Hardware Description Languages (HDL), such as VHDL and Verilog, during the last decade.

### 4.1 Hardware description languages

Been textual, HDLs are more manageable than schematics. One the other hand, both of them support structural descriptions, however, only HDLs allow for higher-level "behavioural" descriptions. Finally, HDLs have specific constructions for modular design and component re-usability. This last characteristic has become crucial, as the size of the standard design has grown from ten or cents of *k*-gates to several million-gates.

Another important characteristic is that high-level HDL descriptions, contrary to schematic descriptions, are technology independent, what allows the designer to synthesize his project over a number of FPGA devices with minor changes at the description level. Different FPGA vendors and architectures can be benchmarked until an optimal implementation is met, with little impact on the design time.

Despite of the use of HDLs, the current design tools and methodologies have became inadequate to effectively manage the tens of millions gates that the silicon technology allows gather together in a single chip, furthermore when the pressure to reduce the design cycle increases continuously.

The tendency has been towards the use of pre-designed and pre-verified cores trying to bridge the gap between available gate-count and designer productivity. Instead of developing a system from scratch, designers are looking at effective methodologies for creating well-verified reusable modules that can be incorporated in a "mix & match" style to the application-specific blocks. These reusable hardware modules are called *cores* or Intellectual Property (IP). To face the design reuse challenge, IP cores must be designed not just application independent, but also technology independent and synthesis/simulator tool independent (Keating & Bricaud, 1999). Beyond typical basic blocks, modules are being designed specifically to be sold as independent articles. These include microprocessors (ARM, MIPS, PowerPC), communication interfaces (PCI, USB, Ethernet), DSP algorithms (FIR/IIR filters, FFT, wavelets), memory elements (SDRAM, FIFO), etc. One of the more complete on-line IP repositories can be found in (Design & Reuse, 2009). OpenCores is another important repository, based the concept of freely usable open source hardware (OpenCores, 2009).

### 4.2 System level specification and codesign

The design process based on HDLs like VHDL, Verilog, etc., is not exempt of difficulties, as these traditional methodologies still require deep hardware skills from the designer. Moreover, the high integration levels of current chips have transformed the concept of System On a Chip (SoC) into reality, increasing design complexity up to an unprecedented level. A typical SoC consists of one or several microprocessors/microcontrollers, multiple SRAM/DRAM, CAM or flash memory blocks, PLL, ADC/DCA interfaces, function-specific cores, such as DSP or 2D/3D graphics, and interface cores such as PCI, USB and UART (Fig. 1).

The intensive use of predesigned IP cores can just mitigate the problem, but in a SoC project, designers can not describe the hardware-specific modules at the Register Transfer Level (RTL), as the HDL methodologies propose, and then wait for a hardware prototype before interacting with the software team to put the design together. New EDA (Electronic Design Automation) tools must incorporate system-level modelling capabilities, such that the whole system, software and hardware, can be verified against its specifications right from the beginning of the design process. This requires an integrated hardware-software co-simulation platform that permits to confer hardware engineers the same level of productivity of software engineers.

To meet the challenges posed by the SoC complexity, new languages, tools and methodologies with greater modelling capabilities are been developed. In the area of design languages, there has been a lot of discussion about the role and applicability area of the various existing and new languages. SystemC, SytemVerilog, Verilog 2005, Analogue and Mixed-Signal versions of Verilog and VHDL, or Vera are some of the new proposals.

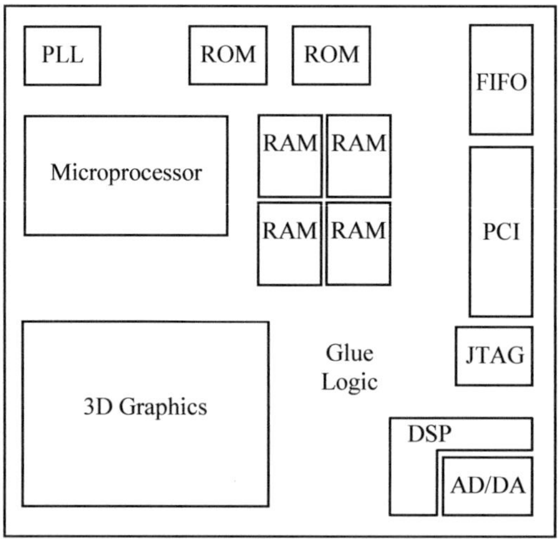


Fig. 1. Structure of core-based system on a chip

One of the most promising alternatives is been developed by the Open SystemC Initiative (OSCI), a collaborative effort launched in 1999 among a broad range of companies to establish the new standard for system-level design. SystemC (OSCI, 2006) (Black & Donovan, 2004) is a modelling platform consisting of C++ class libraries and a simulation kernel for design at the system and register transfer levels. Been a C-based language, SystemC can bring the gap between software engineers used to work with C and C++, and hardware engineers, that use other languages such as Verilog or VHDL. Furthermore, a common specification language would favour the creation of design tools that allow designers to easily migrate functions from hardware into software and vice versa.

Following this approach, a new generation of tools for highly complex circuit design is been developed. This new methodology, known as ESL (Electronic System Level), aims to target the problem of hardware-software co-design from system-level untimed descriptions, using different flavours of High Level Languages (HLLs), such as C, C++ or Matlab. The main difference between tools is the projection methodology used to implement a given algorithm, that is, the approach used to partition and accelerate that algorithm; some tools used a fixed processor based architecture that can be expanded with custom application-specific coprocessors; other are best tailored to create just custom hardware IP modules that could be later integrated in larger systems; some provide a flexible processor architecture whose instruction set can be expanded with application specific instructions supported by custom ALUs/coprocessors; finally, some of them are intended to provide a complete SoC design environment, giving support for custom hardware modules design, standard microprocessors, application software and the necessary hw-to-hw and hw-to-sw interfaces. A detailed review of these tools is beyond the scope of this chapter, so we will just summarize some of them in no particular order, in Table 1. The interested reader can find an exhaustive taxonomy of the design methodologies and ESL design environments commercially or educationally available in (Densmore & Passerone, 2006).

| Company | Web page | Product |
|---|---|---|
| Bluespec | www.bluespec.com | Bluespec Development Workstation |
| CriticalBlue | www.criticalblue.com | Cascade |
| Codetronix | www.codetronix.com | Mobius, XPSupdate |
| Impulse Accelerated Tech. | www.impulseaccelerated.com | CoDeveloper |
| Mitrionics | www.mitrionics.com | Mitrion Software Development Kit |
| Nallatech | www.nallatech.com | DIME-C |
| Poseidon Design Systems | www.poseidon-systems.com | Triton Builder |
| System Crafter | www.systemcrafter.com | SystemCrafter SC |
| ARC International | www.teja.com | ARChitect, others |
| Xilinx Inc. | www.xilinx.com | AccelDSP, System Generator |
| Mentor Graphics | www.mentor.com | Catapult C |
| Cadence Design System | www.cadence.com | C-to-Silicon Compiler |

Table 1. Some companies providing ESL tools.

### 4.3 ImpulseC programming model

In this section, we analyze the main features and workflow of CoDeveloper™, an ESL tool from Impulse Accelerated Technologies, Inc. (Impulse, 2009) used for hardware-software co-design, to evaluate its suitability for the non-hardware specialist scientist in general, as in the case of most AR researches. From our experience, we then provide some keys to get better results with this tool, which may be easily generalized for similar tools, with the aim of making the reconfigurable hardware approach for embedded AR solutions a bit closer for a broaden number of researchers.

ImpulseC compiler uses the communicating sequential process (CSP) model. An algorithm is described using ANSI C code and a library of specific functions. Communication between processes is performed mainly by data streams or shared memories. Some signals can be transferred also to other processes like flags, for non continuous communication. The API provided contains the necessary functions to express process parallelization and communication, as standard C language does not support concurrent programming.

Once the algorithm has been coded, it can be compiled using any standard C compiler. Each of the processes defined is translated to a software thread if the operating system supports them (other tools do not have this key characteristic, and can only compile to hardware).

The entire application can then be executed and tested for correctness. Debugging and profiling the algorithm is thus straightforward, using standard tools. Then, computing intensive processes can be selected for hardware synthesis, and the included compiler will generate the appropriate VHDL or Verilog code for them, but also for the communication channels and synchronization mechanisms. The code can be generic of optimized for a growing number of commercially available platforms. Several *pragmas* are also provided that can be introduced in the C code to configure the hardware generation, for example, to force loop unrolling, pipelining or primitive instantiation.

The versatility of their model allows for different uses of the tool. Let us consider a simple example, with 3 processes working in a dataflow scheme, as shown in Fig. 2. In this case, Producer and Consumer processes undertake just the tasks of extracting the data, send them to be processed, receive the results and store them. The computing intensive part resides in the central process, which applies a given image processing algorithm. A first use of the tool would consist in generating application specific hardware for the filtering process that would be used as a primitive of a larger hardware system. The Producer and Consumer would then be "disposable", and used just as a testbench to check, first, the correct behaviour of the filtering algorithm, and second, the filtering hardware once generated.

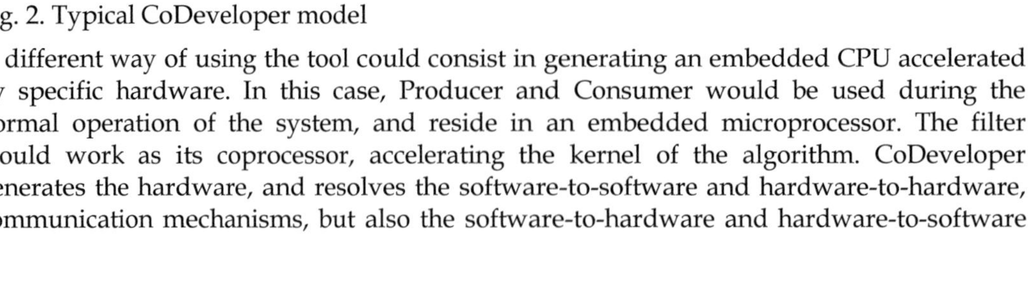


Fig. 2. Typical CoDeveloper model

A different way of using the tool could consist in generating an embedded CPU accelerated by specific hardware. In this case, Producer and Consumer would be used during the normal operation of the system, and reside in an embedded microprocessor. The filter would work as its coprocessor, accelerating the kernel of the algorithm. CoDeveloper generates the hardware, and resolves the software-to-software and hardware-to-hardware, communication mechanisms, but also the software-to-hardware and hardware-to-software

interfaces, for a number of platforms and standard buses. This is a great help for the designer that gets free of dealing with the time-consuming task of interface design and synchronization.
Finally, the objective can be accelerating an external CPU by means of a FPGA board. In this case, the software processes would reside on the host microprocessors, which would communicate to the application specific hardware on the board by means of a high performance bus (HyperTransport, PCI, Gigabit Ethernet, etc.). As in the previous case, software, hardware and proper interfaces between them (in the form of hardware synchronization modules and software control drivers) are automatically generated for several third party vendors.

### 4.4 Key rules for a successful system-level design flow

The results obtained in our experiments with different applications shown that AR-like algorithms can benefit from custom hardware coprocessors for accelerating execution, as well as for rapid prototyping from C-to-hardware compilers. However, to obtain any advantage, both, an algorithm profiling and a careful design are mandatory. These are the key aspects we have found to be useful:

- The algorithm should make an intensive use of data in different processing flows, to make up for the time spent in the transfer to/from the accelerator.
- The algorithm should make use of several data flows, taking advantage of the massive bandwidth provided by the several hundred o I/O bits that FPGA devices include.
- The working data set should be limited to 1-2MB, so that it may be stored in the internal FPGA memory, minimizing access to external memory.
- The algorithm should use integer or fixed point arithmetic when possible, minimizing the inference of floating point units that reduce the processing speed and devour FPGA resources.
- The algorithm must be profiled to identify and isolate the computational intensive processes. All parallelizing opportunities must be identified and explicitly marked for concurrent execution. Isolation of hardware processes means identifying the process boundaries that maximize concurrency and minimize data dependencies between processes, to optimize the use of onchip memory.
- Maximize the data-flow working mode. Insert FIFO buffers if necessary to adjust clock speeds and/or data widths. This makes automatic pipelining easier for the tools, resulting in dramatic performance improvement.
- Array partitioning and scalarizing. Array variables usually translate to typical sequential access memories in hardware, thus if the algorithm should use several data in parallel, they must be allocated in different C variables, to grant the concurrent availability of data in the same clock cycle.
- Avoiding excessive nested loops. This could difficult or avoid correct pipelining of the process. Instead, try partitioning the algorithm in a greater number of flattened processes.

## 5. FPGA applications

### 5.1 FPGA applications in image processing and computer vision

The nature of image processing demands the execution of intensive tasks that in many cases (as it is AR) must meet the requirement of high frame rate. This encourages the use of specific hardware in order to improve the performance of the intended applications. Indeed, the correct choice of hardware can raise dramatically the system performance. Current systems offer different benefits and limitations depending on the type of processing performed and its implementation. In this sense, general-purpose CPUs are the best alternative for sequential tasks where it is necessary to perform complex analysis of images and to run highly branched algorithms. However, in applications of 3D image processing and fast rendering scenes, the Graphics Proccesor Units (GPU) are more suitable because they have specific processing architectures designed to perform vector operations on large amounts of data. FPGAs are especially suitable for performing pre-processing tasks like colour format conversion, image filtering, convolution, and more in general, any repetitive operation that does not require highly complex algorithms, even in those cases when these algorithms are parallelizable and can benefit from the use of unconventional specific architectures. The large number of memory blocks available on FPGAs provides parallel processing support and enables very fast access to data stored in these caches. Developers can leverage the high bandwidth I/O on these devices and thus increase the speed of the functions and data rate that traverse the FPGA on GPUs or CPUs. Thanks to the versatility to develop dedicated circuits and the high degree of parallelism, FPGAs can achieve performances similar to some other hardware alternatives that run at higher frequencies of operation. These reasons explain why the implementation of many algorithms is the focus of a wide number of works since the last decade, and why from early stages of the evolution of reconfigurable hardware, several FPGA-based custom computing machines have been designed to execute image processing or computer vision algorithms (Arnold et al., 1993; Drayer at al., 1995).

Of high interest for AR applications is the implementation of object tracking algorithms, where different approaches have been followed. For example, the authors in (Dellaert & Tarip, 2005) present an application where a multiple camera environment is used for real time tracking with the aim of assisting visually impaired persons by providing them an auditory interface to their environment through sonification. For this purpose an octagonal board can support up to 4 CMOS cameras, an Xscale processor and a FPGA which handles the feature detection in parallel for all cameras. Another FPGA-based application for counting people using a method to detect different size heads appears in (Vicente et al., 2009). More examples of FPGA-based approaches to object tracking can be found in the literature: for colour segmentation (Garcia et al., 1996; Johnston et al., 2005); for implementing an artificial neural network for specifically hand tracking (Krips et al., 2002; Krips et al., 2003); for recognizing hand gestures (In et al., 2008); and for increasing pixel rate to improve real-time objects tracking by means of a compression sensor together with an FPGA (Takayuki et al., 2002).

Similarly, the human exploration in virtual environments requires technology that can accurately measure the position and the orientation of one or several users as they move and interact in the environment. For this purpose a passive vision FPGA-based system has been proposed by Johnston et al. (Johnston et al., 2005). The aim of this system is to produce a generalised AR system in the sense that accurate estimation of a mobile user's position relative to a set of indoor targets is accomplished in real time. FPGA-based systems are also used to develop a system for tracking multiple users in controlled environments (Tanase et al., 2008).

Vision-based algorithms for motion estimation, optical flow, detection of features like lines or edges, etc. are also widely used in AR. Recently, several motion estimation alternatives have been proposed to be implemented on a FPGA platform. Some of them are compared in

(Olivares et al., 2006). Some other good examples interest of the recent literature on this issue can be found in (Yu et al., 2004), where mobile real-time video applications with good trade-off between the quality of motion estimation and the computational complexity are presented, and (Akin et al., 2009), that focuses on the reduction of the computational complexity of a full search algorithm from 8 bits pixel resolution to one. Optical flow can also be used to detect independent moving objects in the presence of camera motion. Although many flow-computation methods are complex and currently inapplicable in real-time, different reliable FPGA-based Real-time Optical-flow approaches have been proposed in the recent years (Martin et al., 2005; Diaz et al., 2006). Furthermore, other processing image techniques like super resolution, atmospheric compensation and compressive sampling may be useful in enhancing the images and to reconstruct important aspect of the scenes. These techniques are highly complex and the use of FPGAs is encouraged to achieve the necessary acceleration. These topics are covered in detail in several articles dedicated to reconfigurable computing (Bowen et al., 2008; Bodnar et al., 2009; Ortiz et al., 2007).

### 5.2 FPGA applications in computer graphics and multimedia

Computer graphics is another field that can benefit from the flexibility of software programmable devices. This explains the increasing attention paid to FGPAs in the last years for the purpose of graphics acceleration, traditionally assigned to GPUs or graphics cards.

The suitability of FPGAs for the implementation of graphic algorithms has been analysed since the mid 90s. Singh and Bellec (Singh & Bellec, 1994) introduce the notion of *virtual hardware*, a methodology to execute complex processes on limited physical resources, using the dynamic reconfigurability of FPGAs. More recently, Howes (Howes., 2006) compare the performance of different architectures based on FPGAs, GPUs, CPUs and Sony Playsation 2 vector units on different graphic algorithms using a unified description based on A Stream Compiler (ASC). This work shows how the FPGAs provide fast execution of the graphics algorithm with clocks at lower frequencies than its competitors. Nevertheless, performances are particularly dependent on the possibilities of optimization for each design.

Radiosity high computational cost has been improved using FPGA devices by Styles et al. (Styles & Luk., 2002). Ye and Lewis (Ye & Lewis, 1999) proposed a new architecture for a 3D computer graphic rendering system which synthesizes 3D procedural textures in an FPGA device, enhancing the visual realism of computer rendered images, while achieving high pixel rate and small hardware cost. In order to improve the efficiency of 3D geometric models represented by a triangle mesh, some mesh compression/decompression algorithms were developed. Mitra and Chiueh (Mitra & Chiueh, 2002) proposed the BFT algorithm and presented a novel FPGA-based mesh decompressor.

Styles and Luk. (Styles & Luk., 2000) analyzed the customization of architectures for graphics applications for both general and specific purposes, and prototyping them using FPGAs. Based on their results, the authors remark the suitability of FPGAs. In the same work an API that allows the execution of OpenGL graphics applications on their reconfigurable architecture is also presented.

### 5.3 FPGA applications in computer graphics and multimedia

Computer graphics is another field that can benefit from the flexibility of software programmable devices. This explains the increasing attention paid to FGPAs in the last

years for the purpose of graphics acceleration, traditionally assigned to GPUs or graphics cards.
The suitability of FPGAs for the implementation of graphic algorithms has been analysed since the mid 90s. Singh and Bellec (Singh & Bellec, 1994) introduce the notion of *virtual hardware*, a methodology to execute complex processes on limited physical resources, using the dynamic reconfigurability of FPGAs. More recently, the authors of (Howes at al., 2006) compare the performance of different architectures based on FPGAs, GPUs, CPUs and Sony Playsation 2 vector units on different graphic algorithms using a unified description based on A Stream Compiler (ASC). This work shows how the FPGAs provide fast execution of the graphics algorithm with clocks at lower frequencies than its competitors. Nevertheless, performances are particularly dependent on the possibilities of optimization for each design. Radiosity high computational cost has been improved using FPGA devices by Styles et al. (Styles at al., 2002). Ye and Lewis (Ye & Lewis, 1999) proposed a new architecture for a 3D computer graphic rendering system which synthesizes 3D procedural textures in an FPGA device, enhancing the visual realism of computer rendered images, while achieving high pixel rate and small hardware cost. In order to improve the efficiency of 3D geometric models represented by a triangle mesh, some mesh compression/decompression algorithms were developed. Mitra and Chiueh (Mitra & Chiueh, 2002) proposed an algorithm and presented a novel FPGA-based mesh decompressor. Styles et al. (Styles at al., 2000) analyzed the customization of architectures for graphics applications for both general and specific purposes, and prototyping them using FPGAs. Based on their results, the authors remark the suitability of FPGAs. In the same work an API that allows the execution of OpenGL graphics applications on their reconfigurable architecture is also presented.

### 5.4 FPGA applications in communications

FPGA technology has appeared to be also very useful for communication systems. Two important factors encourage its expansion in this field: the falling prices of the devices and the inclusion of DSP capabilities. Typical communication problems such as data formatting, serial to parallel conversion, timing and synchronization can be faced naturally in a FGPA device thanks to its specific features. Furthermore, FPGAs are convenient for the development of the necessary glue logic for the interconnection of processors, modems, receivers, etc. Several examples can be found in the literature of the field. In (Ligocki et al, 2004) the authors describe the prototype development of a flexible communication system based on a FPGA. The main focus of this work is on software concerns, considering that FPGA technologies are the core of the project. Other authors exploited the spatial/parallel computation style of FPGAs for wireless communications. Due to the computational complexity of WLAN (Wireless local area network), and taking into account the capabilities of modern microprocessors, an implementation based exclusively on microprocessors is not convenient, requiring a large number of components. Parallel computation allows improving the efficiency of the implementation of the discrete components, and makes it possible to accelerate some complex parts of WLANs (Masselos & Voros, 2007).
Of special interest results the benefits of FPGAs for embedded software radio devices. In (Hosking, 2008), it is shown how its inherent flexibility makes of FGPA devices an excellent choice for coping with the increasing diverse array of commercial, industrial, and military electronic systems. Additionally, the large number of available IP cores offer optimized algorithms, interfaces and protocols which can shorten significantly the time-to-market.

### 5.5 FPGA applications in wearable computing

It is a common understanding that the concept of wearable computing comes from the tools developed to intensify the experience of seeing, what led to augmented reality. However, it can be noticed that in the literature different authors understand the concept of wearable systems in very different manners. Some authors claim that a system is wearable as long as it can be transported by a human. According to this, some authors present wearable solutions based on small variations of desktop applications in a back-up with a laptop (Feiner et al, 1997; Hoellerer et al, 1999). However, let us focus in this chapter on only wearable devices which do not constraint the mobility of the user. For this purpose, the use of FPGAs results of the highest interest. In wearable systems, the problem of combining simultaneously high performance and low power consumption requirements in small dimensions can be overcome with FPGAs. Contrary to ASICs (application specific integrated circuit), reconfigurable logic offers more flexibility to adapt dynamically the processes and the possibility of integrating different processing units in only one device. This way, it is possible to reduce the number of chips in a system, which can be an important advantage.

An interesting study on the improvements regarding energy saving when implementing critical software processes on reconfigurable logic can be found in (Stitt et al, 2002). The LART board, presented in (Bakker et al, 2001) combines a low-power embedded StrongARM CPU with an FPGA device, which offers a better power/MIPS ratio, pursuing power consumption reduction. The FPGA is used for dedicated data processing and for interconnecting several LARTs working in parallel. In a step forward, the authors in (Enzler et al, 2001) analyze the applications of dynamically reconfigurable processors in handheld and wearable computing. They consider a novel benchmark which includes applications from multimedia, cryptography and communications. Based on that work, the authors of (Plessl et al, 2003) presented the concept of an autonomous wearable unit with reconfigurable modules (WURM), which constitutes the basic node of a body area computing system. The WURM hardware architecture includes reconfigurable hardware and a CPU. In the prototype, the implementation is done on only one FPGA, including the CPU as a soft core.

Finally, let us remark the importance of networking for wearable computing. Indeed, the constraints in power consumption, size and weight of wearable computers increase the need for network capabilities to communicate with external units. A study about the interest of FPGA approaches for network on chip implementations across various applications and network loads is presented in (Schelle & Grunwald, 2008). Recently, several authors have followed FPGA-based approaches in their solutions. In (Munteanu & Williamson, 2005), an FPGA is exploited to provide consistent throughput performance to carry out IP packet compression for a network processor. (Wee et al, 2005) presents a network architecture that processes in parallel cipher block chaining capable 3DES cores by using about the 10% of the resources of an FPGA Xilinx Virtex II 1000-4. Within the frame of the European Diadem Firewall Project, IBM suggests the use of standalone FPGA-based firewalls in order to achieve an accelerated network architecture (Thomas, 2006).

## 6. FPGA-based platform for the development of AR applications

We have proposed a platform for developing fully FPGA-based embedded systems aimed for image and video processing applications. It is a hardware/software system created for speeding up and facilitating the development of embedded applications. As the survey of works in previous sections highlights, FPGA devices are very suitable for the implementation of the processing tasks involved in AR. The adoption of an FPGA-based approach allows executing different tasks and algorithms in parallel, which ensures the best performance and the optimum power consumption. The platform acquires video in standard analogue formats, digitizes, and stores it in external memory devices. In order to confer versatility to the embedded system, the platform includes as a key component an interface which allows for user interaction. This interface makes it possible to display text and, by means of hand pose recognition or voice recognition, to choose options and configure parameters. Thanks to it, the user can customize the functionality of the hardware at run-time.

### 6.1 Frame grabber

Video is a primary input to AR systems and can be typically used to develop video see-through systems, to execute vision-based tracking algorithms or as input to a user interface. In order to process video we have developed a frame grabber which accepts standard analogue video signal, converts it into digital and stores it in memory.

The frame grabber is based on the SAA7113 video input processor, from Philips Semiconductors, which is able to decode PAL, SECAM and NTSC from different sources (CVBS, S-video) into ITU-R BT 601. It is configured and controlled through I2C bus, so an I2C controller module must be included to properly manage the SAA7113. The SAA7113 presents video data at an 8 bit digital video port output, with 720 active pixels per line in YUV 4:2:2 format and a number of lines in a frame depending on the video standard (PAL, NTSC). The 4:2:2 output format implies that there is a luminance Y value for each pixel, but only a chrominance pair UV for two pixels. The YUV colorspace is used by the PAL and NTSC colour video standards. However, RGB is the most prevalent choice for computer graphics. Therefore, we have included a converter from YUV to RGB in the design. It just implements the corresponding linear equations, which can be found, e.g., in (Jack, 2005).

The image from the SAA7113 must be stored in a frame buffer. In our platform it is made of external asynchronous SRAM memory devices. A memory interface for generating the memory control signals and read / write operations was implemented on the FPGA.

Colour data stored in the memory is in YUV format since it optimizes the space and the access to memory. While in RGB format a pixel is defined with 24 bits, the YUV format from the video codec uses 32 bits to define two pixels, with exactly the same colour information in both RGB and YUV colorspaces. As physically each frame buffer consists of a 32 bit 256 KB SRAM, it is more efficient to store colour information in YUV colorspace, since it is possible to store two pixels in just one address, and so halving the number of access to the memory.

### 6.2 General purpose user interface

Unlike PC-based solutions, where visualization of text information is completely usual, this is not so natural in hardware-based solutions. Most of the present FPGA-based embedded systems do not offer an interface to the user. Sometimes they just consider a UART to connect with a computer and transfer some information. However, the use of a PC simply for running the software that manages the communications and the interface is a poor, very low efficient solution, even unfeasible in embedded systems. With the aim of overcoming this drawback of FPGA-based embedded systems, we have designed a hardware core which facilitates the addition of a user interface to FPGA-based systems. The core is based on MicroBlaze, a standard 32 bit RISC Harvard-style soft processor developed for Xilinx FPGA devices. This gives flexibility and versatility, and ensures fast re-design of the hardware architecture for enhanced or new applications. The core is made up of hardware components and software functions in different levels. Thanks to the core it is possible to present text information in a VGA monitor to the user, who can navigate through menus, select options and configure parameters by means of a pointer device. So, it provides the flexibility of adapting the systems to the user requirements or preferences. Next, its basic modules are described.

**Display of text and text fonts**

In order to display text, all the bitmaps associated to the font characters were previously defined and stored in a ROM memory using FPGA internal logic resources. The ROM works as a MicroBlaze peripheral, using a dedicated Fast Simplex Link (FSL) channel.

To display text, we have considered a text screen, which manages the visualization of the strings. In the default mode, it is a 640×480 array, whose elements correspond to the pixels in the VGA output. A 64 colours palette has been considered, which implies 6 bits for each pixel. Due to its size, the array is stored in external SRAM.

The text screen is defined as a peripheral and connected to the MicroBlaze microprocessor by means of the On-chip Peripheral Bus (OPB). The hardware of this peripheral includes the SRAM memory interface to control write and read operations and the logic to interpret the data from MicroBlaze into address and data buses values. It carries out two different tasks:

- it receives data from MicroBlaze, and manages the write operations in the SRAM memory just when a modification in the text information displayed is done.
- it reads data from the memory to show the text screen in the VGA monitor. These data are sent to the VGA Generator module. This process is independent on MicroBlaze.

In order to create the interface presented to the user, the function mb_OutTextXY has been prototyped to be instantiated in the software application running in MicroBlaze. It is similar to the equivalent standard C function, and it allows to define a text string and to specify its colour and position in the screen. When the mb_OutTextXY function is executed, the writing instruction of the text screen peripheral is called to write in the SRAM the colour values of the pixels which correspond to each element of the string, according to its position and its colour.

Once the strings are stored in the text screen, the basic user application waits for an interrupt from pointer device. When it happens, an interrupt handler classifies the interrupt and reads the coordinates of the pointer position. Since the position of each text string is known, it is possible to determine in the software application which one has been selected by the user, and then to reply with the desired actions.

**The pointing device**

A pointing device is required to interact within the user interface. With this aim, we have proposed a hand-based interface designed for mobile applications. It detects the user hand with a pointing gesture in images from a camera, and it returns the position in the image where the tip of the index finger is pointing at. In an augmented reality application the camera will be placed on a head mounted display worn by the user. A similar system is proposed in (Piekarski et al, 2004), but our approach is based on skin colour, without the need of glove or coloured marks. Our hand-based interface is aimed for performing pointing and command selection in the platform for developing FPGA-based embedded video processing systems herein described.

Vision-based algorithms have been used to build the hand and the pointing gesture recognizers. The image from the camera, once acquired, digitalized and stored by the previously described frame grabber, is segmented using an ad-hoc human skin colour classifier. Human skin colour has proven to be useful in applications related to face and hands detection and tracking. With this colour skin approach we try to generalize the use by eliminating external accessories, what reduces costs. The skin colour classifier is made of sub-classifiers, each one defined as a rule-based algorithm built from histograms in a colourspace. The rules in each colourspace define a closed region in the corresponding histogram: a pixel of an image is classified as skin if its colour components values satisfy the constraints established by the rules. Classifiers in the YIQ, YUV and YCbCr colorspaces have been considered, so three sub-classifiers have been implemented. To generate a unique output image, their outputs are merged using logical functions. The use of different colorspaces is aimed at achieving invariance to skin tones and lighting conditions. Further details can be found in (Toledo et al, 2006).

Once the image has been segmented the next processing task is to look for the pointing gesture. The solution adopted consists of convoluting the binary image from the skin classifier with three different templates: one representing the forefinger, other the thumb and the third the palm (Toledo et al, 2007). This modularity makes easier the addition of new functionality to the system through the recognition of more gestures. Due to the size of the hand and the templates, an optimized solution for the FPGA-based implementation of large convolution modules has been specifically developed. It can convolve binary images with a three-value template in one clock cycle independently of the template size. It is based on distributed arithmetic and has been designed using specific resources available in Xilinx FPGAs. The maximum size of the template depends on the FPGA device. In this application images are convoluted with 70×70 templates. Each convolution module sends to the MicroBlaze soft processor its maximum value and its coordinates on the image. A software algorithm running on MicroBlaze decides that a hand with the wanted gesture is present when the maximum of each convolution reaches a threshold and their relative positions satisfy some constraints derived from training data. Then, the algorithm returns the position of the forefinger. Otherwise, it reports that no pointing hand is detected.

The software application on MicroBlaze also includes an algorithm for dynamically adapting the skin classification and the parameters for hand recognition. Taking into account the number of pixels classified as skin in the image, the maximum value and the coordinates of each convolution and the detection or not of the pointing hand pose, it tunes each skin classifier and the merging of their binary output images in order to achieve the optimum classification rates, and it also tunes the values of the different constraints to their right values in order to find the desired hand posture. The FPGA implementation of these tasks allows taking advantage of parallelism in each processing stage at different levels. For example, the three classifiers for skin recognition are executed at the same time on an input pixel. Since the constraints of a classifier are all evaluated at the same time, the time required to classify a pixel is just the maximum delay associated to a constraint, three clock cycles in our case. Besides, the three convolutions that look for the hand position are performed in parallel, and the operations involved in each convolution are all executed at the same time in only one clock cycle. Meanwhile, the software application in MicroBlaze is using the

information extracted by the hardware modules as input parameters to the algorithm which estimates the presence and position of the hand. Thanks to exploiting the parallelism inherent to FPGA devices, the hand detection algorithm can process 640×480 pixel images at more than 190 frames per second with a latency of one frame. It also makes it feasible that new processing cores can be added to the system with small performance penalty.
In addition to the hand-based interface, a controller for a generic PS/2 mouse has been implemented and added to the MicroBlaze system as an OPB peripheral.

### 6.3 Generation of video signals

The platform can generate signals for displaying video on monitors and analog screens. The generation of the synchronization and RGB signals for a VGA monitor is carried out by the VGA generator module, which can be configured to generate different resolutions. The platform also includes the SAA7121, an integrated circuit from Philips which encodes digital video into composite and S-video signals. The video generator module also deals with the mixing of the video from the different sources included in the platform.

## 7. Portable real time system for helping visually impaired people

We have validated the usefulness of the described platform in an application for people affected by a visual disorder known as tunnel vision. It consists in the loss of the peripheral vision, while retaining clear and high resolution central vision. As shown in Fig. 3, it is like looking through a keyhole or a ring in the mid-periphery. Tunnel vision is associated to several eyes diseases, mainly glaucoma and retinitis pigmentosa, and reduces considerably the patient's ability to localize objects, which inevitably affects the patient's relationship with people and the environment.

Fig. 3. Simulation of patient affected by tunnel vision view. A residual 10° field of view has been considered to simulate the tunnel vision effect. The severe reduction of the visual field (right) can be observed comparing with the normal vision (left).

To aid affected people, it is necessary to increase the patient's field of view without reducing the usefulness of the high resolution central vision. With this aim, (Vargas-Martín & Peli, 2001) proposed an augmented view system where the contour information obtained from the image of a camera is superimposed on the user's own view. In their work, contours are generated by an edge detection algorithm performed by a four-pixel neighborhood gradient filter and a threshold function, running on a laptop PC (Vargas-Martín & Peli, 2002). They draw the conclusion that, although patients consider the system useful for navigating and obstacle avoiding, a specifically designed system to perform image processing and increase frame rate is necessary. Obviously, an effective improvement of the user's environment perception requires real time processing. To achieve it, we have used our FPGA-based hardware platform, which ensures the video frame rate and the low latency that the mobility of the application required.

Fig. 4. Simulation of patient's view through the HMD for outdoor and indoor environments. A residual 10° field of view has been considered to simulate the tunnel vision effect.

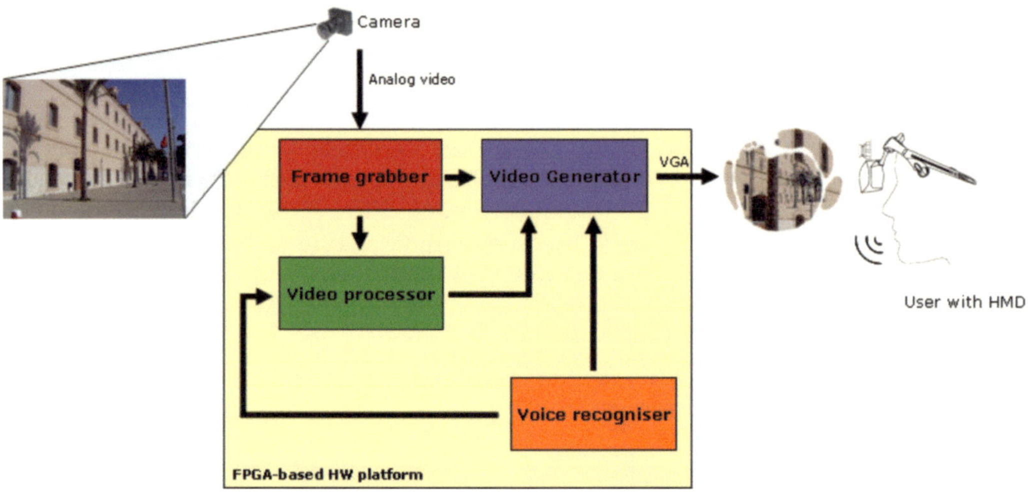


Fig. 5. Overall system schematic showing the main modules and the output view presented to the user.

In our system, the image acquired with the frame grabber is processed to extract contour information and it is used to enhance the user's perception of the environment by the superimposition on his own view of the entourage seen with a see-through head mounted display. To carry out the required processing we proposed the use of a Cellular Neural Network (CNN), which can be tuned to produce customized results and allows increasing the versatility of the system through the possibility of using different templates. The difficulties that rise when designing digital hardware implementation of CNNs are addressed in (Martínez et al, 2007; Martínez et al, 2008), where a novel approach is also proposed. It has been later optimized in (Martínez et al, 2009). After processed, the image from the camera must be properly zoomed out in order to be shown to the user in his residual central vision. A digital zooming algorithm has been included in the design with this purpose. It has been designed to minimize the number of access to the external memory where the original input data are stored.
The image resulting from the processing with the CNN, suitably minified, is sent to the VGA output available in the hardware platform. Fig. 4 shows some examples of the system output.

Due to the special characteristics of the target application, a vision-based interface such as the described in the previous section is not a suitable approach for interacting with this system. Instead, we have developed a voice recognition system which, as the whole of the herein described system, is implemented in FPGA. Since the aid device is conceived as a personal system, an easy and high-reliable speaker dependent recognition algorithm has been designed. In a simple and fast initial step, the user records a customized set of keywords. They are stored in external non-volatile flash memory, so the user only has to do it for the first time use. Later, in operating mode, the algorithm detects when the user says a word and convolves it with all the previously recorded ones. The latency response depends on the number of key words, but it is typically in the order of the milliseconds, fast enough to not appreciating any significant delay.

This user interface makes it feasible to adapt the functionality to the user preferences through, for example, basic modifications in the CNN processing, the minification factor or the colour and intensity of the contour information superimposed in his view.

The great amount of resources available in FPGA devices and their inherent parallelism make it possible to fulfill the requirements of the application without compromising the performance in speed, size and power consumption.

A simplified diagram of the whole system is shown in Fig. 5. The current prototype has been built with boards from Avnet, which populates Xilinx devices and the additional integrated circuits mentioned. The prototype also uses a Sony Glasstron PLMS700E as head mounted display to superimpose the video output on the user view. At the present moment, the system is under test and validation by visually impaired people, offering very successful initial results and improving the patients' ability to localize objects, orientate and navigate. Once passed the tests, a commercial device will be manufactured and packed into a small shoulder bag or belt bag.

## 8. References


Akin, A.; Dogan, Y. & Hamzaoglu, I. (2009). High performance hardware architectures for one bit transform based motion estimation, *IEEE Transactions on Consumer Electronics,* Vol. 55, No. 2, (May 2009), pp. (941-949), 0098-3063

Arnold, J.; Buell, D. & Hoang, D. (1993). The Splash 2 Processor and Applications, *Proc. of International conference on Computer Design,* pp. 482-485, 0-8186-4230-0, Los Alamitos, USA, 1993, IEEE

Assad, M.; Carmichael, D.; Cutting, D. & Hudson, A. (2003). AR phone: Accessible Augmented Reality in the Intelligent Environment, *Proc. of Australiasian Computer Human Interaction Conference,* pp. 232-235, Queensland, Australia, 2003

Bakker, J.; Langendoen, K. & Sips, H. (2001). LART: flexible, low-power building for wearable computers. *Proc. Int. Workshop on Smart Appliances and Wearable Computing,* pp. 255–259. Scottsdale, USA

Barfield, W. & Caudell, T. (2001). *Fundamentals of wearable computers and augmented reality,* Lawrence Erlbaum, 0805829016, USA

Black, D. & Donovan, J. (2004). *SystemC: From the Ground Up.* Kluwer Academic Publishers, ISBN: 978-0-387-29240-3

Billinghurst, M.; Hakkarainen, M. & Woodward, C. (2008). Augmented Assembly using a Mobile Phone, *Proc. of International Conference on Mobile and Ubiquitous Multimedia,* pp. 84-87, 978-1-60558-192-7, Umea, Sweden, december 2008, ACM

Bowen, O. & Bouganis, C. (2008). Real-Time Image Super Resolution Using an FPGA, *Proc. of International Conference on Programmable Logic and Applications*, pp. 89-94, 978-1-4244-1960-9, Heidelberg, Germany, September 2008, IEEE

Bodnar, M.; Curt, P.; Ortiz, F.; Carrano, C. & Kelmelis, E. (2009). An Embedded Processor for Real-Time Atmoshperic Compensation, *Proc. of SPIE conference on Visual Information Processing XVII*, pp. 1-8, Orlando USA, April 2009, SPIE

Dähne, P. & Kariginannis, J. (2002). Archeoguide: system architecture of a mobile outdoor AR system, *Proc. of International Symposium on Mixed and Augmented Reality*, pp. 263-264, 0-7695-1781-1, Darmstadt, Germany, September 2002, IEEE CS

Dellaert, F. & D. Tarip, S. (2005). A Multi-Camera Pose Tracker for Assisting the Visually Impaired, *Proc. of IEEE Computer Society Conference on Computer Vision and Pattern Recognition*, pp. 31–39, 0-0-7695-2372-2, San Diego, USA, June 2002, IEEE

Dawood, A.; Visser, S. & Williams, J. (2002). Reconfigurable FPGAS for real time image processing in space. *Proc. IEEE Int. Conf. Digital Signal Processing*, pp. 845–848, ISBN: 0-7803-7503-3, Greece, July 2002

Densmore, D. & Passerone, R. (2006). A Platform-Based Taxonomy for ESL Design. *IEEEDesign & Test of Computers*, Vol. 23, No. 5, pp. 359–374, ISSN: 0740-7475

Design & Reuse (2009). *Design & Reuse*. Web page: www.design-reuse.com

Diaz, J.; Ros, E.; Pelayo, F.; Ortigosa, E. & Mota, S. (2006). FPGA-based real-time optical-flow system, *IEEE Transactions on Circuits and Systems for Video Technology*, Vol. 16, No. 2, (Feb 2009), pp. (274-279), 1051-8215

Drayer, T.; King, W.; Tront, J. & Conners, R . (1995). A Modular and Reprogrammable Real Time Processing Hardware, MORRPH, *Proc. of IEEE Symposium on FPGA's for Custom Computing Machines*, pp. 11–19, 0-8186-7086-X, Napa Valley, USA, 1995.

Enzler, R.; Platzner, M., Plessl, C., Thiele, L. & Tröster, G. (2001). Reconfigurable processors for handheld and wearables: application analysis. *Proc. SPIE Conf. on Reconfigurable Technology: FPGAs and Reconfigurable Processors for Computing and Communications*, vol. 4525.

Feiner, S.; MacIntyre, B., Höllerer, T. & Webster, A. (1997). A touring machine: Prototyping 3d mobile augmented reality systems for exploring the urban environment. *Proc. of the First International Symposium on Wearable Computers (ISWC)*, pp. 74–81, Cambridge, Massachusetts, USA.

Foxlin, E; & Harrington, M. (2000) WearTrack: A Self-Referenced Head and Hand Tracker for Wearable Computers and Portable VR. *Proc. of the Fourth International Symposium on Wearable Computers (ISWC'00), pp.155.*

Garcia, R.; Batlle, J. & Bischoff, R. (1996). Architecture of an Object-Based Tracking System Using Colour Segmentation, *Proc. of International conference on Image and Signal Processing*, pp. 299-302, 0-4448-2587-8, Manchester, UK, November 1996, Elsevier Science

Guimarães, G.F.; Lima, J.P.S.M. & Teixeira, J.M.X.N., (2007). FPGA Infrastructure for the Development of Augmented Reality Applications *Proc. of the 20th annual conference on Integrated circuits and systems design*. pp. 336 – 341. Copacabana, Rio de Janeiro. ISBN:978-1-59593-816-9.

Hartenstein, R. (2002). Configware/Software Co-Design: Be Prepared for the Next Revolution, *Proc. of the 5th IEEE Workshop Design and Diagnostics of Electronic Circuits and Systems*, pp. 19–34, ISBN: 80-214-2094-4, Brno, Czech Republic, April, 2002.

Hartenstein, R. (2004). The digital divide of computing, *Proc. of the 1st conference on Computing frontiers*, pp. 357 - 362, ISBN:1-58113-741-9, Ichia, Italy, 2004, ACM, NY

Hoellerer, T.; Feiner, S., Terauchi, T., Rashid, G. & Hallaway, D. (1999) Exploring mars: developing indoor and outdoor user interfaces to a mobile augmented reality system. *Computers & Graphics 23* pp. 779–785.

Hosking, R.; (2008). Designing Software Radio Systems With FPGAs. www.pentek.com

Howes, L.; Price, P.; Mencer, O.; Beckmann, O. & Pell, O. (2006). Comparing FPGAs to Graphics Accelerators and the Playstation 2 Using a Unified Source Description, *Proc. of International Conference on Field Programmable Logic and Applications*, pp. 1-6, 1-4244-0312-X, Madrid, Spain, Aug 2006, IEEE

Hsiung, P.A.; Santambrogio, M.D. & Huang, C.H. (2009). *Reconfigurable System Design and Verification*. CRC Press, ISBN-13: 978-1420062663

In P.; Jung K.. & Kwang H. (2008). An Implementation of an FPGA-Based Embedded Gesture Recognizer Using a Data Glove, *Proc. of the 2nd International Conference on Ubiquitous Information Management and Communication*, pp. 496-500, 978-1-59593-993-7, Rennes, France, July 2008, ACM

ImpulseC (2009). *Impulse Accelerated Technologies*. Web page: www.impulseaccelerated.com

Jack, K. (2005). *Video Demystified*, LLH Technology, 2005, 1-878707-23-X, USA

Johnston C.; Gribbon, K. & Bailey, D. (2005). PGA Based Remote Object Tracking for Real-Time Control, *Proc. of International Conference on Sensing Technology*, pp. 66–72, Palmerston North, New Zealand, November 2005

Johnston, D.J.; Fleury, M., Downton, A.C. & Clark, A.F. (2005). Real-time positioning for augmented reality on a custom parallel machine. *Elsevier Image and Vision Computing*, No. 23 (2005) pp. 271-286, doi:10.1016/j.imavis.2003.08.002.

Keating, M. & Bricaud, P. (1999). *Reuse Methodology Manual*. Kluwer Academic Publishers, ISBN-13: 978-0792381754

Krips, M.; Lammert, T. & Kummert, A. (2002). FPGA Implementation of a Neural Network for a Real Time Hand Tracking System. *Proc. of IEEE International Workshop on Electronic Design, Test, Applications*. pp. 313–317, 0-7695-1453-7, Christchurch, New Zealand, 2002, IEEE CS

Krips, M.; Velten, J. & Kummert A. (2003). FPGA Based Real Time Hand Detection by Means of Colour Segmentation, *DOKLADY of Belarussian State University of Informatics and Radioelectronics*, (November 2003), pp. (156–162), 1729-7648

Ligocki, N.P.; Rettberg, A., Zanella, M., Hennig, A. & de Freitas, F.A.L., (2004). Towards a Modular Communication System for FPGAs, *Proc. of the Second IEEE International Workshop on Electronic Design, Test and Applications*, pp. 71.

Luk, W.; Lee, T.K., Rice, J.R., Shirazi, N. & Cheung P.Y.K. (1998). A Reconfigurable Engine for Real-Time Video Processing. *Proc. of the Seventh Annual IEEE Symposium on Field-Programmable Custom Computing Machines* pp. 136. Springer-Verlag.

Luk, W.; Lee, T.K., Rice, J.R., Shirazi, N. & Cheung, P.Y.K. (1999). Reconfigurable Computing for Augmented Reality. FCCM archive. ISBN:0-7695-0375-6 IEEE Computer Society Washington, DC, USA.

Martín, J.; Zuloaga, A.; Cuadrado, C.; Lázaro, J. & Bidarte, U. (2005). Hardware Implementation of Optical Flow Constraint Equation Using FPGAs, *Computer Vision and Image Understanding*, Vol. 98, No. 3, (2005), pp. (462-490)

Martínez, J.J.; Toledo, F.J. & Ferrández, J.M. (2007). Discrete-Time Cellular Neural Networks in FPGA, *Proc. of IEEE Symposium on Field-Programmable Custom Computing Machines (FCCM07)* pp. 293-294, 0-7695-2940-2, Napa, CA, USA, april 2007, IEEE CS

Martínez, J.J.; Toledo, F.J.; Fernández, E. & Ferrández, J.M. (2008). A retinomorphic architecture based on discrete-time cellular neural networks using reconfigurable computing, *Neurocomputing,* vol. 71, 2008, pp. 766-775, 0925-2312.

Martínez, J.J.; Toledo, F.J.; Fernández, E. & Ferrández, J.M. (2009). Study of the contrast processing in the early visual system using a neuromorphic retinal architecture, *Neurocomputing,* vol. 72, 2009, pp. 928-935, 0925-2312.

Masselos, K.; & Voros N. S. (2007). Implementation of Wireless Communications Systems on FPGA-Based Platforms. Hindawi Publishing Corporation EURASIP Journal on Embedded Systems Volume 2007, Article ID 12192, 9 pages. doi:10.1155/2007/12192.

Matsushita, N.; Hihara, D., Ushiro, T., Yoshimura, S., Rekimoto, J. & Yamamoto, Y. (2003). ID CAM: A Smart Camera for Scene Capturing and ID Recognition. *Proc. of the Second IEEE and ACM International Symposium on Mixed and Augmented Reality (ISMAR '03)* pp. 227-236, Tokyo, Japan, October 7-10. IEEE CS, Los Amitos, CA.

Mitra, T. & Chiueh, T. (2002). An FPGA Implementation of Triangle Mesh Decompression, *Proc. of IEEE Symposium Symp. on Field–Programmable Custom Computing Machines,* pp. 22–31, 0-7695-1801-X, Napa, USA, April 2002, IEEE

Möhring, M.; Lessig, C. & Bimber, O. (2004). Video See-Through AR on Consumer Cell-Phones, *Proc. of IEEE/ACM International Symposium on Mixed and Augmented Reality,* pp. 252-253, 0-7695-2191-6, Arlington, USA, november 2004, IEEE CS

Munteanu, D.; & Williamson, C. (2005). An FPGA-based Network Processor for IP Packet Compression. http://pages.cpsc.ucalgary.ca/~carey/papers/2005/FPGA.pdf

Olivares, J.; Benavides, I.; Hormigo, J.; Villalba, J. & Zapata, E. (2006). Fast Full-Search Block Matching Algorithm Motion Estimation Alternatives in FPGA, *Proc. of International Conference on Field Programmable Logic and Applications,* pp. 1-4, 1-4244-0312-X, Madrid, Spain, Aug 2006, IEEE

OpenCores (2009). Opencores. Web page: www.opencores.org

Ortiz, F.; Kelmelis, E. & Arce G. (2007). An Architecture for the Efficient Implementation of Compressive Sampling Reconstruction Algorithms in Reconfigurable Hardware, *Proc. of SPIE conference on Visual Information Processing XVI,* pp. 1-11, 0-8194-6697-2, Orlando USA, April 2007, SPIE

OSCI. (2009). *Open SystemC Initiative.* Web page: www.systemc.org

Passman, W. & Woodward, C. (2003). Implementation of an Augmented Reality System on a PDA, *Proc. of IEEE/ACM International Symposium on Mixed and Augmented Reality,* pp. 276-277, 0-7695-2006-5, Tokyo, Japan, october 2003, IEEE CS

Piekarski, W.; & Thomas, B.H. (2001). Tinmith-evo5: A software architecture for supporting research into outdoor augmented reality environments, *Technical Report, Wearable Computer Laboratory,* University of South Australia.

Piekarski, W.; Smith, R.; Wigley, G.; Thomas, B. & Kearney D. (2004). Mobile hand tracking using FPGAs for low powered augmented reality, *Proc. of 8th IEEE Int. Symposium on Wearable Computers (ISWC04)* pp. 190-191, 0-7695-2186-X, Arlington, VA, USA, november 2004, USA

Plessl, C.; Enzler, R., Walder, H., Beutel, J., Platzner, M., Thiele, L. & Tröster, G. (2003). The case for reconfigurable hardware in wearable computing. Personal and Ubiquitous Computing, vol.7, no. 5, pp. 299–308. Springer-Verlag.

Riess, P. & Stricker, D. (2006). AR on-demand: a practicable solution for augmented reality on low-end handheld devices, *Proc. of AR/VR Workshop of the German Computer Science Society*, pp. 119-130, 3-8322-5474-9, Coblence, Germany, 2006

Schelle, G.; & Grunwald, D. (2008). Exploring FPGA network on chip implementations across various application and network loads. *Proc. of the Field Programmable Logic and Applications (FPL '08)* . pp. 41-46. Sept. 2008. ISBN: 978-1-4244-1960-9 DOI: 10.1109/FPL.2008.4629905.

Singh, S. & Bellec, P. (1994). Virtual Hardware for Graphics Applications Using FPGAs, *Proc. of IEEE Workshop FPGAs for Custom Computing Machines*, pp. 49–58, 0-8186-5490-2, Napa, USA, April 1994

Smith, R.; Piekarski, W. & Wigley, G. (2005). Hand Tracking for Low Powered Mobile AR User Interfaces, *Proc. of the Sixth Australasian User Interface Conference (AUIC '05)* pp. 7-16, Newcastle, Australia, January 31st - February 3rd, 2005, Australian CS, Sydney, NSW.

Stitt, G.; Grattan, B., Villarreal, J. & Vahid, F. (2002). Using on-chip configurable logic to reduce embedded system software energy. *Proc. IEEE Symp. on Field-Programmable Custom Computing Machines*, pp. 143–151. Napa, USA.

Styles, H. & Luk, W. (2000). Customising Graphics Applications: Techniques and Programming Interface, *Proc. of IEEE Symposium on Field-Programmable Custom Computing Machines*, pp. 77–90, 0-7695-0871-5, Napa, USA, 2000

Styles, H. & Luk, W. (2002). Accelerating radiosity calculations using reconfigurable platforms, *Proc. of IEEE Symposium on Field-Programmable Custom Computing Machines*, pp. 279–281, 0-7695-1801-X, Napa, USA, September 2002, IEEE

Takayuki, S.N. & Aizawa, K. (2002). Real time Objects Tracking by Using Smart Image Sensor and FPGA, *Proc. of International Conference on Image Processing*, pp. 441–444, 0-7803-7622-6, Rochester, New York, 2002, IEEE

Tanase, C.; Vatavu, R., Pentiuc, S. & Graur, A. (2008). Detecting and Tracking Multiple Users in the Proximity of Interactive Tabletops, *Advances in Electrical and Computer Engineering*, Vol. 8, No. 2, (2008), pp. (61-64)

Thomas D.; (2006). FPGA Network Firewalling. Report of the Diadem Firewall Project. *www.doc.ic.ac.uk/~dt10/public/diadem.ppt.*

Toledo, F.J.; Martínez, J.J. & Ferrández, J.M. (2007). Hand-based Interface for Augmented Reality, *Proc. of IEEE Symposium on Field-Programmable Custom Computing Machines (FCCM07)* pp. 291-292, 0-7695-2940-2, Napa, CA, USA, april 2007, IEEE CS

Toledo, F.J.; Martinez, J.J., Garrigos, J. & Ferrandez, J. (2005). FPGA Implementation of an Augmented Reality Application for Visually Impaired People. *Proc. of the Fifteenth International Conference on Field Programmable Logic and Applications (FPL '05)* . pp 723-724. Tampere, Finland, August 24-26, 2005. IEEE CS, Los Amitos, CA.

Toledo, F.J.; Martínez, J.J.; Garrigós, F.J., Ferrández, J.M. & Rodellar, V. (2006). Skin color detection for real time mobile applications, *Proc. of Int. Conference on Field Programmable Logic and Applications (FPL06)* pp. 271-274, 1-4244-0312-X, Madrid, Spain, august 2006

Vargas-Martín, F. & Peli, E. (2001). Augmented view for tunnel vision: device testing by patients in real environments, *Digest of Technical Papers, Society for Information Display International Symposium* pp. 602-605, San José, CA, USA, 2001

Vargas-Martín, F. & Peli, E. (2002). Augmented-view for restricted visual field: multiple device implementations, *Optometry and Vision Science,* vol. 79, no. 11, 2002, pp. 715-723, 1040-5488

Veas, R. & Kruijff, E. (2008). Vesp'R: design and evaluation of a handheld AR device, *Proc. of IEEE/ACM International Symposium on Mixed and Augmented Reality,* pp. 43-52, Cambridge, UK, September 2008, IEEE

Vicente, A.; Munoz, I.B.; Molina, P.J. & Galilea, J.L.L. (2009). Embedded Vision Modules for Tracking and Counting People, *IEEE Transaction on Instrumentation and Measurement,* Vol. 58, No. 0, (September 2009), pp. (3004-3011), 0018-9456

Villasenor, J.; Shoner, B.; Chia, K.N.; Zapata, C.; Kim, H.J.; Jones, C.; Lansing, S. & Mangione-Smith, B. (1996). Configurable Computing Solutions for Automatic Target Recognition, *Proc. IEEE Symp. FPGAs for Custom Computing Machines,* pp. 70–79, ISBN: 0-8186-7548-9, Napa, USA, 1996

Wagner, D.; Pintaric, T., Ledermann, F. & Schmalstieg, D. (2005). Towards Massively Multi-user Augmented Reality on Handheld Devices. *Proc. of the Third International Conference on Pervasive Computing (PERVASIVE '05)* pp. 208-219, Munich, Germany, May 8-13, 2005, Springer Berlin/Heidelberg, New York, NY.

Wee, C.M.; Sutton, P.R. & Bergmann, N.W. (2005). An FPGA network architecture for accelerating 3DES - CBC. *Proc. of the IEEE 15th International Conference on Field Programmable Logic and Applications (FPL),* Tampere, Finland, pp. 654-657. August 2005. ISBN: 0-7803-9362-7

Ye, A. & Lewis, D. (1999). Procedural Texture Mapping on FPGAs, *Proc. of the 1999 ACM/SIGDA Seventh International Symposium on Field-Programmable Gate Arrays,* pp. 112 - 120, 1-58113-088-0, Monterey, USA, 1999, ACM

Yu, N.; Kim, K. & Salcic, Z. (2004). A new motion estimation algorithm for mobile real-time video and its FPGA implementation, *Proc. of IEEE Region 10 Conference: Analog and Digital Techniques in Electrical Engineering,* pp. 383-386, 0-7803-8560-8, Chiang Mai, Thailand, November 2004, IEEE

Zhou, F.; Been-lirn Duh, H. & Billinghurst, M. (2008). Trends in Augmented Reality Tracking, Interaction and Display: A Review of Ten Years of ISMAR, *Proc. of IEEE/ACM International Symposium on Mixed and Augmented Reality,* pp. 193-202, Cambridge, UK, September 2008, IEEE

# 4

# A Virtual Harp for Therapy in An Augmented Reality Environment

Tanasha Taylor[1] and Shana Smith[2]
[1]*Iowa State University*
[2]*National Taiwan University*
[1]*U.S.A.*
[2]*Taiwan*

## 1. Introduction

In the United States, between thirty-four and forty-three million people have some type of disability, with physical, sensory, mental, and self-care effects ranging from mild to severe. For people over age sixty-five, nearly 13.9 million people, or thirty-five percent, have some level of disability (Statistics of Disability, 2007). According to the U.S. Department of Commerce, a person is considered to have a disability when that person has difficulty with any of the following tasks (Kraus et al., 1996):

1. Normal body functions, such as seeing, hearing, talking, or walking
2. Activities of daily living, such as bathing or dressing
3. Instrumental activities of daily living, such as shopping or doing laundry
4. Certain expected roles, such as doing housework, school work, or working at a job
5. Performing usual activities, such as driving or taking a bus

In the U.S., an estimated four percent of the non-institutionalized population age five and over, that is 9.2 million individuals, need personal assistance with one or more activities. People who need assistance with instrumental activities of daily living, also considered independent living activities, number over 5.8 million, while 3.4 million people need assistance in activities of daily living, which are personal functioning activities (Kraus et al., 1996). Several different factors can contribute to developing some level of disability, for example, strokes, arthritis, or injuries, or individuals may be born with disabilities such as cerebral palsy.

There are many different treatment methods to reduce or correct disabilities. The most common treatment method is to enrolling the disabled individual in some type of therapy program, such as physical, occupational, recreational, musical, or speech therapy.

Many traditional therapeutic interventions used in rehabilitation programs have demonstrated that intensive and repeated practice may be necessary to modify neural organization, effect recovery of functional motor skills, and promote functional recovery (Jack et al., 2000). With traditional therapy, patients usually visit a therapist once or twice a day for half hour sessions. Their visit frequency drops to once or twice a week when they become outpatients. Finally, when they reach a predetermined level of function, their access to therapy is terminated even if residual deficits remain. It has been reported that while in sessions, common problems during therapy, such as boredom, fatigue, lack of motivation, or cooperation, result in low interaction function between the patient and the environment (Sveistrup, 2004).

Due to decreasing equipment costs and increasing processor speed, computer simulations have become more common over the last decade. Such technology is currently being explored for potential benefits in therapeutic intervention for retraining coordinated movement patterns (Jack et al., 2000). Virtual reality (VR) can create the most appropriate individualized treatment needs and training protocols by providing an environment in which the intensity of feedback and training can be systematically manipulated and enhanced (Jack et al., 2000; Sveistrup, 2004; Kuhlen & Dohle, 1995). In addition, VR-based rehabilitation systems can provide a unique experience that is engaging, functional, and purposeful, in a manner similar to computer games, which is important for stimulating patient motivation. Additionally, VR systems can provide precise real-time feedback, which further increases the motivating effect for patients (Kuhlen & Dohle, 1995).

As an example, Todorov et al. (1997) used a VR system to create a computer animation of a table tennis task for training a difficult multi-joint movement. The system had a virtual ball and virtual paddles which provided the teacher and the trainee the movement variables most relevant for successful performance of the task by the trainee. The system also used augmented feedback. Their results showed that virtual environment training provided better training for the task compared to a comparable amount of training in a real environment.

In a different virtual environment training study, two patients with hemiplegia were trained on an upper-extremity reaching task (Holden, 1999). The two patients were evaluated pre- and post-VR training using motor recovery and functional ability tests and a real-world test. During the training, subjects practiced a virtual task similar to the real task, trying to imitate a virtual teacher's performance. Post-training, reaching errors during real-world performance were reduced by 50%. Both subjects improved in the trained task, indicating transfer of skills from the virtual environment to real world performance. On the other hand, motor recovery and functional scores showed little to no change. However, one subject acquired the ability to perform several functional tasks. The results suggest that virtual environment training has a positive impact in stroke rehabilitation.

Reiss and Weghorst (1995) used augmented reality (AR) to help patients with akinesia Parkinson's disease overcome difficulties stepping over objects in their paths when initiating and sustaining walking. They found that a stable cue appearing about six inches in front of the toes was required to initiate the first step, while cues scrolling toward the feet were needed to sustain walking. In addition, the effectiveness of the visual cue was dependent on the degree and type of akinesia, showing that cues that are more realistic are needed as the severity of akinesia increases.

For individuals with spinal cord injuries, a VR-enhanced orthopedic appliance was developed linking a gait-inducing exoskeleton to a HUD. The exoskeleton used a semi-rigid sling to support the bust and lower limbs of the user and move the lower extremities to support and induce human gait. In preliminary study results, a 26-year old with complete paraplegia showed improvements in self-confidence, increased relaxation, and activity scores, and higher levels of optimism and motivation (Riva, 1998).

VR assessment and intervention tools have also been developed. A hand system with force feedback was developed in a virtual environment to complete various tasks such as a virtual PegBoard and reach-to-grasp exercises. The system was useful for augmenting rehabilitation chronic-phase patients following strokes. Skills also transferred to a functional clinical outcome measure as well as improvement on a variety of movement parameters (Adamovich, 2003).

Luo et al. (2005) conducted a pilot experiment on finger extensions for three male stoke survivors participating in 30-minute training sessions held three times per week for six weeks. Users were placed in an AR environment trying to grasp 15 virtual objects followed by 15 real objects, one using assistance from a body-powered orthosis (BPO), one using assistance from a pneumatic-powered device (PPD) and one using only AR. Their results show an encouraging trend of improvement for finger extension capability in the impaired hand after 6 weeks of training in functional tests scores, peak angular extension speed, maximal displacement, and BPO assistive force.

Environments in VR are being used in therapy treatment for anorexia, psychological ailments, post-traumatic stress disorder, and pain. Using real-world scenarios in the treatment for post-traumatic stress disorder and phobias patients would have enough exposure for habituation to occur and overcome their ailment to help live their lives. In order to help individuals with pain such as burn patients VR is being used for distraction. When the patients explored the VR winter environment, their pain tolerance lowered allowing their painful wounds to be debrided. Patients with anorexia are placed in a VR house with many doors to meet various person-sized animations. These animations include their judged ideal size, this help the patient form more accurate mental pictures of themselves (Westerhoff, 2007).

For individuals with spinal cord injuries, a video-capture virtual reality system was used for balance training. The study had 13 participants experience three virtual environments, birds and balls, soccer, and snowboard, compared to a group of 12 non-disabled participants. The participants expressed interest in having additional sessions suggesting this enhances motivation and enjoyment during a therapy-like session. The amount of effort exerted from the participants performing the three environments at different levels of difficulties without having any frustrations or discouragement shows that the ability to adjust the level of difficulty of environments and the related proper motor responses corresponds to the key rehabilitation principle (Kizony, 2005).

VR in rehabilitation has unique attributes for achieving many rehabilitation goals including the encouragement of experiential, active learning; the provision of challenging but safe and ecologically valid environments; the power to motivate patients to perform to their utmost ability; and the capacity to record objective measures of performance (Weiss & Katz, 2004).

In this paper, a realistic virtual harp was created to assist individuals with disabilities for their rehabilitation therapy using augmented reality technology and a haptic device. In our prior study, we created a prototype computer-generated harp for interactive musical experiences (Taylor, et al., 2007). A simple harp was created and force feedback was provided using a Sensable Phantom Omni haptic device.

## 2. Augmented reality

Head Mounted Device (HMD). Such a device presents an image acquired by a camera mounted on the HMD, producing the effect of seeing through the video display while allowing virtual objects to be displayed. When users interact with a special marker in the real world, this marker is tracked by the system allowing the overlay of computer graphics with respect to the marker. The user can thus move virtual objects in and with respect to the real world by simple manipulation of the marker. The movements of the camera or the movement of the marker will move the virtual harp. This allows the user to manually move the harp to "zoom" in or out, or to select its exact position in their view.

A popular open source package for tracking such markers and handling the see-through video display is the ARToolkit (Lamb, 2007). The system is cross platform and transparently handles the video capture, video display and marker extraction, and calculates the marker transform relative the camera. It is possible to use many different markers, which are then individually identified and tracked, for the simultaneous tracking of multiple marked objects in the real world.

ARToolKit uses computer vision algorithms to track the users' viewpoint, using video tracking libraries to calculate, in real time, the real camera position and orientation relative to physical markers. ARToolKit tracking works by capturing camera video of the real world allowing the computer to search through each video frame for any square shape. Then, it calculates the position of the camera relative to a black square, which draws a computer graphics model from that position to render graphics overlaid on the real world (Kato & Billinghurst, 1999).

The challenge is to integrate the video capturing and marker tracking of ARToolkit with the computer graphics and haptic feedback. The software package H3D API is chosen for graphical rendering and haptics. H3D API is an X3D based open source system for handling multi modal rendering and simulation with support for a wide range of display technologies and haptic devices. It is available for the three major operating systems and allows for programming at three different levels: X3D for scene graph definition and modeling, Python for interactive behavior, animation, and dynamics, and C++ for the extension and implementation of base functionality.

A bridge called HART handles the connection between ARToolkit and H3D API. The bridge is implemented in C++ and provides a set of X3D scene graph nodes for the convenient representation of basic ARToolkit functionality inside of H3D API. With HART an augmented reality applications can be easily built which take advantage of all the power provided by the H3D API with the ease of using ARToolkit.

The bridge connects the H3D API functionality with ARToolkit through a singleton object, which is represented by a "Bindable" node in the H3D scene graph. One and only one such node is required for the system to work. As this node is created and initialized the required initialization of ARToolkit is performed and all the properties specified for the node through X3D are used to configure the video capturing and loading marker for the ARToolkit. Any other node representing a functionality of ARToolkit make calls to the singleton node to perform their respective action.

There are two general types of nodes in the bridge: a see-through background node (SeeThroughBackground) for displaying the camera image as a background, and various nodes for using marker transforms. The presented prototype uses a see-through viewpoint node (SeeThroughViewpoint) that updates the viewpoint of the virtual environment to match the viewpoint of the camera in the real world relative the coordinate system defined by a specified marker. This way the actual coordinate system for the virtual environment will be stationary regardless of marker movements. This is done by querying ARToolkit for the viewpoint transform that matches the selected marker and applying that to the viewpoint in H3D. Using the SeeThroughViewpoint node together with the SeeThroughBackground node produces an augmented reality environment, as shown in Fig. 1.

Since the coordinate system for the virtual environment does not change as the HMD moves relative the marker, the harp object will not move relative the haptics device. This is essential for the stability of the haptic rendering of the harp since the positional precision required for haptic rendering is several magnitudes higher than the precision, which can be provided by optical tracking today.

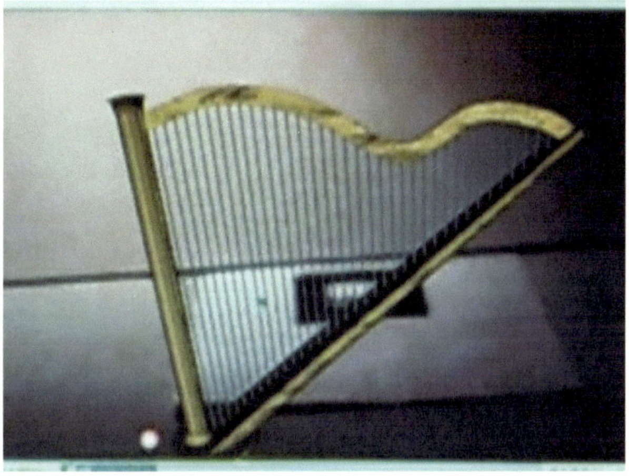

Fig. 1. Harp in augmented environment

## 3. Harp string node and vibration model

Originally, a Python code was used to produce the string vibration animations (Taylor et al., 2007). However, the first limitation was the code needed to have each string coded with all the necessary properties to do the animations and routed to the X3D file. The next limitation was caused by the fact that each string and their properties had to be written in the Python code; any change to the strings properties in the X3D file or movement to the harp's placement on the screen would cause the haptic device to be unable to pluck the harp strings. This code did not have any of the vibration model equations implemented, and the code was limited in which mathematical functions it had to use. The final harp design required the use of thirty-six strings and realistic real-time vibrations. These limitations in Python would have made the code very long and confusing for using thirty-six strings, resulting in the loss of the ability to allow the users to move the harp in any position without providing the real-time vibrations. Therefore, a H3D node for the string animation was written in C++ to eliminate the limitations found in using the Python code.

The string is modeled as a mass-spring system where having N number of masses would produce N number of modes of transverse oscillations. For this computer-generated harp, the first six modes of oscillation are considered for the string vibration animation interaction to minimize the computation time. Each mass-spring section will be considered as a mass point along the string and can only move in one plane. On a harp, the strings are fixed at both ends of the instrument and since the string is modeled with many mass points along the line, the vibration motion will be analyzed using a Fourier analysis for each point along the line.

Since the strings on a realistic harp are not positioned on a starting base location, it was needed to take into account a starting position and an ending position in order to draw the strings in the proper location as a realistic harp. Using the y-axis starting point position ($P_2$) and the y-axis ending point position ($P_1$) the string length $L$ will be $P_1$-$P_2$. As shown in Fig. 2, this simulates the realistic pulling motion limit variables in the string to provide the calculation of the pulling limit along the string.

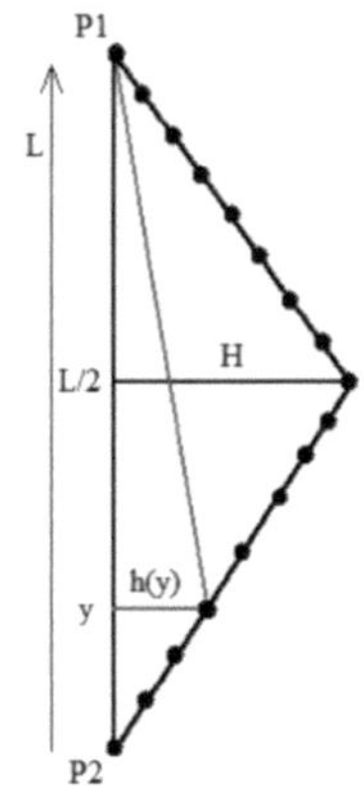


Fig. 2. String pulling limit

The string pulling limit now needs to take into account the y-axis starting point position and the y-axis ending point position in order to use this equation for any string in any position on the harp model. The maximum pulling limit (H) is based on half of the distance between two strings before hitting the next string along the x-axis. The string pulling limit equation requires the use of two equations for the lower half and the upper half as in Eq. (1).
String pulling limit:

$$h(y) = \begin{pmatrix} \left(2H/L\right)(y - P2), P2 \le y \le L/2 \\ \left(-2H/L\right)(y - P1), L/2 \le y \le P1 \end{pmatrix} \tag{1}$$

The periodic function of the string was defined based on the pluck location with the fundamental frequency having a wavelength of 2L giving the limit on the y-axis of $-L$ and $L$ as shown in Fig. 3. This diagram leads to three sets of equations based on the pluck location in the periodic function used to do the analysis of the Fourier coefficient for the first six modes of oscillation, as shown in Eq. (2).
Fourier coefficient:

$$C_n(y) = 1/2L \int_{-L}^{L} y(z)\sin(nk_n z)dz =$$
$$\begin{pmatrix} 1/2L\left[\left(h(y)/y\left(\sin(nk_1z)/n^2k_1^2 - z*\cos(nk_1z)/nk_1\right)\right)\right]_{-L}^{L}, -y < z < y \\ 1/2L\left[\left(h(y)/(L-y)\left((z-L)*\cos(nk_1z)/nk_1 - \sin(nk_1z)/n^2k_1^2\right)\right)\right]_{-L}^{L}, y < z < L \\ 1/2L\left[\left(-h(y)/(L-y)\left(\sin(nk_1z)/n^2k_1^2 - (L+z)*\cos(nk_1z)/nk_1\right)\right)\right]_{-L}^{L}, -L < z < -y \end{pmatrix} \tag{2}$$

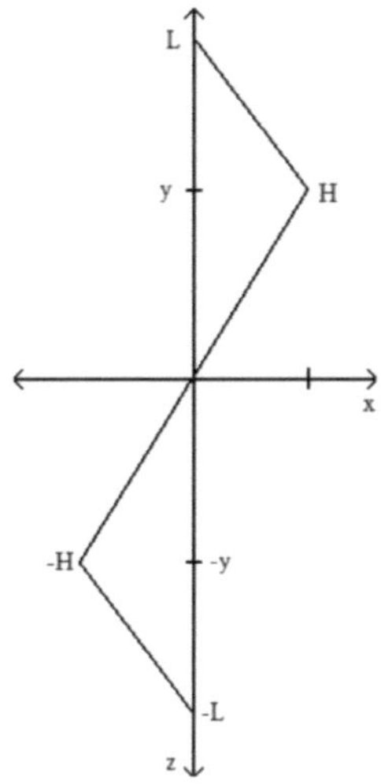


Fig. 3. Periodic motion diagram

To simulate the vibration motion for each time frame for each node along the string, the Fourier coefficient values are calculated in the Fourier analysis by Eq. (3). The string properties, wavenumber by Eq. (4), and eigenfrequency by Eq. (5), also known as harmonics would be defined as functions calls to be used during the Fourier analysis calculation. The damping term ($\Gamma$) value was defined on a trial and error basis by matching the vibration decay to the sound decay, and the frequency ($f$) value in the eigenfrequency equation was defined using the MIDI note frequency definition for each string. The string's note frequency is placed in a list and selected based on the user's string number input.
Fourier analysis:

$$x(y,t) = \sum_{n=1}^{N} C_n(y)\sin(k_n z)\cos(2\pi * v_n t)e^{-\Gamma t} \tag{3}$$

Wavenumber:

$$k_n = {n\pi}/{L} \tag{4}$$

Eigenfrequency:

$$v_n = n * f \tag{5}$$

A flow chart for describing the process is shown in Fig. 4. The program can be divided into three sections with section one handling the line drawing for the string called Harpline, section two handling the forces for the string called Harpforce, and section three handling the sound for the string called Harpsound, all being place in the group node called Harp.
When the program starts Harpline, an IndexedLineSet node initially draws the string with a vertical line using two hundred points equally spaced from the line length equation being divided by the number of points in the direction of the y-axis. To manipulate the line's points, the IndexedLineSetIsTouched feature is routed in the X3D code and is initially set to false, and the haptic device is informed if the line is touched which starts the animation for pulling the string. One example is shown in Fig. 5.

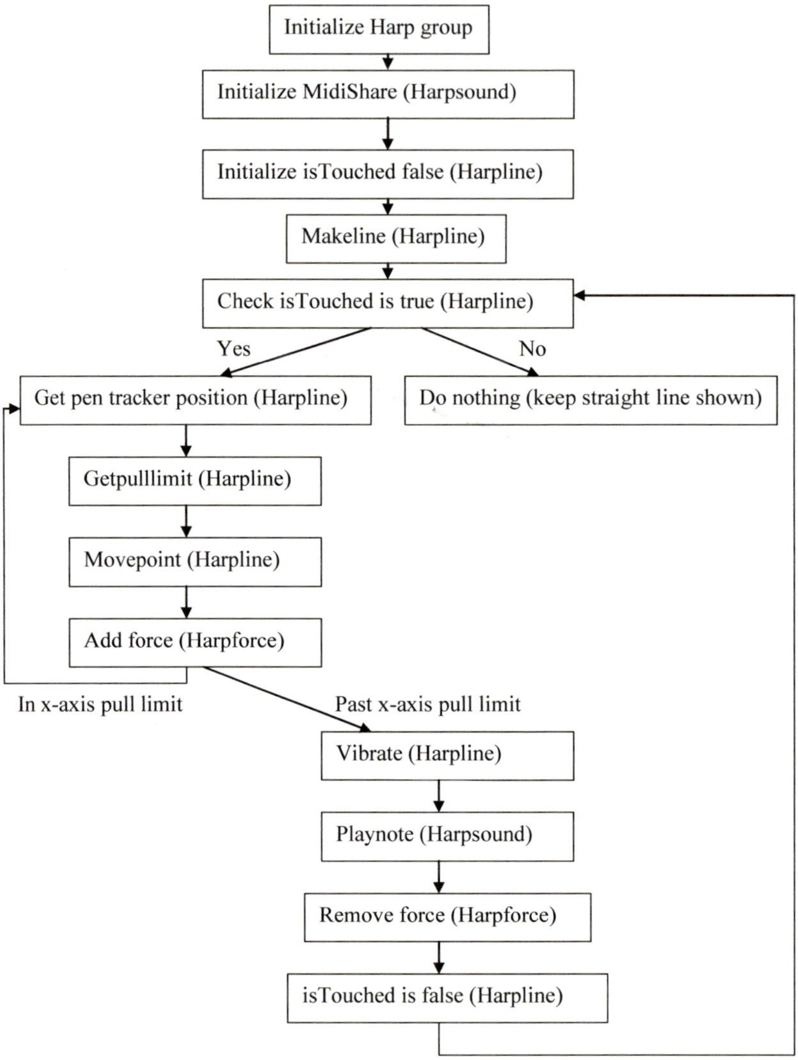


Fig. 4. Program flow chart

Fig. 5. Plucking harp string

During the pulling of the string, Harpforce an H3DForceEffect node is activated. It creates a spring effect by using the distance difference from the initial position to the current position multiplied by the spring constant to give the users the feeling of string tension while the line is pulled within the pulling limit using the Phantom Omni's haptic device. Once the user reaches the string's calculated pulling limit, the string would start the vibration animation removing the spring effect and producing the appropriate MIDI harp note sound.
The vibrate function in Harpline starts a real-time timer loop for drawing each of the two hundred points along the string in the correct position from the Fourier analysis equations, for which the timer is reset every time the string is touched. The vibration damping term value was found by matching the MIDI sound decay to the visual string vibration decay.

## 4. Realistic harp design and sound

To model the realistic harp, SolidWorks 2001 was used, and it was able to convert the model file into an X3D file that H3D uses. Using a model guide, the harp frame was divided into four parts consisting of the column, base, soundboard, and string frame. This SolidWorks assembly file was then converted into an X3D file for which now the model is a series of IndexFaceSets points with a wood texture applied on the face. The strings were colored a light gray color to resemble the color of metal strings.
The Harpsound node created in C++ used MIDIShare for the sound output. The harp's sound range is from C2 to C7 on the MIDI sound range scale. When the program starts Harpsound, an X3DChildNode node initially opens the MIDIShare system and changes the sound output to produce harp type MIDI sounds. When the string's calculated pulling limit is reached, the MIDI pitch value of the string was sent to the playnote function in Harpsound. Once the vibration animation starts, there is a switch to activate the sound.

## 5. Virtual therapist

In most therapy sessions, the therapist would prompt the individual in therapy to perform an exercise and observe the individual during therapy exercises for errors and improvements. Once the individual leaves the therapy sessions, the therapist wants the individual in therapy to continue performing the exercises on their own. Therapy exercises are repetitive, causing the individual performing the therapy exercises to become bored and unmotivated to continue performing the exercises on their own. Therefore to allow the individual to engage in self-motivating therapy exercises outside the therapy sessions and have the therapist observe the individual during therapy exercises without musical knowledge, in this study, a virtual therapist feature was developed.
The virtual therapist feature includes a sequence of colored strings. The patients can play a song by plucking the harp by following the colored strings. Here, Python is used to create the virtual therapist guiding feature because Python allows the users to modify the string sequence easily using a text editor and the program does not need to be compiled again.
The virtual scene uses a 3D sphere as a 3D button to active the virtual therapist feature. As shown in Fig. 6, touching this 3D sphere allows individuals to follow a sequence of notes by following the colored strings to help the user identify the notes, similar to playing the Simon game. In this study, the virtual therapist will highlight the strings and guide the users to play the song "Joy to the World".

### 5.1 User study

This study consisted of 20 participants, requirements of our participants included having upper limb limitations or any disability affecting their arm or hand. The age group ranged from ages 18-60. The total age distributaries are 55% of participants in the age range of 18 and 30, 10% in the range of 31 and 40, 15% in the range of 41 and 50, and 20% in the rage of 51 and 60. Of these participants, 80% have been in traditional therapy where Fig. 6 shows the distribution of years.

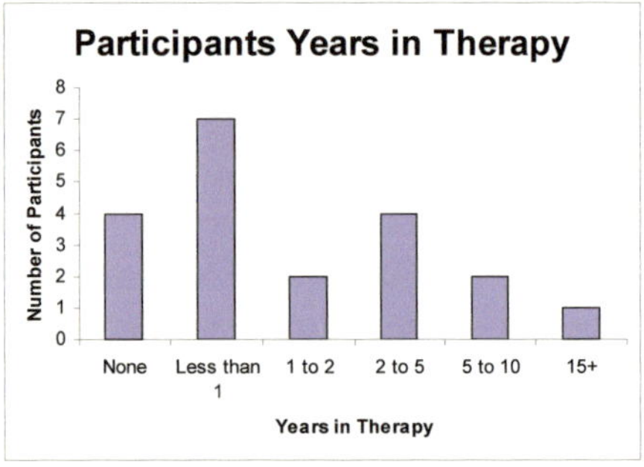


Fig. 6. Years in therapy

In addition, 15 participants (75%) had have some type of musical experience, 17 participants (85%) have not used any type of computer-aided music software or equipment, and the remaining 3 participants (15%) had experience with computer software such as sheet music writing, keyboarding, and Guitar Hero.

There were 12 females and 8 males that participated in the study. The user study testing procedure consisted of the four following sections:

1. Greeting and background questionnaire
2. Orientation
3. Performance test
4. Participant debriefing

The participant were greeted and made to feel comfortable while the study was explained. Each participant was required to sign a consent form before the study began. During this time, the participants were informed on the issues of confidentiality and allowed an opportunity to ask any questions they might have concerning the test. Each participant was asked to fill out a short questionnaire gathering basic background information before using the system. Participants were given an explanation of the virtual harp therapy system equipment so that they would become familiar with the technology and understand how it is being used. This was followed by an informed discussion about how the system will work and an explanation of the interface with the equipment. During the observed testing, the participants were positioned in front of the virtual harp setup. In order to help adjust to the unique instrument, participants were asked to familiarize themselves with the harp and its interface by freely playing the virtual harp.

After the familiarization period, the participants were asked to follow a simple sequence of notes using the virtual therapist feature, as shown in Fig. 7. After the testing tasks were complete, the participant were asked to fill out a brief questionnaire pertaining to the usability of the virtual harp, development of skills, improvement in range of motion, and entertainment value.

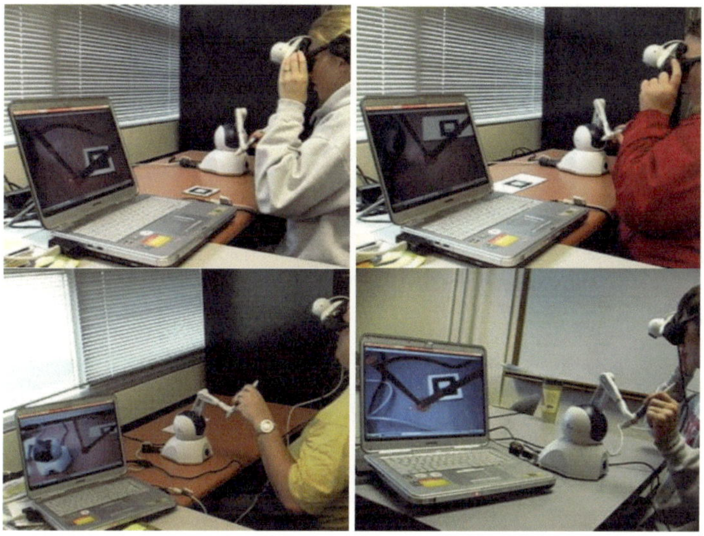

Fig. 7. User study participants playing the virtual harp

### 5.2 Study results

Based on the participants' type of disability they were formed into two groups. There were 9 participants classified with long-term disability (cerebral palsy, arthritis) and 11 participants classified with short-term disability (pinched nerves, injuries). Statistical analysis was done using one sample t-test for the whole study group (20) and to compare the long-term disability and short-term disability. For users with either long-term disability or short-term disability the hypotheses are the following:

1. The virtual harp system would be easy and comfortable from using to the users
2. The users would improve their range of motion and skills
3. Users would be motivated to continue playing the system for therapy

The following questions are used as a composite result related to the ease and comfort from using for testing for the first hypothesis.

1. How would you describe the level of difficulty in using the virtual harp?
   (1=very easy, 5= very difficult)
2. Did you find that the virtual harp acted in a predictable manner?
   (1=strongly agree, 5= strongly disagree)
3. How satisfying was the virtual harp to use?
   (1=very satisfying, very unsatisfying)
4. Was the virtual harp comfortable to use physically?
   (1=strongly agree, 5= strongly disagree)
5. Were you able to play notes or individual strings with little or no error?
   (1=strongly agree, 5= strongly disagree)

The following questions are used as a composite result related to the improvement in range of motion and skills for testing for the second hypothesis.

6. Did you experience any improvement in your range of motion?
   (1=much improvement, 4= no improvement)
7. Did you experience any improvement in your skill level?
   (1=yes, 3=no)

The following questions are used as a composite result related to the user motivation from playing for testing for the third hypothesis.

8. I felt motivated to continue playing this harp over traditional therapy exercises.
   (1=strongly agree, 5= strongly disagree)
9. I would recommend this along with traditional therapy.
   (1=strongly agree, 5= strongly disagree)
10. I would recommend this augmented reality format for other therapy.
    (1=strongly agree, 5= strongly disagree)
11. Would you like to play the virtual harp or another musical instrument presented in augmented reality again in the future?
    (1=yes, 3=no)

The composite result for questions 6-7 related to the improvement in range of motion and skills was calculated by Eq. (6). The composite result for questions 8-11 related to the user motivation from playing was calculated by Eq. (7). These two equations change the composite result questions scale from 0-1 in order to find the average mean since the questionnaire scale was different between the questions.

Composite result for questions 6-7:

$$x_i = \frac{1}{2}\left(\frac{1}{4}x_6 + \frac{1}{3}x_7\right) \tag{6}$$

Composite result for questions 8-11:

$$x_t = \frac{1}{2}\left(\frac{1}{5}\left(\frac{(x_8 + x_9 + x_{10})}{3}\right) + \frac{1}{3}x_{11}\right) \tag{7}$$

Table 1 shows the results of the one sample t-test for the whole study group, the long-term disability, and short-term disability on the three hypotheses.

Users with either long-term disability or short-term disability felt the virtual harp system was neither easy nor difficult when using, so the first hypothesis is rejected. Short-term disability users gained improvement in their range of motion and skills. Long-term disability users did not show improvement. However, overall, as a group, users did show improvement, so the second hypothesis is accepted. Users with either long-term disability or short-term disability were motivated to continue playing the system for therapy, so the third hypothesis is accepted.

| α= .05 | Whole Group | Long Term | Short Term |
|---|---|---|---|
| Composite results for problems 1-5<br>Ho: μ=3<br>Ha: μ<3 | μ=3.21<br>*p*=.9<br>not sig. | μ=3.13<br>*p*=.7<br>not sig. | μ=3.27<br>*p*=.88<br>not sig. |
| Composite results for problems 6-7<br>Ho: μ=.875<br>Ha: μ<.875 | μ=.68<br>*p*=.0004<br>sig. | μ=.73<br>*p*=.036<br>not sig. | μ=.65<br>*p*=.0034<br>sig. |
| Composite results for problems 8-11<br>Ho: μ=.8<br>Ha: μ<.8 | μ=0.443<br>*p*=.0001<br>sig. | μ=.44<br>*p*=.0001<br>sig. | μ=.44<br>*p*=.0001<br>sig. |

Table 1. One-sample t-test results

## 6. Discussion

The use of the virtual harp therapy system had an impact on the participants in the program, most were very excited when they first arrived. While almost all of the participants have received some form of traditional therapy training, most have never experienced virtual or augmented reality before and were therefore, able to look at the therapy training that they have seen before in a different way. Part of the problem with traditional therapy training exercises is that patients get bored or fatigued with the repetitive activity and lose motivation to continue with the training exercises.

This augmented reality based therapy system allows participants not only to experience a new type of technology with a hands-on therapy exercise, but also to be motivated to continue exercising through playing the virtual harp. During the observational testing, users playing performance did increase as they continued plucking the harp strings. They would start the test searching for the strings with long periods of pauses between notes gradually being able to shorten the period of pauses or strumming the harp. Participants were able to follow the virtual therapist feature with little error from selecting the wrong string. There were social interactions from the users such as asking questions, emotional expressions, and non-verbal communication while playing the harp.

Most of the participants stated that they enjoyed the experience; however, there were a few complaints that seemed to come up often. The primary two of these were the haptic device cursor sinking through the harp and the flashing background making it hard to see our harp. The model we used was very detailed and producing realistic vibrations with the haptics in the augmented scene is a memory intensive operation so at times the program can be slow. Haptics was used over optical finger tracking to reduce the challenge of trying to find the correct string in the air; since haptics provides force feedback and could have the benefit of muscle resistance exercises. Other glove haptic devices could be used to provide a more realistic plucking action but this device was used to minimize cost and system complexity in order to be used at various therapy facilities.

Another common complaint was the headset was too heavy and big, making it hard to keep in place. Based on the results for the level of difficulty in using the virtual harp, the users felt it was difficult using the system. Some of the users' comments mentioned that this will take awhile to get used to, but there could be good skills learned and that it was more interesting than traditional therapy because playing the harp gives an immediate reward for trying. One reason may have been the equipment was new to them and since the users had to hold up the head mounted display on their head the accuracy of tracking the marker did have an affect on the playing difficulty. Another comment mentioned with improvement the system would be versatile for use in therapy like hand/eye coordination.

Measuring improvement and learned skills is one of the greatest challenges of a training program. In the survey the participants were asked to rate how much they improved and learned during the experience. Even though the study lasted about thirty minutes for one session, users expressed they experienced some improvement in their range of motion but really noticed improvement in their skills. While this is not a concrete measure of skills and improvement acquired since repetitive sessions are needed, it suggests that participants at least felt that they had gained a great deal of information utilizing our program. Despite these issues, most participants indicated that the VR training as their favorite method of therapy training. Most participants thought the system was entertaining and desired to continue playing the harp after the testing session. In addition, users would recommend this along with traditional therapy and like to play the virtual harp or another musical instrument presented in augmented reality again in the future.

## 7. Conclusion and future work

The virtual harp system was an attempt to provide interactive musical experiences and development of skills during therapy for individuals with disabilities in a motivating and fun method. This system provides individuals a means to engage in a self-motivating therapy exercises outside the therapy room and therapists without musical knowledge to observe the individual during therapy exercises. Virtual reality technology has the potential benefit as a therapeutic intervention for retraining coordinated movement patterns because it has the unique capability to be engaging, functional, and purposeful for patient motivation, the virtual harp system results associate with the statement. The system is coupled with music to increase the therapeutic goals from music therapy and to help stimulate and motivate the use of therapy exercises. The users from the study did have some frustrations using the system but felt that they could improve with practice over time. They felt this system was more enjoyable, interesting, and a fun challenge over traditional therapy. Although measuring improvement skills in therapy can be difficult, individuals cannot forget the experience and rewards they received using this system.

The virtual harp therapy system would benefit being used at a healthcare facility such as the hospital or nursing home along with an individuals' traditional therapy program. The virtual harp therapy system would benefit from an assessment of how the video camera image is conducted for the ARToolKit background image in H3D to keep the background image from flashing. While the current method worked better on the computer used for the user testing, users still had difficulties and frustrations with using the system. In addition, the head mounted display should be replaced with a lighter version to provide users with more comfort. The virtual therapist system could also be extended to represent different difficulty levels of pieces of music by adding more three-dimensional buttons that provide different difficulty levels in therapy. In addition, this system could be expanded to include different types of instruments or different types of therapy scenarios such as lifting different weighted objects. Overall, the virtual harp system would be a beneficial extension to a therapy program.

## 8. Nomenclature

| | |
|---|---|
| H | Defined pulling limit value (m) |
| Ho | Null hypothesis |
| Ha | Alternative hypothesis |
| L | Length of string (m) |
| N | Number of mass points on string |
| h(y) | Pulling limit based from position (m) |
| n | Number of mode |
| $p$ | P-value for T-test |
| t | Time (s) |
| x | Position (m) |
| y(z) | Node position along y and z-axis (m) |
| z | Node position along z-axis (m) |

| | |
|---|---|
| $a$ | Significance level |
| Γ | Damping term |
| μ | Mean |

## 9. References

Adamovich, S.; Merians, A.; Boian, R.; Tremaine, M.; Burdea, G.; Recce, M. & Poizner, H. (2003). A virtual reality based exercise system for hand rehabilitation post-stroke, *Proceedings of the Second International Workshop on Virtual Rehabilitation,* Piscataway, pp. 74-81.

Holden, M.; Todorov, E.; Callahan, J. & Bizzi, E. (1999). Virtual environment training improves motor performance in two patients with stroke: case report," Neurology Report, Vol23, No. 2, pp. 57-67.

Jack, D.; Boian, R.; Merians, A.; Adamovich, S.; Tremaine, M.; Recce, M.; Burdea, G. & Poizner, H. (2000). A virtual reality-based exercise program for stroke rehabilitation, *Proceedings of ASSETS 2000: Fourth ACM SIGCAPH Conference on Assistive Technologies*, Arlington, Virginia, pp. 56-63.

Kato, H. & Billinghurst, M. (1999). Marker tracking and HMD calibration for a video-based augmented reality conferencing system, *Proceedings of the 2nd International Workshop on Augmented Reality (IWAR 99),* October 1999, San Francisco.

Kizony, R.; Raz, L.; Katz, N.; Weingarden, H. & Tamar Weiss, P. (2005). Video-capture virtual reality system for patients with paraplegic spinal cord injury, *Journal of Rehabilitation Research & Development,* Vol. 42, No. 5, pp. 595-608.

Kraus, L.; Stoddard, S. & Gilmartin, D. (1996). Chartbook on disability in the united states, 1996, An InfoUse Report, U.S. Naional Institute on Disability and Rehabilitation Research, Washington, DC.

Kuhlen, T. & Dohle, C. (1995). Virtual reality for physically disabled people, *Computers in Biology and Medicine*, Vol. 25, No. 2, pp.205-211.

Lamb, P. (2007). ARToolKit, Human Interface Technology Laboratory (HIT Lab), University of Washington.

Luo, X.; Kline, T.; Fischer, H.; Stubblefield, K.; Kenyon, R. & Kamper, D. (2005). Integration of augmented reality and assistive devices for post-stroke hand opening rehabilitation, *Proceedings of the 27th International Conference of the IEEE Engineering in Medicine and Biology Society (EMBC05),* Shangai, China.

Riess, T. & Weghorst, S. (1995). Augmented reality in the treatment of parkinson's disease, *Proceedings of Medicine Meets Virtual Reality*, pp. 298-302.

Riva, G. (1998). Virtual reality in paraplegia: a VR-enhanced orthopaedic appliance for walking and rehabilitation," *Virtual Environments in Clinical Psychology and Neuroscience*, pp. 209-218.

Statistics of Disability (2007). Medical University of South Carolina, http://www.muschealth.com/gs/HealthTopic.aspx?action=showpage&pageid=P01183

Sveistrup, H. (2004). Motor rehabilitation using virtual reality, *Journal of NeuroEngineering Rehabilitation,* Vol. 1, No. 1, 1:10.

Taylor, T.; Smith, S. & Suh, D. (2007). A virtual harp with physical string vibrations in an augmented reality environment, *Proceedings of the ASME 2007 International Design*

*Engineering Technical Conferences & Computers and Information in Engineering Conference (IDETC/CIE 2007)*, September 4-7, 2007, Las Vegas, Nevada.
Todorov, E.; Shadmehr, H. & Bizzi, E. (1997). Augmented feedback presented in a virtual environment accelerates learning of a difficult motor task, *Journal of Motor Behavior*, Vol. 29, No. 2, pp. 147-158.
Weiss & Katz (2004). The potential of virtual reality for rehabilitation, *Journal of Rehabilitation Research & Development*, Vol. 41, No. 5, pp. vii-x.
Westerhoff, N. (2007). Fantasy Therapy, *Scientific American Mind*, pp. 71-75.

5

# Augmented Reality for Minimally Invasive Surgery: Overview and Some Recent Advances

Pablo Lamata[1,2], Wajid Ali[3], Alicia Cano[1], Jordi Cornella[3], Jerome Declerck[2], Ole J. Elle[3], Adinda Freudenthal[4], Hugo Furtado[5], Denis Kalkofen[6], Edvard Naerum[3], Eigil Samset[3], Patricia Sánchez-Gonzalez[1], Francisco M. Sánchez-Margallo[7], Dieter Schmalstieg[6], Mauro Sette[8], Thomas Stüdeli[4], Jos Vander Sloten[8] and Enrique J. Gómez[1]

*[1]Universidad Politécnica de Madrid, Spain*
*[2]Siemens, United Kingdom*
*[3]University of Oslo, Norway*
*[4]Delft University of Technology, Netherlands*
*[5]Medical Centre Ljubljana, Slovenia*
*[6] Graz University of Technology, Austria*
*[7]Minimally Invasive Surgery Centre Jesús Usón, Spain*
*[8]University of Leuven, Belgium*

## 1. Introduction

The advent of minimally invasive surgical (MIS) revolution has changed the way surgery is practiced. Technological advances in optics, instrumentation, materials, robotics, computer systems, etc, are bringing new means and possibilities to the Operating Room. These advances are conferring considerable advantages on the patient, but they are also imposing an additional difficulty on the physician, who needs to develop new skills and dexterity in order to adapt to a limited workspace. This chapter focuses on activity to facilitate minimally invasive treatment: the development and application of augmented reality (AR) technologies for guidance and navigation during surgical procedures.

The first section describes AR technologies and concepts from a surgical application perspective, and reviews current systems and prototypes. Tracking technologies and systems, image to physical registration methods, visualization strategies and clinical user interfaces are developed and assembled in computer-assisted navigation systems. These solutions are clinically applied in different surgical disciplines, like neurosurgery, interventional radiology and orthopaedics.

The second section presents the use of robotic devices to enhance the surgeons' capabilities in terms of dexterity and accuracy. The development of haptic feedback in tele-robotics, semi-autonomous robots and robotic systems cross-linked with image data are presented and results discussed.

The third section presents the process and methodology to develop AR systems for surgical applications. It highlights the importance of the multidisciplinary approach to this field of research, which requires the engagement of physicians, engineers and ergonomists. The experience of the ARIS*ER[1] European consortium is presented, providing some valuable lessons learned about workflow centred design and the importance of field studies. The study of human factors, sensorial and cognitive capabilities, is also briefly addressed.

The last section of the chapter describes four recent advances in the field: (1) a new videobased method for tracking surgical tools, which eliminates the extra burden introduced by existing solutions at a cost of some accuracy loss; (2) an advanced visualization strategy by means of novel collision detection feature for enhancing the safety and accuracy of radiofrequency ablation of tumours; (3) the development of the Endoclamp positioning system for minimally invasive cardiac procedures, which is designed to increase the safety of the procedure by providing real-time visualization and control of catheters reducing also the need of radiation exposure; and (4) the clinical adoption of the Resection Map, a navigation system for liver procedures, which efficiently increases the orientation of the surgeon.

## 2. AR in surgery: technologies, concepts and current systems

Augmented reality (AR) refers to a perception of a physical real-world environment whose elements are merged with (or augmented by) virtual computer-generated stimuli (visual or haptic), creating a mixed reality. While Paul Milgram and his colleagues (Milgram & Kishino, 1994) characterize AR as being a fusion of real and virtual data within a real world environment, Azuma and his colleagues base their definition of AR on the attributes of the AR application (Azuma et al., 2001). In addition to a mixture of real and virtual information, an AR application has to run in real time and its virtual objects have to be aligned (registered) with real world structures. Both of these requirements guarantee that the dynamics of real world environments remain after virtual data has been added. In order to both register the data and fuse virtual and real imagery in real time, special devices implementing a variety techniques are used by today's AR systems.

### 2.1 Visual AR display technology

To combine visual information in real time, one of the following three techniques is used in AR display devices. *Optical See Through* devices project the current rendering of the virtual data onto a semi-transparent mirror (Fig. 1a). This special mirror allows the user to perceive the real world through it while at the same time it passes on the virtual content to the eyes of its user. In contrast, *Video See Through* devices capture the real world information with a video camera (Fig. 1b). Before the final result is presented to the user, the captured video will be blend with the rendering of the virtual content by the device. *Direct Augmentations* use projectors and the surfaces of the environment to present the virtual information directly in the 3D real world environment (Raskar et al., 2001).

Display devices can also be distinguished by where they are installed in 3D space. Displays worn on the head (Head Mounted Display or HMD) usually integrate video or optical see through technology into a helmet (Cakmakci & Rolland, 2006). Small carried displays (or Handheld Displays) are equipped with a video camera and a 2D screen supporting video

[1] European Marie Curie Research Training Network for Augmented Reality in Minimally Invasive Surgery. www.ariser.info.

see through systems. Nevertheless, both head mounted and handheld displays depend on additional hardware which is usually either heavy or uncomfortable to wear, or in case of handheld displays suffer from a small physical screen size.

MIS technologies include in many cases the use of miniaturised cameras and tools, like in laparoscopy or arthroscopy. This makes potentially the *Video See Through* approach the most suitable one for these applications. Nevertheless, percutaneous procedures, like in radiofrequency ablation of liver tumours, can benefit from the other AR visual approaches.

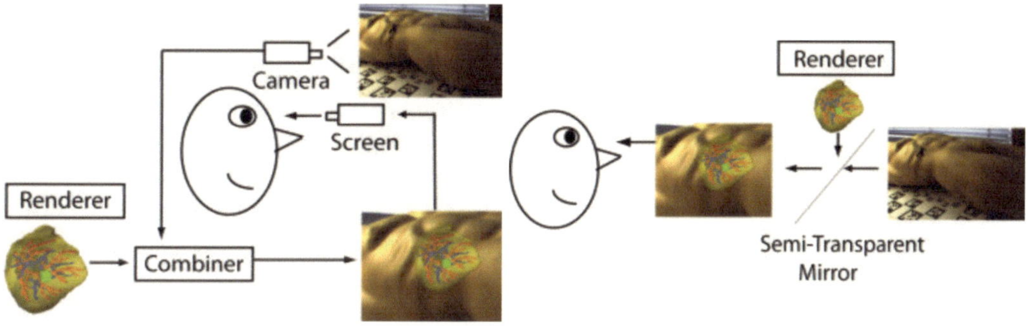


Fig. 1. Techniques for combining visual information (a) Video See Through (b) Optical See Through.

### 2.2 Registration methods for the alignment of real and virtual realities

The second main requirement for an AR application is a three dimensional registration of its virtual content relative to the real world objects. Therefore, AR systems estimate the position of either the virtual objects relative to the video camera or of both the video camera and the virtual objects relative to a common coordinate system (e.g. to also allow registered augmentations using optical see through devices). Virtual models are generated by image segmentation of medical image studies of the patient (Massoptier & Casciaro, 2008).

Up to now a number of different technologies have been developed to support the registration of 3D objects, ranging from analyses of the real world environment to evaluations of intentionally introduced fiducials. For example, computer vision algorithms are able to compute the position of a video camera directly from the images it delivers to the system (Davison et al., 2007). To be able to compute a 3D position, the algorithms have to select features (landmarks, shades, silhouettes…) directly out of the images and analyze them. Since feature detection and its subsequent processing is a computationally expensive and often noisy operation, some other technologies can help by adding artificial landmarks into the 3D environment (Teber et al., 2009b). Those aids (called fiducials) add a specific stimulus to the environment which is easier and faster to detect and evaluate. A number of different types of stimuli have already been used as sources for fiducial tracking. For example, retro-reflective spheres allow for quick and precise visual identification (see Fig. 2). Even audio sources (Doussis, 1993) or magnetic fields (natural as well as syntactically induced) have been used. The downside of adding fiducials to the environment is the artificial modification of the environment as well as the preparation required along with the need for specialized receivers. However, since the operation room allows preparing the environment, most medical AR application make use of the advantages of intentionally introduced tracking targets.

Registration is one of the current main challenges to solve in soft tissue surgery, like laparoscopy, where organs and tissues are deformed, cut, dissected, etc. Automatic tracking and compensation of these changes are required for a stable AR overlay. The greater the differences between the virtual reconstructed models and the real organs of the patient in the OR, the more difficult this challenge is.

### 2.3 AR systems for MIS

AR and Virtual Reality (VR) applications are capable of not only supporting an intervention itself, but also its preparation and a number of follow up procedures. However, AR is a rather complex aggregate technology, and research on AR-guided treatment is typically targeted at a single phase or aspect in a surgical procedure. Thus, embedding AR into a clinical workflow requires careful design of a software architecture that provides consistent services for image processing, visualization, tracking etc. throughout a variety of situations and requirements.

The challenge here is to provide useful, high-performance components that are also sufficiently flexible to allow re-use across different applications. Componentization also allows more careful testing of components in isolation (unit tests), and makes approval of software components for clinical evaluation more straight forward.

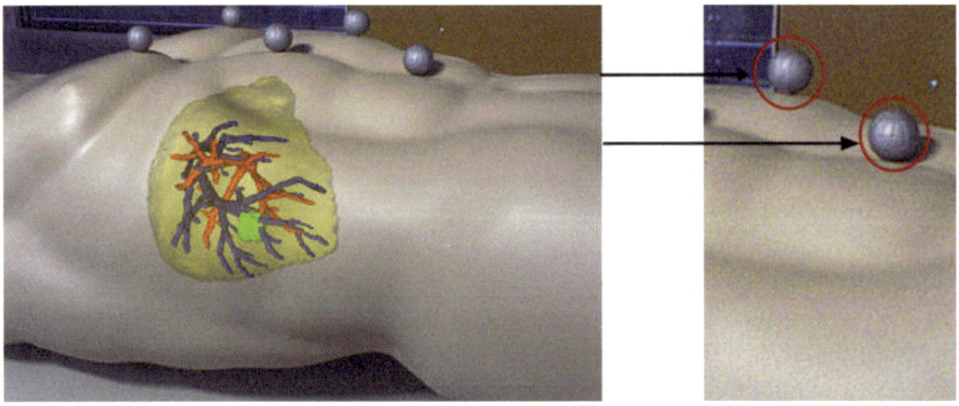

Fig. 2. Tracking using retro-reflective markers. This data is used to register the virtual counterparts of the liver with two vessel trees and a tumour. This AR application supports the insertion of a needle to ablate the tumour (see section 5.2)

An AR system for supporting medical applications has generally three main components:

- **Consistent data models**. The requirements of surgical planning, navigation and simulation go beyond the simple display of volumetric data acquired in previous image scans. Anatomical and pathological structures must be explicitly modeled and manipulated. Physicians demand predictable and reproducible results, so all these representations must be kept in a consistent state throughout the medical workflow while permitting arbitrary changes on the data.
- **Real-time data acquisition**. In contrast to modalities such as CT or MR, which are normally not acquired in real time, AR applications require the management of streaming input data such as tracking, US or video data. The handling of such data requires real-time algorithms and also careful synchronization, in particular between simultaneously acquired data from heterogeneous sources.

- **Visualization**. Compared to conventional screen-based navigation, AR has elevated requirements for visualization. Techniques must be independent of the viewing mode and display type, and must be able to simultaneously display all kinds of data models in real time.

### 2.4 Application areas

One of the main strengths of AR in medical applications is its ability to overcome difficulties related to hand-eye coordination (Johansson et al., 2001). For example, AR displays are able to present, by means of registration of virtual objects within real world environments, the information exactly where the hands have to act. Fig. 3 shows examples of this concept. Another possibility is to bring the support into the 'classical' 2D screen, as done in the support of needle ablation of tumours (see section 5.2).
This section reviews the current main areas of AR applications in surgery. It presents the applications characteristics, and it discusses the data used in the main components of the AR system.

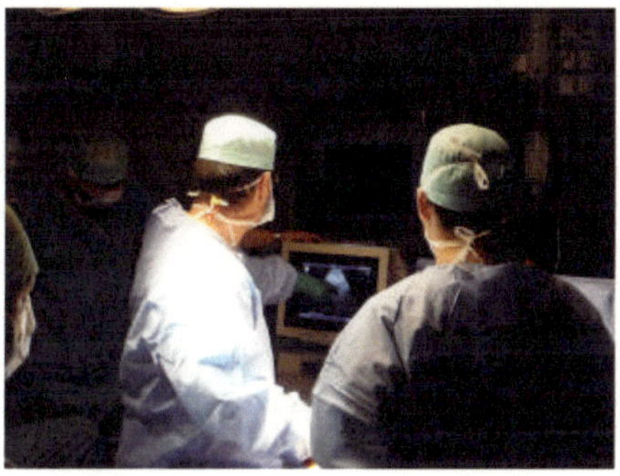
(a)

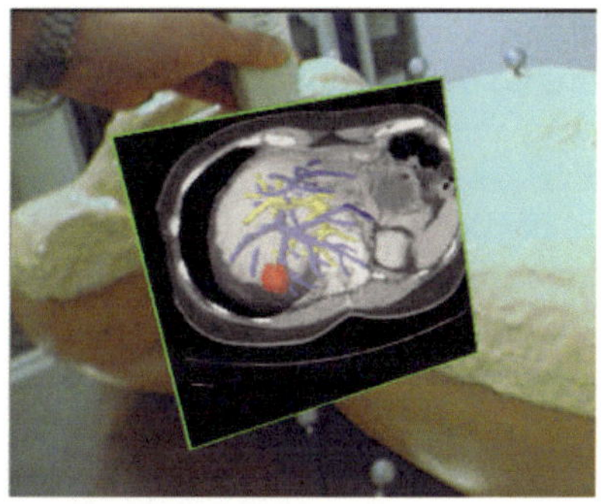
(b)

Fig. 3. Overcoming the problem of hand-eye coordination using Augmented Reality (a) Typical examination using sonography. (b) The AR display enables the user to see the data at the same location where his/her hands operate.

**Neurosurgery and orthopedics**

AR and computed assisted surgery has already found a place in open and minimally invasive procedures (Teber et al., 2009a). Nowadays, these systems are used in neurosurgical, craniomaxillofacial and orthopedic interventions. The use of navigation technologies reports substantial improvement regarding safety, aesthetic and functional aspects in a range of surgical procedures, like dental implantology, arthroscopy of the temporomandibular joint, osteotomies, distraction osteogenesis, image guided biopsies and removals of foreign bodies (Ewers et al., 2005). Applications in this category are able to use a virtual counterpart of hidden real structure which was generated before the intervention was started. Thus, these applications are able to make use of high qualitative 3d models.
Notice, the usage a 3d model, which is generated from pre-operatively acquired volumetric scans (e.g. CT-data) is only possible because no deformation modifies the structure between the scan of the patient (using e.g. CT) and the surgical procedure where the data is visualized. Consequently if rigid structures are in the focus of attention the acquired data almost perfectly represents the intra-operative scenario. This is the reason for the extensive

use of AR systems in those applications. The surgical field is composed or framed by rigid structures, which implies an easier alignment between the virtual reconstruction of the patient and the operating field (the registration step).
BrainLab (Feldkirchen, Germany) and Medtronic Navigation (Louisville, USA) demonstrate that applications in this area are even able to move from a research center to an industrial application. Both companies develop commercialized surgical navigators for rigid structures.

**Soft tissue surgery**

In soft-tissue surgery additional technical challenges exist. Current research focuses on intra-operative deformations, shifting, and topological changes done to the organs (Baumhauer et al., 2008). Due to those additional difficulties, only some research prototypes are able to offer a real-time navigation environment in an immobilized anatomy, displaying tools' location on preoperative or intra-operative 3D images (Beller et al., 2007; Cash et al., 2007). To be able to present virtual counterparts of real world organs the virtual model has to adapt to the real deformations. Consequently, besides the three main components of a medical AR systems the data model used to generate the AR imagery has to be updated regarding to the current deformation of the organs.
Currently, most soft-tissue navigation systems are focused on liver surgery, due to its clinical relevance. Indeed, liver cancer is one of the most important causes of death (El-Serag & Rudolph, 2007). As discussed before, there is a need of enhancing the prognosis by a better control of resection margins and risk areas (important vessels) during the intervention. The guidance of the needle in tumour ablation procedures, which can be also done under a laparoscopic approach, is a more controlled problem that is quite addressed using AR technology (Maier-Hein et al., 2008). These navigation environments can increase the accuracy of the needle placement (Stüdeli et al., 2008). For a more detailed review on the field of navigation in endoscopic soft tissue surgery the reader is referred to (Baumhauer et al., 2008).

**Catheterised interventional procedures**

Interventional procedures are minimally invasive procedures in which the medical doctor, typically a radiologist, performs a procedure by means of a small catheter introduced into the blood vessels. Most of the interventional procedures aim the treatment of aneurisms, stenosis and radio-frequency ablations in different anatomical districts.
In most of the cases the procedure is visualized by means of angiographic imaging, allowing having a visualization of both catheter and anatomical structures. Typically this is based on either X-ray fluoroscopy, computed tomography (CT), magnetic resonance imaging (MRI) or Ultrasound (US) Imaging and often uses contrast agent. However, these three classical imaging techniques have the disadvantage of being either bulky, being based on ionizing radiation or having poor resolution.
A valid alternative to those visualization procedures is represented by the AR. Several commercial systems implementing these technologies are currently available. As pure example we report names of commercial system for model generation EnSite NavX (St. Jude), Carto (Biosense Webster), LocaLisa (Medtronic). The systems are based on the combination of three different components. The first component is a tracking device that is able of giving information on position and orientation of a tracked object, the tracking is then integrated with a geometrical model and then visualized with the help of a visualization unit.

There exists on the market different solution for the tracking in interventional environments, using acoustical, inertial, electrical or electromagnetic technology. On the other hand, no interventional catheter procedure takes place before the patient undergoes a pre-procedural scan through means of MRI or CT. To reduce the mental workload, the obtained patient data can be pre-processed by a computer program and a set of geometrical models can be computed automatically. With the adequate visualization technology it is provided an intuitive representation of the catheter location within its environment. Fluoroscopy, providing a real-time visualization has been the gold standard for years, although its application was restricted as radiation exposure has to be minimized.

## 3. Robotic devices to enhance the surgeons' capabilities

Compared to open access surgery, MIS imposes a set of constraints that strongly limit the information provided by the natural human senses of sight and touch. In MIS, the organs are accessed by long instruments inserted by small incisions in the patient's skin (ports). As a result, small tremors are amplified and the forces exerted on the tissue can be only partially transmitted to the tool's handle (Picod et al., 2005). Ports, which act as fixed pivot points, limit the range of motion of instruments and introduces the fulcrum effect in the manipulation of tools. This makes the hand-eye coordination skill difficult to learn.

During the last decade, robots have been appearing in the operating rooms to overcome some of the current problems in MIS, covering nowadays a wide range of surgical specialties (neurosurgery, orthopaedic surgery, cardiac surgery and urology, among others (Diodato et al., 2004)). Due to disparate characteristics of surgical operations, robots have been used in different modes, ranging from teleoperation to true autonomous robots. In this line, *Image-guided surgical robots* are the type of robots that presents more degree of autonomy, although this autonomy is restricted to specific tasks within specific procedures. This kind of robots have been mainly applied in neurosurgery (Finlay & Morgan, 2003) (Karas & Chiocca, 2007) and orthopaedic surgery (Kazanzides et al., 1995; Kwon et al., 2001)since bones and the skull are relatively easy to image and the rigidity allows an easy registration between preoperative and intra-operative images (as already discussed in previous section). In abdominal procedures, autonomous robots have been used in applications such as automatic positioning of the laparoscopic camera (Krupa et al., 2003) or percutaneous procedures using visual servoing techniques (Loser & Navab, 2000).

Since several decisions have to be taken during the course of the operation, a more conservative approach is the development of telesurgical systems, where the motions of the surgeon through a master console are reproduced by the slave robot. In this way, the surgeons can make use of the benefits that a robot offers but preserving the human capability to react to any unexpected event. These characteristics make the telesurgical systems very attractive and two commercial systems with FDA approval have been developed until now: Zeus (ComputerMotion Inc., Goleta, CA, USA) and Da Vinci (Intuitive Surgical, Montain View, CA, USA).

A trade-off between image-guided surgical and telesurgical robots are *synergetic robots*, also called *hands-on robots*, where the robot is driven by the cooperation of an automatic controller and the surgeon. Synergetic robots can be found in a wide range of medical applications such as pericardial puncture (Schneider & Troccaz, 2001), knee arthroplasty (Ho et al., 1995), retinal surgery (Iordachita et al., 2006) or positioning of pedicle screws (Ortmaier et al., 2006).

This section presents the use of augmented reality and robotic devices to enhance the surgeon's capabilities in terms of dexterity and accuracy. Haptic feedback in tele-robotics will increase surgeon's capability of perceiving the tissue properties and of performing more intricate surgical tasks; the use of virtual models cross-linked with image data allow a better visualization of the operating area and the development of high accuracy image guided interventions; finally, haptic feedback and augmented reality can be merged, obtaining haptic guidance tools where virtual forces are generated in order to guide the movements of the surgeon according to a preoperative plan.

### 3.1 Haptic feedback in telesurgical systems

The word *haptic,* from Greek *ἁπτικός* (*haptikos*), means pertaining to the sense of touch and comes from the verb *ἅπτεσθαι* (*haptesthai*) meaning "*to contact*" or "*to touch*". There are two different kind of haptic feedback (Rosenbaum, 1990):

- *Kinesthetic feedback:* This is generated mainly by the proprioceotive receptors and describes the force exerted by a part of the body on the environment; in engineering it can be identified as the exerted force and torque.
- *Tactile feedback:* This is represented mainly by the esteroceptive information and describes the pressure distribution between the body and the environment; in this case, tactile feedback can be described with a pressure map.

There are many surgical tasks that require the surgeon to use the hands to acquire haptic (both kinesthetic and tactile) information from the patient's body. One of the most important tasks is palpation, which implies the surgeon explores organ's and anatomical surfaces looking for difference in the tissue stiffness, being harder tissues often diseased; as example, it has been demonstrated that palpation is the best technique to identify, during a surgical procedure, the location of liver metastases in colorectal cancer. The palpation of blood vessels and nerve path is also an important task in order to locate them and avoid accidental resections. Haptic feedback is also important when a resection is carried out, in order to sense the resistance between the blade and the tissue, or when the surgeon pulls the tissue with a forceps, closes a blood vessel with a clamp, or tights a suture knot. In all these cases, it is very likely that the applied force is causing the exceeding of the breaking stress and leading to harmful consequences.

When a minimally invasive procedure is performed with a telesurgical system, the surgeon is physically decoupled from the patient and the haptic feedback can be restored only with artificial devices. In this case, it is necessary to acquire the information on the patient's side, elaborate the data stream with a processing unit and present the information to the surgeon trough a master console. This represents a technological challenge that includes the development of appropriate master consoles and sensing devices, as well as the control schemes of the overall system. Although research has been very active in this field for long time, a suitable solution has not yet been found.

There exist several commercial master and slave devices for kinesthetic feedback. Whereas in most applications the mounting of force sensors on the robots is easy, it represents a challenge in teleoperated MIS since the reliable measure of the interaction forces requires to place the sensor close to where they are produced, i.e. the tip of the instrument. A robotic instrument for MIS typically has a diameter of less than 10mm, and today there are no commercially available force sensors of comparable size. Also, sterilizability and disposability are difficult to achieve with force sensors, for technical reasons and cost reasons respectively.

Hence, an interest in force estimation emerges as a potential substitute technique. The estimation of interaction forces between a robot and its environment must necessarily be based on information from other types of sensors. The most common approach is to estimate interaction forces from the knowledge of the dynamics of the robot and the measurement/estimation of position, velocity and acceleration (Hacksel & Salcudean, 1994; Smith et al., 2006; Naerum et al., 2008). The success of this approach depends on our ability to accurately identify and compute the dynamic parameters of the robot. A different approach is to consider the behaviour of the robot's environment instead of the robot during interaction. In this case, the knowledge of the environment's dynamics is required, together with a sensor system to measure displacement. For example, a vision system can measure the deformation of the environment as the robot applies a force to it, and the interaction force is computed with the help of a known force-displacement relationship (Kennedy et al., 2002; Gaponov et al., 2008). Again, force estimation performance relies on the accuracy of the dynamic model of the environment.

Different are the technological bottlenecks for the tactile feedback, the research in this field is still in its primitive step trying to build the fundamental hardware: tactile sensors and displays with performances suitable for medical application (Peeters et al., 2008). Particularly interesting are the solutions developed for the tactile sensing, among others there is the example of a sensor based on piezo-resistive rubber (Fig. 4.a) (Goethals et al., 2008). The novel idea in a tactile sensor based on tactile data extrapolation from intraoperative ultrasound images, in an early stage of prototype development as shown in Fig. 4.b, has an interesting potential (Sette et al., 2007).

(a) (b)

Fig. 4. Tactile feedback technology. (a) Elastoresistive tactile sensor (Goethals et al., 2008). (b) Ultrasound probe for tactile feedback (Sette et al., 2007)

### 3.2 Image-guided surgical robots

The advances in medical imaging technology allow the visualization of anatomic structures with a high degree of accuracy. By means of computer image processing and modelling, the location of the pathologies and essential structures can be revealed and presented to the clinician in a suitable form. This preoperative information can be fully exploited by guiding the movements of a robot in order to augment the overall precision and accuracy of the surgical intervention (orthopaedic and neurosurgery being the main surgical areas of application).

As it was shown in the previous chapter, the use of AR can provide clinicians with interactive 3D visualizations in all phases of the treatment. Besides the visualization tools, AR can be used together with robotic systems in order to develop path-planning algorithms that automatically calculate the optimal surgical plan (Kazanzides et al., 1995)
Once the registration of the image data with the position of the patient and robot is properly done, AR can be useful to monitor the movements of the robot inside the body and to detect deviations between the real position and the preoperative plan.

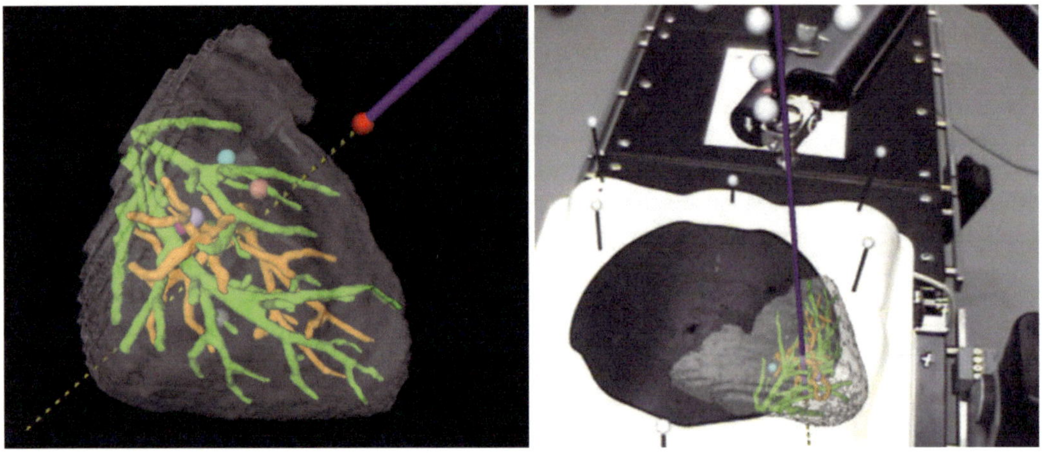

Fig. 5. Augmented reality tools for preoperative planning and correlation with the intraoperative robot.

Fig. 5 shows an example of using AR for increasing the accuracy of a Zeus telesurgical robot when it executes tasks autonomously (Cornellà et al., 2008). A virtual liver model was used as preoperative information and then correlated with the intra-operative robot. In this case, the errors in the registration, the noise in the signals provided by the tracking system and the inaccuracies in the kinematics chain of the robot, were corrected by means of an adaptive control algorithm based on a Kalman filter, obtaining a final accuracy much better than the own accuracy of the robot alone. This demonstrates that AR can provide real benefits to image guided surgical robots.

### 3.3 Augmented reality for haptic guidance generation

Teleoperated systems with haptic feedback allow the user to feel the contact forces between the slave manipulator and the remote environment. Additionally, the user may feel some virtual forces generated from a virtual model with the objective of guiding his movements and help him to complete the task successfully. This approach, which is known as *haptic guidance* or *virtual fixtures*, is more conservative than a true autonomous robot, since in this case the user has the control of the robot, but it is a step further than haptic feedback, since his/her movements are guided according to a preoperative plan. In this case, virtual environments and augmented reality tools can be used to detect the deviations between the real position and the preoperative plan and to generate the guiding forces to the user. Fig. 6 shows a conceptual diagram of a teleoperated system with haptic guidance and the relations between its elements.

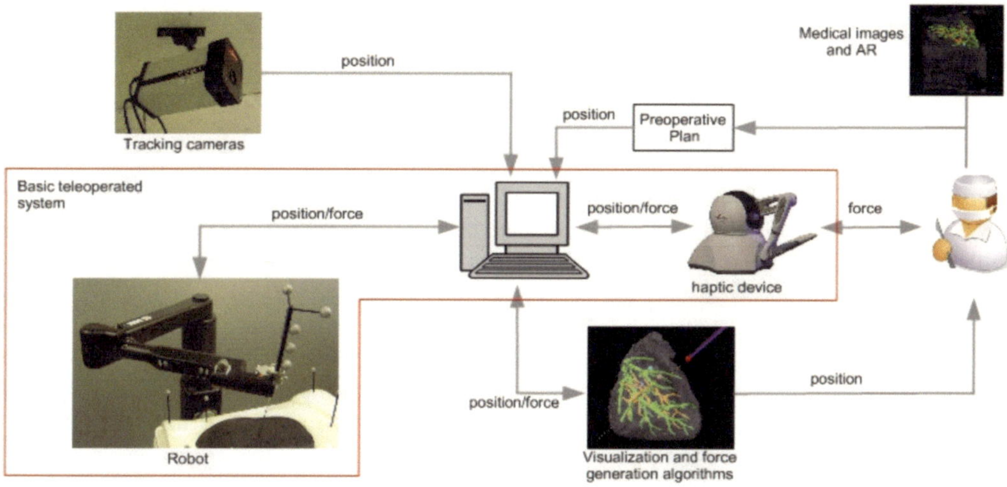


Fig. 6. A basic teleoperated system is made up by the master haptic device and the slave robot. In this case, the slave robot follows the movement of the surgeon, who feels the interaction forces from the remote size through the haptic device. A haptic guidance system introduces new elements: first, a preoperative planning based on medical images and AR in order to guide the movements of the surgeon; second, a tracking system to monitor the position of the robot; finally, force generation algorithms based on AR models that compute the appropriate force according the preoperative plan and the real position of the robot. AR models can also be used to provide another visual feedback to the surgeon of the movements of the robot inside the body.

Haptic guidance has been proven as a very effective technique for increasing the performance of teleoperated systems. Among other benefits, it increase speed and precision, reduce operator workload and the effects of time delays (Rosenberg, 1995) (Sayers & Paul, 1994). Haptic guidance has also been used in several telesurgical applications, ranging from limiting the movements of the manipulator into restricted regions (Payandeh & Stanisic, 2002) to increase the accuracy in microsurgery (Bettini et al., 2004).

The constraints that restrict the movements of the user can be defined taking into account different aspects. The first one, and the most obvious, is considering the Cartesian position of the slave manipulator and the task to be performed (Turro et al., 2001). In this case, the haptic guidance can be divided in three basic forms: if the movements of the slave are constrained in all the three degrees of freedom, then the slave manipulator must remain in a fixed point; constraining the movements in two degrees of freedom, the operator can move the slave manipulator along a line; finally, if just one degree of freedom is constrained, then it can move over a surface. In addition to the number of degrees of freedom, the forces can be either attractive or repulsive. Attractive forces drive the operator towards the constraint and can be useful to increase the accuracy of the procedure. Repulsive forces restrict to be outside certain zones, which can increase the safety of the operation by means of defining forbidden regions where the robot is not able to move.

Instead of considering the Cartesian position, the constraints can be based on other parameters involved in a teleoperated system, like the relative velocity between master and slave devices, which increase the coordination between master and slave movements (Nuño

& Basañez, 2006), or limits and singularities of the devices, which increase the safety in the slave side, especially when the kinematic configuration of the master and slave devices are very different (Turro et al., 2001).

## 4. Multidisciplinary user centred design process

Development and design processes of novel computing systems with integrated Augmented and Virtual Reality Technology (AR/VR-technology) in the medical domain is complex and highly iterative, generally involving multiple disciplines and partners. In this section we share experiences gathered during an exemplary development project over four years: the European research training network "Augmented Reality in Surgery" (ARIS*ER) aimed to develop next generation novel imaging guidance (augmented reality built from various modalities, such as ultrasound, MRI and video-endoscopy) and cross linked robotic systems (automatic control loops guided by radiological data of the patient) to improve minimally invasive interventions and surgery. The technologies involved are: image processing, image fusion, interactive 3D visualization and navigation, robotics and haptics. *"Through this research, a group of young researchers is being trained to work internationally and multidisciplinary. The team is working across the boarders of medical interventions, information and communication technology development, and user interface design."* (www.ariser.info)

The ARIS*ER consortium consisted of over 40 researchers and eight partner institutions. Over 4 years 10 PhD candidates and 6 PostDoc researchers worked on "*building blocks*" addressing key technological problems as well as the integration of these different modules into different systems (demonstrators and showcases). The aim was to develop, in multidisciplinary teams for each medical case, systems of specific surgical navigation and information support with augmented reality technology.

In this section we will discuss three important aspects of user centred design of surgical support tools, as learned in our ARIS*ER project. (1) These systems are meant to enable better medical procedures. Therefore these supports will influence the procedures themselves. In order to get the most wanted effect of the technological possibilities, the procedures themselves have to be redesigned as well, parallel and in relation to the development of their supportive tools (section 4.1). (2) A multidisciplinary co-design approach is advised, involving multiple engineering disciplines, medical experts from different fields, as well as Ergonomics / Human Factors Engineering (section 4.2). (3) To be able to increase safety and efficiency of MIS approaches it is important to conduct during the development process ergonomic studies to identify requirements for design (e.g. analyses of current tasks), as well as evaluations of proposed new information and actuation tools and new related procedures (section 4.3).

### 4.1 Workflow centred design

One important aspect of the user centred approach within ARIS*ER was the systems approach in the investigations on future user needs and the context analysis. The intervention suit or operation theatre has been treated as a (work) system with technology components, procedures of usage, procedures of handling complications (problem solving), team roles and tasks. Investigations started by studying the actual system with current user, task, context, current technological solutions, current problems and desires for change as well as the current workflow.

A medical workflow can be described as a logical and effective sequence of tasks that follows surgical routines and rules. Medical procedures traditionally follow detailed protocols that are built on practical and scientific experiences. These protocols try to maximize the benefits and minimize the risks. But protocols are more rules than reality and are not binding on details, e.g., in case of complications the surgeon might need to deviate from the protocol or his foreseen planed procedure. Surgical tasks might therefore change substantially. Clinical judgement is complex, and based on extensive knowledge, only partially journalized. Considerable effort is actually undertaken to investigate surgical workflows to better understand these surgical routines but also to build the base for the development of intelligent surgical information systems (Neumuth et al., 2006).

Within ARIS*ER we implicitly used some of these well-known methodologies for investigating clinical workflows, like surgical process descriptions (Neumuth et al., 2006) and task analysis according to ISO 13407 (Stüdeli et al., 2007). Also multiple visualization styles such as storyboards, flow-charts and tables were used but our prime communication tools were matrixes and storyboards. The Workflow Integration Matrix (WIM) was proposed in ARIS*ER as a effective framework aimed to assist the analysis of user requirements and surgical problem solving processes as well as communication between surgeons, technology engineers and designers of a multidisciplinary team (Jalote-Parmar et al., 2007).

Within ARIS*ER the consideration of the workflow was part of the user centred approach. Recorded actual medical workflows have been used to derive specific user needs and offered valuable context information. Additionally visualizations of workflows on tables and storyboards were used to transfer medical know-how to technical engineers (easier than documented verbal medical protocols). Ergonomics/Human Factors (HF) experts were in charge of streamlining the parallel design and development of technology and work procedures. Workflow centred design can have its focus on a re-design of clinical workflow (optimized to the technology) or just on carefully considering existing clinical workflows in the design of the supportive tool.

To conclude: A continuous consideration of workflow aspects during design process can support the process in many ways. This applies not only for entire technical work systems like the 'operation room of the future' (Cleary et al., 2005) but also to supportive tools on a smaller scale. Visualization of medical workflows can offered an easy access to the medical field for the engineers and gives a natural insight in the dynamics of the work system. Knowledge about actual workflow is also knowhow about clinical needs (user requirements). And last but not leased the optimal design solution might be in the combination of new technology solution and an adapted or re-designed workflow.

### 4.2 The ARI*SER multidisciplinary example

The ARIS*ER development and design process was both user driven and technology driven. The collaboration between the researchers was organized according to the co-design approach, as depicted in Fig. 7. Speed of getting a prototype out had priority, following 'action research' approach. In this approach prototypes were compiled from the various technical domains and integrated, based on user guidance, which is known as 'participatory design'.

Parallel to the developments of these sub-systems Ergonomics/HF specialists investigated the medical procedure of the study cases to specify requirements for the envisioned target

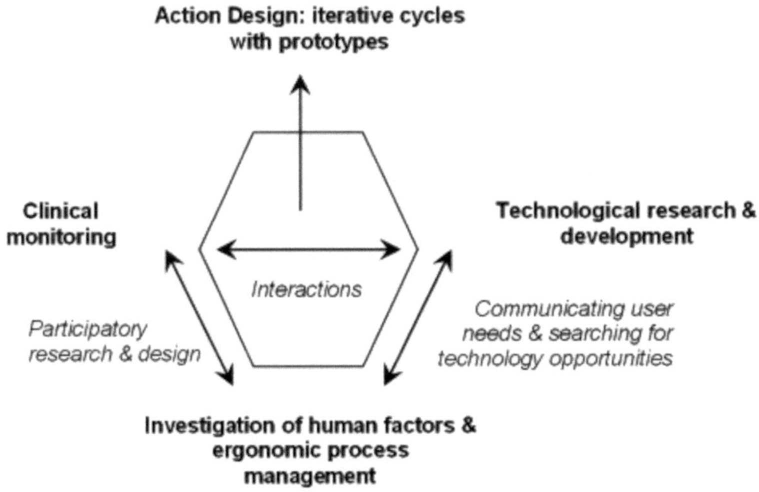


Fig. 7. The co-design approach in ARIS*ER (Augmented reality in surgery - EU research training network). In this approach we intended to bridge the gap between user and technology developer (Jalote-Parmar et al., 2007). The measures are two fold. Human Factors specialists are involved to bridge the gap. Also direct interaction between users and technology developers take place. In both situations the users are involved as co-designers. (Adapted figure from (Freudenthal et al., 2007))

systems. They guided and designed user interfaces and performed ergonomic interventions, including workflow driven design. Clinical users were involved to guide the design work: clinical experts conducted clinical monitoring. Many clinicians were consulted from within ARIS*ER consortium partners and from outside.

This mixture of technology driven (technology components) and user driven methods (application projects) speeded up the investigation and development. This approach allowed us to reach animal and patient testing in a limited time. It solves one of the common problems in participatory design, which is that medical users encounter a lot of difficulty envisioning what a new non-existing technology will look like and behave in actual use. They need presentations to (imagine the) experience of actual interaction. Actual prototypes, even ones that are faulty in many respects, allow them to experience the interactions. It allows them to envision adapted versions they would like and comment on problems with the current proposal. These comments can then be processed by the HF specialists and used in next versions. The requirement list and the solutions quality develop quicker this way. The more and the earlier prototype test rounds can be run - the better.

To conclude: The co-design approach in ARIS*ER included partners from all essential technology component domains, medical users and human factors/design. Both components and integrated demonstrators were developed - in parallel. User input came from field studies 'up front', but was also based on evaluative studies of demonstrators and prototypes. Since users have problems envisioning the possibilities of novel technologies, prototypes are crucial to gather user feedback and speed up development.

### 4.3 Human factors studies

Human Factors is a synonym of Ergonomics (HF/Ergonomics). Having his roots traditionally as "science of work", today Human Factors (engineering) covers all areas of human life. The most commonly used definition is from the council of the International Ergonomics Association (IEA)[2]: "*Ergonomics (or human factors) is the scientific discipline concerned with the understanding of interactions among humans and other elements of a system, and the profession that applies theory, principles, data, and other methods to design in order to optimize human well-being and overall system performance. Ergonomists contribute to the design and evaluation of tasks, jobs, products, environments and systems in order to make them compatible with the needs, abilities and limitations of people.*"

The discipline HF/Ergonomics is divided broadly into three domains: Physical Ergonomics, Cognitive Ergonomics (engineering psychology) and Organizational Ergonomics (macroergonomics), each of which can be found relevant to product design in the medical domain. Methods are often manifold and not limited to one specific domain but combine elements different scientific disciplines. In order to increase MIS safety and efficiency as well as to reduce workload HF/Ergonomics interventions are conducted.

Most technology developers are well aware of the general aim of HF/Ergonomics, which is to meet user/clinical needs and human limitations. Most developers indeed do (occasionally) visit a doctor or have an early demonstrator / prototype evaluated. But the majority still has a limited view on HF/Ergonomics methods, scope and possibilities. The role of the ergonomist in large design and development projects is generally weakly defined. A common mistake in ICT related development and design processes is to limit HF/Ergonomics methods to usability evaluations that are widely and successfully used in practice. Usability research is indeed an important and powerful method, but it focuses only on the conduct of a proper test to evaluate use-related requirements of a product or prototype such as learnability (ease-of-use), efficiency, memorability, errors, and satisfaction in use (Nielsen, 1994; International Standards, 1999). In addition to this HF/Ergonomics methods also aim to generate a thorough understanding of the usage context (Stüdeli & Alexander, 2008) and through this also provide guidance in finding solutions.

In ARIS*ER HF/Ergonomics was meant to guide the development work in the three applications. Secondly, methodological knowledge on ergonomics of complex medical systems had to be developed. Two main ergonomic challenges were addressed (1) How to analyze surgical procedures in a way that decisions for the design of supportive technology but also workflow issues can be treated (see section 4.1 on clinical workflow design) (2) How to best introduce ergonomic evaluations and usability tests into the development and design process? The second question can not be generally or finally answered. However our experiences within the ARIS*ER project show some main issues for the ergonomic evaluation of complex medical systems with AR/VR technology:

- **Selection of evaluation criteria**. General work characteristics of MIS are demands on information processing and communication (team work), high workload (duration, intensity) as well as high demands in accuracy and prudence. Therefore evaluations focussing on accuracy, cognitive load, fatigue and safety aspects were chosen (Stüdeli et al., 2007).
- **Ergonomic evaluations** should already be prepared from the first analysis of the work system (section 4.1). Analyses should not be restricted to the actual procedures but also consider technological opportunities of the future and potential new workflows. This

[2] IEA is the parent organization of the national associations. Definition of Ergonomics (August 2000): http://www.iea.cc/

approach is in line with a common designers approach to work with 'dream scenario' (Stüdeli & Freudenthal, 2009)

- **Usability testing** of prototypes or existing products and ergonomic evaluations can be combined successfully. Prototyping phase with user studies and task simulations can then be e.g. used to refine evaluation criteria. Working with (early) prototypes allows the further development of the usability metrics during development process. The integration of prototyping activities in the evaluation process can concretize and refine know-how on the context-of-use (Stüdeli & Freudenthal, 2009).
- In order to guide a **complex design and development process** efficiently, scope of ergonomic evaluation has to be handled flexible. Analysis and interventions on the level of the work systems as well as on a single (but important) interaction between the user and the system are needed.

In ARIS*ER the prime focus was on decision support, but equally important is teaching support. Due to the high demands on fine-motor and cognitive skills, also training of surgeons (users) is an issue of immense importance. New developments on MIS therefore have to consider aspects of surgical training. For example, the analysis of the perception of surgical interaction forces is of key importance for the design of training systems (i.e. Virtual Reality simulators) and for understanding the development of perceptual surgical skills (Lamata et al., 2008a).

To conclude: HF/Ergonomics bridges different disciplines with different methodological approaches such as psychology, engineering, design and medical. Usability research can and should be used in all stages of the design. Thereby knowledge of the work system will increase in time and evaluation criteria will develop parallel to the design and development process.

## 5. Some recent advances

### 5.1 Video-based tracking of surgical tools

Operating rooms are overloaded of systems and technology, while efficient workflows and use of space are mandatory. Current AR systems rely on additional hardware systems with different limitations, as described in section 2 of this chapter. Here, an alternative to existing systems for tracking surgical tools is described, which is based on an analysis of the surgical video signal.

The challenge of the approach is to extract the 3D position and orientation of a rigid cylindrical tool from the 2D information of the surgical scenario captured by endoscope. Concretely, proposed method exploits the model and properties of a perspective image analysis applied to the cylindrical shape of tools, allowing the assessment of the instruments' position and orientation. Proposed approach can be decomposed in solving two main problems: (1) extraction of relevant 2D information from the image through segmentation techniques, and (2) estimation of 3D coordinates of the tool with this information. The first step is, more specifically, to segment the contours of surgical tools and to localise the tip location in the image (see Fig. 8.a). Different image processing techniques can be applied for obtaining a fast and robust method for near real time applications (Voros et al., 2007). It is also possible to introduce colour markers fixed on the instrument to facilitate image processing stage (Tonet et al., 2007).

The second step is to determine the 3D tool position through geometrical equations elaborated on the analysis of the projection of the instrument in the image plane (see Fig.

8.b). Segmented tool edges and camera field of view (FoV) define a tool 3D orientation, and the tip's 3D position is determined by its image 2D coordinates and the tool's physical diameter (5 or 10 mm usually in laparoscopic tools).

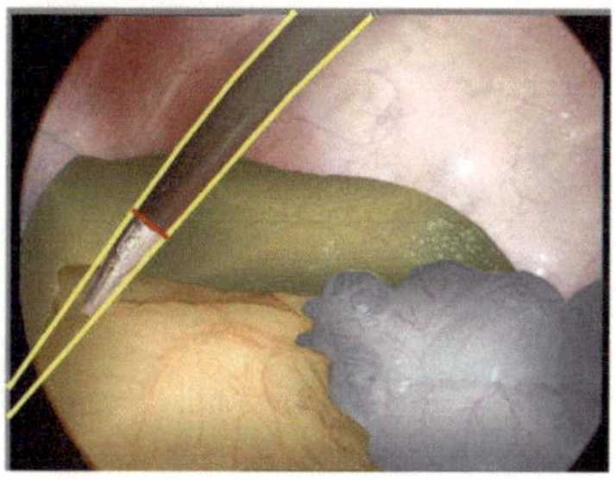

(a)

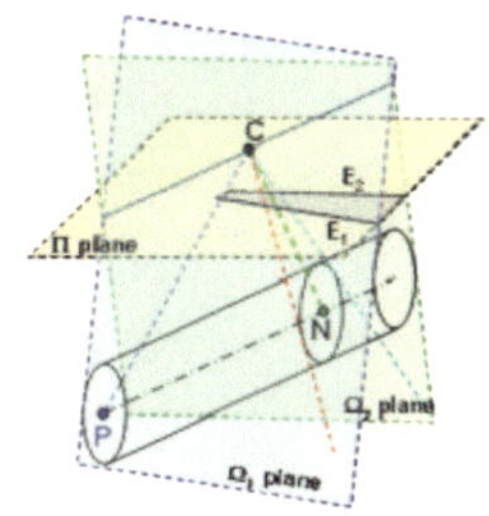


(b)

Fig. 8. Video-based tracking of surgical tools (Cano et al., 2008). (a) Image processing for extracting 2D information (b) Model of the laparoscopic tool used for calculate the 3D position and orientation of the tools; C: optical center, P: tip of the tool; N: point of the cylinder axis which projective line is perpendicular to this axis; $\Omega_1$, $\Omega_2$: planes of sight of the tool edges; Π plane: image plane; $E_1$, $E_2$: projective tool edges.

Current tracking performance of proposed method is sufficient for gesture analysis and an objective evaluation of surgical manoeuvres, with an accuracy of around 3 mm (Cano et al., 2008). The main benefit of this approach is the lack of extra elements which disturb surgeon's performance in the clinical routine, reducing the complexity and cost of physical tracking instruments.

### 5.2 Advanced guidance of radio frequency ablation needles

Radio-frequency ablation (RFA) has become an important minimally invasive treatment for liver cancers. RFA can be performed on inoperable hepatic tumors, both primary and metastatic. The procedure is performed under conventional ultrasound image guidance which leaves the interventionist with the challenging task of correlating pre-operative findings with intra-operative imaging while navigating the RFA probe to the target tumor. This problem is tackled with a computer aided surgery system called ARIS*ER RFA (Ali et al., 2009), which supports a complete interventional workflow including pre-operative, intra-operative and post-operative visualization and fusion of different imaging modalities for guidance of RFA interventions.

The system can perform complex image data visualization and fusion, virtual navigation, image and RFA needle calibration, and registration for inserting the RFA probe as accurately as possible in a single workflow during ablation of liver tumors percutaneously (see Fig. 9 for different example views supported by ARI*SR RFA system). The ARIS*ER RFA system was developed using the Studierstube Medical framework (Kalkofen & Schmalstieg, 2006), which is useful for developing both Virtual Reality (VR) and Augmented Reality (AR) applications for medical procedures due to its flexible and modular design.

Within the development of the ARIS*ER RFA system two directions of interfaces were explored, and both interfaces were subject to user testing. One was explicitly based on WIM (section 4.1): three flat screens (US, CT and in the middle a fusion of the two) (Jalote-Parmar et al., 2009)., and the second based on WIM and a cognitive model of (needle) navigation strategies: a 2D screen with three needle related slices and a 3D scene as seen in Fig. 9.b (Stüdeli et al., 2008), but without image fusion.

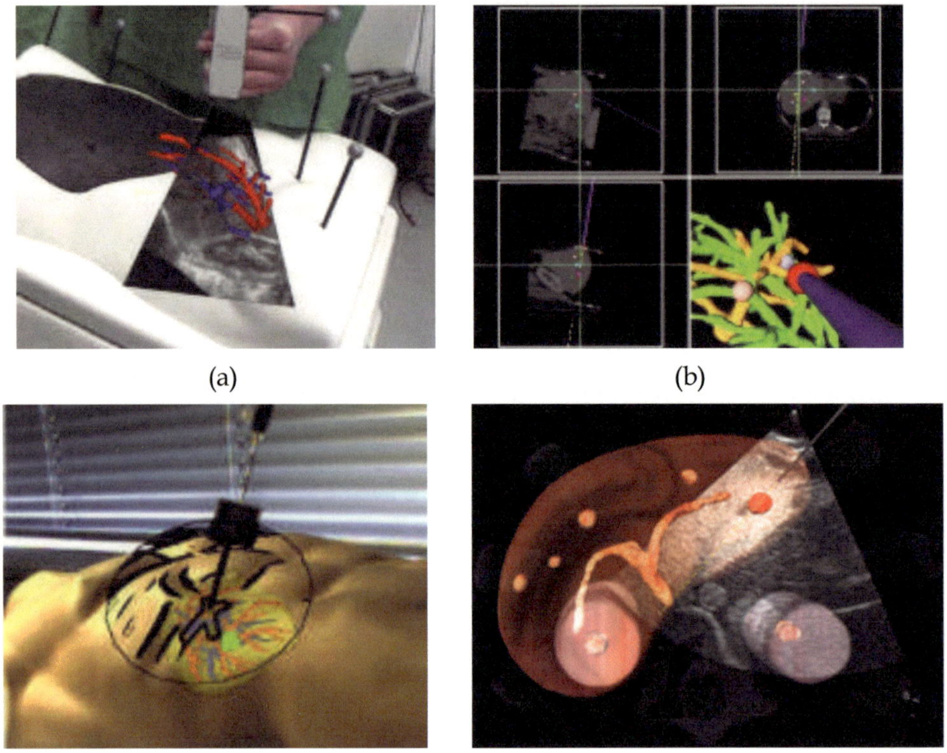

(a) (b) (c) (d)

Fig. 9. Example views of the capabilities of the ARIS*ER RFA system. a) First demonstrator (Kalkofen et al., 2007), b) Visualization concept 2D/3D (Stüdeli et al., 2008), c) Visualization concept HMD (Kalkofen et al., 2009), d) Fusion of US and 3D model generated from CT (Jalote-Parmar et al., 2009).

The developed system also introduces a novel Collision Detection (CD) feature in order to avoid hitting major vessels and vital organs (E.g. ribs) with the RFA probe (Morvan et al., 2008). It also developed and integrates an intra-operative image to tracker space registration, as well as realtime tracked Ultra-Sound (US) video texture for data fusion and for ultrasound augmentation. Although the framework is specifically made to support percutaneous RFA interventions, it could also be used for other needle biopsy procedures. The developed system could also be used as a surgical simulator to train novice interventionists using abdominal phantoms. In addition, ARIS*ER RFA system is also capable to support augmented ultrasound thus the interventional radiologist could easily find a target tumor and the augmented tip of the RFA needle in an ultrasound plane.

### 5.3 Endoclamp positioning system

In minimally invasive mitral valve surgery the heart has to be stopped and the aorta has to be sealed (clamped) to isolate the heart from the rest of the circulation. Unlike in the open chest procedure, the aorta cannot be clamped from the outside. This can be done with an endoclamp (Edwards Lifesciences, Irvine,USA), a catheter with an inflatable balloon at its tip. Once inflated in the aortic arch, the balloon provides the required sealing (Grossi et al., 2000).

This technique (Port-Access™ -PA- technique) is used nowadays as a standard procedure in several hospitals worldwide but it presents two main difficult steps: initial **placement**, and **monitoring** of balloon migrations. Initial **placement** is normally done using Trans-Esophageal Echography (TEE) as visual guidance with good results, but it is a hard task with a long learning curve mainly due to difficulties in **maneuvering** (difficult to control the balloon while there is still blood flow) and **visualizing** the balloon (with TEE it is only possible to see the balloon on a very small section of the artery) (Gulielmos et al., 1998; Aybek et al., 2000). **Monitoring** the balloon position during the surgery is even a harder challenge as TEE is unusable (there is air inside the heart and abdomen) so it is done indirectly through comparison of arterial pressures. Monitoring is extremely important as there can be damage to the aortic valve or to the central nervous system (even resulting in death) as a result of migration. Better monitoring and control of balloon position is needed to provide a safe and uncomplicated sealing of the aorta in this type of surgery.

To cope with these difficulties, a combined information and positioning system was developed within ARIS*ER, which is based on augmented reality technology and robotics (Furtado et al., 2010). The system was designed specifically for minimally invasive cardiac surgery. It provides constant, real-time monitoring of balloon position during the entire procedure, automatic position control to a specified target and automatic balloon pressure control. We believe that such a system helps overcome some of the most important difficulties in the PA technique and has the potential to make it the technique of choice for minimally invasive cardiac surgery. The system was developed using user centred design techniques where surgeons, engineers and human factor specialists were involved in all the development phases: concept, design, implementation and testing (Stüdeli & Freudenthal, 2009), as described in section 4.

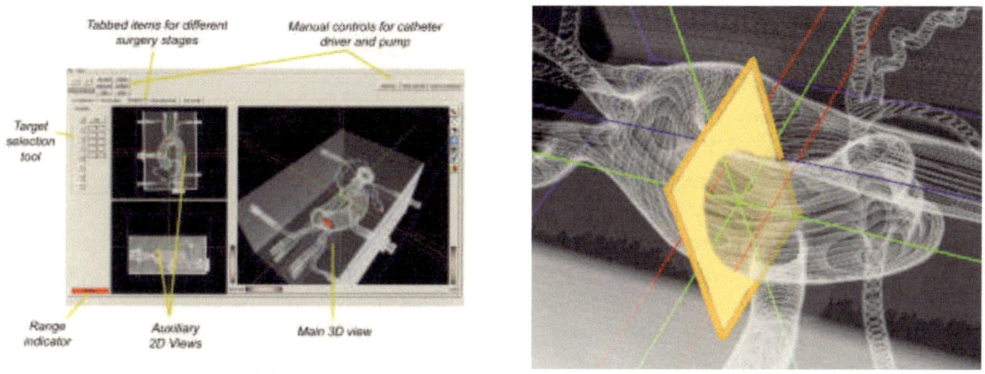


(a) (b)

Fig. 10. Endoclamp positioning system developed in ARIS*ER (Furtado et al., 2010). a) User interface of the system with explanation of the key concepts and b) and a close up of the target region (right).

The balloon position is measured in real time with an electromagnetic (EM) tracking system where the EM sensor coil is placed inside the balloon. Using this measurement, a model of the balloon is superimposed on a 3D rendered model of the patient's thorax, showing its actual position inside the vessel at all times. Fig. 10 shows the complete user interface, with two views of the anatomy and position of the balloon following the EM measurements. Using the buttons, the user can define a target (green lines and yellow plane) and the tolerance (red lines) for the balloon position. When control is on, the system places the balloon automatically in the target but the user also has the option to do everything manually. In this application, the deformation of the structures of interest is small, thus, a point-based rigid registration algorithm is enough to align tracking data with the rendered model.

A robotic inserter was custom designed to be able to push and pull the catheter inside the vessel (see Fig. 11.b). As explained before, the user defines a target position and the robotic catheter inserter places and maintains the balloon in this position, based on the EM sensor measurements. If there is a migration, the inserter automatically takes care of repositioning in the target location. The pressure inside the balloon is also automatically controlled to a defined target pressure using pressure sensor measurements and estimations taking into account the dynamics of the system catheter-balloon-aorta (Sette et al., 2009).

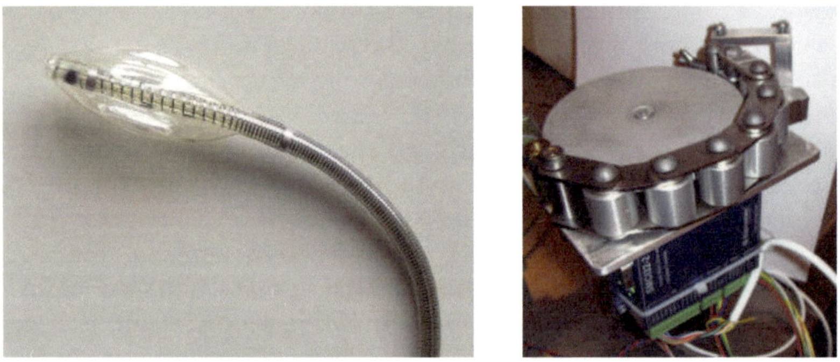

(a) (b)

Fig. 11. a) Endoclamp balloon and b) catheter driver (Sette et al., 2009).

So far, the system was tested several times in different scenarios. The first group of tests were performed on a silicon phantom with correct aortic anatomy (Fig. 12.a). The users performed several insertions with three types of visual support: looking directly inside the aorta, with the 3D view of the system and with a simulation of the view the surgeons currently have (simulated TEE). The users place the catheter faster and more accurately with the 3D view than with the simulated TEE view. The results are comparable to those obtained by looking directly inside the transparent aorta of the phantom. This has shown that the system gives back to the users the visual information they have lost by performing the surgery with the closed chest. Experiments on two animals (pigs) were also performed with the purpose of simulating a normal surgical workflow using the system in close-to-real conditions (Fig. 12.c). The system could effectively be used to guide the insertion of the catheter even in such a rough setting.

The proposed system presents clear benefits regarding the current situation where balloon position management is done with poor visual support. It provides a clear and intuitive notion of the balloon's position and corrects positioning errors automatically. This eases up strenuous monitoring tasks and catheter handlings and reduces work rhythm brakes of the surgeon during actual surgery at the heart. More extensive tests will be performed but for the time being we believe that this application has the potential to make the technique safer and simpler reducing the learning curve for the surgical teams and effectively increasing the safety of the procedure.

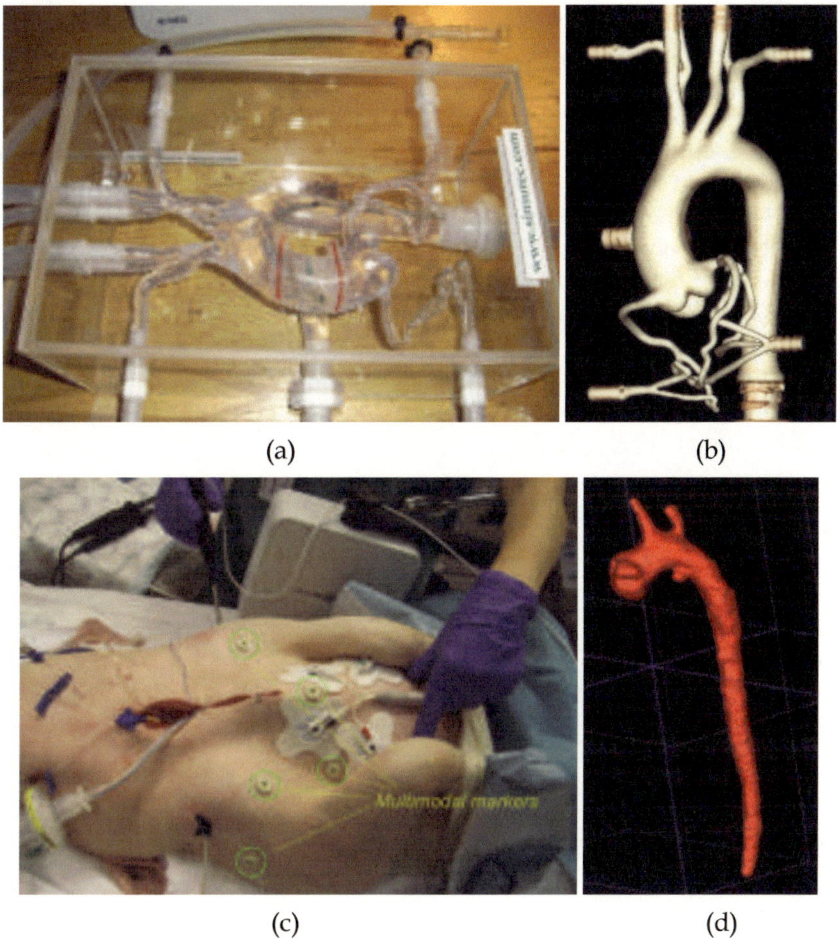


Fig. 12. User studies subjects and datasets obtained: a, b) silicon phantom c, d) pig.

### 5.4 The resection map for guidance in hepatectomies

Surgical demand exists for computer aided surgical systems in both open and laparoscopic liver resections. Surgeons expect orientation and visualization support during operations that allow for a more accurate and secure execution of the planned operation, especially in non anatomical resections. The Resection Map (see Fig. 13) is a solution that addresses this clinical need of intraoperative navigation for safer liver resections. It is an interactive 3D carthograpy of the patient's anatomy, a system for simplified and effective visualization of the critical structures and the path that has been preoperatively planned for the resection.

The concept of the Resection Map is somehow similar to the use of a navigation system while driving a car, but without the positioning information, without knowing the corresponding location of the tools in the map. Our strategy is to harness the rich preoperative planning information during the surgical procedure with an intuitive cartography, and without the need of any additional hardware or equipment. The system thus relies on the surgeon's capacity to perform a mental alignment between the Resection Map and the operating field. A detailed description of the design process and concept of this system can be found in (Lamata et al., 2008b).

Its integration in the Operating Room is seamless, and preliminary results show a perceivedincrease in the safety and confidence of the surgeon (Lamata et al., 2009a). We believe that the Resection Map could be very helpful for the education of inexperienced liver surgeons, for the adoption of a laparoscopic approach, for an easier implantation of a living donor programme, and for the complex cases of an experienced surgeon. The tool could even substitute some of the uses of the intraoperative US, like the identification of the key vessels that are going to be cut in the resection. Nevertheless, this imaging modality will be still required for the verification of the position and size (possible growth) of known tumours and the identification of new ones.

Research efforts are also being conducted towards the registration (alignment) of the virtual reconstruction of the liver with the patient's anatomy under the laparoscopic view. The objective is to do so without any additional hardware, as done in the localization of tools (see section 5.1), by exploiting the video information. Some preliminary promising results are presented in (Lamata et al., 2009b).

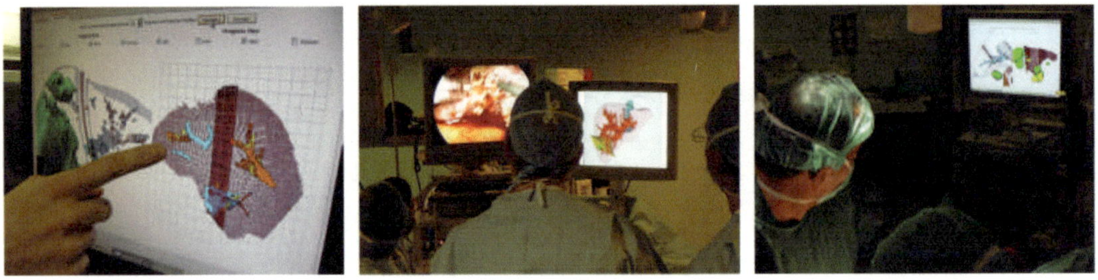

(a) (b) (c)

Fig. 13. Three liver resection interventions assisted by the Resection Map. (a) Close detailed view of the Map, (b) laparoscopic and (c) open procedures. (Lamata et al., 2009a).

## 6. Conclusions

Surgery is evolving towards a safer minimally invasive approach, driven by different technological advances. Augmented reality systems are gradually being adopted by surgeons to support their orientation and improve their accuracy, like the example of the Resection Map for the support of hepatectomies. There are also several AR prototypes, like the Endoclamp Positioning System and the ARIS*ER RFA system, with a great potential to reduce errors and increase safety in MIS heart clamping and needle ablations/biopsies respectively. The development and adoption of AR technologies is one of the main drivers in today's surgical revolution.

Research efforts in this field are directed in several directions. One crucial aspect is the reduction of the technological burden in the OR, with solutions like the tracking of surgical tools based in video analysis. Another is to find the scientific and technological grounds to provide haptic and tactile feedback in robotic systems. And one of the most difficult challenges is to solve the problem of organ deformation and shift during soft tissue surgery. And last but not least, it is necessary to highlight the importance in this field of research of a fluent and coordinated multidisciplinary dialogue and effort in the R&D team. User centred design techniques, where surgeons, engineers and human factor specialists are involved in all the development phases (concept, design, implementation and testing), are strongly advised.

## 7. References


Ali, W., Morvan, T., Risholm, P., et al. (2009). A visualization and fusion system for image guided RFA procedures. *Int J Image & Graphics*, Vol. (in press).

Aybek, T., Dogan, S., Wimmer-Greinecker, G., et al. (2000). The micro-mitral operation comparing the port-access technique and the transthoracic clamp technique. *Journal of Cardiac Surgery*, Vol. 15, No. 1, 76-81.

Azuma, R., Baillot, Y., Behringer, R., et al. (2001). Recent advances in augmented reality. *Ieee Computer Graphics and Applications*, Vol. 21, No. 6, 34-47, 0272-1716.

Baumhauer, M., Feuerstein, M., Meinzer, H.P., et al. (2008). Navigation in endoscopic soft tissue surgery: Perspectives and limitations. *Journal of Endourology*, Vol. 22, No. 4, 751-766, 0892-7790.

Beller, S., nerbein, M., Lange, T., et al. (2007). Image-guided surgery of liver metastases by three-dimensional ultrasound-based optoelectronic navigation. *British Journal of Surgery*, Vol. 94, No. 7, 866-875, 00071323 (ISSN).

Bettini, A., Marayong, P., Lang, S., et al. (2004). Vision-Assisted Control for Manipulation Using Virtual Fixtures. *IEEE Transactions on Robotics*, Vol. 20, No. 6, 953-966.

Cakmakci, O. and Rolland, J. (2006). Head-Worn Displays: A Review. *J. Display Technol.*, Vol. 2, No. 3, 199-216.

Cano, A., Gayá, F., Lamata, P., et al. (2008). Laparoscopic Tool Tracking Method for Augmented Reality Surgical Applications. *Lecture Notes in Computer Science*, Vol. 5104, 191-196.

Cash, D.M., Miga, M.I., Glasgow, S.C., et al. (2007). Concepts and preliminary data toward the realization of image-guided liver surgery. *J Gastrointest.Surg.*, Vol. 11, No. 7, 844-859.

Cleary, K., Kinsella, A. and Mun, S.K. (2005). OR 2020 workshop report: Operating room of the future. *International Congress Series*, Vol. 1281, 832-838.

Cornellà, J., Elle, O.J., Ali, W., et al. (2008). Intraoperative Navigation of an Optically Tracked Surgical Robot. *Lecture Notes in Computer Science*, Vol. 5242, 587-594.

Davison, A.J., Reid, I.D., Molton, N.D., et al. (2007). MonoSLAM: Real-time single camera SLAM. *Ieee Transactions on Pattern Analysis and Machine Intelligence*, Vol. 29, No. 6, 1052-1067, 0162-8828.

Diodato, M.D., Prosad, S.M., Klingensmith, M.E., et al. (2004). Robotics in surgery. *Current Problems in Surgery*, Vol. 41, 752-810.

Doussis, E. (1993). An Ultrasonic Position Detecting System for Motion Tracking in Three Dimensions, Tulane University.

El-Serag, H.B. and Rudolph, K.L. (2007). Hepatocellular carcinoma: epidemiology and molecular carcinogenesis. *Gastroenterology.*, Vol. 132, No. 7, 2557-2576.

Ewers, R., Schicho, K., Undt, G., et al. (2005). Basic research and 12 years of clinical experience in computer-assisted navigation technology: a review. *Int J Oral Maxillofac Surg*, Vol. 34, No. 1, 1-8, 0901-5027 (Print).

Finlay, P.A. and Morgan, P. (2003). Pathfinder Image Guided Robot for Neurosurgery. *Industrial Robots: An International Journal*, Vol. 30, No. 1, 30-34.

Freudenthal, A., Pattynama, P.M.T., Samset, E., et al. (2007). Technology assessment as guidance in product development for real time radiology based information for the surgeon. In: *Novel Technologies for Minimally Invasive Therapies*. S. Casciaro and E. Samset (Ed.), 180-188, Lupiensis Biomedical Pubs., 978-88-902880-0-5, Lecce, Italy.

Furtado, H., Stüdeli, T. and Sette, M. (2010). Endoclamp balloon visualization and automatic placement system. *Proc. of SPIE Medical Imaging*, San Diego, CA, USA.

Gaponov, I., Ryu, J.-H., Choi, S.-J., et al. (2008). Telerobotic system for cell manipulation. *Proc. of IEEE/ASME Int Conf on Advanced Intelligent Mechatronics, AIM*, pp. 165-169, Xi'an, China.

Goethals, P., Sette, M.M., Reynaerts, D., et al. (2008). Flexible elastoresistive tactile sensor for minimally invasive surgery. *Haptics: Perception, Devices and Scenarios, Proceedings*, Vol. 5024, 573-579, 0302-9743.

Grossi, E., Ribakove, G., Galloway, A., et al. (2000). Minimally invasive mitral valve surgery with endovascular balloon technique. *Operative Techniques in Thoracic and Cardiovascular Surgery*, Vol. 5, 176-189.

Gulielmos, V., Dangel, M., Solowjowa, N., et al. (1998). Clinical experiences with minimally invasive mitral valve surgery using a simplified port access(TM) technique. *European Journal of Cardio-thoracic Surgery*, Vol. 14, No. 2, 141-147.

Hacksel, P.J. and Salcudean, S.E. (1994). Estimation of environment forces and rigid-body velocities using observers. *Proc. IEEE Int Conf on Robotics and Automation*, pp. 931-936, San Diego, CA, USA.

Ho, S.C., Hibberd, R.D. and Davies, B.L. (1995). Robot Assisted Knee Surgery. *IEEE Engineering in Medicine and Biology*, Vol. 14, No. 3, 292-300.

International Standards, O. (1999). ISO 13407. Human Centred Design Process for Interactive Systems.

Iordachita, I., Kapoor, A., Mitchell, B., et al. (2006). Steady-Hand Manipulator for Retinal Surgery. *MICCAI, Medical Robotics Workshop*, pp. 66-73, Copenhaguen, Denmark.

Jalote-Parmar, A., Badke-Schaub, P., Ali, W., et al. (2009). Cognitive processes as integrative component for developing expert decision-making systems: A workflow centered framework. *Journal of Biomedical Informatics*, Vol. (in press).

Jalote-Parmar, A., Pattynama, P.M.T., Goossens, R.H.M., et al. (2007). Bridging the gap: A design approach to developing technological solutions to support minimally invasive surgeries. In: *Novel Technologies for minimally invasive therapies*. S. Casciaro and E. Samset (Ed.), 93-101, Lupiensis Biomedical Publications, Lecce, Italy.

Johansson, R.S., Westling, G., Backstrom, A., et al. (2001). Eye-Hand Coordination in Object Manipulation. *J. Neurosci.*, Vol. 21, No. 17, 6917-6932, 1529-2401.

Kalkofen, D., Mendez, E. and Schmalstieg, D. (2009). Comprehensible visualization for augmented reality. *IEEE Transactions on Visualization and Computer Graphics*, Vol. 15, No. 2, 193-204.

Kalkofen, D., Milko, S., Massoptier, L., et al. (2007). "ARIS*ER Demo Radio Frequency Ablation." from http://www.ariser.info/projects/rfa_demo.php

Kalkofen, D. and Schmalstieg, D. (2006). *An Augmented Reality Framework for Medical Interventions*, Minimally Invasive Therapies & Novel Embedded Technology Systems, ARISER Summer School Textbook.

Karas, C. and Chiocca, E.A. (2007). Neurosurgical robotics: a review of brain and spine applications. *Journal of Robotics Surgery*, Vol. 1, 39-43.

Kazanzides, P., Mittelstadt, B.D., Musits, B.L., et al. (1995). An integrated system for cementless hip replacement. *IEEE Transactions on Biomedical Engineering*, Vol. 14, No. 3, 307-313.

Kennedy, C.W., Hu, T. and Desai, J.P. (2002). Combining haptic and visual servoing for cardiothoracic surgery. *Proc. IEEE Int. Conf. of Robotics and Automation, 2002. ICRA '02.*, pp. 2106-2111, 0-7803-7272-7, Washington, DC, USA.

Krupa, A., Gangloff, J., Doignon, C., et al. (2003). Autonomous 3-D Positioning of Surgical Instruments in Robotized Laparoscopic Surgery Using Visual Servoing. *IEEE Transactions on Robotics and Automation*, Vol. 19, No. 5, 842-853.

Kwon, D.S., Yoon, Y.S., Lee, J.J., et al. (2001). ARTHROBOT: a new surgical robot system for total hip arthroplasty. *Proc. of IEEE/RSJ Int. Conf on Intelligent Robots and Systems*, pp. 1123-1128, 0-7803-6612-3, Maui, HI, USA.

Lamata, P., Gomez, E.J., Lamata, F., et al. (2008a). Understanding perceptual boundaries in laparoscopic surgery. *IEEE Trans.Biomed.Eng*, Vol. 55, No. 3, 866-873.

Lamata, P., Jalote-Parmar, A., Lamata, F., et al. (2008b). The Resection Map, a proposal for intraoperative hepatectomy guidance. *Int.J of CARS*, Vol. 3, No. 3, 299-306.

Lamata, P., Lamata, F., Sojar, V., et al. (2009a). Use of the Resection Map as guidance during hepatectomy. *Surg.Endosc.*, Vol. In press.

Lamata, P., Morvan, T., Reimers, M., et al. (2009b). Addressing shading-based laparoscopic registration. *Proc. Medical Physics and Biomedical Engineering World Congress 2009*, pp. (in press), Munich, Germany.

Loser, M.H. and Navab, N. (2000). A New Robotic System for Visually Controlled Percutaneous Interventions under CT Fluoroscopy. *Proc. MICCAI.* , pp. 887-896.

Maier-Hein, L., Tekbas, A., Seitel, A., et al. (2008). In vivo accuracy assessment of a needlebased navigation system for CT-guided radiofrequency ablation of the liver. *Medical Physics*, Vol. 35, No. 12, 5385-5396, 0094-2405.

Massoptier, L. and Casciaro, S. (2008). A new fully automatic and robust algorithm for fast segmentation of liver tissue and tumors from CT scans. *European Radiology*, Vol. 18, No. 8, 1658-1665.

Milgram, P. and Kishino, F. (1994). Taxonomy of mixed reality visual displays. *IEICE Transactions on Information and Systems*, Vol. E77-D, No. 12, 1321-1329, 09168532 (ISSN).

Morvan, T., Reimers, M. and Samset, E. (2008). High Performance GPU-based Proximity Queries using Distance Fields. *Computer Graphics Forum*, Vol. 27, No. 8, 2040-2052, 1467-8659.

Naerum, E., Cornellà, J. and Elle, O.J. (2008). Contact force estimation for backdrivable robotic manipulators with coupled friction. *Intelligent Robots and Systems, 2008. IROS 2008. IEEE/RSJ International Conference on*, pp. 3021-3027, ISBN: 978-1-4244-2057-5, Nice, France.

Neumuth, T., Durstewitz, N., Fischer, M., et al. (2006). Structured recording of intraoperative surgical workflows. *Progress in Biomedical Optics and Imaging - Proceedings of SPIE*, pp. 61450A.

Nielsen, J. (1994). Usability Engineering. San Francisco, USA, Morgan Kaufmann.

Nuño, E. and Basañez, L. (2006). Haptic guidance with force feedback to assist teleoperation systems via high speed networks. *IFR/DGR International Symposium on Robotics*, pp. 213.

Ortmaier, T., Weiss, H., Hagn, U., et al. (2006). A Hands-On-Robot for Accurate Placement of Pedicle Screws. *Proc IEEE Int Conf on: Robotics and Automation, 2006. ICRA 2006.* , pp. 4179-4186, 0-7803-9505-0.

Payandeh, S. and Stanisic, Z. (2002). On Application of Virtual Fixtures as an Aid for Telemanipulation and Training, pp. 18-23, Symposium on Haptic Interfaces for Virtual Environment and Teleoperator Systems.

Peeters, K., Sette, M., Goethals, P., et al. (2008). Design considerations for lateral skin stretch and perpendicular indentation displays to be used in minimally invasive surgery. *Haptics: Perception, Devices and Scenarios, Proceedings*, Vol. 5024, 325-330, 0302-9743.

Picod, G., Jambon, A.C., Vinatier, D., et al. (2005). What can the operator actually feel when performing a laparoscopy? *Surgical Endoscopy and Other Interventional Techniques*, Vol. 19, No. 1, 95-100, 0930-2794.

Raskar, R., Welch, G., Low, K.-L., et al. (2001). Shader Lamps: Animating Real Objects With Image-Based Illumination. *Eurographics Workshop on Rendering*, pp. 89-102.

Rosenbaum, D.A. (1990). *Human Motor Control*, Academic Press.

Rosenberg, L.B. (1995). *The use of Virtual Fixtures to Enhance Operator Performance in Time Delayed Teleoperation*, Armstrong Laboratory.

Sayers, C. and Paul, R. (1994). An Operator Interface for Teleprogramming Employing Synthetic Fixtures. *Presence*, Vol. 3, No. 4, 309-320.

Schneider, O. and Troccaz, J. (2001). A six-degree-of-freedom passive arm with dynamic constraints (PADyC) for Cardiac Surgery application: preliminary experiments. *Computer Aided Surgery*, Vol. 6, 340-351.

Sette, M., D'hooge, J., Langeland, S., et al. (2007). Tactile feedback in minimally invasive procedures using an elastography-based method. *Int J CARS*, Vol. S504.

Sette, M., Furtado, H., Stüdeli, T., et al. (2009). Physiological Parameters Based Control Scheme For Automatic Intravascular Balloon Inflation. *Proc. Medical Physics and Biomedical Engineering World Congress 2009*, pp. (in press), Munich, Germany.

Smith, A.C., Mobasser, F. and Hashtrudi-Zaad, K. (2006). Neural-network-based contact force observers for haptic applications. *IEEE Trans. Robot.*, Vol. 22, No. 6, 1163-1175.

Stüdeli, T. and Alexander, T. (2008). Actual ergonomic research in applied virtual and mixed reality systems - with a special focus on navigation and control aids in 3D. In: *Minimally Invasive Techs. & Nanosystems for Diagnosis & Therapies*. S. Casciaro and E. Samset (Ed.), 1-11, Lupiensis Biomedical Pubs., 978-88-902880-2-9, Lecce, Italy.

Stüdeli, T. and Freudenthal, A. (2009). Defining the role of the Ergonomist in the development of medical mixed reality systems - Aspects to be considered during the development of enabling technology in the operation theater. *17th World Congress On Ergonomics IEA 2009*, Beijing, China.

Stüdeli, T., Freudenthal, A. and de Ridder, H. (2007). Evaluation Framework of Ergonomic Requirements for Iterative Design Development of Computer Systems and their User Interfaces for Minimally Invasive Therapy. *8th International Conference on Work With Computing Systems - WWCS 2007* Stockholm, Sweden.

Stüdeli, T., Kalkofen, D., Risholm, P., et al. (2008). Visualization tool for improved accuracy in needle placement during percutaneous radio-frequency ablation of liver tumors - art. no. 69180B. *Medical Imaging 2008: Visualization, Image-Guided Procedures, and Modeling, Pts 1 and 2*, Vol. 6918, B9180-B9180, 0277-786X.

Teber, D., Baumhauer, M., Guven, E.O., et al. (2009a). Robotic and imaging in urological surgery. *Current Opinion in Urology*, Vol. 19, No. 1, 108-113, 0963-0643.

Teber, D., Guven, S., Simpfendorfer, T., et al. (2009b). Augmented Reality: A New Tool To Improve Surgical Accuracy during Laparoscopic Partial Nephrectomy? Preliminary In Vitro and In Vivo Results. *European Urology*, Vol. 56, No. 2, 332-338, 0302-2838.

Tonet, O., Thoranaghatte, R.U., Megali, G., et al. (2007). Tracking endoscopic instruments without a localizer: A shape-analysis-based approach. *Computer Aided Surgery*, Vol. 12, No. 1, 35-42, 1092-9088.

Turro, N., Khatib, O. and Coste-Maniere, E. (2001). Haptically augmented teleoperation. *Proc. Ieee Int Conf on Robotics and Automation*, pp. 386-392, 1050-4729.

Voros, S., Long, J.A. and Cinquin, P. (2007). Automatic detection of instruments in laparoscopic images: A first step towards high-level command of robotic endoscopic holders. *International Journal of Robotics Research*, Vol. 26, No. 11-12, 1173-1190, 0278-3649.

# 6

# Using Augmented Reality to Cognitively Facilitate Product Assembly Process

Lei Hou and Xiangyu Wang
*The University of Sydney*
*Australia*

## 1. Introduction

Assembly task is an activity of collecting parts / components and bringing them together through assembly operations to perform one or more of several primary functions. In practice, part drawing is still performing as a main means for assembly guidance nowadays. As an emerging and powerful technology, Augmented Reality (AR) integrates images of virtual objects into a real world. Due to its self characteristic features, AR is envisaged to afford great potentials and to be an alternative of traditional means in assembly task. This chapter speculates the issues and discrepancies involved in the present practice of assembly task, recommends a novel utilization of AR animation technology in this area, and discusses the potentials of using AR animation in guiding product assembly task.

## 2. State-of-the-art review of visualization methods for product assembly

This section presents the issues and discrepancies involved in the present practice of assembly task, and compares the state-of-the-art of the two advanced visualization technologies in their applications in assembly process: Virtual Reality and Augmented Reality.

### 2.1 Traditional method for assembly

In practice, assembly drawing (manual) is still performing as a main means for assembly guidance nowadays (Laperriere & EI Maraghy, 1992). Assembly drawing delivers the holistic constructional knowledge of a machine and its separated components / parts, as it is an essential technological file for the technicians to enact assembly craft, conduct assembly task and evaluate assembly result. A well-formulated assembly drawing should necessarily present at least four categories of assembly information, a set of visual percepts of product components / parts, their parameters or dimensions, technical requirements in quality, installation and testing and other auxiliary information.

Confined in a fixed-size two dimensional (2D) drawing, a large quantity of information concerning product parts and components can be quite redundant, cumbersome and crowded, especially when the comparatively complex assembly tasks are referred. This traditionally creates a hardship of fast information orientation and understanding complex assembly relations (He et al., 1989). From the perspective of the technicians (e.g., designers / assemblers), there needs to be a large number of subjective information retrieval behaviors and relative mental processes added into the proceeding of understanding the assembly information context owing to the complex information flows during manual-based cognition. It is widely accepted that the form of capacity of selective information retrieval and filtering does not occur until a long-term accumulation of assembly experiences and expertise. Sometimes, it even needs extra targeted training activities (Croft et al., 1991). However, using such a manual is not easy to train the expert assemblers, especially for assembly processes that require problem-solving skills (Johnson-Laird., 1983). It often takes months or even years for a novice assembler to develop expert knowledge for assembling processes that involve high complexity (Hoffman et al., 1998). In some cases, even the expert assemblers must constantly refer to the instructions from assembly manual for infrequently performed procedures or procedures with high difficulty, not to say for those novice assemblers.

Previously, researches have indicated that assembly under drawing guidance consumed a mass of invalid time (behaviors not related to workpieces) and also found that such an assembly based on 2D assembly drawing relatively failed to consider the cognitive issues comprehensively (Abe & Tsuji, 1987). In practice, implementation of assembly task consists of workpiece activities and non-workpiece activities. In each assembly step, while conducting a series of physically workpiece operations like observing, grasping, installing and so on, an assembler should also conduct several mentally manual-related processes such as comprehending, translating and retrieving information context (Neumann & Majoros, 1998). Once finishing the present step, he or she will resume these physical and mental behaviors in next assembly steps. Neumann and Majoros (1998) claimed that information-related activities tend to be cognitive, workpiece activities tend to be kinesthetic and psychomotor and the time allocated to each portion was measured by Towne (1985), who came to the conclusion that the information-related activities (cognitive workload) accounted for 50 percent of the total task workload. Other researchers have indicated a large number of switchovers between physical (workpiece) and mental (manual) process generally result in operational suspensions and attention transitions to the novice assemblers (Shalin et al., 1996). Ott (1995) concluded that 45 percent of every technicians' shifts actually spent on finding and reading procedural and related information when assembling the repaired hardware. Neumann and Majoros (1998) also uncovered that individual technicians differed in how much time they devoted to cognitive / informational chores, but differed little in how much time they devoted to manual. Apart from the consumption between physical and cognitive process, mental tiredness can come into being after a long exposure to the drawings, since information retrieval difficulty generally exists in complex assembly drawings, especially to the novice assemblers (Gick & Holyoak, 1980). At the same time, the likelihood of incorrect assemblies typically exists in assembly task when novice assemblers continue to bear the mental pressure and focusing, since a successive cognitive process of handling manual information could trigger the mental tiredness and negligence, which in turn cause error assembly procedures. The evidence was supported by development of Aviation Safety Reporting System (a NASA-conducted method for airline personnel to report problems anonymously), which reported that 60 percent of errors were procedural errors, most of which were due to negligence in understanding drawing (Veinott & Kanki, 1995). Last but not least, the task motivation in this traditional method is to some extent suppressed because of the cognitive baldness and behavioral repetition in between the unilateral information retrieval and the corresponding operation (Locke & Edwin, 1968).

### 2.2 Virtual reality in assembly

As the development of computer graphics, an entirely new technology, Virtual Reality (VR) has emerged. Described as a technology for which "the excitement to accomplishment ratio remains high" (Durlach and Mavor, 1995), VR is now rapidly outgrowing its computer games image and finding applications in a variety of contexts and in fields as diverse as engineering (Frederick & Brooks, 1999), design (Sherman & Craig, 2003), architecture (Calvin et al., 1993), medicine (Satava1995), education (Psotka, 1993), rescuing (Bliss et al., 1997), military (Hue et al., 1997) and so on (Goldberg, 1994). The kernel of VR is computer simulation, which combines the three dimensional (3D) graphics, motion tracking technology and sensory feedback (Pahl & Beitz, 1997). Accordingly, VR attempts to replace the user's perception of the surrounding world with computer-generated artificial 3D virtual environments (VEs). The use of VEs allows the user total control of both the stimulus situation and the nature and pattern of feedback, and also allows comprehensive monitoring of performance. To date, there are already many well-known applications of VR technology. One of the most famous applications was in NASA's Hubble Space Telescope repairing mission, where an immersive virtual environment was created by NASA to train telescope repair personnel (Veinott & Kanki, 1995). Another one was from the U.S. military. A networked artificial virtual environment was aggressively pursued for the distributed simulation of integrated combat operations, where diverse topographic and climate elements were mixed together by creating a series of complex scenarios which included both real and autonomous agents (Mastaglio & Callahan, 1995). Rose and his colleagues (2000) also found except that, VEs were of a considerable skill transfer effect in implementing training task. In their three experiments, performance of trainees disclosed an equivalent extent of skill transfers from training in virtual environments to real world post-training tasks and from training in real task training to real post-training tasks.

The success of a variety of VR applications has also enabled an attempt in manufacturing industry since the 80s. An initial trial of using VR technology in guiding assembly task instead of the assembly drawing was conducted before it won a praise and a further interest in research perspective. Nowadays, this technology has been commonly used in product assembly area (Ritchie et al., 1999). Through it, product designers are able to create the virtual prototypes of product accessories, modules and parts in VEs, where the virtually trial assembly tasks are enabled for the purpose of facilitating assemblers through the evaluation of varying task difficulties from computer. Coincidentally, simulation and evaluation in the early assembly design stage are also enabled with VR, with a large amount of prototyping cost saved from real prototyping in real environment (Zachmann, 1996). In the world wide, commercial virtual prototyping software such as CAD, Pro/E and IDEAL has been widely used to facilitate the product assembly and aid the product assembly design, and the product technicians are capable of developing various product accessories, modules and parts with different functions and dimensions, and conveniently conducting the product assembly guidance or design based on computers (Pratt, 1995).

Notwithstanding, regardless of the considerable assembly accuracy, this software-guided method also manifests its defects. For instance, VR-based method cannot provide a better understanding of diverse interferences of assembly path and complex real assembly environments. The issues such as assembly task difficulty and assembly workload could not be easily evaluated either. What is more, another shortcoming is the limited level of "realism" experience due to the lack of rich sensory feedback (Wang & Dunston, 2006). The computer-generated virtual components cannot convey other channel of useful feedback such as audio, tactile, and force, etc., which normally exist in the real world. Accordingly, the lack of interactions between virtual and real entities greatly cumbers the furthering development of using VR in product assembly task (Brooks & Jr, 1996).

### 2.3 Augmented reality in assembly

In order to solve this trade-off, researchers have opened up another promising alternative, Augmented Reality (AR) technology, a more expansive form of VR (Milgram & Colquhoun, 1999). As an emerging and cutting-edge technology, AR integrates images of virtual objects into a real world. By inserting the virtual simulated prototypes into the real environment and creating an augmented scene, AR technology could satisfy the goal of enhancing a person's perception of a virtual prototyping with real entities. This gives a virtual world a better connection to the real world, while maintaining the flexibility of the virtual world (Fig. 1. a novel storytelling means).

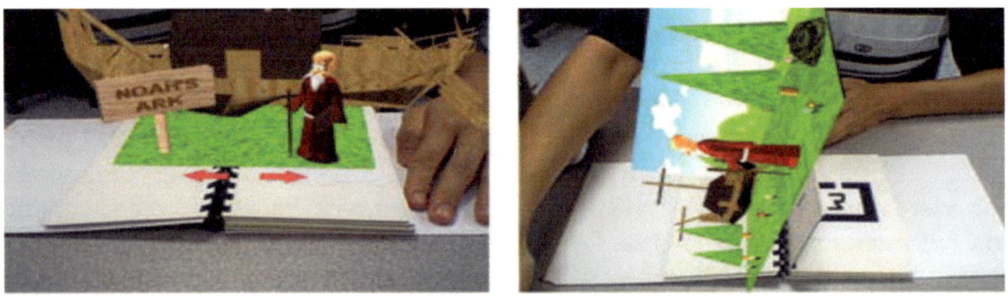

Fig. 1. A novel storytelling means using AR scene (Zhou et al, 2008)

Defined as the combination of the real and virtual scenes, such technology has been explored in the areas such as maintenance (Feiner et al., 1993), manufacturing (Curtis et al., 1998), training (Boud, 1999), battlefield (Urban, 1995; Metzger, 1993), medicine (Mellor, 1995; Uenohara & Kanade, 1995), 3D video conferencing (Regenbrecht et al., 2004), computer assisted instruction (CAI) (Tang et al., 2003), computer-aided surgery (Bajura et al., 1992), entertainment (Wagner & Pintaric, 2005) and so on. Some of the successful AR applications in industry are highlighted as follows. One is integrating AR with manual gas-metal-arc welding technology. Since in the traditional manual gas-metal-arc welding, the welder has a very limited field of view through the dark cartridge used to protect welders' eyes from dangerous UV radiation, Park (2007) applied the AR registration technology to welding helmet to aid welding process by virtually presenting the outline of to-be-welded objects. Based on it, they developed an AR-based welding helmet system --- TEREBES (Tragbares Erweiter tes Realitäts-System zur Beobachtung von Schweißprozessen System), a wearable Augmented Reality System for observation of welding processes. Through TEREBES, the limited real vision was enlarged by virtual vision and the welders could better command an overall welding performance with great ease (Fig. 2. AR welding helmet system). Another successful application of using augmentation is in supporting factory layout planning. Volkswagen (1999) has developed an Augmented Reality supported manufacturing-planning system where a physically existing production environment can be superimposed with virtual planning objects, and planning tasks can thus be validated without modeling the surrounding environment of the production site. By combining and superimposing the result of the ergonomic simulation process, planners can optimize the manual workplace without actually modeling the workplace. The production personnel can participate in this process, and various rearrangements can be benchmarked at the same time (Fig. 3. AR in factory layout) (Doil et al., 2003). Besides, current Augmented Reality was also attempted to combine with x-ray vision to overcome the discrepancies of pure AR registration, e.g. mismatch. Via this combination, users have realized an architectural anatomy, which creates an augmentation that shows users portions of a building that are hidden behind architectural or structural finishes, and allows them to see additional information about the hidden objects (Webster et al., 1996).

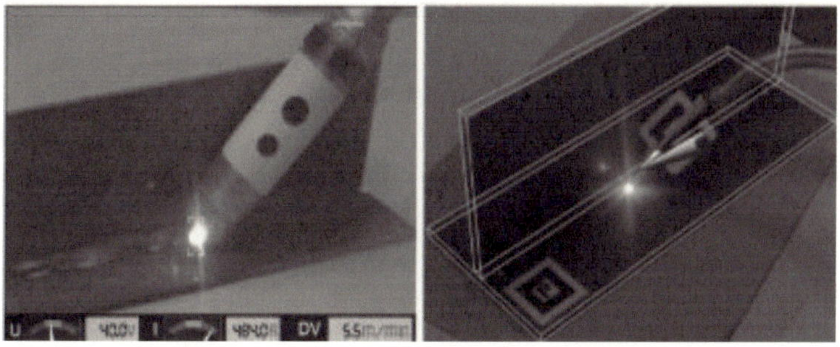

Fig. 2. Using AR in welding process-a user interface of welding helmet system (Hillers et al., 2004)

Fig. 3. Visualization of virtual machinery in real plant-environment (Doil et al.,2003)

Compared with VR which entirely separates the real environment from the virtual environment, AR maintains a sense of presence inside the real world and balances the perception of real and virtual worlds (Raghavan et al., 1999). Through AR, a technician can manipulate the virtual components directly inside the real environment. He or she could identify the potential interferences between the to-be-assembled objects and the existing objects in the real assembly environment. Therefore, in AR environment, a user can not only interact with real environments, but also interact with *Augmented Environments (AEs)* that are structured to offset partial sensory loss in VR to the user. Furthermore, to better support the feedback of augmentation, the additional "non-situated" augmenting elements could be added into the assembly process like recorded voice, animation, replayed video, short tips and arrows, all of which could simultaneously guide the assemblers to conduct assembly task throughout the entire procedural operational process, release their tension and even notify an erroneous assembly sequence. Therefore, the reality being perceived is further augmented. Due to its self characteristic features, AR is envisaged to provide great potentials in product assembly task, which will be discussed in the following sections.

In the past few years, various researches have focused on product assembly area by using Augmented Reality technology. To obtain the optimized assembly sequence, Raghavan, Molineros, and Sharma (1999) adopted AR as an interactive technique for assembly sequence evaluation and formulated the assembly planner and liaison graph. In their research work, they have addressed the issue of automatically generating the most optimized product assembly sequence using AR. A resembled research was also conducted by Liverani, Amati and Caligiana (2004), where a binary assembly tree (BAT) algorithm was developed with the personal active assistant system (PAA) in their project. The BAT in PAA replaced the function of liaison graph and shaped their own assembly sequence optimization method to aid the product assembly design. At the same time, an inline assembly database was created as an attachment of PAA system. Besides, Salonen and his colleagues (2007) used AR technology to conduct their research in the area of industrial products assembly and developed a multi-modality system based on the AR facility, which consisted of a head-mounted display (HMD), a marker-based software toolkit (ARToolKit), an image tracking camera, a web camera and a microphone. In their system, they realized a graphical user interface where three controlling methods were enabled to effectively process the assembly design of the industrial product, including the keyboard control, gesture control and speech control (Liverani et al., 2004). In addition, considering that the utilization of AR in product assembly design was based on the marker registration technology, Kutulakos and Vallino (1998) implemented their research to realize a markerless-based registration technology, for the purpose of overcoming the inconveniences of applying markers as the carrier in assembly design process. Although a markerless-based AR system named calibration-free system was developed, it still could not overcome the relative technical limitations such as the radial camera distortions, perspective projection and so on, which prevented it from a prevailing use. Last but not least, the utilization of AR technology has extended to the assembly guidance of a wide range of products, e.g., furniture assembly design (Zauner et al., 2003), toy assembly design (Tang et al., 2003), and so on (Yamada & Takata 2007). Many past augmented reality developments were based on ARToolKit, a powerful agent for object registration. Via ARToolKit (Kutulakos et al., 1998), the virtual images of product components can be registered onto predefined paper-based markers, then pop up in view of monitors like HMD or computer screen using marker tracking camera.

Notwithstanding, trials have achieved fruitful results, there are still some issues that could not be well resolved in terms of assembly area. For instance, current trials have not thoroughly eliminated the assemblers' cognitive workload when using AR as an alternative guidance of manual or VR. A reasonable explanation is that because the virtual images of to-be-assembled objects are registered as static image individuals onto pre-defined markers on the basis of the actual registration technology, cognition is still prevented from utmost because the augmented clews are independently exhibited from each other. Accordingly, to acquire the sequent information context such as assembly paths and fixation forms of components (augmented clews), the assemblers still need a positive cognitive retrieval before reorganizing these augmented clews in mind. In order to address this long-standing and critical cognitive problem, the rest of this chapter introduces a more expanded form of traditional AR called AR with animation (rather than abandoning the mature AR technology), and argues its unparalleled potentials of being guideline compared with manual, VR and AR.

## 3. Potentials

The following cognitive aspects are critical involved the product assembly process. Augmented Reality is discussed in the following cognitive aspects regarding its great potentials in facilitating product assembly process.

### 3.1 Enhancement of information retrieval capacity

Personal information retrieval capacity differs greatly since it depends on personal expertise, rather than merely on complexity of assembly task itself. An effective retrieval capacity refers to a series of fast mental behaviors, i.e., searching information, analyzing information, extracting information and so on. Actually, the level of personal retrieval capacity generally handicaps the transition from informational novel to information expert (Neumann & Ott, 1995). To solve this trade-off, this revolutionary alternative, AR animation guidance brings a qualitative change in terms of the way to retrieve information where the subjective one-sided information pick-up behavior is taken over by a mutual interaction between computer and people.

#### 3.1.1 Information context formed in assembly task

To accomplish assembly task, a series of visual percepts of components / parts is the first section of information context that needed to retrieve. They encapsulate the components / parts' functionality, assembled relations and their main structures and are exhibited using proper, complete, clear and concise expression. Followed are the parameters of each components / parts e.g. texture, material, color and weight. Another equally important information context is the technique requirements of product or its segments, including requirements in quality, assembly, testing, using and so on. They fit together, coordinate with each other and shape a sequent information context in assembly task.

#### 3.1.2 Relations in information context

To be specific, the information context consists of the sub-assembly relations among each to-be-assembled component when referring to organizing a coherent information context. Accordingly, it is ultimately implemented to the parts fitting relations, which are the dimensional and functional fits between the contacting surfaces of assembled and to-be-assembled components. For example, a nut matches a bolt, thus, retrieving the diameter information of a bolt could lead to a successful nut and bolt assembly. A concave matches a convexity. Thus, picking the components that maintain the same contacting surfaces could typically bring lead to a successful assembly. Besides, expertise or experiences accumulated are also contributing to assembly relations, e.g. a rigid component is opt to bracing a rigid component and one type of color generally corresponds to the proximate color in views of aesthetics consideration.

#### 3.1.3 Context information retrieved using AR animation

The information context would be intermitted if clues are carelessly overlooked or mistakenly retrieved. In AR animation, it provides a dynamic exhibition of consistent information context via animation segments displayed in each assembly step. Observers could detect the existing dimensions from real positioned components as well as the registered ones attached to the virtual to-be-positioned components from the see-through HMD. At the same time, animation dynamically demonstrates the assembly process in HMD by approaching the virtual to-be-assembled objects to the real assembled ones settled in the ideal positions. This enables technicians to mimic each assembly step and complete real assembly operation with great ease. Through demonstrating a series of virtual animation segments registered in the real environment, AR compensates for the mental and cognitive gaps between individual differences in info-retrieval capacity and lowers the influences that a task difficulty imposes on information retrieval. Consequently, it eases the information retrieval and meanwhile, provides a synchronized means for implementation.

### 3.2 Synchronized assembly guidance

Synchronization is another characteristic feature of AR animation used in place of traditional manual in assembly task. In view of each assemble step, AR animation scenario dynamically ushers the coherent spatial position changes of components in space within each animation segment that can be triggered by the operators themselves. When completing each animation segment, AR animation scenario turns into an augmented presentation tool, in which the previous mobile virtual components are registered or mapped on the final positions statically, as well as the individual attached information. The scenario is temporarily suspended to wait for the next trigger from assemblers. During each time intervals (when finishing the last bout of guidance), the assemblers get sufficient time to pick up the real to-be-assembled component from the resting and positioning it to the destination under the guidance of previous animation segment. Accordingly, the assembly operations and augmented guidance could proceed collaboratively, which embodies the characteristic of parallel task mode in AR animation.

### 3.3 Reduction of assembly error

One research finding value made by Miller and Swain (1986) is the influence of working stress on task implementation. It conveys a fact that novices and experts are equally likely to err in performance under low stress, but novices are more likely to err under high stress. In practice, when first facing a new assembly task that is not familiar with, an assembler typically begins with understanding sub-assembly relations from assembly drawing. However, suffering from scarcity of personal expertise and practical experiences, a novice could spend a lot of time in cognitive process ahead of operation. When driven by the actual constrains like working efficiency and qualification rate, a novel assembler would sustain a high stress mentally and make mistakes in information retrieving process and assembly operation. In addition, a resumed step of information retrieval follows the wrong retrieval and is a byproduct of previous assembly error, which further strengthens their intension and exacerbates their performances. As an attempt to address these problems, animation in AR platform better supports the augmentation at virtual and real interface, lowers the cognitive workload, enables a synchronized guidance and releases the working stress. For the purpose of acquiring distinctiveness to the important dimensions, the virtual components can be intentionally rendered with different striking colors. Via exemplars principle that altering the color of target objects does not influence performances unless the task requires encoding of color (Logan et al., 1996), the irrelevant dimensions become less distinguishable and the difficulty of cognition is reduced without harming the task performances. On the other side, as improvements in performances are frequently due to reduces processing of irrelevant stimuli (Haider & Frensch, 1996), while the important dimensions are registered in our AR animation system, the less important counterparts that possibly interrupt the perceptual attention could be omitted to register. Last but not least, as an intuition (empirical support) has indicated that experts in a field have several differentiated categories where the novice has only a single category (Tanaka & Taylor,1991), the possibility of differentiating the important and less important information context could be aided through AR animation scenario based on what is mentioned above (using selective dimension rendering). The outcome is that mental ignorance existed in retrieval behaviors would seldom happen, task performance would rise and assembly errors would be possibly reduced.

### 3.4 Stimulation of motivation

The fun of interactive experience in AR animation might stimulate the task motivation. As Chignell and Waterworth (1997) stated that multimedia could produce a rich sensory experience that not only conveyed information but also increased the motivation and interest to its operator or viewer. We believe that AR animation is a good media to increase motivation by replenishing manifestation of abundant information context, by offering lifelike assembly guidance environment and by enabling interactive operation to assemblers. On one hand, the dimension of virtual components registered could be designed with noticeable manifestations, i.e., color and font, and the graphical arrows could be added in aim of reinforcing the assemblers' focus and improving discrimination with surrounding environments. On the other hand, environmental augmented elements like lighting, object shadow could be rendered via OSGART and as a part of real environments conveniently. Since the improvement of interactivity are contributive to the enhancement of assembly motivation (Neumanm & Majoros, 1998), functioning buttons could be added into the augmented interface, such as the play / back buttons (triggering / repeat animation segment), vocal button (turn on / turn off vocal hints) and so on. This way, the users will be readily to try such a novelty.

### 3.5 Improvement of spatial cognition and reduction of cognitive workload

To decrease information-related activities (cognitive workload), the relationship among a virtual object, a spatial location and spatial cognition is carried out by numerous researchers. Anderson (1980) came to the conclusion that when putting and arranging the imagery-related spatial object (positioning and changing spatial layout of virtual rendered objects) is subject to particular human ability of spatially physical cognition. Repetitive encounters with a spatial space could make people (usually without any conscious effort and probably as an adjunct to attention) build up an enduring, internal representation or "cognitive map" of the space (Thorndyke, 1980). Neumann and Majoros (1998) also disclosed that people like to know where the information is and the information shown spatially underpins the attention of this information patch. As far as attention is concerned, via incorporating virtual objects into real-world scenes, the objects could become part of the world scene and become almost spatially defined entities just as other actual elements do. Many research work and literature have provided an evidence that it is the nature of attention to work spatially and attention can be conceived when working spatially. By combining them with the real context, the cues concerning the property of the virtual objects can also be added to the registered objects that they do not possess independently of the real context. With AR animation platform, the 3D components / parts could become embodiment in real assembly environment. Furthermore, because of the feedback of other "non-situated" augmenting elements like recorded voice, animation, replayed video, short tips and arrows, AR could simultaneously guide the assembly designers through the entire assembly operation, release their tension and even notify an erroneous assembly, and more importantly, ease the assemblers' spatial recognition. This can be achieved by virtual prototyping technology (Pratt, 1995), which supports the virtual construction on computer by using business software. Therefore, the above reviews and discussions have provided us a theoretically solid foundation for the potential conclusion that comparing with the assembly drawing and VR, AR animation could be the plausible and effective choice to enhance spatial cognition and release cognitive workload in assembly task guidance. The augmentation functionality can be realized by AR-Toolkit and OSGART, which enable the static and dynamic registration of graphically virtual objects and their assembly paths on the pre-defined markers in real environment. This way, an immersive augmentation between real and virtual interface is constructed where the assemblers are able to conduct real assembly task while observe a series of immersive virtual assembly processes. Through realizing all the possibilities in 3D space, any one is able to perform complex assembly work independently.

## 4. Summary

This chapter speculates the issues and discrepancies involved in the present practice of assembly task, recommends a novel utilization of AR animation technology in this area, and discusses the potentials of using AR animation in guiding product assembly task. These potentials include its unparalleled information retrieval technique, just-in-time assembly guidance, reduction of error assembly, low cognitive workload, high skill transfer, improved task motivation and so on. On the basis of these great potentials, AR animation could facilitate the product assembly from cognitive perspective by lowering assemblers' cognitive workload.

## 5. References

Abe, N. & Tsuji, S. (1987). Toward Understanding of an Instruction Manual in Mechanical Asemblies, *Proceedings of IEEE Trans on Robotics and Automation,* pp. 1413-1418

Anderson, J.R. (1980). Cognitive psychology and its implications. San Francisco : W.H. Freeman

Bajura, M.; Fuchs, H. & Ohbuchi, R. (1992). Merging Virtual Reality with the Real world: Seeking Ultrasound Imagery Within the Patient. *IEEE Computer Graphics,* 26(2),pp. 203-210

Bliss, J.P.; Tidwell, P.D. & Guest, M.A. (1997). The effectiveness of virtual reality for administering spatial navigation training to fire-fighters, *Presence : Teleoperators and Virtual Environments,* 6, pp. 73-86

Boud, C. (1999). Virtual Reality and Augmented Reality as a Training Tool for Assembly Tasks. *Proceedings of the 1999 International Conference on Information Visualization Page:* 32 Year of Publication: 1999 ISBN:0-7695-0210-5

Brooks & Jr, F.P. (1996). The computer scientist as Toolsmith two. *CACM 39,* 3 (March), pp. 61-68

Calvin, J.; Dickens, A.; Gaines, B.; Metzger, P.; Miller, D. & Owen, D. (1993). The SIMNET virtual world architecture. *IEEE Virtual Reality Annual International Symposium,* pp. 450-455, ISBN 0-7803-1363-1, USA

Chignell, M.H. & Waterworth, J.A. (1997). Multimedia. In G. Salvendy (Ed.), *Handbook of Human Factors and Ergonomics,* 2nd ed,.pp.1808-1861, New York : Jobh Wiley

Croft, W.; Turtle, H.R. & Lewis, D.D. (1991). The use of phrases and structured queries in information retrreval, *Proceedings of the 14th annual international ACM SIGIR conference on research and development in information retrieval,* pp. 32-45, Chicago, Illinois, United States, October 13-16, Chicago

Curtis, D.; Mizell, D.; Gruenbaum, D. & Janin, A. (1998). Several devils in the detail : Making an ar application work in the airplane factory. *In proc. International Workshop on Augmented Reality' 98*

Doil, F.; Schreiber, W.; Alt, T. & Patron, C. (2003). Augmented Reality for manufacturing planning. *Proceedings of the workshop on Virtual environments,* Zurich, Switzerland, ACM, New York, ISBN :1-58113-686-2, pp. 71-76

Durlach, N.I. & Mavor, A.S. (1995). *Virtual Reality: Scientific and Technological Challenges,* National Academy Press

Feiner, S.; MacIntyre, B. & Seligmann, D. (1993). Knowledge-based augmented reality. In ACM(Ed.), Special issue on computer augmented environments back to the real world, pp. 53-62. NY, USA : ACM Publishing

Frederick, P. & Brooks. (1999). What is real about virtual reality. *IEEE Computer Graphics and Applications,* Vol 19., pp. 16-27

Gick, M. & Holyoak, KJ. (1980). Analogical problem solving. *Cognitive psychology,* Vol 12(3)., pp. 306-355

Goldberg, S. (1994). Training dismounted soldiers in a distributed interactive virtual environment, *US Army Research Institution Newsletter,* 14(April), pp. 9-12

Haider, H. & Frensch, P.A. (1996). The role of information reduction in skill acquisition *Cogn. Psychol.* 30 :304-337

He, S.; Abe, N. & Kitahashi, T. (1989). Understanding Illustrative Deagrams in an Assembly Manual, *Proceedings of IEEE International Workshop on Industrial Applications of Machine Intelligence and Vision,* pp. 133-138, Tokyo, Japan

Hoffman, R.R.; Crandall, B. & Shadbolt, N. (1998). Use of the critical decision method to elicit expert knowledge : a case study in the methodology of cognitive task analysis. *Human Factors.,* pp. 254-277

Hue, P.; Delannay, B. & Berland, J.C. (1997). Virtual reality training simulator for long time flight, in R.J.Seidel and P.R.Chantelier (eds), *Virtual Reality, Training's Future ?* pp. 69-76., New York

Johnson-Laird, P.N. (1983). Mental models. Cambridge : Cambridge University Press

Kutulakos, K. & Vallino, J. (1998). Calibration-free augmented reality. *IEEE Transactions on Visualization and Computer Graphics.*

Laperriere, L. & El Maraghy, H.A. (1992). Planning of Products Assembly and Disassembly. Annals of CIRP, Vol., 41., 5

Liverani, G.; Amati, G. & Caligiana. (2004). A CAD-augmented Reality Integrated Environment for Assembly Sequence Check and Interactive Validation. *Concurrent Engineering*, Vol. 12, no.1,pp. 67-77

Locke & Edwin, A. (1968). Toward a theroy of task motivation and incentives. Organizational Behavior & Human Performance, Vol 3(2)., pp. 157-189

Logan, G.D.; Taylor, S.E. & Etherton, J.L. (1996). Attention in the acquisition and expression of automaticity. *J. Exp. Psychol : Learn. Mem. Cogn.*22pp620-638

Mastaglio, T.W. & Callahan, R. (1995). A large-Scale Complex Virtual Environment for Team Training. *Computer,* Vol. 28, no. 7, pp. 49-56, July

Mellor, J.P. (1995). Enhanced reality visualization in a surgical environment (Tech. Rep). MIT Artificial Intelligence Laboratory

Metzger, P.J. (1993). Adding reality to the virtual. *Paper presented at Virtual Reality Annual Symposium,* WA, USA

Milgram, P. & Colquhoun, H. (1999). Ataxonomy of real and virtual world display integration, In Y Ohta and H Tamura (eds), *Mixed Reality : Merging Real and Virtual Worlds,* Ohmsha Ltd and Springer Verlag, pp. 5-30

Miller, D. & Swain, A. (1986). Human error and human reliability. *In G. Salvendy (Ed.), Handbook of Human Factors,* pp. 219-252. NY : John Wiley

Neumann, U. & Majoros, A. (1998). Cognitive, Performance, and Systems Issues for Augmented Reality Applications in Manufacturing and Maintenance, *Proceedings of IEEE Virtual Reality Ann,* pp. 4-11, Los Alamitos, Calif

Ott, J. (1995). Maintenance executives seek greater efficiency. *Aviation Week and Space Technology,* 142 (20), pp. 43-44

Pahl, G. & Beitz, W.K. (1997). Methoden und Anwendungen, 4, Auflage, Berlin: Springer, 1997

Park, M.; Schmidt, C. & Luczak, H. (2007). Design and Evaluation of an Augmented Reality Welding Helmet. *Human Factors and Ergonomics in Manufacturing,* Vol. 17(4), pp. 317-330

Pratt, M.J. (1995). Virtual prototypes and product models in mechanical engineering. In J. Rix, S. Haas, and J. Teixeira, editors, *Virtual Prototyping-Virtual environments and the product design process,* chapter 10, pp. 113-128

Psotka, J. (1993). Immersive training systems : virtual reality and education and training, *Instructional Science,* 23, pp. 405-431

Regenbrecht, H.; Lum, T.; Kohler, P.; Ott, C.; Wagner, M.; Wilke, W. & Mueller, E. (2004). Using Augmented Virtuality for Remote Collaboration, Presence: *Teleoperators & Virtual Environments,* 13(3): pp. 338-354

Ritchie, J.M.; Dewar, R.G. & Simmons, J.E.L. (1999). The generation and practical use of plans for manual assembly using immersive virtual reality. *Proceedings of the Institution of Mechanical Engineers, Part B : Journal of Engineering Manufacture,* Vol.213, ISSN 09544054, pp. 461-474

Rose, F.D.; Attree, E.A.A.; Brooks, B.M.; Parslow, D.M.; Penn, P.R. & Ambihaipahan, N. (2000). Training in virtual environments : transfer to real world tasks and equivalence to real task training. *Ergonomics*, Vol 43., no. 4., pp. 494-511

Salonen, T.; Sääski, J. & Hakkarainen, M. (2007). Demonstration of Assembly Work Using Augmented Reality. *Conference On Image And Video Retrieval archive. Proceedings of the 6th ACM international conference on Image and video*, pp. 120 – 123

Satava, R.M. (1995). Medical applications of virtual reality. *Journal of Medical Systems*, pp. 275-280

Shalin, V.L.; Prabhu, G.V. & Helander, M.G. (1996). A cognitive perspective on manual assembly, *Ergonomics*, Vol. 39., No.1., pp. 108-127

Sherman, W.R. & Craig, A.B. (2003). Understanding Virtual Reality Interface, Application and Design, In : *Presence*, Morgan Kaufman, pp. 441-442, ISBN 1-55860-350-0, US

Tanaka, J. & Taylor, M. (1991). Object categories and expertise : Is the basic level in the eye of the beholder ? *Cogn. Psychol.* 23 :457-482

Tang, A.; Owen, C.; Biocca, F.; & Mou, W. (2003) .Comparative Effectiveness of Augmented Reality in Object Assembly Conference on Human Factors in Computing Systems archive. *Proceedings of the SIGCHI conference on Human factors in computing systems table of contents* Ft. Lauderdale, Florida, USA . SESSION: New techniques for presenting instructions and transcripts table of contents. pp. 73 – 80

Thorndyke, P.W. (1980). Performance models for spatial and locational cognition, *(Reprot No. R-2676-ONR)*. Washington, DC : Rand

Towne, D.M. (1985). Cognitive workload in fault diagnosis, Los Angeles, CA : Behavioral Technology Laboratories, University of Southern California

Uenohara, M. & Kanade, T. (1995). Vision-based object registration for real-time image overlay. *Computer Vision, Virtual Reality and Robotics in Medicine*, pp. 14-22

Urban, E.C. (1995). The information warrior. *IEEE spectrum*, 32(11), pp. 66–70

Veinott, E.S. & Kanki, B.G. (1995). Identifying human factors issues in aircraft maintenance operations. *Poster presented at the 39th Annual Meeting of the Human Factors and Ergonomics Society*, San Diego, CA

Wagner, D. & Pintaric, T. (2005). Towards the Massively Multi-user Augmented Reality on Handheld Devices. *LNCS*, Springer Berlin, ISBN. 978-3-540-26008-0, pp. 208-219

Wang, X. & Dunston, P.S. (2006). Compatibility issues in Augmented Reality systems for AEC : An experimental prototype study. *Automation in Construction.*, pp. 314-326

Webster, A.; Feiner, S.; MacIntyre, B. & Massie, W. (1996). Augmented Reality in Architectural Constructions, Inspection and Renovation. *Proc. ASCE Third Congress on Computing in Civil Engineering, Anaheim*, CA, 17-19, pp. 913-919

Yamada, A. & Takataa, S. (2007). Reliability Improvement of Industrial Robots by Optimizing Operation Plans Based on Deterioration Evaluation. *Waseda University Available online*

Zachmann, G. (1996). A language for describing behavior and interaction with virtual worlds. *In proceedings of ACM conference.* VRST 96, Hongkong

Zauner, J.; Haller, M.; Brandl, A. & Hartman, W. (2003). Authoring of a Mixed Reality Assembly Instructor for Hierarchical Structures. *Mixed and Augmented Reality, 2003. Proceedings.The Second IEEE and ACM International Symposium on Publication* Date: 7-10, pp. 237- 246

# 7

# Tangible Interfaces for Augmented Engineering Data Management

Michele Fiorentino, Giuseppe Monno and Antonio E. Uva
*DIMeG, Politecnico di Bari*
*Italia*

## 1. Introduction

To maintain a competitive edge in global market, manufacturing enterprises must leverage their digital information assets, which include a tremendous amount of engineering data: CAD models, FEM analysis, tolerances, annotations, etc.. An emerging technology called *Digital Master* embeds all the engineering knowledge about a product into its CAD model. Tools and process to efficiently manage, distribute, and modify this information are essential. The digital master, which virtually eliminates the stacks of technical drawings, is not yet completely adopted in industrial practice, mainly because engineering software do not support at best all phases of the virtual product development process. At present time, Engineering Data Management (EDM) tools use standard desktop-based GUI, which demonstrated the following limits: scarce usability for not CAD professionals, low cooperation level, limited management for different expertises and low integration between real and virtual models.

As far as regards usability, current Graphical User Interfaces (GUI) in EDM are mainly based on part features tree view and spreadsheets operations. This GUI may not be user friendly to navigate and perceive complex CAD models or to be used in manufacturing environments. Moreover desktop GUI does not facilitate team working, because of the physical barrier of the computer screens (called "immediate individual environment"). Effective EDM tools should provide a better digital cooperative workspace similar to a meeting table and should improve communication among experts in different fields.

Another issue to face in current EDM systems is the information overload. A new generation of software tools is needed to simplify the visualization and database access according to users' roles and expertises.

An additional drawback of current EDM software is the lack of a unique workspace where virtual models, technical drawings and physical products can coexist for discussion. This scenario is common in industry because a virtual shape (i.e. CAD model) often needs to be compared with physical mock-ups.

According to the authors' vision, the ideal collaborative drawing-less workspace for EDM could benefit from Augmented Reality (AR) technology (Fig. 1).

Born in military and aerospace applications to augment information-dense environments with digital data, AR can provide an ideal solution for *Digital Master* exploration. In fact, Dunston demonstrated with engineering user tests, that the perception of 3D design can be improved using AR (Dunston et al., 2002).

Fig. 1. Tangible interface for a CAD model with Technical annotations.

Moreover AR system can provide different levels of model perception according to the type of display and the viewpoint control. Lee categorized them in three main configurations (Lee et al., 2005). In *mobile* configurations the viewpoint is coincident to the user's eyes. This can be achieved by see-through displays or by using projectors (spatial augmented reality). The users are free to change their viewpoint while the digital content is overlaid onto the real scene. In *fixed* configurations, the real scene is acquired by a fixed camera positioned accurately to cover the entire workspace. The augmented scene is visualized on a display, usually a large screen, decoupled from the real world. The user is not compelled to wear or hold any device. Finally the *tele-mobile* configuration is similar to the *fixed* one, but with the user moving the camera.

Several different industrial showcases of AR are reported in the ARVIKA project (www.arvika.de). They demonstrated that one of the most important aspect of AR is the possibility to use tangible interfaces. A Tangible User Interface (TUI), is a user interface in which a person interacts with digital information through the physical environment. TUIs have emerged as an alternative paradigm to the more conventional Graphical User Interfaces (GUI) letting users manipulate objects in virtual space using real, thus "tangible", objects (Ullmer et al., 2000). The early developments of TUIs date back to the early 1980s, when Frazer explored different approaches to parallel physical and digital interactions with his 3D data input devices (Frazer, J., 1995).

The ARIEL system (Mackay et al., 2000) was one of the first examples in literature of TUI applied to technical augmented reality environments. ARIEL is based on a graphics tablet for capturing user gestures and on a projector to overlay 2D multimedia annotations onto real technical drawings. Their experiments proved the benefits of a tangible medium (i.e. the paper drawings) when augmented with digital content.

Terry presented JUMP, a tangible interface for augmented paper-based architectural documents (Terry ad al., 2007). He presented a novel set of tangible tools for the navigation and interaction using 2D augmented technical drawings. In JUMP, filter tokens can be placed on the paper to modify the visualization of electrical, mechanical, and structural information. They developed also a physical rectangular selection tool by framing a portion of the drawing with physical brackets.

Some researchers have proved by user tests that gesturing, navigation, annotation and viewing are the four primary interactions with design artefacts in technical meeting (Tory et al., 2008). According to their studies, the form of the design information (2D vs. 3D, digital vs. physical) has minimal impact on gesture interactions, although navigation varies significantly with different representations. They spotted bottlenecks in the collaborative design process when meeting participants attempted to navigate digital information, interact with wall displays, and access information individually and as a group.
However, most researches in literature are proof-of-concept prototypes which hardly progress beyond the lab-phase. For this reason, the attention of commercial EDM software producers is more and more focused on user-friendly interfaces in order to deal with the growing database complexity. Dassault Systemes, for example, in its latest EDM commercial products, lets users intuitively browse, zoom, select and inspect the product definition dynamically using virtual 3DLive turntables. 3DLive turntable is an innovative interface, specifically developed for 3D model understanding and tangible rotation using a touch-screen.
But TUI cannot replace completely the common GUI. Precise selection, text and numerical input, very common in EDM system are more efficient using a common GUI based (keyboard and mouse) interaction.
By means tangible interfaces and AR we developed a novel and efficient interaction paradigm with the digital master for better perceive, understand and add contents to EDM knowledge.

## 2. Tangible interfaces for engineering

Tangible interfaces are a novel approach to access EDM contents efficiently and user friendly. In our idea, the user can introduce a tangible element with a unique visual ID in the workspace (office desk, meeting table, production workbench, etc.). This visual ID can be a binary coded image, the marker, working as spatial reference for the AR visualization overlay. These markers can be printed or attached as stickers on paper, i.e., technical drawings. We decided to use these tangible interfaces, for three main reasons: (i) because drawings are currently used in any EDM stage, (ii) because technical users are used to handle, store and sort sheets of paper (iii) because of simplicity and the low costs of implementation. We implemented such interfaces in our AR engineering framework (Fiorentino et at, 2009a).

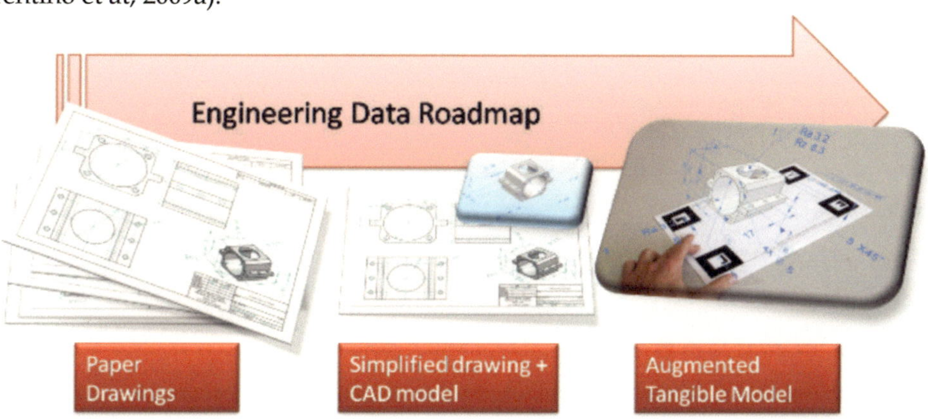


Fig. 2. From paper drawings to augmented tangible data

EDM model and data are displayed in real time as 3D info spatially referenced to the tangible interface. Data navigation (pan and zoom) is easily achieved by physically handling the tangible marked drawings (Fig. 3).

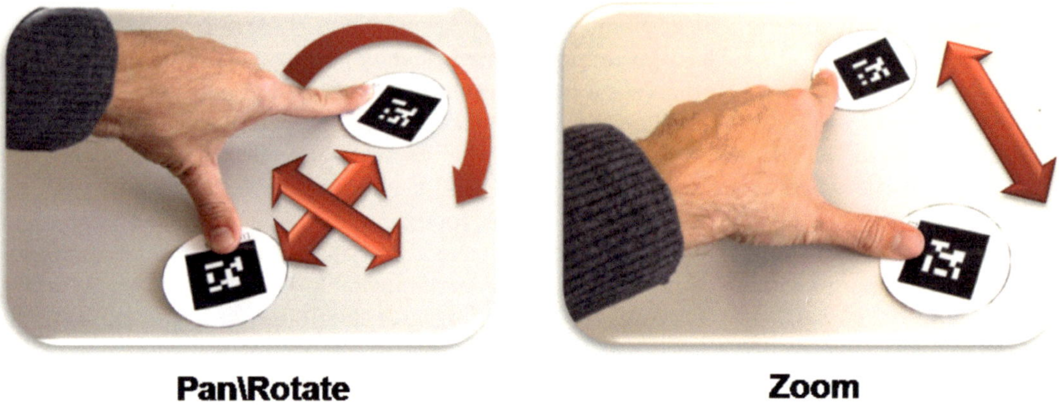


Fig. 3. Tangible interface model navigation using two paper markers

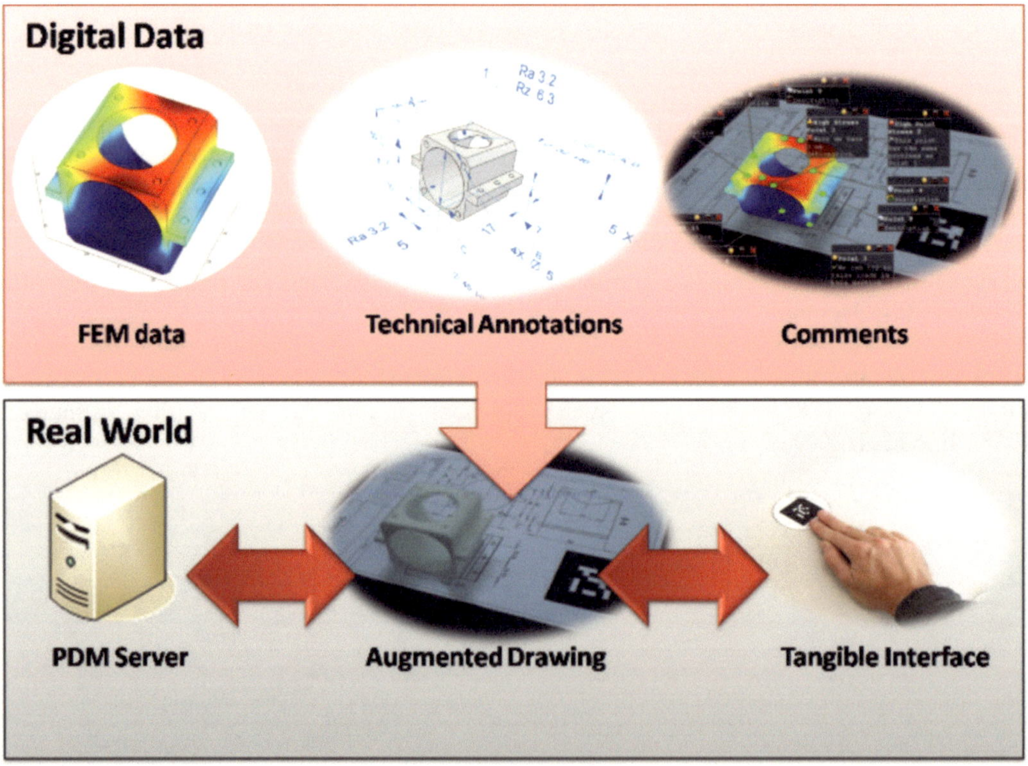


Fig. 4. Tangible Interfaces in Engineering Data management.

Accessing directly to the digital master has three main advantages compared to traditional paper drawing: always up-to-date information, access to multimedia content and web 2.0 technology, and custom\role oriented interface.

Collaboration can be fostered by sharing the digital workspace using personal TUI or by sharing a common TUI. In the first case all the users of the team are able to see and annotate the digital master with their data in their personal AR environments. In the second case, exchanging ideas in a common physical workspace is promoted using face to face dialogue and supported by augmented visualization and annotations.
Another TUI can be also a real mock-up, augmented by sticking a set of identification markers. For example, in design review a real product can be augmented with simulation data (Fig. 4).
The only TUI does not support at best all EDM activities. Therefore we adopted an hybrid user interface with a combination of GUI/TUI to benefit from the advantages of each approach. The user may exploit TUI for intuitive model navigation and GUI for precise control (i.e. through touchscreen, digital pen, mouse, keyboard).

## 3. Engineering scenarios

Product development brings together a large number of activities and a single workspace does not satisfy all the user requirements. In this section we present a non-exhaustive list of possible scenarios for tangible interface applications in EDM. For each scenario we outline the following aspects: hardware configuration, viewpoint type, TUI\GUI interaction level, application field, physical collaboration support and remote co-working capabilities.

### 3.1 Augmented user

The user wears see-through AR glasses connected to a wearable PC. See-through displays allow the user to be aware of the real industrial environment (Fig. 5a). This configuration allows maximum mobility for the user letting him\her work in a large workspace with free hands. EDM database is accessed via wireless network. The interaction is achieved mostly by TUI with none or limited GUI. Suggested applications for this setup are: inspection, training, etc. Disadvantages may include the display resolution, the limited field of view and the optical tracking robustness in hostile manufacturing environments (e.g. dust, electrical noises, bad lighting, etc.).
In another setup the user holds a handheld (flashlight-like) camera and a wearable PC connected to the network. The user is free to move in the industrial environment and to

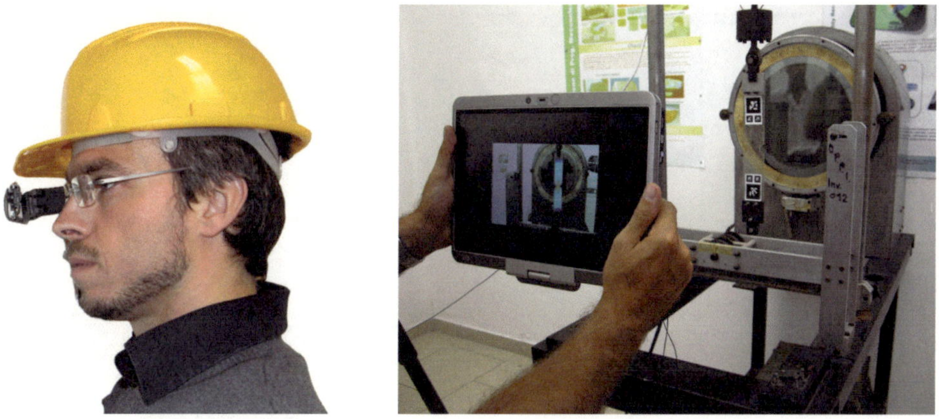

Fig. 5. HMD engineering setup(a) and personal mobile window (b)

teleconference with other users remotely logged. The difference compared to previous setup is the viewpoint mobility. The user can move the camera in the industrial environment, reaching potentially every location under wireless coverage. Local tracking is provided by markers (in future may be RFID active markers) and broadcasted to the system. This scenario is particularly important in maintenance, where remote experts can guide and assist the user. The user loads his\her customized visualization of the model and broadcasts it remotely. The main advantage of this configuration is the maximum mobility for point of view. This may also lead to an unsteady point of view due to the fact that the user must hold the camera. TUI and GUI interaction is also rather limited.

### 3.2 Mobile window

The user holds a tablet PC with a camera on the back side (Fig. 5b). Tablet displays allow the user to be fully aware of the real industrial environment. This configuration allows a good mobility for the user letting him/her work in a large workspace but it requires that at least one hand holds the tablet. EDM database is accessed via wireless network. The interaction is achieved mostly by GUI with the tablet pen. Suggested applications for this setup are: design review, inspection, etc. Disadvantages may include the weight of the tablet and the single-handed interaction limitation.

### 3.3 Augmented desktop

The user works on a desktop workstation with a camera pointing on a free area on the desk which will be the augmented workspace (Fig. 6a). The AR workspace is limited to the user's desktop and the model interaction is achieved by moving the TUI (augmented technical drawings) and by the traditional desktop GUI with a mouse and a keyboard. In normal use, the TUI is just a support to the ordinary GUI. For this reason, this scenario is suggested for all EDM tasks which involve an heavy use of keyboard entry of numerical or text data: e.g. detailed design, engineering, numerical analysis, etc. The main advantage of this setup is the similarity with the traditional working environment, allowing an easy access even for a non technical user. Users, in fact, find much easier and intuitive the navigation of 3D models using a tangible metaphor. A limiting factor is that it must be implemented in an office-like environment.

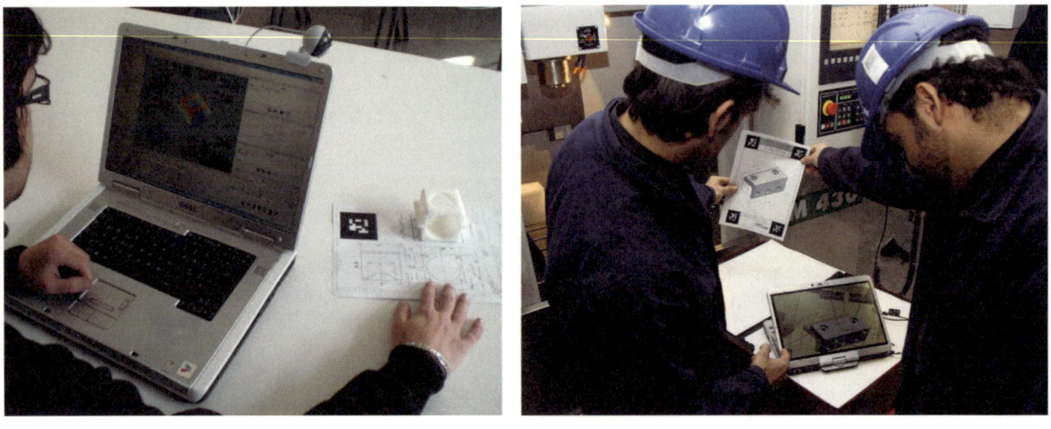

Fig. 6. Augmented desktop(a) and augmented workshop(b)

### 3.4 Augmented workshop

This scenario is similar to the augmented desktop as regards the hardware setup, but it is designed for a production stage environment (Fig. 6b) instead of a clean office desk. The user is on a workbench on the production line where no keyboard or mouse is present. The user can interact by touch screen on industrial monitor and by tangible augmented drawings. An industrial buttonbox can also be used. The main advantages are: both hands free for the user, possibility to display high resolution rendering of the 3D model and EDM data, comfortable working environment, similar to a non augmented one. Ideal applications may be quality check or guided assembly.

### 3.5 Augmented collaborative table

This scenario supports collaborative workspace at best. It consists of a meeting table with the function of shared augmented area and of a large screen. The screen can be vertical or horizontal and eventually have stereographic or holographic display. The configuration is depicted in Fig. 7a. All users can access to the augmented shared area with their tokens and they can annotate the model using their own PC laptop for precise GUI input. Remotely located users can join the group and participate with virtual meeting tools. The system will take care of the synchronization of the digital master data including annotations, chat and history. The main applications of this scenario are marketing and design review: the shared workspace can contain virtual CAD models, real pre-production mock ups, on-line technical content and simulation results for collaborative discussion. The main advantages of this scenario are the high collaboration support, the coexistence of real and virtual products and the social contact of real meetings.

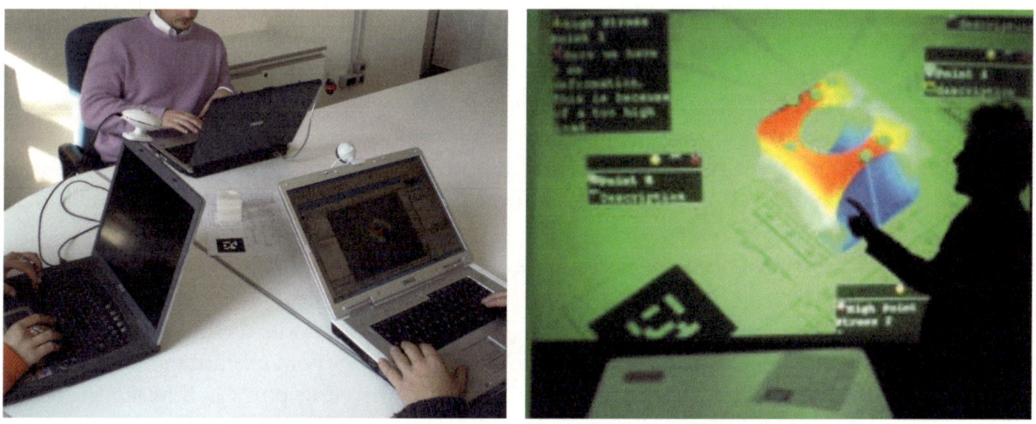

Fig. 7. Augmented collaborative table(a) and augmented presentation (b)

### 3.6 Augmented presentation

This scenario considers a speaker who wants to present a solution to a large audience. A large screen is the main visualization device. The data management is achieved mainly by TUI in form of digital drawing or mock-up placed on the speaker's stand (Fig. 7b). The audience can access to the same digital data with personal visualization devices and can add annotations which are updated in real time for all the members of the discussion.

The characteristics of each scenario are summarized in Table 1.

| Scenario | Viewpoint | TUI Level | GUI Level | Collaboration Level | Remote co-working |
|---|---|---|---|---|---|
| Augmented User | mobile | high | low | low | medium |
| Mobile Window | mobile | low | high | medium | medium |
| Augmented Desktop | fixed | medium | high | low | high |
| Augmented Workshop | fixed | medium | low | low | low |
| Augmented Collab. Table | fixed | high | medium | high | medium |
| Augmented Presentation | fixed | high | low | medium | medium |

Table 1. Tangible interface scenarios.

## 4. Engineering digital contents

The standards (ASME Y14.41-2003 and ISO 16792:2006) define three levels of product data documentation:

- *Drawings only*: paper drawings are supported to define a product, with the addition of Geometric Dimensioning and Tolerancing (GD&T) symbols, axonometric views as dimensionable views, and supplemental geometry;
- *Models and Drawing* (or reduced content drawings): an engineering drawing is available, but does not contain all the necessary information (i.e. free forms sections) which must be retrieved from the CAD model;
- *Models Only*: the practices, requirements, and interpretation of the CAD data when there is no engineering drawing.

By defining a models only documentation (Fig. 2), these standards formalize practices already in use in aerospace and automotive industry, with the main advantage of paving the way to the full digital model integration. One important missing point is that standards do not regulate interactive interfaces. For example, 3D annotations must be placed above fixed datum planes defined once by the user.

Another significant standard for technical publications is the S1000D (www.s1000d.org). Originally developed by the aerospace and defence industries for military aircraft maintenance and operations, the S1000D provides the guidance and rules for the presentation and use of technical information. It defines two main types of documentation: page-oriented presentation on paper or screen and interactive electronic technical publications presentation on screen. This second section provides guidance for software developers of interactive digital technical documentation. It supports desktop based GUIs

(mouse, keyboard, touch screen, etc.) and defines in detail screen layout, title\menus bar, dialog boxes, etc. S1000D standard is rather limited in the definition of 3D CAD model navigation and web based tools. In fact it rules 3D visualization in terms of 2D static or animated graphical figures (prospective or orthographic), fly-through (3D model navigation) and helper applications (e.g. Adobe Acrobat) or plug-ins (e.g. Arbortext IsoView). User annotations are supported in the form of: action complete indicator, personal data annotation, and redlining. Callouts are supported to show where a component is located. Due to their novel implementations and the scarce knowledge about their deployment, actual standardization do not support all means of "digital master" navigation, considering recent interfaces such augmented reality or tangible interface.
In next sections we present a technical ontology related to EDM data which can be displayed on the model.

### 4.1 Ontology of engineering data associated to the model

The digital master is a CAD model which contains two different kinds of information: *nominal geometry* and *product data*. The first type contains the mathematical representation of the ideal (i.e. no production faults) shape. Product data are additional technical information such as: material, simulation constraints and boundary conditions, surface finish, tolerances, quality control, simulation parameters, etc. These data are strictly connected to the CAD model features like faces, holes, rounds, chamfers, etc. Technical annotations can be divided in three main functional types: dimensions, geometric tolerances and general annotations.

### 4.2 Dimensions

Spatial dimensions of the model are fundamental elements in design, production and inspection phases. Examples of dimensions are: distance between, angle between, coordinate dimension, angular coordinate, symmetry. Dimensions can be derived from CAD exact geometry or by a formula or by a variable defined in the EDM database.
Dimensions items use, as reference, model features such as: edges, key points, sketches, construction surfaces, axes and coordinate systems. If dimensions are functional, they contain tolerances values, which provide information about the acceptable variation in the size or location of a feature on a part, according to standards (ISO 286-2). While paper drawings represent dimensions by distributing and organizing them among different views (one instance for each dimension is allowed), a unique 3D CAD model representation requires an optimal visualization in order to avoid confusion and overlapping. Dimensioning needs differ also during product lifecycle according to the application. For example in design dimensions must be related to structural stress, while in inspection only the checked features need to be displayed.

### 4.3 Geometric tolerance

Geometric tolerance is a technical annotation used to establish the relationships among features or datum of parts according to the standards (ASME Y14.5-1994 and ISO 1101:2004). In 2D drawing, standards require that geometric tolerance must be indicated using two or more rectangular boxes containing the following information: geometric characteristic symbol, datum reference, tolerance zone symbol, tolerance value, material condition symbol.

### 4.5 Annotations and linking

An large part of the manufacturing process involves different users (experts from design to inspection) to provide digital master with a variety of EDM information in form of text, notes, graphics, sketches, reference, audio\video content, etc.
EDM data annotations can be arrangement on the base of the application: (i) manufacturing (surface finish, welding notations), (ii) inspection (key locations points), (iii) assembly instructions (iv), product information (materials, suppliers, part numbers), etc.
Annotations can be associative or non-associative. An associative annotation is semantically attached to model faces, surfaces, curves, edges, and sketch elements, and even to existing dimensions and annotations. Annotations with leaders have the following components: leader line, break line, terminator, and annotation. An annotation can have more than one leader. The terminator end must move with the element it is connected. Most used associative annotations are Leader, Balloon, Callout, Surface Texture Symbol, Weld Symbol, Edge Condition, Feature Control Frame, Datum Frame, Datum Target. Differently, non-associative annotations are usually located in free space.

| Graphic Element | Dimension | Geometric Tolerance | Annotation |
|---|---|---|---|
| Quote | X | X | |
| Leader | | X | X |
| Symbol | | X | X |
| Datum | | X | |
| Link | | X | X |
| Multimedia\Web | | | X |

Table 2. Graphical annotations

Annotations are often related to linking functionality. An example is the connection of the model geometry to data as cross-references tables, simulations data, images, 2D view and even external links to web pages or to pdf based digital documentation.

### 4.6 Data filtering

A three-dimensional digital master requires an optimal visualization in order to avoid confusion and overlapping. "Information overload" is a term coined by Alvin Toffler which refers to an excess amount of information being provided, making the perception of information very difficult for the individual because sometimes the user can not see the validity behind the information. A correct dynamic data filtering is essential for each phase of product lifecycle which requires different dimensioning and annotations. For example, the design phase needs dimensions for assembly, while the inspection phase needs only the dimensions under control.

## 5. Issues and solutions

In our implementation of tangible interface in AR based engineering frameworks (Uva et al., 2009; Fiorentino et at, 2009a) we addressed several issues proposing our solutions as follow.

### 5.1 Real time tangible engineering simulation

We decided to implement and evaluate the novel idea of "touch and see" real time FEM analysis (Fiorentino et at, 2009b). The main goal was to allow the user to modify the simulation parameters via a tangible interface and immediately visualize the results overlaid on the real object. Augmented reality visualization techniques display the results as a video overlay "attached" to the real model which can be handled naturally by the user to explore the data.
In our implementation a specific module extracts the data from an engineering simulation software (COMSOL Multiphysics ®) and uploads them to the visualization system.

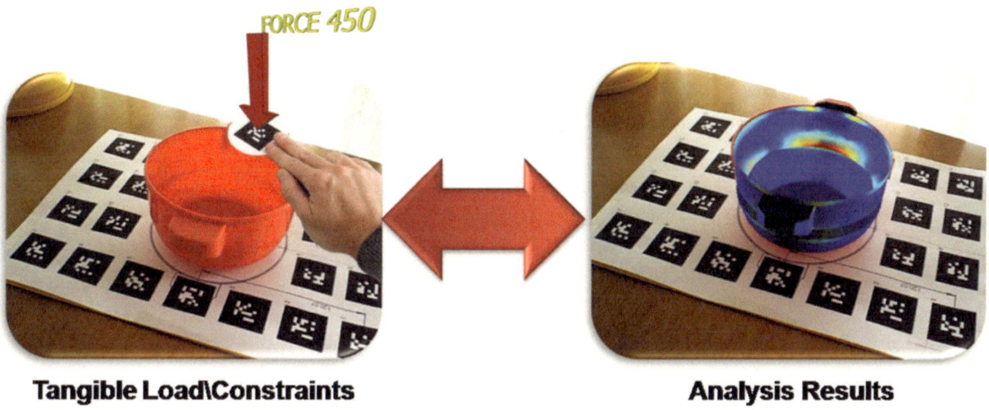


Fig. 8. Engineering simulation workflow

The user can modify the simulation parameters via a tangible interface and instantly visualize the results overlaid on the real object. The benchmarks demonstrated that the application is 'real time' (simulation refresh rate > 6Hz; visualization refresh rate > 30Hz) and the user is not aware of the simulation latency.

### 5.2 Tracking integration

We decided to manage the tracking system as a plug-in which handles 3D position, orientation and ID of tangible interfaces. We developed a tracking plug-in for the ARToolkitPlus marked based tracking system (Wagner & Schmalstieg, 2007). Other tracking systems (e.g. markerless) may be supported in our framework by simply adding new plug-ins. We implemented a macro in the EDM system which generates and manages the markers ID for each cad part. For example during the 2D draft creation, markers are automatically embedded in the Title Block. When a known marker enters the AR working area, the system automatically retrieves the EDM data, visualizing the 3D geometry and the associated technical annotations. The markers are used to track the location (pose estimation) of the tangible interface. We found that better results can be achieved with multi-marker tracking. The pose estimated from a single marker is not always stable enough, moreover, a single marker can exit the view area. Using multi-marker tracking, the pose estimation stability and precision are dramatically improved by merging information extracted from several pre-calibrated markers. We developed and tested a drawing template with four markers.

### 5.3 Contents management

An important issue is related to the visualization of technical content associated to the model. These contents can be added as floating 2D labels overlaid on the scene. In our implementation, the rendering of 2D data is based on a standard web browser technology which is stable, widely-documented and popular. We embed the Mozilla FireFox engine into our labels using a library called "NaviLibrary".

An important benefit of this solution is the integration of web 2.0 based applications into our AR workspace. Chat, forum, web browsing, document viewers, online technical manuals can be accessed with TUI.

Our AR workspace (Uva et al, 2009) uses a server/client architecture to exploit collaboration. Each user may have a different AR configuration while the digital master is hosted on a server and shared/updated among the clients (even geographically distributed). The data on the server side are received by a PHP front-end, that serializes it to a back-end MySQL database. At any data change, the server broadcasts the modified data to the logged clients.

To improve the broadcast of modifications in EDM we presented a novel approach we called *product feed* (Fiorentino et at, 2009a). This idea extends to EDM the concept of web feed, widely adopted for notification of web contents. A web feed is a document which contains data (full or summarized text, plus metadata such as publishing dates and authorship) with web links to update versions. This technology is undervalued in the EDM community and in enterprises. Today's web feed is used for non technical content (blog, news, podcasting, etc.), but feeds could be enhanced by CAD or EDM data. In our implementation when a user subscribes to (with the appropriate permissions) a set of product feed, it is visualized using an aggregator. A feed aggregator, also known as a feed reader, is a client module which aggregates syndicated EDM contents in a single location for easy viewing. For any change, e.g. a price change for a supplied part, the EDM database syndicates the updates to the authorized and interested users.

### 5.4 Augmented label placement

The placement of 2D labels on 3D objects is a complex task because of occlusion and readability problems. Several studies (Azuma et al., 2003; Götzelmann et al., 2007) have been presented in literature but only a few for technical annotations. This issue is even more critical in AR because the user's point of view and the background can vary continuously. A three-dimensional model and, specifically, an industrial prototype can assume rather complex structures and can present a considerable amount of information. Showing all labels together would result in overlapping and overloading the scene with information and in losing desirable clearness and effectiveness.

We implemented a dynamic labelling management with view-driven filtering and placement (Fig. 9) in a specific plug-in. We considered the label placement as a cost minimization problem. The cost function is a linear combination of several aspects of layout quality.

This algorithm handles the continuous variability of both the virtual scene and background that occurs in AR applications when using tangible interfaces. In order to avoid information overload for complex models, our algorithm does not visualize the labels whose anchor point is occluded in the current view. This adaptive filtering helps the user to perceive clearly and univocally the label association to model features.

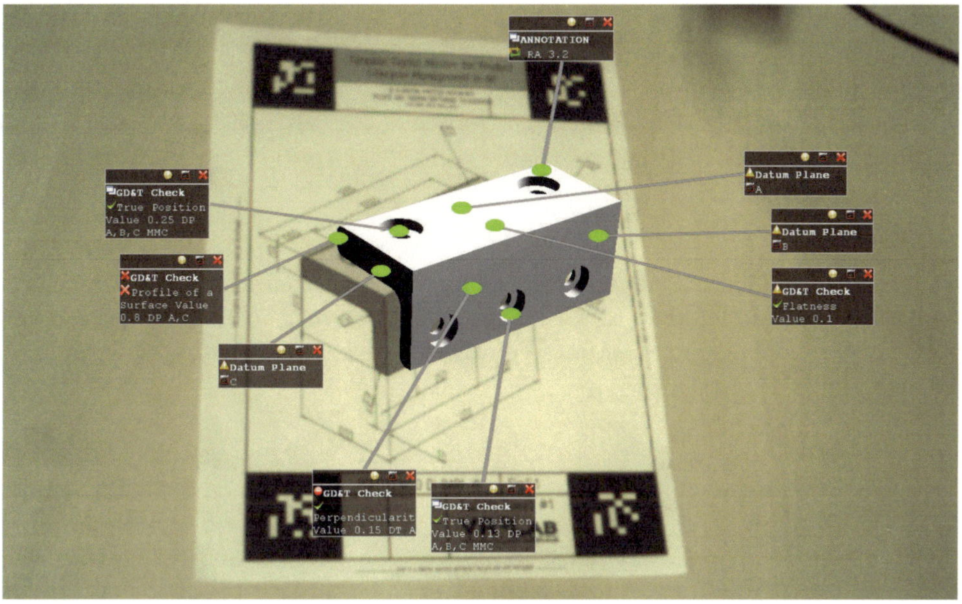


Fig. 9. Example of labels placement

### 5.5 Augmented badge

In a EDM system, for security and competence reasons, data access must be granted according to the user profile. Users should be allowed to view/assign/modify data with a different level of access according to:

- Expertise profile (engineer, design, manager, etc.)
- Group: R&D, Engineering, Operations, Manufacturing, Quality
- Skill Level (advanced, medium, essential)
- Security & digital signatures (internal, staff, guest, etc.)

We implemented a plug-in for user management and logging via the *augmented badge.* The permission to view or to modify data is granted by showing the badge in the AR environment. The augmented badge loads also user's preferences (layers, GUI settings, personal notepad, etc.) and personal information and 3d avatar. This is extremely useful in a distributed collaborative environment because remote users can visualize information about the person logged. Security can be enforced by additional systems (RFID, smart card, etc.)

All the personal annotations are included in EDM database and synchronized in real time among all the participants of the workgroup using the product feed.

### 5.6 Tangible layers

To manage the visualization of the massive amount of data in EDM, we implemented a layering system with tangible interface. Our layers are EDM feed aggregators. We manage the activation/deactivation of layers in three tangible modes: (i) *layer chip tokens, (ii) layer tabs, (iii) augmented badge.*

*Layer chip tokens* look like gambling chips with a marker associated to a specific layer. By dropping a chip in the AR working area, the associated layer is visualized in AR (Fig. 10). The layer can be switched off by simply flipping the chip (hiding the marker) on the table.

*Layer Tabs*, with small markers, can be embedded in technical drawings. By simply folding or unfolding tabs the user can hide/show the associated layers.
In the third modality, each user, instead of physical managing multiple tokens, can select a set of preferred layers. His/her company badge has a marker (*augmented badge*) and works as a token to activate the user's layer preferences.

## 6. Conclusion

In last decade, digital data in engineering problems has grown in complexity and computer assisted tools demonstrated their limits: low usability for non CAD experts, low cooperation support, limited understanding of 3D geometries and low integration between real and virtual models.

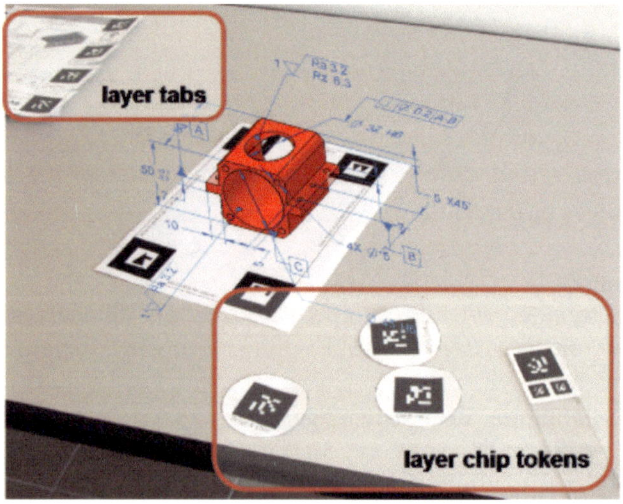


Fig. 10. Activation/deactivation of layers using tangible interaction.

We presented a novel approach in Engineering Data Management based on two key technologies: Augmented Reality and Tangible Interfaces. The first allows to add information directly on the physical model or on a physical contexts as technical drawings. The second provides a direct EDM data navigation and visualization using intuitive and collaborative metaphors such as rotating or moving a real object on a meeting table. We explored new tangible approaches using marker-based recognition. The users can access, navigate and annotate the 3D CAD model, can define structural stress\constraint, can manage layers and explore the simulation results in a highly collaborative workspace without the limit of mouse or keyboard. Tangible interfaces cannot replace completely the common GUI. Precise selection, text and numerical input, very common in EDM system are more efficient using a common GUI based (keyboard and mouse) interaction. To assist different industrial activities a flexible framework which can combine graphical (i.e. forms) and tangible interfaces is required. We developed a novel and efficient interaction paradigm with digital master for better perceive, understand and add contents to EDM knowledge.
We implemented and tested different industrial scenarios according to specific engineering activities: collaborative technical discussion, interactive FEM analysis and remote

maintenance. The marker-based tracking allows a simple and low-cost integration in the industrial lifecycle process. The novel interface required to address new challenging issues. We presented our solutions to: real time simulation, tracking integration, content management, labels placement and EDM data filtering and access. We tested the system in a manufacturing enterprise with a highly configurable products. We supported product variability in three main phases: early design, marketing and assembly. The main benefits experienced have been the significant reduction of paper drawings and the increased speed of the revision phases. Limiting factors with current hardware systems are the marker-based tracking which may be not robust enough for manufacturing environment and displays issues (i.e. limited resolution and field of view). Emerging technologies like marker-less tracking, RFID, pico-projectors, may solve these issues in the next future.

## 7. References

Azuma, R.; Furmanski, C. (2003). Evaluating label placement for augmented reality view management, *Proceedings of the 2nd IEEE and ACM international symposium on mixed and augmented reality*, pp. 66-75, Washington, IEEE Computer Society

Dunston, P.; Wang, X., Billinghusrt, M. & Hampson B. (2002). Mixed Reality Benefits For Design Perception. *Proceedings of 19th international symposium on automation and robotics construction*, pp. 191-196

Fiorentino, M.; Monno, G. & Uva, A. E. (2009a). Tangible Digital Master for Product Lifecycle Management in Augmented Reality. *International Journal on Interactive Design and Manufacturing*, Vol. 3, p. 121-129, ISSN:1955-2513

Fiorentino, M.; Monno, G. & Uva, A. E. (2009b). Interactive "touch and see" FEM Simulation using Augmented Reality. *International Journal of Engineering Education*, ISSN: 0949-149X

Frazer, J. (1995). *An Evolutionary Architecture*, Architectural Association Publications, Themes VII

Götzelmann, T.; Hartmann, K. & Strothotte, T. (2007). Annotation of animated 3D objects, *Proceedings of 18th Conference on Simulation and Visualization*, pp. 209-222

Lee, G. A.; Kim, G. J., & Billinghurst, M. (2005). Immersive authoring: What You eXperience Is What You Get (WYXIWYG), *Commun. ACM*, 48, 7, pp. 76-81

Mackay, W. E.; Pagani, D. S., Faber, L., Inwood, B., Launiainen, P., Brenta, L. & Pouzol, V. (2000). Ariel: augmenting paper engineering drawings, *Proceedings of Conference Companion on Human Factors in Computing Systems. CHI '95*, New York

Terry, M.; Cheung, J., Lee, J., Park, T., & Williams, N. (2007). Jump: a system for interactive, tangible queries of paper, *Proceedings of Graphics Interface 2007 GI '07*, vol. 234, ACM, New York, pp. 127-134

Tory, M.; Staub-French, S., Po, B. A., & Wu, F. (2008). Physical and Digital Artifact-Mediated Coordination in Building Design, *Proceedings of ACM conference on Computer Supported Cooperative Work*, Vol. 17, No. 4, pp. 311-351

Wagner, D. & Schmalstieg, D. (2007). ARToolKitPlus for Pose Tracking on Mobile Devices, *Proceedings of 12th Computer Vision Winter Workshop*, pp 139–146

Ullmer, B. & Ishii, H. (2000). Emerging Frameworks for Tangible User Interfaces. *IBM Systems Journal*, Vol. 393, No. 3, pp. 915-931, ISSN:0018-8670

Uva, A. E.; Cristiano, S., Fiorentino, M., & Monno, G. (2009). Distributed design review using tangible augmented technical drawings, *Journal of Computer Aided Design*, ISSN:0010-4485, DOI: 10.1016/j.cad.2008.10.015

# 8

# Human Factor Guideline for Applying AR-based Manuals in Industry

Miwa Nakanishi
*Chiba University*
*Japan*

## 1. Introduction

Augmented reality (AR)-based manuals, which replace the paper-based manuals used in the past, is a promising application of AR in industrial settings such as manufacturing, maintenance and so on. In our previous research, we conducted experiments to compare the case where workers referred to a traditional paper-based manual with that where they referred to an AR-based manual in the tasks of assembling, wiring and inspection (Nakanishi & Okada, 2006; Nakanishi et al., 2007). We confirmed that, in the latter case, they completed each type of task in around 15% less time and made fewer errors than in the former case. Further, we found that psychological stress in referring to the manual was mitigated in the latter case. This is possibly because the AR-based manual enabled workers to view task-related information superimposed on real objects and made it easy to cognitively link the objects and information.

For these reasons, AR-based manuals are expected to serve as effective tools for increasing efficiency, preventing human errors and promoting comfort in industrial settings. However, before practical use of such manuals, it is necessary to clarify human factor requirements concerning workers, the environment and the information presented.

Thus, we have been examining basic human factor requirements through a series of experiments, particularly under the assumption that workers see an AR-based manual using monocular see-through head-mounted displays (HMDs). In this chapter, we review how the performance of workers using AR-based manuals is changed by differences in the workers themselves, the work environment and the information presented by HMDs, based on behavioural, physiological and psychological data. Furthermore, we summarise a human factor guideline for applying AR-based manuals. The guideline can give suggestions for smooth and effective introduction of AR technology to industries.

## 2. Data on improvement of workers' performance using AR-based manuals

First, we introduce an experimental result that shows that workers' performance is improved by using an AR-based manual instead of a traditional paper-based manual.

### 2.1 Method

The experimental task was to insert plugs into a panel according to information in the manual. Five colours of cables (red, green, blue, white and yellow) with plugs on both ends were prepared (Fig. 1). The panel had 37 holes on the left side and 43 on the right (Fig. 2). Subjects inserted one end of each cable into a left-side hole and the other into a right-side hole following the manual shown in Fig. 3. In this manual, two numbers and a character appear inside each circle corresponding to each hole on the left side. The upper-left-hand number indicate the order in which one end should be inserted, the upper-right-hand character indicate the plug colour, and the lower number indicate the hole on the right side into which the other end should be inserted. Subjects inserted both ends of 37 plugs into the panel in a task. Then they performed the task lying on their back (Fig. 5), as seen in some actual situations such as maintenance or inspection.

In this experiment, basic and comparative conditions were prepared. In the basic condition, subjects performed the task using the paper-based manual. In the comparative condition, they wore HMDs (NOMAD, made by Microvision, Inc.) and used an AR-based manual, so that they could see the manual superimposed on the panel, as shown in Fig. 4. Subjects (six students with good vision) performed the task using different patterns in the manual in each condition.

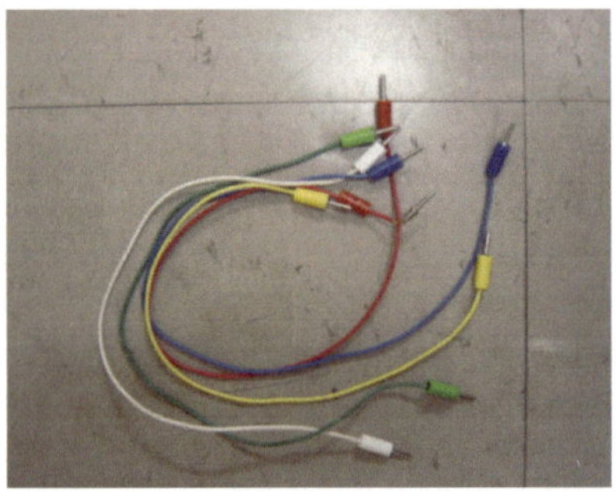

Fig. 1. Plugs

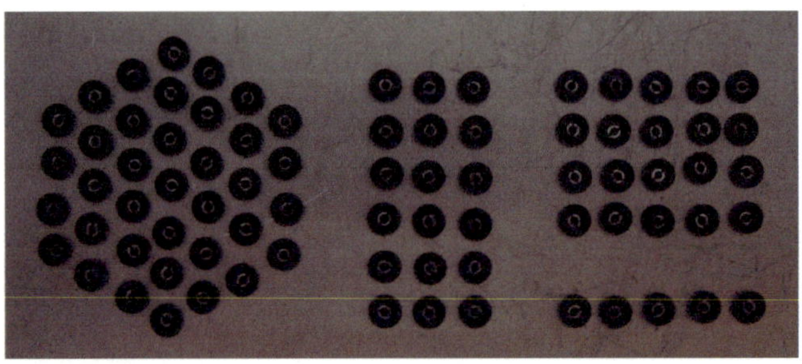

Fig. 2. Operational panel

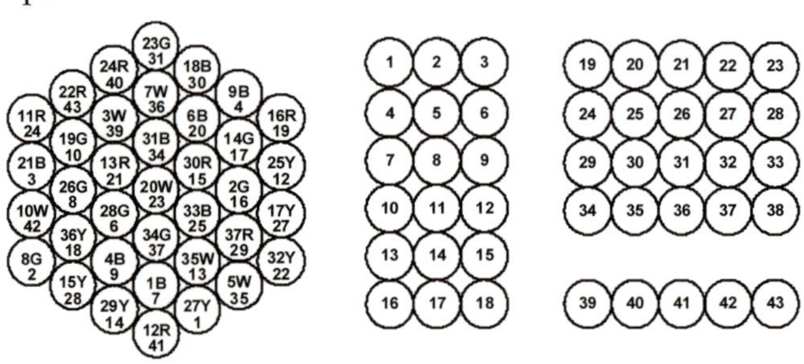


Fig. 3. Manual

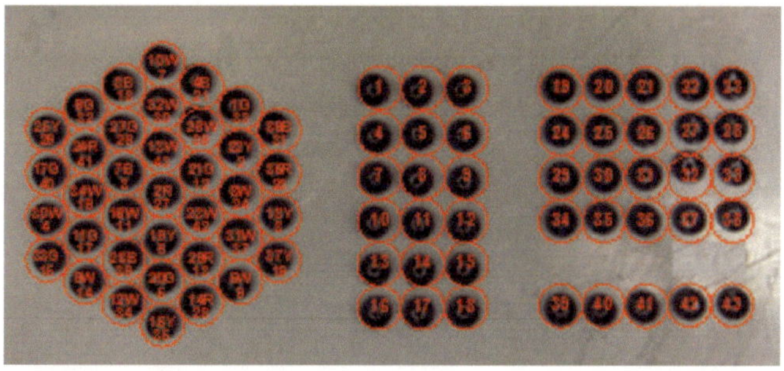

Fig. 4. Overlay of AR-based manual on panel

Fig. 5. Experimental environment

### 2.2 Results

Figure 6 illustrates the process flow for inserting a plug. Based on this process, errors that occurred during the task were classified into four types, as shown in Table 1. Below, the time for a task and the frequency of each error are compared for the two conditions.

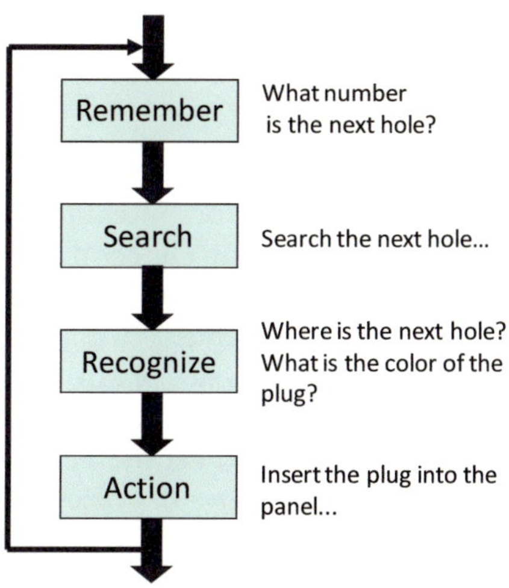


Fig. 6. Process of inserting a plug

| Errors during the task | Type |
|---|---|
| - Forget what number the next hole is. | Error in remembering procedures |
| - Skip the next hole. | |
| - Intentionally insert a plug into a wrong hole. | Error in recognising positions |
| - Intentionally insert a plug in wrong colour into a hole. | Error in recognising objects |
| - Unintentionally insert a plug into a wrong hole. | Error in action |
| - Unintentionally insert a plug in wrong colour into a hole. | |

Table 1. Classification of errors during the experiment

(I) Time for a task

Fig. 7 shows the average time for the task in each condition. It is clear that the time was about 15% less in the comparative condition than in the basic condition. One reason is that subjects' eye movement was reduced because they could see both the manual and the panel at the same time when they used an AR-based manual, whereas they had to see them one after the other when they used a paper-based manual. Another reason is that they could plug into the panel more easily in the comparative condition, which allowed hands-free operation, than in the basic condition, which required them to hold the paper-based manual.

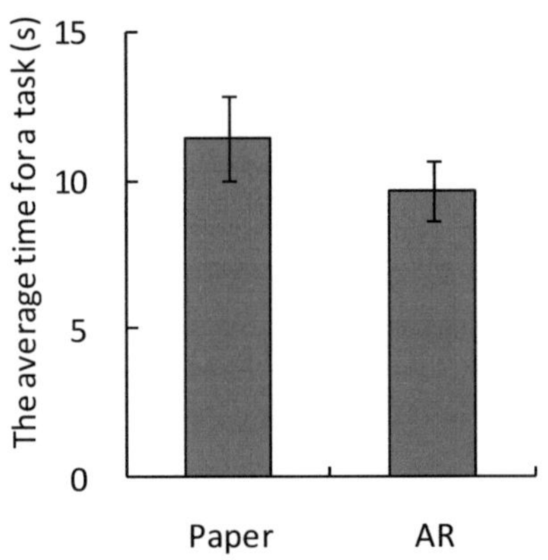


Fig. 7. Average time for the task

(II) Frequency of errors

Fig. 8 shows the frequencies of four types of errors in each condition. First, the error in remembering the procedures was less frequent in the comparative condition than in the basic condition. As described above, subjects could perform the task more smoothly when they used an AR-based manual. Further, it prevented them from forgetting what number hole they should next plug into. Second, the frequency of errors in recognising the positions was smaller in the comparative condition than in the basic condition. When subjects used HMDs, they could see the manual superimposed on the panel so that they could easily check both of them. Third, the error in recognising the objects seldom occurred in either condition. Fourth, the frequency of error in action in the comparative condition was about a quarter of that in the basic condition. This is probably because an AR-based manual made it less difficult to compare the manual and the panel, reducing such careless errors.

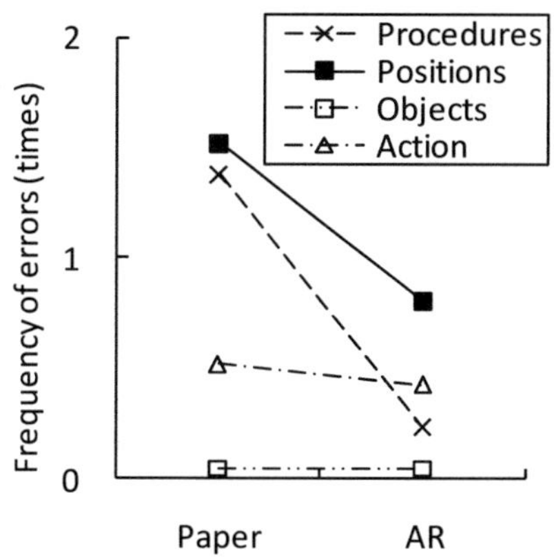


Fig. 8. Average frequency of errors

In addition, we have reported that an AR-based manual can support both skilled and unskilled workers (Nakanishi & Okada, 2006). An AR manual is especially effective for rule-based tasks of the three types described in the SRK task model (Nakanishi, et al., 2009a), and it makes it easy to foresee future situations in dynamic control tasks (Nakanishi & Okada, 2003; Nakanishi & Okada, 2004; Nakanishi & Okada, 2005).

## 3. Examination of human factor requirements for applying AR-based manuals

As shown in the previous section, AR-based manuals are promising as a next-generation tool for both preventing errors and enhancing task efficiency. Based on this prospect, it is necessary and important to clarify the basic human factor requirements before they are put into practical use.

In this section, we describe the conditions required to effectively enhance the performance of the workers who use an AR-based manual. In particular, we discuss what should be considered when they work with HMDs, and also how much information should be provided by HMDs depending on the real view, through experiments (Nakanishi et al., 2007; Nakanishi et al., 2008a).

### 3.1 Points to be examined

The main characteristics of using an AR-based manual are wearing HMDs and superimposing a digital image on the real view. Thus, we focus on the following eight significant points.

(I) Effect of wearing HMDs

When an AR-based manual is used in assembling or inspecting tasks, it is of primary importance that workers can see real objects clearly enough. Accordingly, the use of a monocular transparent HMD is recommended. Thus, we examine the following six points that should be considered when workers wear HMDs.

1. Difficulty in preparing to use AR-based manuals: Does it take more time to prepare to use AR-based manuals with HMDs than paper-based manuals?
2. Effect of eyesight correction: Although it is currently difficult for the workers wearing glasses to also wear HMDs, is it possible to apply AR-based manuals with HMDs to the workers wearing contact lenses?

3. Effect of eye dominance: Is it better for the workers to wear monocular HMDs on their dominant or non-dominant eye?
4. Effect of surrounding illumination: Is the workers' view affected by surrounding illumination when they use HMDs?
5. Workload: Is the workers' workload heavier when they use AR-based manuals with HMDs than when they use traditional paper-based manuals?
6. Attention to surroundings: Is it more difficult to recognise changes in surroundings when they use AR-based manuals with HMDs than when they use paper-based manuals?

(II) Effect of superimposing information on the real view

An AR-based manual allows workers to see an overlay of task-related information and real objects to be manipulated. This characteristic shows a great potential to reduce human errors and enhance task efficiency in actual work situations. However, if too much information is given by an AR-based manual, it may interfere with the real view. Thus, we further examine the following two points for clues to the proper design of AR-based manuals.

1. Effect of information presented by HMDs (static background): How does the workers' performance change depending on the balance between the complexities of digital information and the static real background?
2. Effect of information presented by HMDs (dynamic background): How does the workers' performance change depending on the balance between the complexities of digital information and the dynamic real background?

### 3.2 Method

To answer the above questions, we considered an experimental approach. To examine points (1) to (6), which concern the use of an HMD, we conducted experiments in which subjects performed the same task described in section 2. The detailed settings of the experiment were different for each examined point (described in the following sections).

Further, to examine points (7) and (8), which concern superimposition of digital images on the real view, we prepared another experimental task in which subjects experienced various grades of complexity of the AR-based manual and the real view. Its details are also given in later sections.

### 3.3 Human interface

Current technology offers two easily available human interfaces for AR-based manuals: a see-through display (STD) and a retinal-scanning display (RSD). An STD (Fig. 9) is an HMD that lets a user see images projected from a PC onto a half-mirror in front of his/her eye, and an RSD (Fig. 10) is an HMD that lets a user see images by shining a low-power laser beam directly into his/her retina and scanning it at high speed.

In the experiments for examining points (1) to (6), we asked subjects to perform the task using the AR-based manual with STDs (Dataglass2A, made by SHIMADZU) and RSDs (NOMAD, made by Microvision, Inc). Further, if it was necessary for comparison, we asked them to perform the task while holding the paper-based manual, an A4 paper showing the same image as Fig. 3, in their hand. When they used the AR-based manual, they could see the superimposed image of the manual and the panel, as shown in Fig. 4. The image size was set to the same in every case. However the transparency was different between STDs (approximately 15%) and RSDs (almost 100%). Moreover, in the experiment for examining points (7) and (8), subjects used RSDs whose transparency was higher.

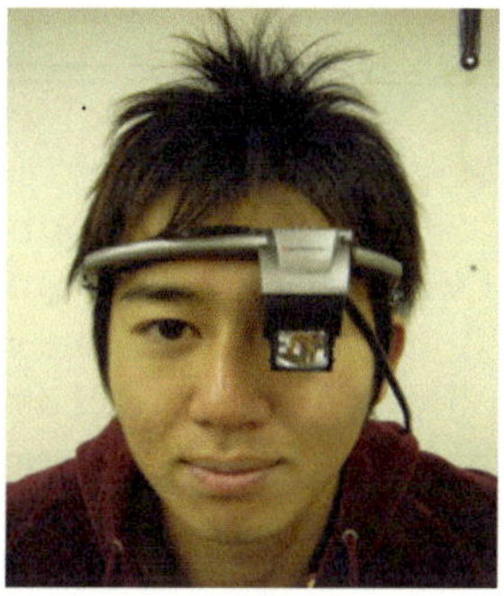

Fig. 9. STD

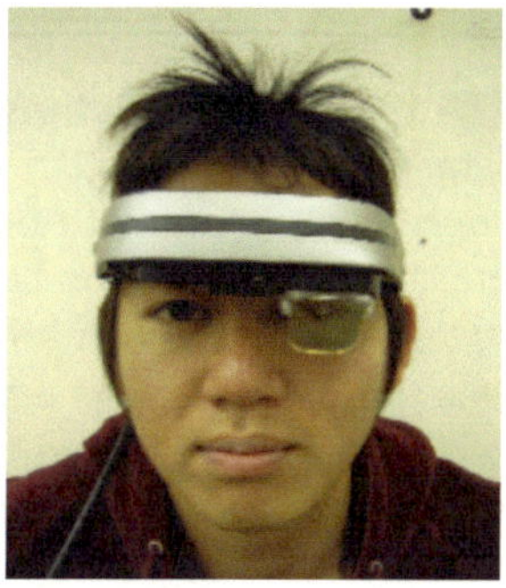

Fig. 10. RSD

In all the experiments, they practiced well in advance of data collection.
In the following sections, the detailed settings of each experiment and their results are described.

### 3.4 Setting details and results

#### 3.4.1 Difficulty in preparing to use AR-based manuals

(I) Setting details

Subjects were nine students whose right eyes were dominant. Each of them sat as shown in Fig. 11 with an STD or RSD in his/her hand. At a signal, they started putting on the STD or RSD on their dominant eye and then adjusted their own position so that they could see the superimposed image of the panel and the manual presented by the STD or RSD. They were asked to say "Wore" when they finished putting on the STDs or RSDs and "Saw" when they could see the superimposed image; the time they said these words were recorded. Each of them repeated the procedure three times.

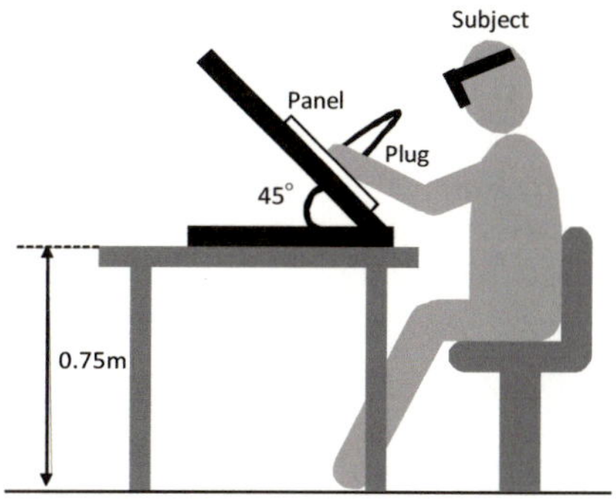


Fig. 11. Position of a subject

(II) Result

The average time until they finished putting on the STDs was 19.7 (s), and that until they finished putting on the RSDs was 19.2 (s). The average time until they could see the perfectly superimposed image was 5.4 (s) when they used STDs and 6.0 (s) when they used RSDs.

From these results, we can say that workers easily prepare to use either STDs or RSDs. Moreover it is expected that in future these HMDs will become simpler, just like glasses, so workers can more easily wear them.

### 3.4.2 Effect of eyesight correction

(I) Setting details

Subjects were nine students with normal eyesight of 1.0 or better (normal group) and nine students with eyesight of 1.0 or better corrected by contact lens (corrected group). Their eyesight was tested with the Landolt C test. Each subject's dominant eye was the right.

Their task was to insert 25 plugs into holes on the panel following the manual as quickly as possible. Two experimental conditions were prepared: a) wearing an STD on the non-dominant eye and b) wearing an RSD on the non-dominant eye. They performed the task once in each condition. The position of a subject and the panel was the same as in Fig. 11.

(II) Result

The error rate per task for both groups was below 1.0 in both conditions. The average time per task for each group is given in Table 2.

| | STD | RSD |
|---|---|---|
| Normal Group | 302.9 | 310.4 |
| Corrected Group | 313.0 | 312.0 |

Table 2. Time per task

These results show no significant difference between the groups in either condition. Thus, we can say that workers whose eyes are corrected by contact lenses as well as workers with good eyesight can use AR-based manuals with either STDs or RSDs.

### 3.4.3 Effect of eye dominance

(I) Setting details

Subjects were 14 students whose right eyes were dominant and 6 students whose left eye was dominant. Their dominant eye was determined by the Rosenbach test.

Their task was to insert 20 plugs into holes on the panel according to the manual as quickly as possible. Four experimental conditions were prepared: a) wearing an STD on the dominant eye, b) wearing an STD on the non-dominant eye, c) wearing an RSD on the dominant eye and d) wearing an RSD on the non-dominant eye. They performed the task once in each condition and after each task five questions were answered by giving scores of −5 to +5. The position of a subject and the panel is shown in Fig. 12.

(II) Result

The error rate per task was below 1.0 in all conditions. The average time per task for each condition is given in Fig. 13.

This chart shows that if they used either STDs or RSDs, the time tended to be shorter when they wore it on their non-dominant eye than when they wore it on their dominant eye. The scores for the five questions are given in Fig. 14. The score for the question "Easy to see the panel or not?" means that they felt it easier to see the panel when they wore STDs or RSDs on their non-dominant eye, while the score for the question "Easy to see the manual or not?" means that they felt it easier to see the manual when they wore STDs or RSDs on their dominant eye. This result is natural, because they can more clearly see an object with their dominant eye. However, focusing on the questions asking about factors that could

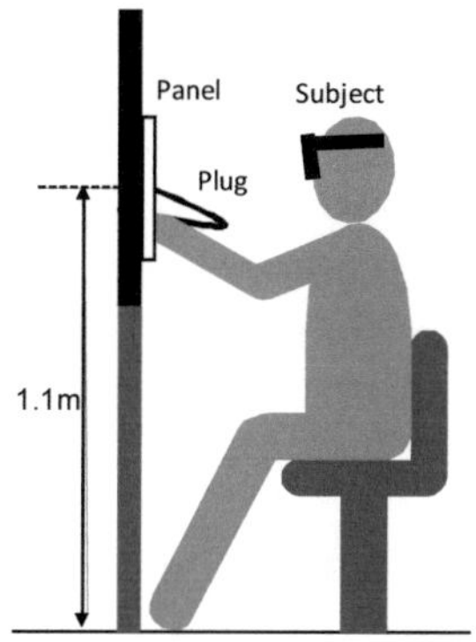


Fig. 12. Position of a subject

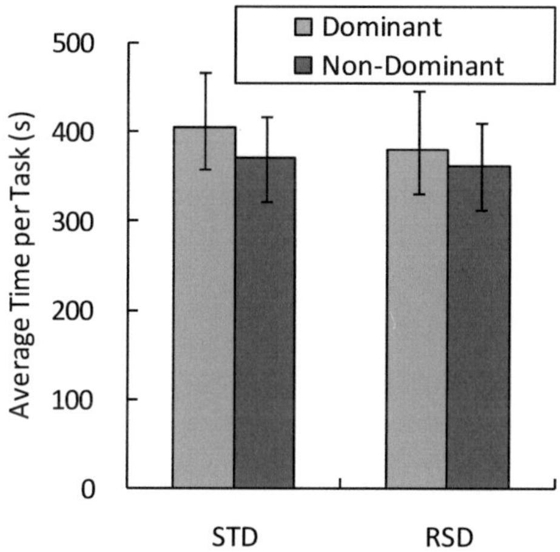


Fig. 13. Average time per task

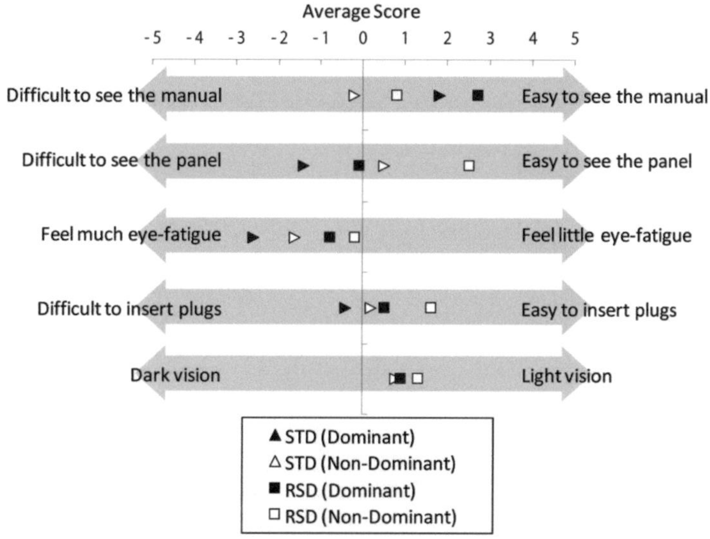


Fig. 14. Scores for the five questions in each condition

potentially influence their overall performance, such as "Feel much eye-fatigue or not?" or "Easy to insert plugs or not?", the scores were found to be more favourable when they wore STDs or RSDs on their non-dominant eye. This seems to be because it was primarily important for them to clearly see the real panel and plugs in this task.
From the above examination, it is recommended that if either STDs or RSDs are used for AR-based manuals in tasks such as assembly or inspection, they should be worn on the non-dominant eye. Accordingly, design of the manuals shown by STDs or RSDs should be simple enough for the workers to easily read them with their non-dominant eye.

### 3.4.4 Effect of surrounding illumination

(I) Setting details
Subjects were 10 students whose right eyes were dominant.
Their task was to insert 25 plugs into holes on the panel according to the manual as quickly as possible. Two experimental conditions were prepared: a) wearing an STD on the non-dominant eye and b) wearing an RSD on the non-dominant eye. The position of a subject and the panel is the same as in Fig. 12.
Japanese Industrial Standard (JIS) Z 9110 specifies that 300 (lx) to 3000 (lx) is recommended as the standard of illumination in assembling or inspecting tasks (Japan Standards Association, 1979). However it does not consider the use of STDs or RSDs, and workers sometimes have to work under low or high illumination. So we set the experimental environment as follows: six grades of indoor illumination [100 (lx), 400 (lx), 800 (lx), 1200 (lx), 1600 (lx)] and outdoor illumination (under the direct rays of the morning sun). Each subject performed the task once each using an STD or RSD under each of seven lighting conditions.
(II) Result
The outdoor illumination level was 68,333 (lx) on average. The error rate per task is given in Fig. 15. The error rate in cases of indoor illumination was below 1.0 when subjects used either STDs or RSDs. However, it was comparatively high when they used STDs under outdoor illumination. The average time per task is given in Fig. 16. We see that the time was more than 150 (s) longer only when they used STDs under outdoor illumination compared with the other cases. This is possibly because an STD sends images to a user's retina via a half-mirror and it is easily affected by surrounding illumination, whereas an RSD sends images directly to the retina and is scarcely affected by surrounding illumination.

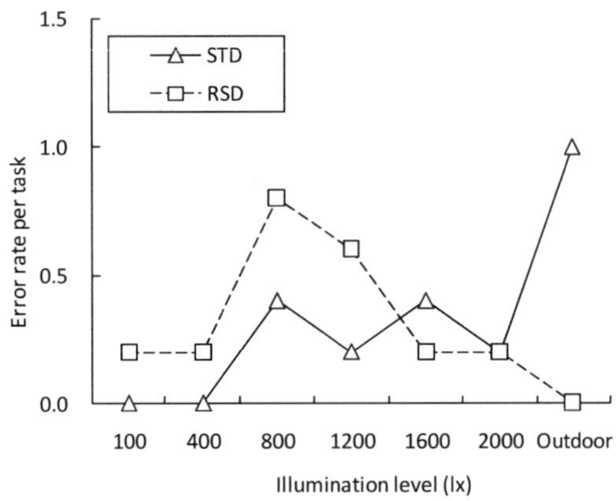


Fig. 15. Error rate per task

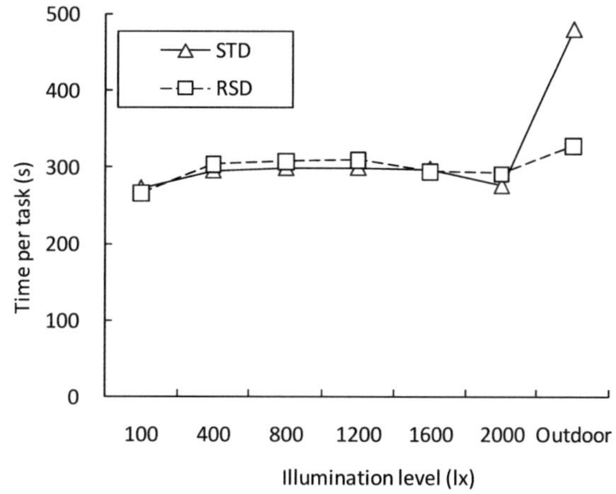


Fig. 16. Average time per task

From the above examination, we can say that there is no evident problem in using either STDs or RSDs under indoor illumination if it is within the range of the standard level. However, when workers use STDs under extremely high illumination, it may be difficult to read the information they present. In such cases, the problem can be solved by using RSDs instead of STDs.

### 3.4.5 Workload

(I) Setting details

Subjects were 10 students whose right eyes were dominant.

Their task was to insert 30 plugs into holes on the panel according to the manual as quickly as possible, and three repetitions of this task were defined as a term. In this experiment, each of them was given three terms, including breaks of two minutes. Before the first term and after each term, an electrocardiogram (ECG) was recorded using EP-202 (made by Parama-Tech), and the critical flicker frequency (CFF) was recorded using 501BTKK (made by Takei Kiki Kogyo). They also answered 22 questions concerning workload such as "heavy head", "stiff shoulders" by giving scores of 1 (light) to 5 (heavy) (Institute for Science of Labour, 1970). Fig. 17 shows the experimental procedure. The experimental conditions were as follows: a) using the paper-based manual, b) wearing an STD on the non-dominant eye and c) wearing an RSD on the non-dominant eye. Subjects experienced each experimental condition on different days following the above procedures. The position of a subject and the panel is the same as in Fig. 11.

(II) Result

Generally, it has been said that workload should be examined using multiple indicators (Hayashi et al., 1981). We adopted the following four indicators to evaluate workload (Ito, 1988).

i. Time per task: As workload is increased, performance drops, and the time should increase.
ii. CFF: As workload is increased, the CFF should decrease. We calculated the average value of top-down CFF and bottom-up CFF for each measurement and focused on the difference from the first value.

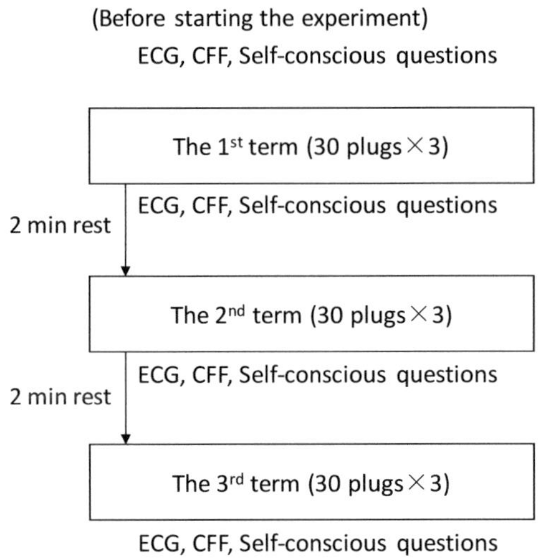


Fig. 17. Experimental procedure

iii. Cardiac wave ratio (W.R.): This is the ratio of waves to the cardiac frequency. As workload is increased, W.R. should increase. We focused on change against the first W.R. W.R. is given by the following expressions.

$$\mathrm{W.R} = \mathrm{WAVE} / \mathrm{N} \tag{1}$$

$$\mathrm{WAVE} = \sum_{i=2}^{N-1} Y(i), \quad i>2 \tag{2}$$

$$Y(i) = 1.: \text{if } \{X(i) < X(i+1)\} \text{ and } \{X(i) < X(i+1)\}$$

$$\text{or if } \{X(i) > X(i+1)\} \text{ and } \{X(i) > X(i-1)\}$$

$$Y(i) = 0.: \text{else } X(i)$$

$$X(i): \text{Time sequential data of RR intervals}$$

$$(i = 1, 2, \ldots, N)$$

$$N: \text{Cardiac frequency}$$

iv. Self-evaluation score: This is the total score for all questions. As workload is increased, the score should increase. We focused on the difference from the first score.

First, the result for indicator (i) is given in Fig. 18. We cannot find any significant change in this chart, so it seems that their performance hardly decreased. Second, the result of indicator (ii) is given in Fig. 19. This chart shows that the CFF gradually decreased when the paper-based manual was used; however, it did not do so when the AR-based manual with an STD or RSD was used. Thus, it seems that their workload did not increase when they used the AR-based manual as much as when they used the paper-based manual. Third, the result of indicator (iii) is given in Fig. 20. This chart shows a similar tendency to Fig. 19. That is, the W.R. in the condition of the paper-based manual increased monotonously, but the W.R. in the conditions of the AR-based manual went up once and back down. Fourth, the result of indicator (iv) is given in Fig. 21. In this chart, we can see that the score in any condition increased as the terms progressed. However, there was some difference in the scores after the third term between the conditions.

From these results, we can understand that the AR-based manual does not add more workload to workers than the paper-based manual. In fact, the AR-based manual saves time for these tasks, so it can reduce their workload compared with the traditional way.

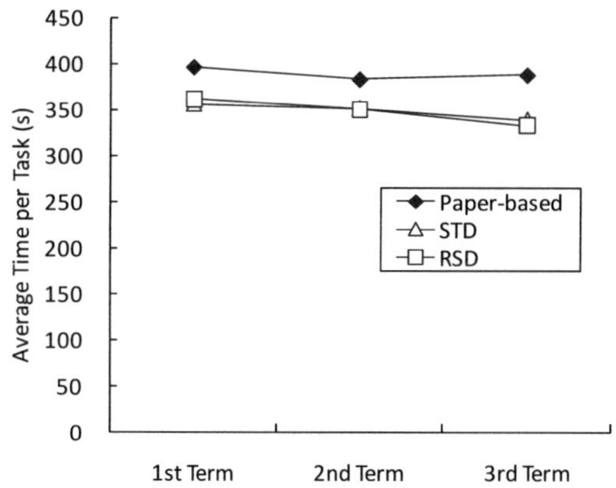


Fig. 18. Shift of average time per task as terms progress

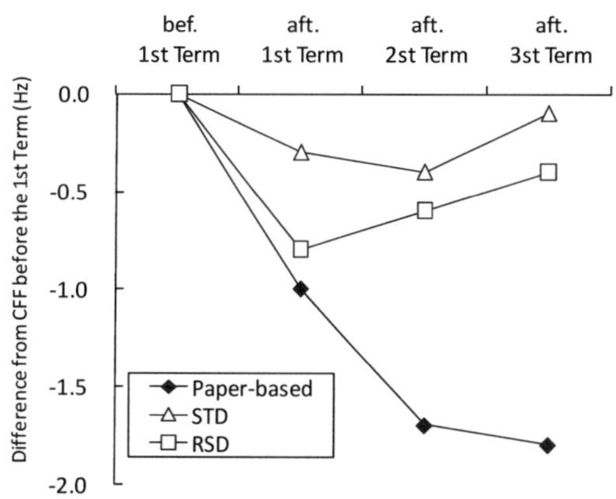


Fig. 19. Shift of CFF as terms progress

### 3.4.6 Attention to surroundings

(I) Setting details

The subjects were 14 students whose right eyes were dominant. The position of a subject and the panel is the same as in Fig. 12. The panel was surrounded by 45 small LED boards (NT-16, made by EK JAPAN), which were positioned in a horizontal range of −90 (deg) to +90 (deg) and a vertical range of −60 (deg) to +60 (deg), as shown in Fig. 22. On each board, 10 LEDs were lined up. During the experiment, the LED boards flashed at random.

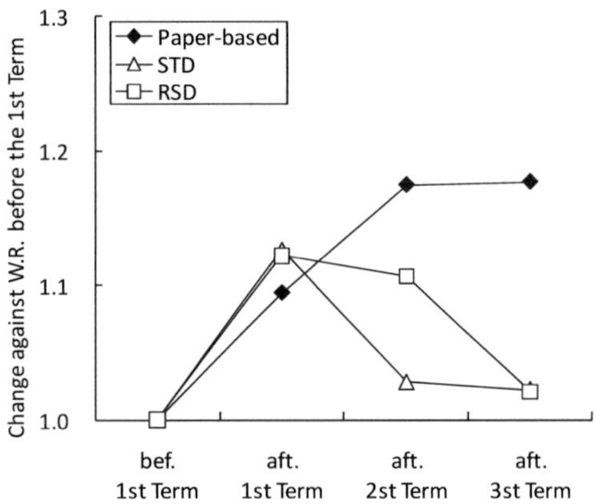


Fig. 20. Shift of W.R. as terms progress

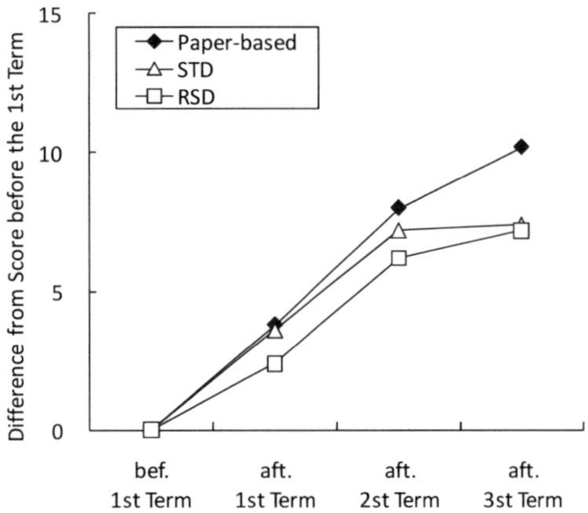


Fig. 21. Shift of self-evaluation score as terms progress

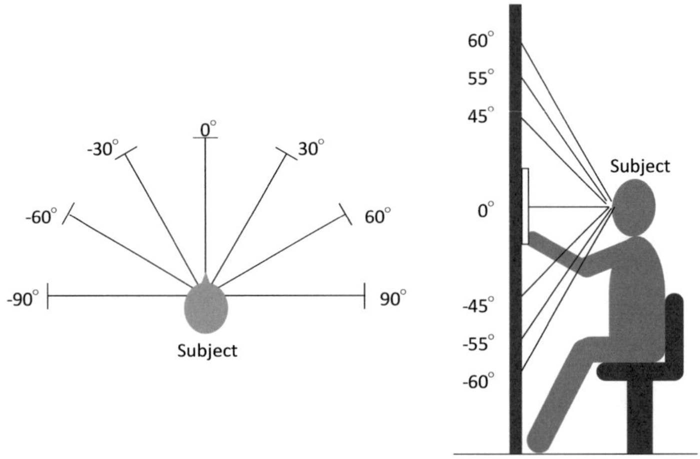


Fig. 22. Positions of a subject and the LED boards: view from the top (left) and view from the side (right)

Their task was to insert 20 plugs into holes on the panel according to the manual as quickly as possible. They were told to concentrate on this task, but if they noticed one of the LED boards flashing, they should say "Found" immediately. The experimental conditions were as follows: a) using the paper-based manual, b) wearing an STD on the non-dominant eye and c) wearing an RSD on the non-dominant eye.

(II) Result

The detection rate of each LED board in the condition of using the paper-based manual is given in Fig. 23, that in the condition of using STDs is given in Fig. 24 and that in the condition of using RSDs is given in Fig. 25. In these charts, the rate can be distinguished by colour. Darker cells represent higher rates. By comparing these charts, we can see that Figs. 24 and 25 include more dark cells than Fig. 23, in particular in the horizontal range of −60 (deg) to +60 (deg) and the vertical range of −45 (deg) to 0 (deg). This is probably because the subjects could keep viewing the panel through the task when they used the AR-based manual. However, we can also observe that when they used RSDs, they could not notice any flash positioned in the vertical range over 55 (deg). This is possibly because their view to the upper front was blocked by the RSD's frame (Fig. 10). Summarising the above results, we can infer that it was easier for workers to notice a change in their surroundings when they used STDs than when they used the paper-based manual. Moreover, when they used RSDs, they could easily notice changes occurring in the vertical range under 50 (deg), but they

| | -90° | -60° | -30° | 0° | 30° | 60° | 90° |
|---|---|---|---|---|---|---|---|
| 60° | 0.00 | 0.06 | 0.00 | 0.00 | 0.00 | 0.00 | 0.00 |
| 55° | 0.00 | 0.00 | 0.00 | 0.12 | 0.05 | 0.00 | 0.00 |
| 45° | 0.00 | 0.17 | 0.19 | 0.40 | 0.27 | 0.29 | 0.00 |
| 0° | 0.47 | 0.35 | 0.39 | | 0.40 | 0.35 | 0.13 |
| -45° | 0.59 | 0.64 | 0.64 | | 0.50 | 0.67 | 0.43 |
| -55° | 0.40 | 0.36 | 0.41 | | 0.71 | 0.44 | 0.20 |
| -60° | 0.25 | 0.12 | 0.10 | | 0.08 | 0.00 | 0.06 |

Fig. 23. Detection rate of each LED board when subjects used the paper-based manual

| | -90° | -60° | -30° | 0° | 30° | 60° | 90° |
|---|---|---|---|---|---|---|---|
| 60° | 0.00 | 0.06 | 0.11 | 0.08 | 0.06 | 0.00 | 0.00 |
| 55° | 0.00 | 0.12 | 0.24 | 0.41 | 0.16 | 0.15 | 0.00 |
| 45° | 0.17 | 0.63 | 0.88 | 1.00 | 0.71 | 0.44 | 0.00 |
| 0° | 0.73 | 1.00 | 0.94 | | 1.00 | 0.90 | 0.33 |
| -45° | 0.21 | 0.67 | 0.86 | | 0.83 | 0.65 | 0.12 |
| -55° | 0.00 | 0.06 | 0.15 | | 0.18 | 0.06 | 0.00 |
| -60° | 0.06 | 0.06 | 0.06 | | 0.00 | 0.00 | 0.00 |

Fig. 24. Detection rate of each LED board when subjects used STDs

| | -90° | -60° | -30° | 0° | 30° | 60° | 90° |
|---|---|---|---|---|---|---|---|
| 60° | 0.00 | 0.00 | 0.00 | 0.00 | 0.00 | 0.00 | 0.00 |
| 55° | 0.00 | 0.00 | 0.00 | 0.00 | 0.00 | 0.00 | 0.00 |
| 45° | 0.15 | 0.63 | 0.07 | 0.41 | 0.25 | 0.29 | 0.00 |
| 0° | 0.82 | 1.00 | 0.94 | | 0.81 | 1.00 | 0.53 |
| -45° | 0.26 | 0.88 | 0.64 | | 0.56 | 0.57 | 0.00 |
| -55° | 0.06 | 0.31 | 0.15 | | 0.22 | 0.00 | 0.00 |
| -60° | 0.00 | 0.00 | 0.06 | | 0.00 | 0.06 | 0.00 |

Fig. 25. Detection rate of each LED board when subjects used RSDs

could not notice those in the vertical range over 55 (deg). However, it is expected that RSDs will become smaller in the near future, so the problem of blocked sight will be improved.

### 3.4.7 Effect of information presented by HMDs (static background)

(I) Setting details

For the experiment, a simple operational panel was displayed on a PC monitor (PCG-241N, made by Sony). A pattern of the operational panel is shown in Fig. 26, and a pattern of the AR-based manual is shown in Fig. 27. In addition, an overlay image of the operational panel and the AR-based manual is shown in Fig. 28. On the operational panel, blocks including buttons numbered from 1 to 6 (Fig. 26-1) were arranged in a matrix of m × m. In the AR-based manual, numbers within the range of 1 to 6 were arranged in the same size matrix as on the operational panel. The matrix size of the operational panel and the number of numbers presented at the same time by the AR-based manual were changed depending on the experimental conditions explained in the following paragraph. Clicking a button that

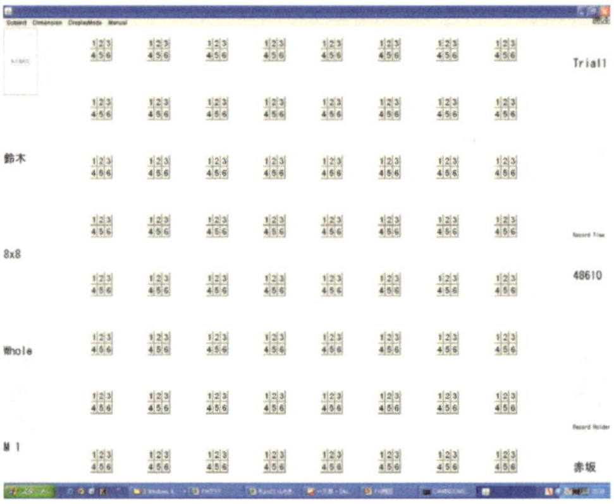


Fig. 26. A pattern of the operational panel

Fig. 26-1. A block on the operational panel

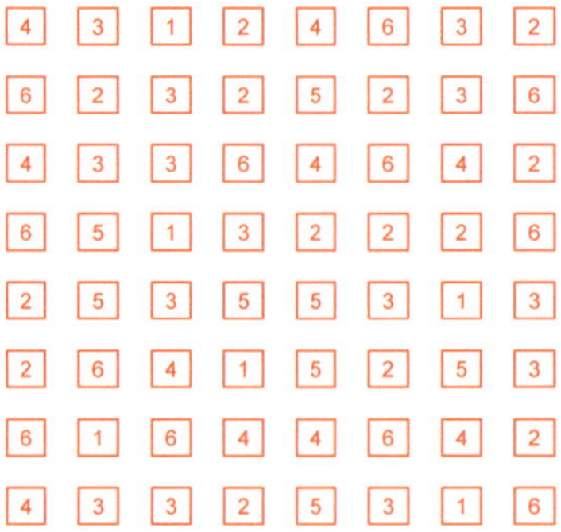


Fig. 27. A pattern of the AR-based manual

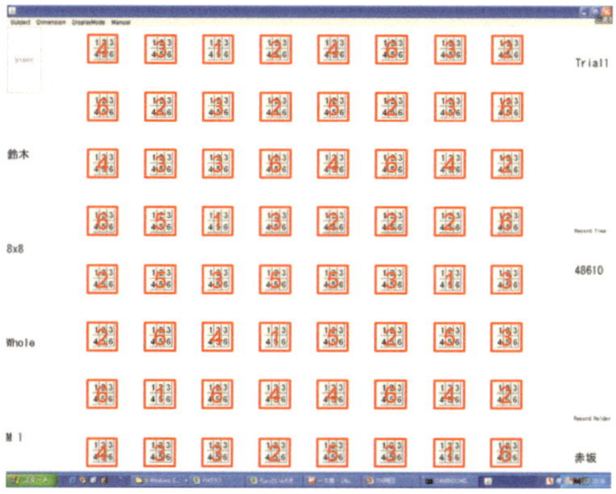


Fig. 28. An overlay of the operational panel and AR manual

had the same number as that given by the AR-based manual was defined as a unit operation for a block. Subjects' task was to complete operation for all blocks correctly as quickly as possible.

We set five levels of complexity for the operational panel by changing the matrix size (m × m): m = 4 (Fig. 29-1), m = 6 (Fig. 29-2), m = 8 (Fig. 29-3), m = 10 (Fig. 29-4) and m = 12 (Fig. 29-5). Further, we set three levels of complexity for the AR-based manual by changing the number of numbers appearing at the same time: the whole indication (m × m) (Fig. 30-1), one-line indication (1 × m) (Fig. 30-2) and individual indication (1 × 1) (Fig. 30-3). In one-line and individual indication, subjects had to switch images of the AR-based manual from one line to the next or from one number to the next with a keystroke.

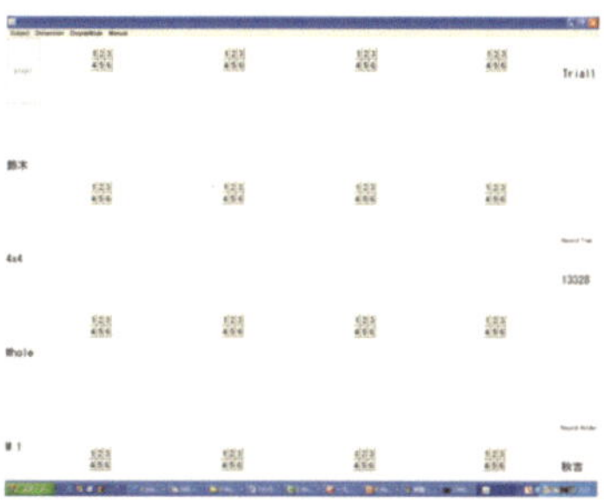

Fig. 29-1. Operational panel (m = 4)

Fig. 29-2. Operational panel (m = 6)

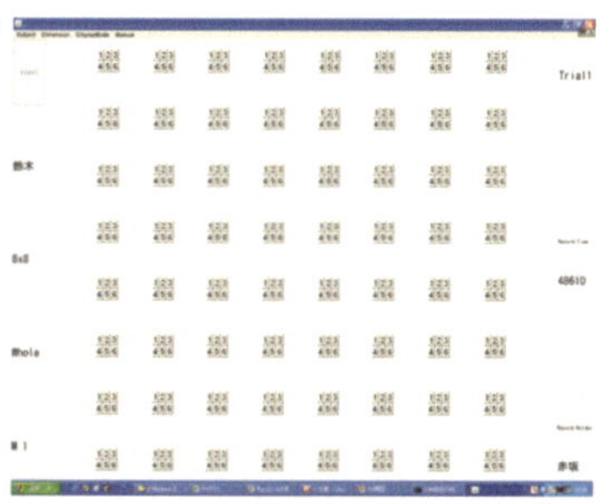

Fig. 29-3. Operational panel (m = 8)

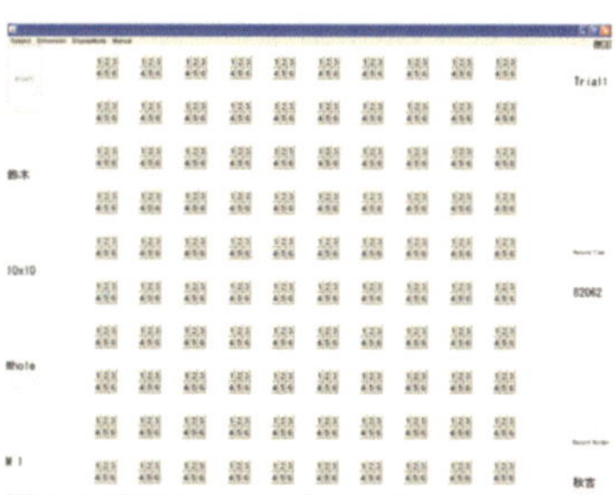

Fig. 29-4. Operational panel (m = 10)

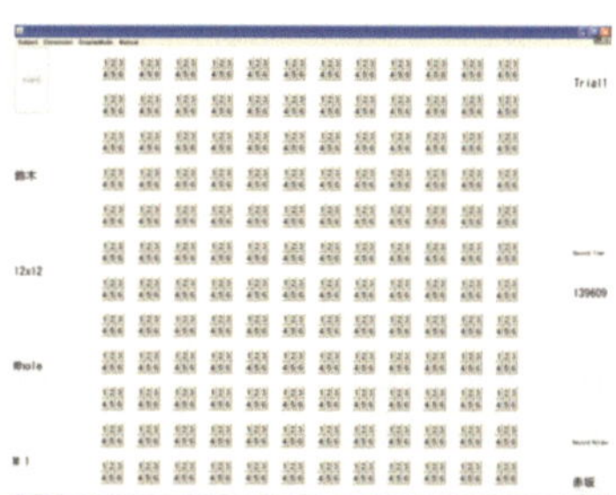

Fig. 29-5. Operational panel (m = 12)

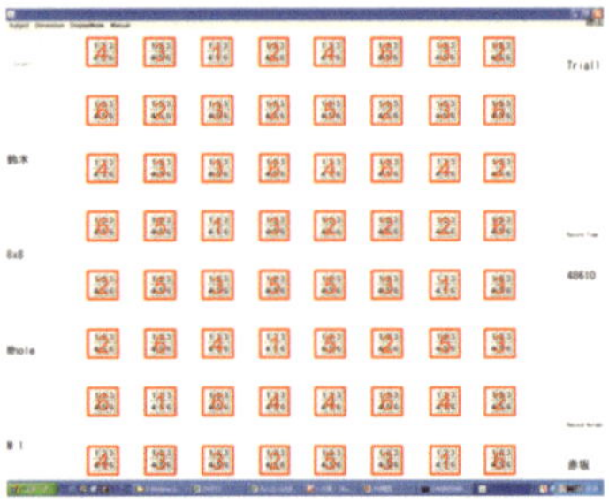

Fig. 30-1. Whole indication (m = 8)

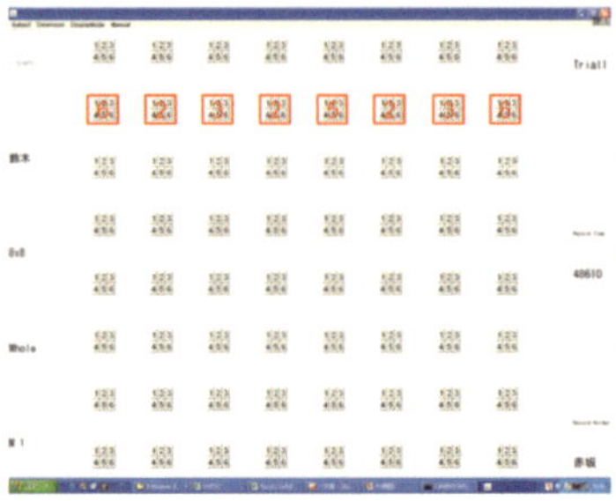

Fig. 30-2. One-line indication (m = 8)

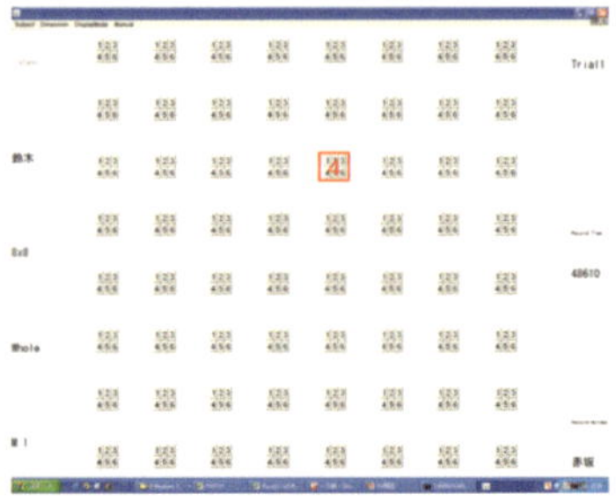

Fig. 30-3. Individual indication (m = 8)

Fifteen conditions were prepared: five levels of complexity of the operational panel × three levels of complexity of the AR-based manual. Subjects were six students whose right eyes were dominant. They wore RSDs on their non-dominant eye, and performed the task five times in each of the fifteen conditions. The numbers presented by the AR-based manual were random. We recorded the operation logs during the task in time sequence. The position of a subject and a PC monitor displaying the operational panel is shown in Fig. 31.

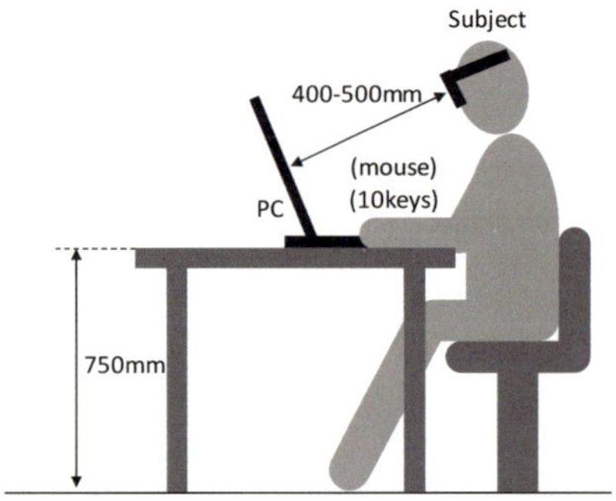


Fig. 31. Position of the PC monitor and a subject

(II) Result

In the present situations, the complexity of the real view is given. Thus, we focused on how subjects' performance changed depending on the conditions of the AR-based manual under each condition of the operational panel.

First, we counted the case where a subject clicked on a different numerical button from the number presented by the AR-based manual as an error and calculated the error rate per unit operation. Figs. 32-1, 32-2, 32-3, 32-4 and 32-5 show the error rates in each condition of the operational panel (m = 4, 6, 8, 10, 12). The vertical axis is scaled individually for each graph so that the error rates can be compared between the conditions of the AR-based manual under different conditions of the operational panel. When the matrix size of the operational panel was 4 and 6 (m = 4, 6), the error rates were comparatively low when the AR-based manual presented the whole indication. This is possibly because in this case subjects did not have to switch images of the AR-based manual and could pay attention to the operational panel throughout the task. On the other hand, when the matrix size was 8, 10 and 12 (m = 8, 10, 12), the error rates were comparatively high when the AR-based manual presented the whole indication. This is possibly because, when many blocks appear on the operational panel, and furthermore numbers were overlaid on each of those blocks by the AR-based manual, too much information was given to subjects at once. Then they tended to click on wrong buttons or mistake operated blocks for unoperated ones.

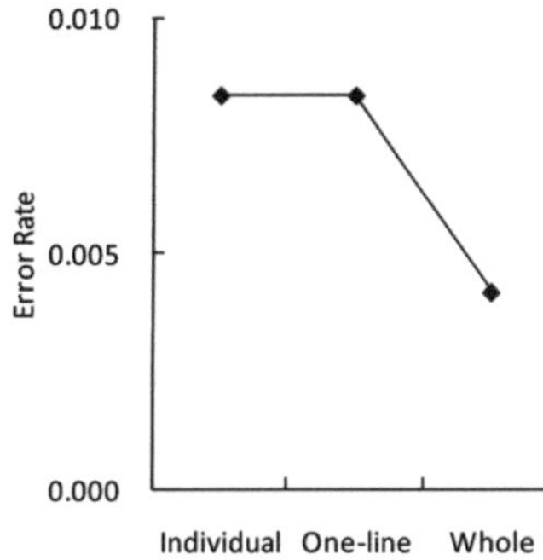


Fig. 32-1. Error rate per operation unit (m = 4)

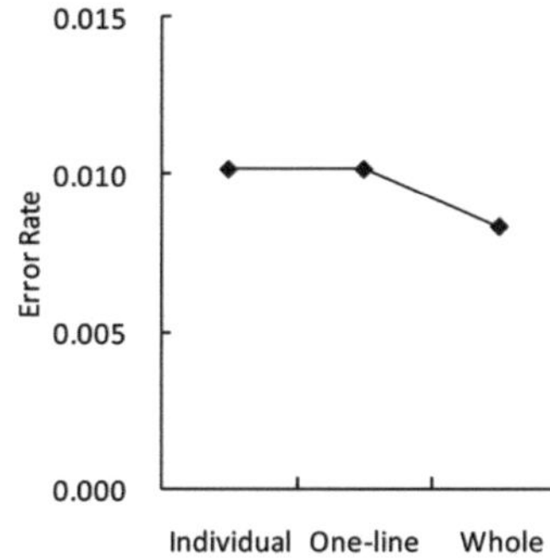


Fig. 32-2. Error rate per operation unit (m = 6)

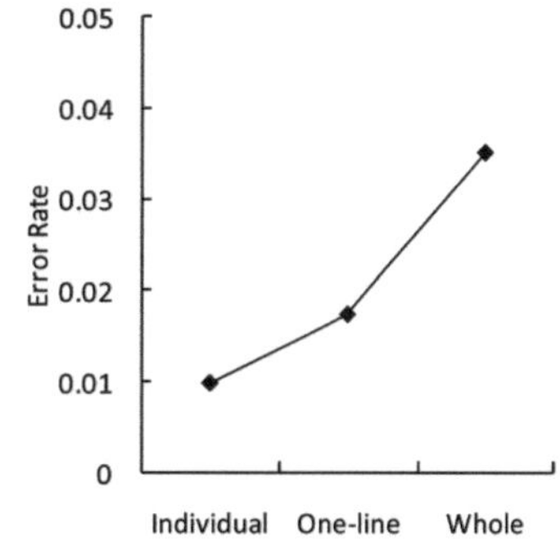


Fig. 32-3. Error rate per operation unit (m = 8)

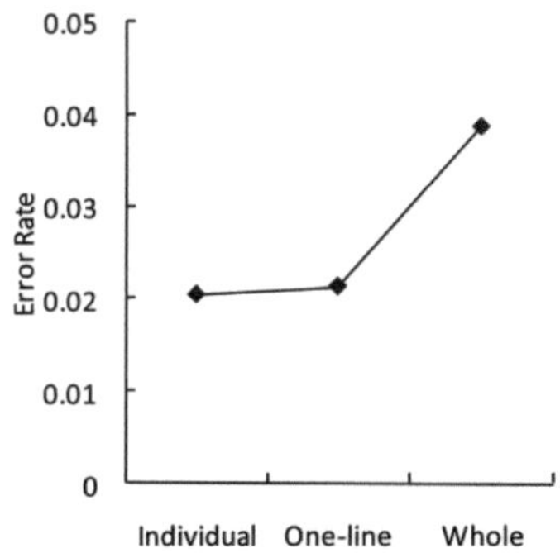


Fig. 32-4. Error rate per operation unit (m = 10)

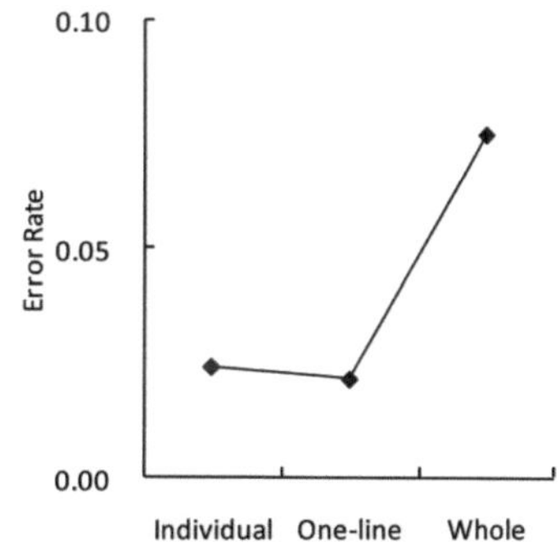


Fig. 32-5. Error rate per operation unit (m = 12)

Second, we analysed time per unit operation. Figs. 33-1, 33-2, 33-3, 33-4 and 33-5 show the average time per unit operation in each condition of the operational panel (m = 4, 6, 8, 10, 12). When the matrix size of the operational panel was 4 and 6 (m = 4, 6), the operation time tended to be longer when the AR-based manual presented the individual indication. On the other hand, when the matrix size was 8, 10 and 12 (m = 8, 10, 12), the operation time was shorter in the case of the one-line indication than in the other cases. Moreover, when the matrix size was 12 (m = 12), the operation time was remarkably longer in the case of the whole indication. We can understand these results as follows. When a small number of blocks appeared on the operational panel, the efficiency of operation was affected more by switching images of the AR-based manual than by viewing much information. Conversely, when many blocks appeared on the operational panel, the efficiency of operation was affected more by viewing much information than by switching images of the AR-based manual. When these two factors were balanced, the efficiency of operation was highest.

The above examination yields the following suggestions for designing AR-based manuals. If the real view is not very complex, giving a large amount of information at a time saves workers the trouble of switching images in an AR-based manual. However, if the real view is rather complex, giving too much information reduces workers' performance, so giving information part by part is recommended. Moreover, in situations where human errors are to be strictly avoided, it will be better to give information one after the other.

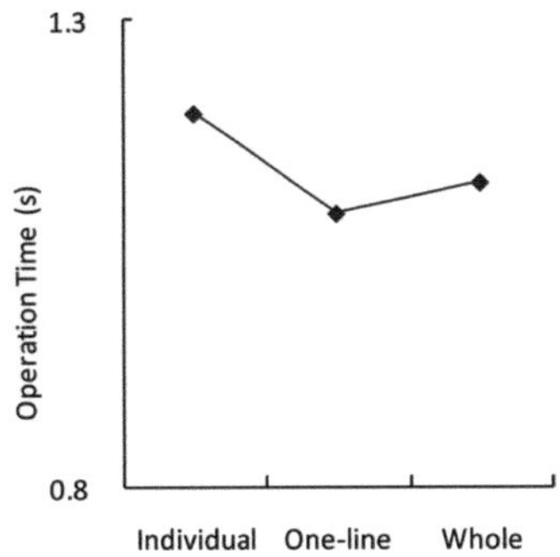


Fig. 33-1. Operation time (m = 4)

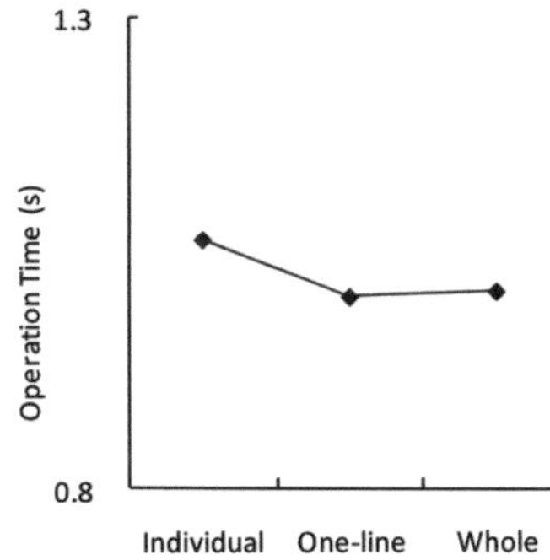


Fig. 33-2. Operation time (m = 6)

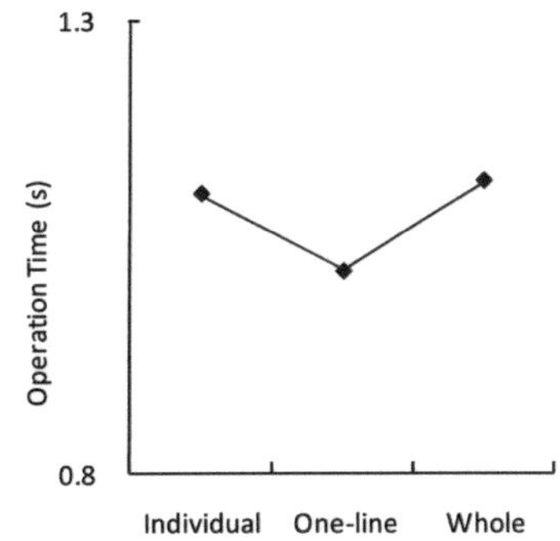


Fig. 33-3. Operation time (m = 8)

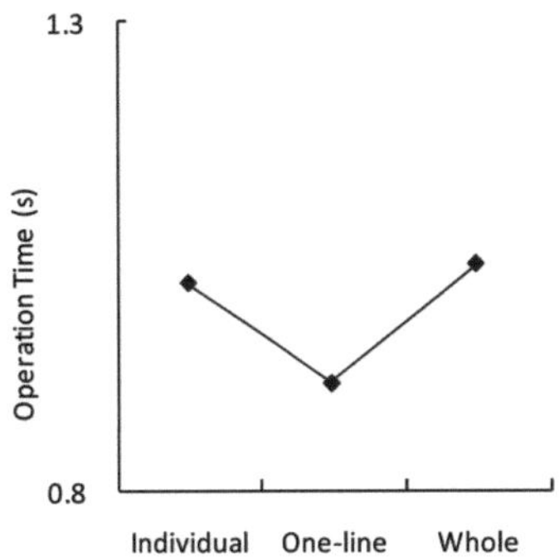


Fig. 33-4. Operation time (m = 10)

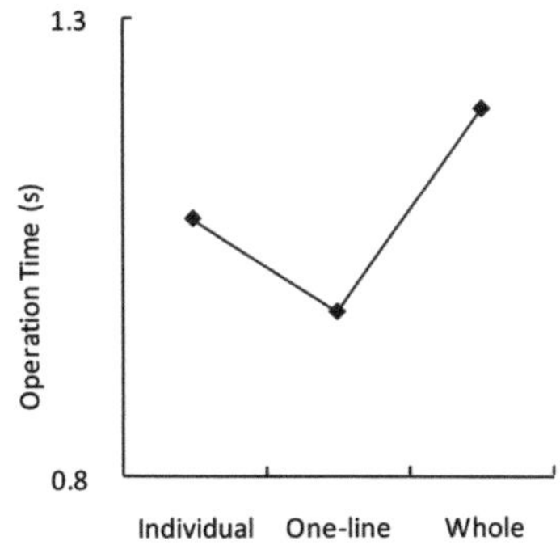


Fig. 33-5. Operation time (m = 12)

As an extra challenge, we attempted to build a model that describes the most effective design of AR-based manuals according to real-world conditions (Akasaka et al., 2007; Tamamushi et al., 2008; Nakanishi et al., 2008b; Nakanishi et al., 2009). First, we considered two aspects of task performance, accuracy (lack of errors) and efficiency (speed). Assuming that both accuracy and efficiency were equally necessary and important, we defined damage to task performance (DP) using both error rates (E) and unit operation time (T).

$$DP = 0.5S(E) + 0.5S(T) \tag{3}$$

S(E): Standardised E

S(T): Standardised T

Second, we quantified the conditions of visual information based on the idea of complexity. In general, the more crowded the items are, the more complex the information looks. Thus, we defined complexity (C) as the number of items to be attended to (n) divided by their dispersion (M). M was defined as the standard deviation of the distance from each item to the centre of the items (di: i = 1, 2,..., n) divided by the mean of the distances ( ), so that C did not depend on measurement of di.

$$C = n/M = n\bar{d}/\sqrt{\sum_{i=1}^{n}(d_i - \bar{d})^2/(n-1)} \quad (4)$$

We examined the experimental data and found that the relationship between the complexity of the real view ($C_R$), the complexity of the AR-based manual ($C_A$) and DP could be expressed by the following equation.

$$\begin{aligned}\overline{DP} = \\ &(2.57\times10^{-4}C_R + 8.71\times10^{-1})(6.63\times10^{-3}C_A - 8.76\times10^{-1}) \\ &+ (1-(2.57\times10^{-4}C_R + 8.71\times10^{-1})(\frac{1.00\times10^{+2}}{C_A + 6.22}) - 3.00)\end{aligned} \quad (5)$$

Moreover, we suggested that when $C_R$ was given, $C_A$ that minimised DP could be determined by the following equation.

min. $\overline{DP}$

$$\hat{C}_A = \sqrt{\frac{1.00\times10^{+2}(1-(2.57\times10^{-4}\,C_R + 8.71\times10^{-1}))}{6.63\times10^{-3}(2.57\times10^{-4}C_R + 8.71\times10^{-1}))}} - 6.22 \quad (6)$$

Equation (6) provides the effective complexity of AR-based manuals according to the complexity of the real view. Accordingly, it can be regarded as the basic model that describes effective design of AR-based manuals using the number and dispersion of information items.

### 3.4.8 Effect of information presented by HMDs (dynamic background)

(I) Setting details

In this experiment, the blocks displayed on the PC monitor moved left to right at a constant speed (Fig. 34). The numbers on the AR-based manual were synchronised with the blocks (Fig. 35). Thus, the subjects could see the correspondence between them (Fig. 36). A unit operation for a block was defined as clicking a button that had the same number as that given by the AR-based manual. The subjects' task was to operate each block as correctly and quickly as possible. The task was continued for three minutes.

Fig. 34. A pattern of the operational panel

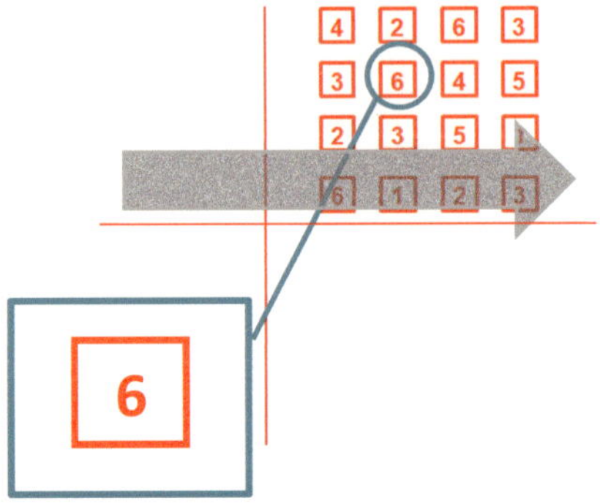


Fig. 35. A pattern of the AR manual

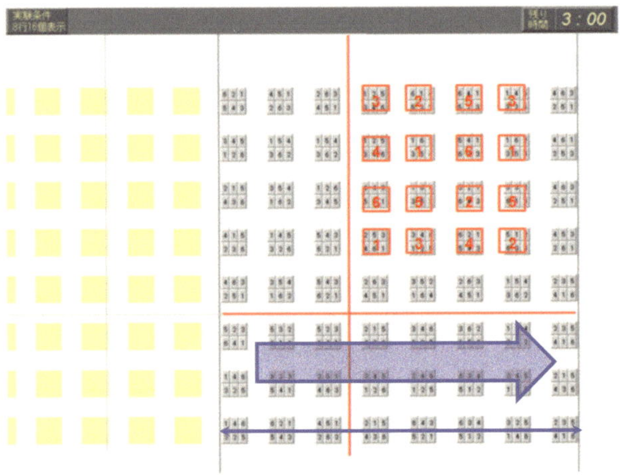


Fig. 36. An overlay of the operational panel and the AR-based manual

We set three levels of complexity for the operational panel by changing the matrix size (m × m): m = 4 (Fig. 37-1), m = 8 (Fig. 37-2) and m = 12 (Fig. 37-3). Furthermore, we set four levels of complexity for the AR-based manual by changing the number of numbers appearing at the same time: 1-indication (1 × 1) (Fig. 38-1), 6-indication (3 × 2) (Fig. 38-2), 8-indication (4 × 2) (Fig. 38-3) and 16-indication (4 × 4) (Fig. 38-4). Twelve conditions were prepared: three levels of complexity of the operational panel × four levels of complexity of the AR-based manual. During the task, if subjects operated the blocks indicated by the AR-based manual, they switched the manual images to refer to the next indication with a keystroke.

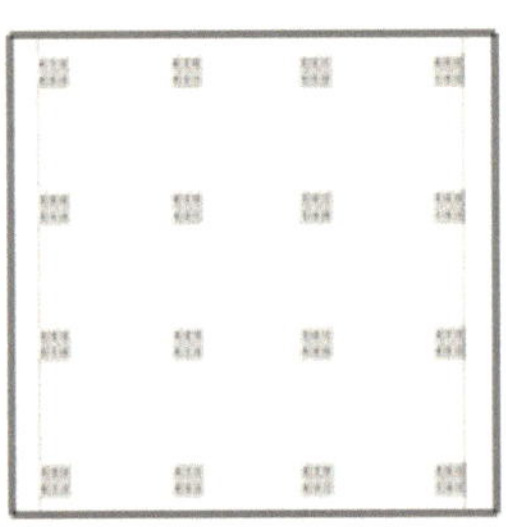

Fig. 37-1. Operational panel (m = 4)

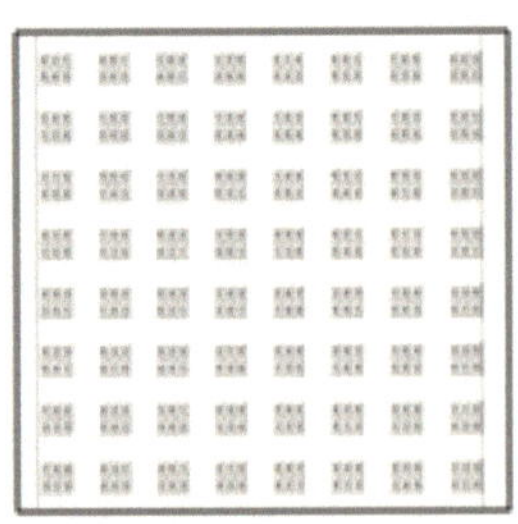

Fig. 37-2. Operational panel (m = 8)

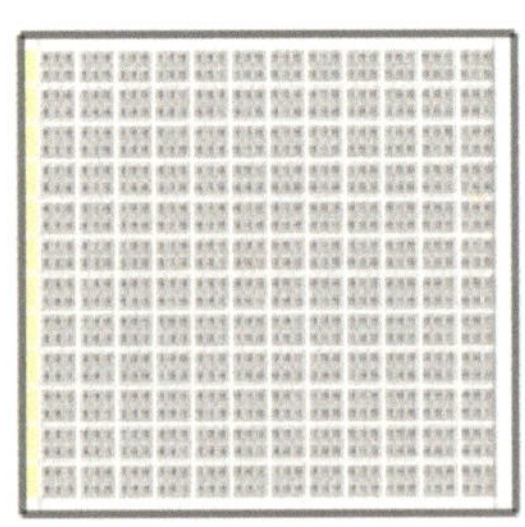

Fig. 37-3. Operational panel (m = 12)

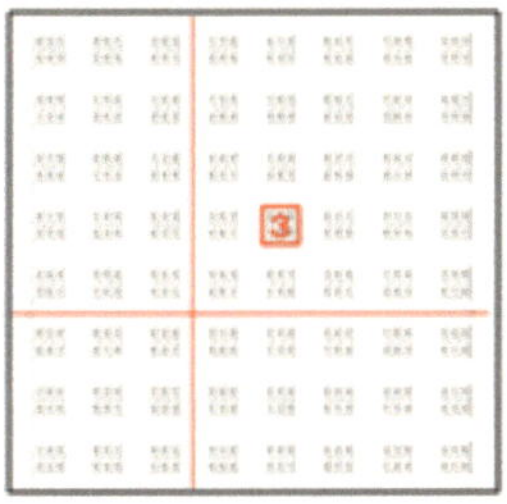

Fig. 38-1.
1-indication (m = 8)

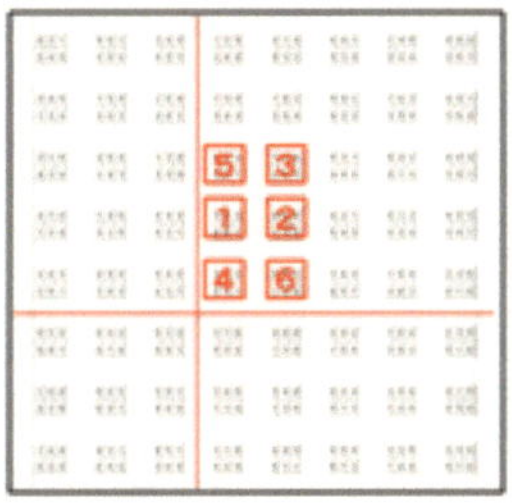

Fig. 38-2.
6-indication (m = 8)

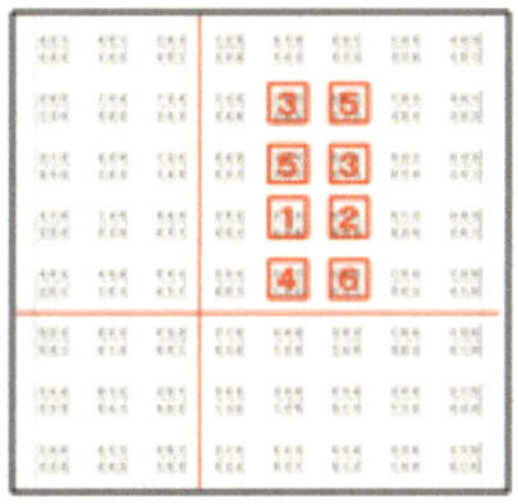

Fig. 38-3.
8-indication (m = 8)

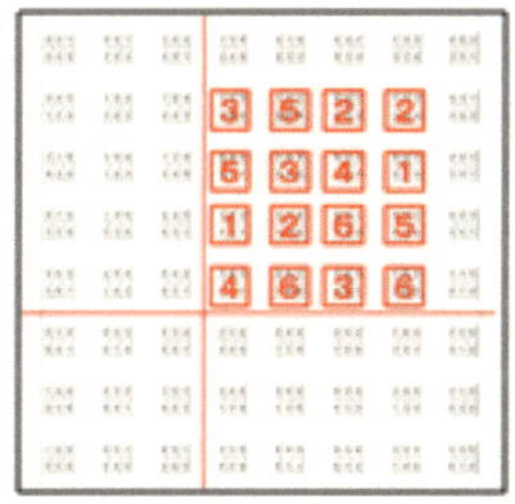

Fig. 38-4.
16-indication (m = 8)

Subjects were 15 students whose right eyes were dominant. They wore RSDs on their non-dominant eye and performed the task once in each of the twelve conditions.

(II) Result

First, we counted the case where a subject clicked on a different numerical button from the number presented by the AR-based manual as an error and calculated the error rate per unit operation. Figs. 39-1, 39-2 and 39-3 show the error rates for each condition of the operational panel (m = 4, 8, 12). The vertical axis is scaled individually for each graph so that the error rates can be compared between the conditions of the AR-based manual under a condition of the operational panel. For any matrix size on the operational panel, the error rate was high when the AR-based manual presented 1-indication. Moreover, as a large number of blocks appeared on the panel, the error rate when the AR-based manual presented 16-indication increased.

Second, we counted the number of blocks that left the PC monitor without any operation as a misoperation and calculated the rate per unit operation. Figs. 40-1, 40-2 and 40-3 show the misoperation rate. These results show a tendency roughly similar to that of the error rate (Fig. 39-1, 39-2 and 39-3).

Because 1-indication required switching the manual images after every operation, it took more time than the other indication patterns. Moreover, because subjects had to adjust the superimposition every time in this case, errors tended to occur. On the other hand, when many blocks existed on the panel, the 16-indication made the distinction between each block more difficult. Further, in particular, when the matrix size was 12 (m = 12) and when the AR-based manual presented 16-indication, the blocks, which were quite close to each other, moved continuously, such that it was not easy for subjects to correctly operate on the block that they intended.

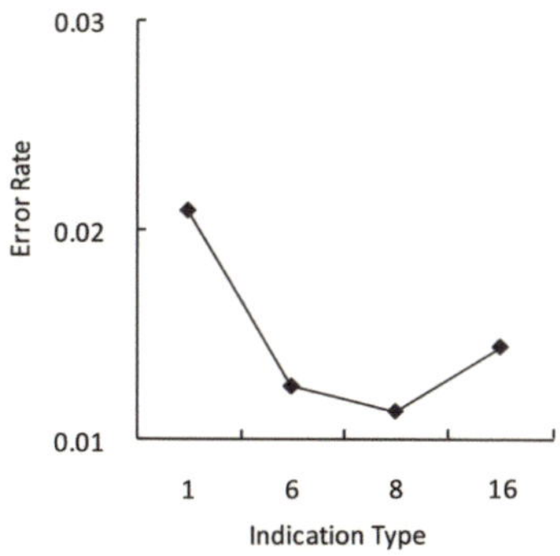


Fig. 39-1. Error rate per operation unit (m = 4)

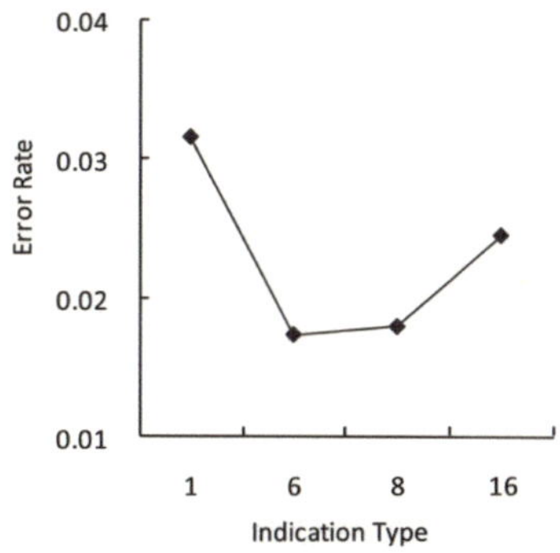


Fig. 39-2. Error rate per operation unit (m = 8)

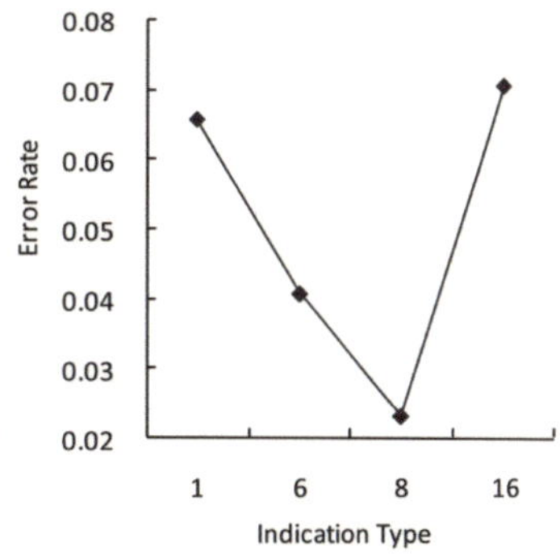


Fig. 39-3. Error rate per operation unit (m = 12)

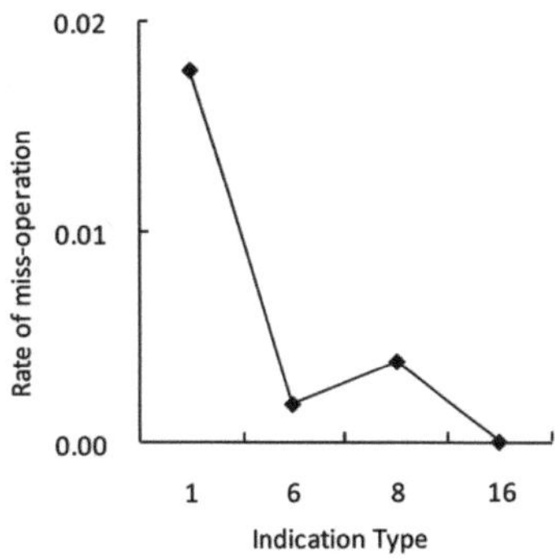


Fig. 40-1. Rate of misoperation (m = 4)

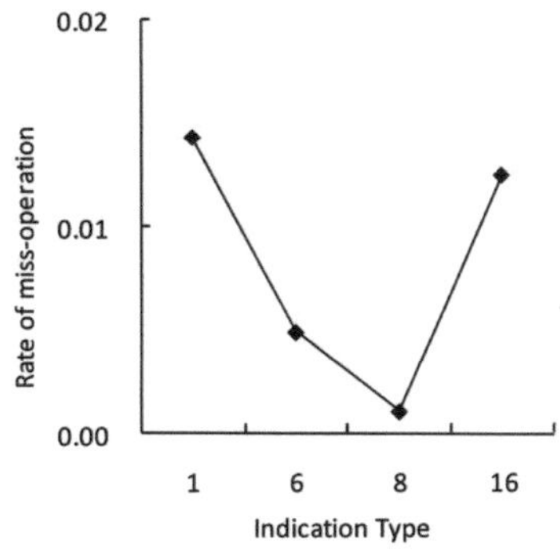


Fig. 40-2. Rate of misoperation (m = 8)

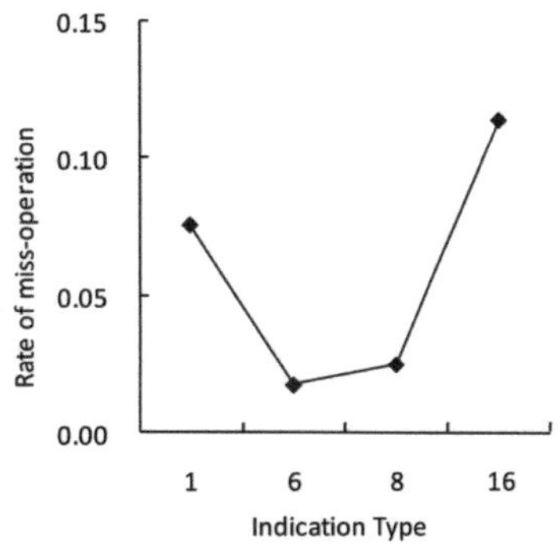


Fig. 40-3. Rate of misoperation (m = 12)

From the above examination, we can understand the relationship between AR manual design and task performance as follows. When the items flow dynamically in real-world conditions, the complexity of visual information depends on the number of items, their dispersion and the distance between neighbouring items. Task performance is damaged if the complexity of the real view and that of an AR-based manual is unbalanced.

As an extra challenge, we tried to build a model that gives the most effective design of AR-based manuals according to real-world conditions (Tamamushi et al., 2009a; Tamamushi et al., 2009b). First, assuming that both aspects of task performance, accuracy (lack of errors) and efficiency (speed), were equally necessary and important, we defined damage to task performance (DP) using both error rates (E) and misoperation rates (L).

$$DP = 0.5S(E) + 0.5S(L) \tag{7}$$

S(E): Standardised E

S(L): Standardised L

Second, we quantified the complexity (C) of visual information that was dynamically flowing using the number of items to be attended to (n), their dispersion (M) and the separation between neighbouring items (s). M was defined as the standard deviation of the distance from each item to the centre of the items ($d_i$: i = 1, 2,..., n).

$$C = \log(e^n / M) = \log(e^n \sqrt{a} / \sqrt{\textstyle\sum_{i=1}^{n} (d_i - \bar{d})^2 / (n-1)}) \tag{8}$$

We examined the experimental data and found that the relationship between the complexity of the real view ($C_R$), the complexity of the AR-based manual ($C_A$) and DP could be expressed by the following equation.

$$\begin{aligned} \overline{DP} &= \\ &(8.66 \times 10^{-1} C_R - 8.02)(1.67 C_A - 6.40) \\ &+ (\frac{-4.40 \times 10^{-1}}{C_A - 6.91 \times 10^{-1}}) + 3.42)(\frac{1.38 \times 10^{+2}}{C_A + 1.38 \times 10}) - 2.14 \times 10^{-3}) \end{aligned} \tag{9}$$

Moreover, we suggested that when $C_R$ was given, $C_A$ that minimised DP could be determined by the following equation.

min. $\overline{DP}$

$$\hat{C}_A = \sqrt{\frac{1.38 \times 10^{+2}(-4.00 \times 10^{-1} / (C_R + 6.91 \times 10^{-1}) + 3.42))}{1.67(8.66 \times 10^{-1} C_R - 8.02)}} - 1.38 \times 10 \qquad (10)$$

Equation (10) provides the effective complexity of AR-based manuals according to the complexity of the real view. Accordingly, it can be regarded as the basic model, which gives effective design of AR-based manuals when the items are dynamically flowing in real-world conditions.

## 4. Human factor guideline for applying AR-based manuals

We clarified experimentally the conditions favourable for the effective use of AR-based manuals in actual work situations, particularly considering that AR manuals require users to wear HMDs and to view digital images superimposed on the real view. Based on the results, a human factor guideline for effective use of AR manuals is proposed as follows.

1. Difficulty in preparing to use AR-based manuals:
   It is easy to prepare to use either STDs or RSDs. Thus, there is no disadvantage compared to traditional paper-based manuals. Simple and compact HMDs just like glasses are expected to be developed in the near future, allowing workers to more easily use AR-based manuals.
2. Effect of eyesight correction:
   Workers with contact lens can use AR-based manuals with either STDs or RSDs as well as workers with good eyesight. Although it is currently difficult for workers wearing glasses to also wear HMDs, this is simply a technical problem. Depending on their needs, it is fully possible to redesign HMDs for workers wearing glasses.
3. Effect of eye dominance:
   Wearing STDs or RSDs on the non-dominant eye is recommended when these are used for presenting AR-based manuals in assembling or inspecting tasks, because it is of primary importance for workers to clearly see real-world objects. Design of the AR-based manuals should be simple enough for the workers to easily read them with their non-dominant eye.
4. Effect of surrounding illumination:
   There is almost no problem in using AR-based manuals under standard illumination. However, under extremely high or low illumination, RSDs should be better. If workers have to perform a difficult task under morning sunshine or a delicate task in a dark laboratory, they may not clearly read a paper-based manual; however, they can clearly read an AR-based manual presented by an RSD.
5. Workload:
   AR-based manuals do not add more workload than paper-based manuals do. In fact, AR-based manuals enable workers to refer to task-related information without using their hands, increasing task efficiency, so they can reduce the workload compared with the traditional way.
6. Attention to surroundings:

Workers can easily notice changes in their surroundings even when they wear STDs or RSDs. In current situations, a problem remains because the frame of these HMDs blocks part of a worker's view; however, the design is fully expected to be improved in the near future.

7. Effect of information presented by HMDs (static background):
   When the real background is static, the effective complexity of AR-based manuals can be determined according to the complexity of the real view, which is described by the following formula.

$$\hat{C}_A = \sqrt{\frac{1.00 \times 10^{+2}(1-(2.57 \times 10^{-4}\, C_R + 8.71 \times 10^{-1}))}{6.63 \times 10^{-3}(2.57 \times 10^{-4} C_R + 8.71 \times 10^{-1}))}} - 6.22 \qquad (6)'$$

   Figs. 41-1, 41-2, 41-3, 41-4 and 41-5 show rough examples of the effective complexity when the background real view is static.

8. Effect of information presented by HMDs (dynamic background):
   When the real background is dynamically flowing, as products move on a conveyer belt, the effective complexity of AR-based manuals can be determined according to the complexity of the real view, which is described by the following formula.

$$\hat{C}_A = \sqrt{\frac{1.38 \times 10^{+2}(-4.00 \times 10^{-1} / (C_R + 6.91 \times 10^{-1}) + 3.42))}{1.67(8.66 \times 10^{-1} C_R - 8.02)}} - 1.38 \times 10 \qquad (10)'$$

Figs. 42-1, 42-2 and 42-3 show rough examples of the effective complexity when the real background view is dynamic.

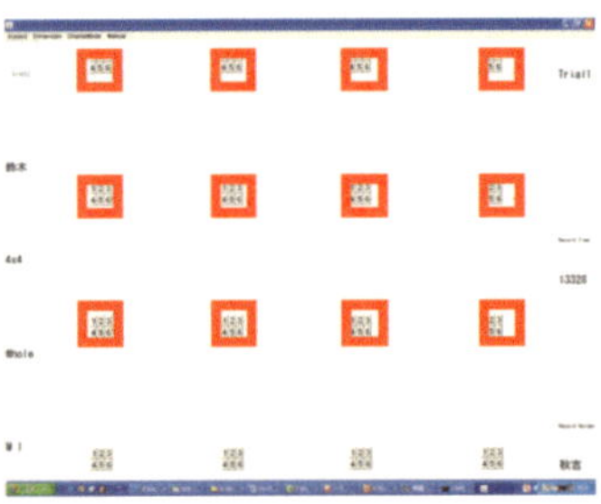

Fig. 41-1. An example of effective complexity (m = 4)

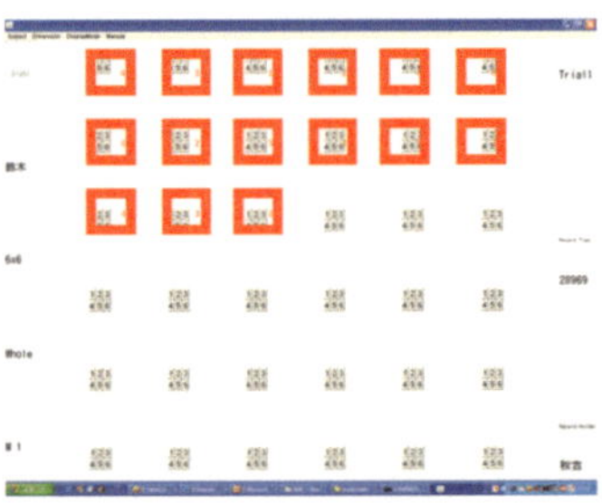

Fig. 41-2. An example of effective complexity (m = 6)

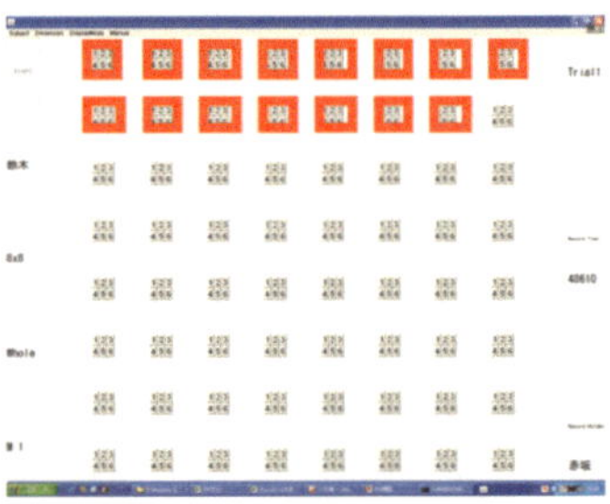

Fig. 41-3. An example of effective complexity (m = 8)

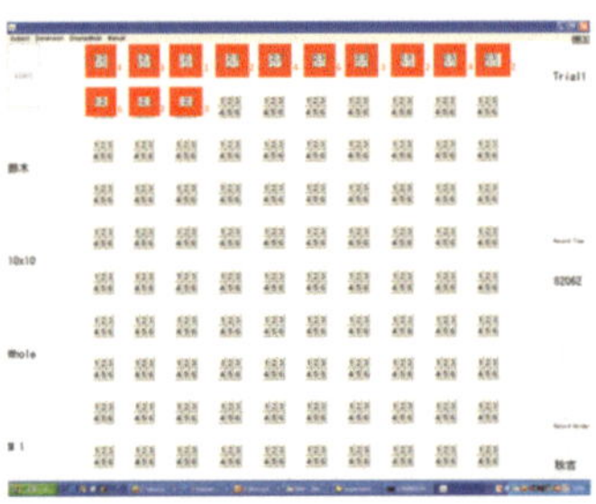

Fig. 41-4. An example of effective complexity (m = 10)

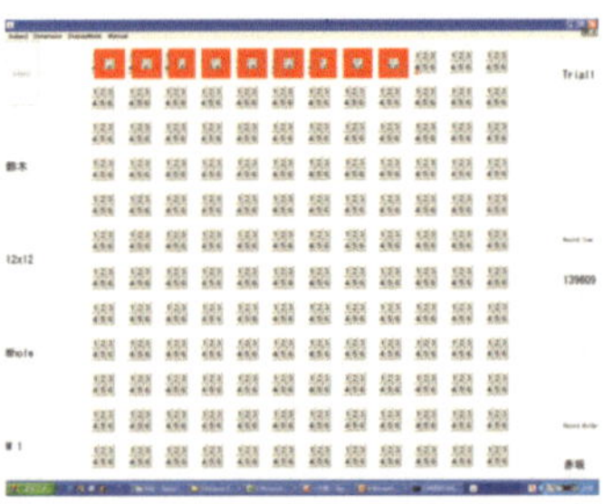

Fig. 41-5. An example of effective complexity (m = 12)

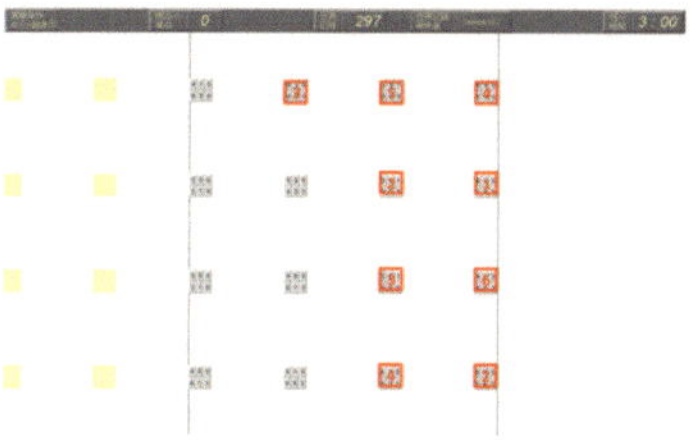

Fig. 42-1. An example of effective complexity (m = 4)

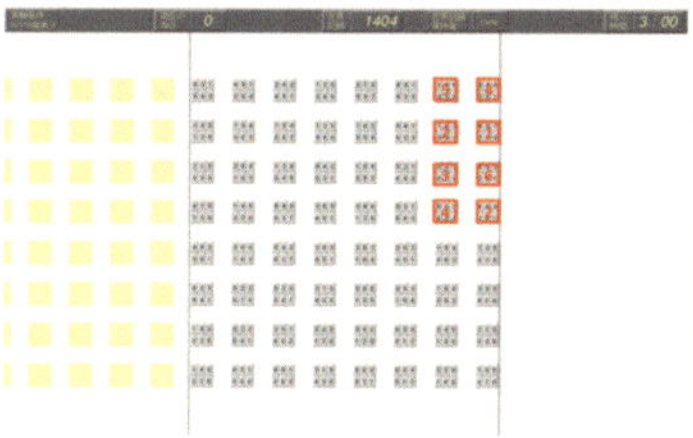

Fig. 42-2. An example of effective complexity (m = 8)

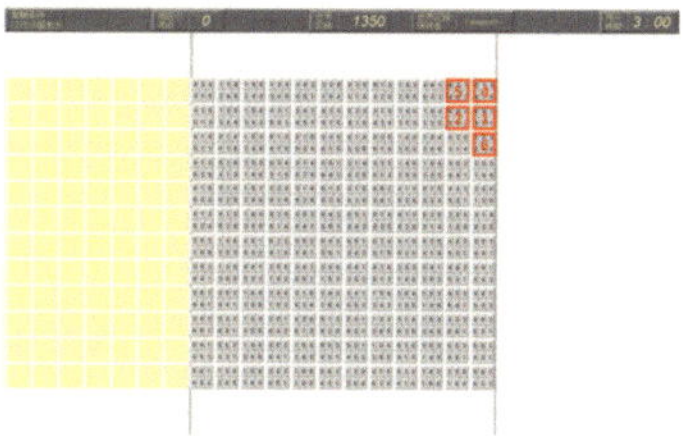

Fig. 42-3. An example of effective complexity (m = 12)

## 5. Conclusion

In this chapter, first, we introduced experimental data showing that an AR-based manual helped reduce errors and enhanced task performance compared to the traditional paper-based manual, and demonstrated that AR manuals show promise for practical use. Second, considering that the main characteristics of using an AR-based manual are wearing HMDs and superimposing a digital image on the real view, we showed the results of detailed experiments conducted to clarify the human factor requirements that should be examined before practical use. Furthermore, we summarised these results and provided a guideline for effective use of an AR-based manual by workers.

Although some imperfect points remain in the usability of an HMD, which plays a major role in an AR-based manual, in current situations these can be addressed by rising demand and continued efforts of developers. In fact, a certain Japanese manufacturing corporation has developed a compact and light HMD that looks like glasses, and some industries are interested in introducing it into their operations.

New application will be expanded into other fields by the mutual advance of both users' needs and technical development. In the case of an AR-based manual, although the technical aspects are maturing rapidly, information concerning the influence of its introduction on workers or the restrictions in using it has not been sufficiently provided to field workers yet. Accordingly, workers have not been able to discuss and judge, based on data, whether they should choose an AR-based manual instead of the paper-based manual used in the past. We are sure that the contents of this chapter complement such information and we hope that it helps workers understand AR-based manuals and triggers dramatic improvement in industrial settings.

## 6. References


Akasaka, T.; Nakanishi, M. & Okada, Y. (2007). Appropriate Complexity of Image Displayed on Head-Mounted Displays in Augmented Reality, *Proceedings of the 12th International Conference on HCI (Human Computer Interaction)*, CD-ROM

Hayashi, Y.; Ogi, K.; Nakamura, S.; Yazu, Y. & Yukimachi, T. (1981). *Ergonomics (in Japanese)*, Japanese Standards Association, pp. 152-167

Ito, Y. (1988). The relationship between the changes of biophysiological reactions and subjective mental workload in the typing tasks under time pressures, *Japan Ergonomics Society*, Vol. 24, No. 4, pp. 253-260

JIS Z 9110-1979. (1979). *Recommended Levels of Illumination*, Japan Standards Association

Institute for Science of Labour. (1970). Questionnaires on Self-Conscious Stress (in Japanese), *Digest of Science of Labour*, Vol.25, No. 6, pp. 12-33

Nakanishi, M. & Okada, Y. (2003). A Study on Application of a Monocular See-Through Head-Mounted Display for Visual Tracking, *Proceedings of IEA (International Ergonomics Association) XVth Triennial Congress*, CD-ROM

Nakanishi, M. & Okada, Y. (2004). A Study on Application of a Monocular See-Through Head Mounted Display for Air Traffic Control System, *Proceedings of the 7th International Conference on WWCS (Work with Computing Systems)*, CD-ROM

Nakanishi, M. & Okada, Y. (2005). Information Sharing by Using Monocular See-Through Head-Mounted Displays for Cooperative Work in Air Traffic Control Systems, *Proceedings of the 11th International Conference on HCI (Human Computer Interaction)*, CD-ROM

Nakanishi, M. & Okada, Y. (2006a). Practicability of using active guidance with retinal scanning display in sequential operations, *Proceedings of IEA (International Ergonomics Association) 2006 Triennial Congress*, CD-ROM

Nakanishi, M. & Okada, Y. (2006b). Development of an Instruction System with Augmented Reality Technology -for supporting both skilled and unskilled workers-, *Proceedings of INSCIT(International Conference on Multidisciplinary Information Sciences and Technologies)*, pp. 112-116

Nakanishi, M.; Miura, T. & Okada, Y. (2007). How does the Digital Manual with Controllability and Perfect-Transparency Effect on Workers' Cognitive Processes? -Application of Augmented Reality Technology to Manufacturing Work-, *Proceedings of the 4th International Conference on CITSA(Cybernetics and Information Technologies, Systems and Applications)*, CD-ROM

Nakanishi, M.; Ozeki, M.; Akasaka, T. & Okada, Y. (2007). Human Factor Requirements for Applying Augmented Reality to Manuals in Actual Work Situations, *IEEE Systems Man & Cybernetics 2007*, CD-ROM

Nakanishi, M.; Akasaka, T. & Okada, Y. (2008). Modeling Approach to "Effective Augmentation" for Designing Manuals with Augmented Reality, *Proceedings of the 2nd International Conference on AHFE (Applied Human Factors and Ergonomics)*, CD-ROM

Nakanishi, M.; Ozeki, M.; Akasaka, T. & Okada, Y. (2008). What Conditions are Required to Effectively Use Augmented Reality for Manuals in Actual Work, *Journal of Multimedia*, Vol.3, No.3, pp. 34-43

Nakanishi, M.; Taguchi, K. & Okada, Y. (2009a). How can visual instruction with see-through HMD be effectively used in safety-critical fields?, *Proceedings of the Asia Pacific Symposium on Safety 2009*, CD-ROM

Nakanishi, M.; Tamamushi, S. & Okada, Y. (2009b). Study for Establishing Design Guidelines for Manuals Using Augmented Reality Technology -Verification and Expansion of the Basic Model Describing "Effective Complexity"-, *Enterprise Information Systems*, pp. 11-16,

Tamamushi, S.; Nakanishi, M. & Okada, Y. (2008a). How to Design of Task-related Information Overlaid by AR Technology -Focusing on Task Characteristics- *Proceedings of the 2nd International Conference on AHFE (Applied Human Factors and Ergonomics)*, CD-ROM

Tamamushi, S.; Nakanishi, M. & Okada, Y. (2008b). Mathematical modelling for determining effective information quantity given by Augmented Reality Manual -Overlay on Dynamic Background-, *Proceedings of Asia Pacific Symposium on Safety 2009*, CD-ROM

Tamamushi, S.; Nakanishi, M. & Okada, Y. (2009). Suitable Amount of Information for an Augmented Reality Manual -Superimposing on Dynamic Actual Field of Vision-, *Proceedings of the 13th International Conference on HCI (Human Computer Interaction)*, CD-ROM

# 9

# AAM and Non-rigid Registration in Augmented Reality

Yuan Tian, Tao Guan and Cheng Wang
*Digital Engineering and Simulation Research Center,*
*Huazhong University of Science and Technology,*
*Wuhan, China*

## 1. Introduction

Augmented Reality copes with the problem of dynamically augmenting or enhancing the real world with computer generated virtual objects [Azuma, 1997; Azuma, 2001]. Registration is one of the most pivotal problems in augmented reality applications. Typical augmented reality applications track 2D patterns on rigid planar objects in order to acquire the pose of the camera in the scene. Although the problem of rigid registration has been widely studied [Yuan et al., 2005; Yuan et al., 2006; Guan et al., 2008a; Guan et al., 2008b; Li et al., 2008], non-rigid registration is recently receiving more and more attention. There are many non-rigid objects existing in the real world such as animated faces, deformable cloth, hand and so forth. How to overlaid virtual objects on the non-rigid objects is particular challenging.

Recently, many related non-rigid registration approaches have been reported. In many cases (e.g. human faces), only a few feature points can be reliably tracked. In [Bartoli et al., 2004], a non-rigid registration method using point and curve correspondences was proposed to solve this problem. They introduced curves into the non-rigid factorization framework because there are several curves (e.g. the hairline, the eyebows) can be used to determine the mapping. The mapping function is computed from both point and curve correspondences. This method can successfully augment the non-rigid object with a virtual object. In [Pilet et al., 2005; Pilet et al., 2007], they presented a real-time method for detecting deformable surfaces with no need whatsoever for a prior pose knowledge. The deformable 2D meshes are introduced. With the use of fast wide baseline matching algorithm, they can superimpose an appropriately deformed logo on the T-shirt. These methods are robust to large deformations, lighting changes, motion blur and occlusions. To align the virtual objects generated by computers with the real world seamlessly, the accurate registration data should be provided. In general, registration can be achieved by solving a point matching problem. The problem is to find the correspondence between two sets of tracked feature points. Therefore, the detection of feature points and the points tracking are the two main problems. Rigid object detection and tracking have been extensively studied and effective, robust, and real-time solutions proposed [Lowe, 2004; Lepetit & Fua, 2005; Lepetit et al., 2005; Rosten & Drummond, 2005]. Non-rigid object detection and tracking is far more complex because the object is deformable and not only the registration data but also a large number of deformation parameters must be estimated.

Active Appearance Models (AAM), introduced a few years ago [Cootes et al., 1998; Cootes et al., 2001], are commonly used to track non-rigid objects, such as faces and hands. There are many methods have been proposed to track non-rigid objects using AAM. A working system for finding and tracking a human face and its features using active appearance models was presented in [Ahlberg, 2001]. A wireframe model is adapted to the face in each image. Then the model is matched to the face in the input image using active appearance algorithm. In [Sung & Kim, 2004], the previous 2D AAM is extended to 3D shape model and modified model fitting algorithm was proposed. In [Markin & Prakash, 2006], occluded images are included into AAM training data to solve the occlusion and self-occlusion problem. This approach can improve the fitting quality of the algorithm.
With known coordinates of 3D points in the world coordinates and the corresponding 2D image points, the camera pose can be estimated. For non-rigid objects, AAM algorithm is a robust method to acquire the 2D image points. It has been proven to be a useful method for matching any of the statistical models to a new image rapidly. The 3D points of the non-rigid objects can be represented by a linear combination of a set of 3D basis shapes. By varying the configuration weights and camera pose parameters, the error between the estimated 2D points (projected by the estimated 3D shapes using estimated camera pose parameters) and 2D tracking points can be minimized.
Many methods have been proposed to recover 3D shape basis from 2D image sequences. In [Tomasi & Kanade, 1992], the factorization method is used to recover shape and motion from a sequence of images under orthographic projection. The image sequence is represented as a measurement matrix. It is proved that under orthography, the measurement matrix is of rank 3 and can be factored into 3D pose and 3D shape matrix. Unfortunately this technique can not be applied to non-rigid deforming objects, since they are based on the rigidity assumption. The technique based on a non-rigid model is proposed to recover 3D non-rigid shape models under scaled orthographic projection [Bregler et al., 2000]. The 3D shape in each frame can be expressed by a linear combination of a set of K basis shapes. Under this model, the 2D tracking matrix is of rank 3K and can be factored into 3D pose, object configuration and 3D basis shapes with the use of SVD.
In this chapter, a novel non-rigid registration method for augmented reality applications with the use of AAM and factorization method is introduced. We focus on AAM algorithm and factorization method which can obtain the 3D shape basis, object configuration and 3D pose simultaneously. The following demonstrations are mainly based on the researches presented in [Tomasi & Kanade, 1992; Cootes et al., 1998; Bregler et al., 2000; Cootes et al., 2001; Xiao et al., 2004; Zhu et al., 2006; Tian et al., 2008]. In section 2, we will have a detailed review of active appearance models and focus on the way of how to track non-rigid objects. In section 3, we will illustrate how to compute the 3D shape basis, the camera rotation matrix and configuration weights of each training frame simultaneously from the 2D tracking data using factorization algorithm. In section 4, we will introduce how to compute the precise configuration weights and camera rotation matrix by optimization method and the experimental results are also given.

## 2. Tracking non-rigid objects using AAM

Tracking non-rigid objects using AAM includes five main steps. The first step is to obtain landmarks in training image set. Then establish the shape model and texture model separately. These two models are unified into one appearance model in the next step. Finally the difference between the closest synthesized AAM model and input image is minimized to get the accurate tracking result. The flowchart is shown in Fig. 1.

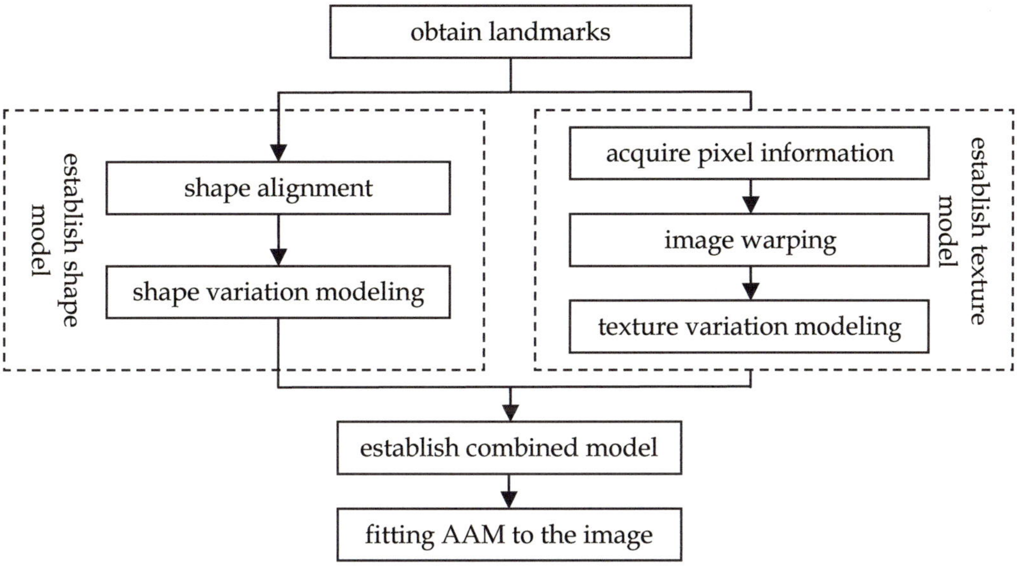


Fig. 1. The flowchart of tracking non-rigid objects using AAM.

## 2.1 Obtain landmarks

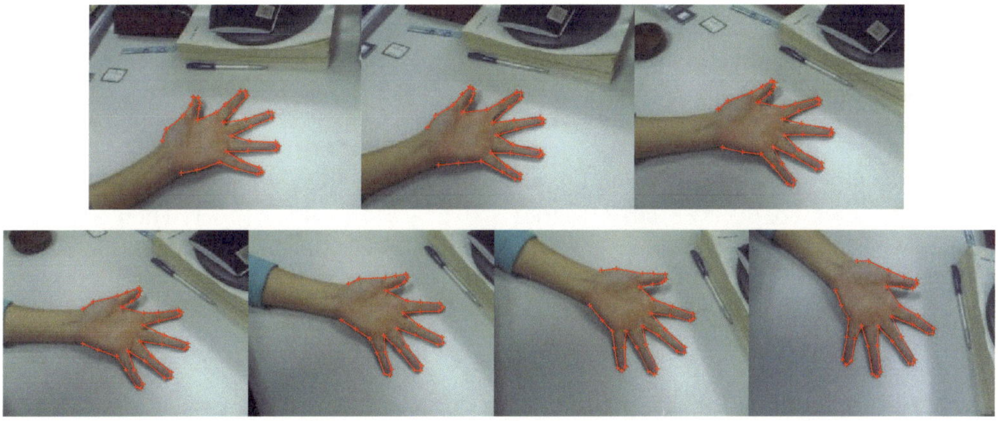

Fig. 2. Examples of traning images manually labeled with consistent landmarks.

Before establishing the models, we should place hundreds of points in each 2D training image. The landmarks in each image should be consistent. We usually choose the points of high curve or junctions as landmark points which will control the shape of the target object strictly. The acquisition process is cumbersome especially when it is done manually. Researchers have looked for different ways to reduce the burden. Ideally, one only need to place points in one image and the corresponding points in the remain traning images can be found automatically. Obviously, this is impossible. However many semi-automatic methods

have been proposed and can successfully find the correspondences accross an image set. Here we focus on the tracking procedure, more details about semi-autometic placement of landmarks can be found in [Sclaroff & Pentland, 1995; Duta et al., 1999; Walker et al., 2000; Andresen & Nielsen, 2001]. The examples of training images manually labeled with consistent landmarks are shown in Fig. 2. We use 7 training images taken from different viewpoints. Each image is labeled with 36 landmarks shown as the " × " in the figures.
Given a training image set with key landmark points are marked on each example object, we can establish the shape and texture variations. These approaches will be detailedly illustrated in the following sections.

### 2.2 Establish shape model

Suppose $L$ denotes the number of shapes in a training image set and $m$ is the number of key landmark points on each image. The vector representation for each shape would then be:

$$X_i = \left[x_1, x_2, \ldots, x_m, y_1, y_2, \ldots, y_m\right]^T, \; i = 1, 2, \ldots, L \tag{1}$$

Then the training image set $\Omega = (X_1, X_2, \ldots, X_L)$.
The shape and pose (include position, scale and rotation) of the object in each training image is different, so the shapes should be aligned to filter out the pose effects. We will first explain how to align two shapes and then extend it to a set of shapes.
If $X$ and $X'$ are two shape vectors, the goal is to minimize the square sum of corresponding landmarks after alignment using similarity transformation technique. That is to minimize $E$:

$$E = \left|T(X) - X'\right|^2 \tag{2}$$

where

$$T\begin{pmatrix} x \\ y \end{pmatrix} = \begin{pmatrix} u & -v \\ v & u \end{pmatrix}\begin{pmatrix} x \\ y \end{pmatrix} + \begin{pmatrix} t_x \\ t_y \end{pmatrix} \tag{3}$$

Choose three kinds of transformation factors: scale factor-$s$, rotation factor-$\theta$ and translation factor-$t$. And $u = s \cdot \cos\theta$, $v = s \cdot \sin\theta$. Hence $s^2 = u^2 + v^2$, $\theta = \tan^{-1}(v/u)$. Then equation (2) can be rewritten as:

$$E(u, v, t_x, t_y) = \left|T(X) - X'\right|^2 = \sum_{i=1}^{m}(ux_i - vy_i + t_x - x'_i)^2 + (vx_i + uy_i + t_y - y'_i)^2 \tag{4}$$

To solve the minimum value of equation (4) is equivalent to let the partial derivative equals to zero. Then the transformation parameters are:

$$u = \frac{(x \cdot x')}{|x|^2}, \; v = \frac{\sum_{i=1}^{m}(x_i y'_i - y_i x'_i)}{|x|^2}, \; t_x = \frac{1}{m}\sum_{i=1}^{m} x'_i, \; t_y = \frac{1}{m}\sum_{i=1}^{m} y'_i \tag{5}$$

The alignment of a set of shapes can be processed by iterative approach suggested by [Bookstein, 1996]. The detailed process is shown in Table 1.
So the new training image set $\hat{\Omega} = (\hat{X}_1, \hat{X}_2, \ldots, \hat{X}_L)$. The mean shape is calculated by:

Step 1: Choose one shape as the initial estimate of the mean shape.
Step 2: Scale the mean shape so that $|\bar{X}_0| = 1$.
Step 3: Align all the remaining shapes to the mean shape using the method described above.
Step 4: Re-estimate the mean shape from aligned shapes.
Step 5: Scale the new mean shape so that $|\bar{X}_{new}| = 1$.
Step 6: If the new calculated mean shape doesn't change significantly, convergence is declared; else return to step 3.

Table 1. The process of aligning a set of shapes.

$$\bar{X} = \frac{1}{L}\sum_{i=1}^{L}\hat{X}_i \tag{6}$$

The covariance matrix can thus be given as:

$$\sum\nolimits_s = \frac{1}{L-1}\sum_{i=1}^{L}(\hat{X}_i - \bar{X})(\hat{X}_i - \bar{X})^T \tag{7}$$

Calculate the eigenvalue $\lambda_{s,i}$ of $\sum_s$ and the corresponding eigenvector $\eta_{s,i}$:

$$\sum \eta_{s,i} = \lambda_{s,i}\eta_{s,i} \tag{8}$$

Sort all the eigenvalues in descending order:

$$\lambda_{s,i} \geq \lambda_{s,i+1}, \; i = 1,2,\ldots,2m-1 \tag{9}$$

The corresponding set of eigenvectors is $\mathrm{H}_s = [\eta_{s,1}, \eta_{s,2}, \ldots, \eta_{s,2m}]$.

To reduce the computational complexity, the principal component analysis (PCA) method is used to reduce the space dimensions. Choose $t$ largest eigenvalues which satisfy the following condition:

$$\sum_{i=1}^{t}\lambda_{s,i} \geq 0.98\left(\sum_{i=1}^{2m}\lambda_{s,i}\right) \tag{10}$$

Then any shape instance can be generated by deforming the mean shape by a linear combination of eigenvectors:

$$\hat{X} \approx \bar{X} + \Phi_s b_s \tag{11}$$

where $\Phi_s$ is a matrix of dimension $2m \times t$ and contains $t$ eigenvectors corresponding to the largest eigenvalues, $\Phi_s = (\varphi_{s,1} | \varphi_{s,2} | \ldots | \varphi_{s,t})$. $b_s$ is a $t$ dimensional vector and the eigenvectors are mutually orthogonal, so it can be given by:

$$b_s = \Phi_{-1}^{s}(\hat{X} - \bar{X}) = \Phi_s^T(\hat{X} - \bar{X}) \tag{12}$$

By varying the elements of $b_s$, new shape instance can be generated using equation (11).

### 2.3 Establish texture model

To establish a complete appearance model, not only the shape but also the texture should be considered. We should firstly acquire the pixel information over the region covered by the landmarks on each training image. Then the image warping method is used to consistently collect the texture information between the landmarks on different training images. Finally establish the texture model using the PCA method.

The texture of a target object can be represented as:

$$g = [g_1, g_2, \ldots, g_n]^T \tag{13}$$

where $n$ denotes the number of pixel samples over the object surface.

In an image, the target object may occupy a small region of the whole image. The pixel intensities and global changes in illumination are different in each training image. The most important information is the texture that can reflect the characteristic of the target object. Due to the number of pixels in different target region is different and it is difficult to acquire the accurate corresponding relationship between different images, the texture model can not be established directly. We need to obtain a texture vector with the same dimension and corresponding relationship. So we warp each example image so that its control points match the reference shape. The process of image warping is described as follows:

Firstly, apply Delaunay triangulation to the reference shape to obtain the reference mesh which is consisted of a set of triangles. We choose the mean shape as the reference shape.

Secondly, suppose $v_1$, $v_2$ and $v_3$ are three vertices of a triangle in the example mesh, any internal point $v$ of the triangle can be written as:

$$v = v_1 + \beta(v_2 - v_1) + \gamma(v_3 - v_1) = \alpha v_1 + \beta v_2 + \gamma v_3 \tag{14}$$

where $\alpha + \beta + \gamma = 1$. Constrain $0 \le \alpha, \beta, \gamma \le 1$ because $v$ is inside the triangle. Given $v = [x, y]^T$, $v_1 = [x_1, y_1]^T$, $v_2 = [x_2, y_2]^T$, $v_3 = [x_3, y_3]^T$, then $\alpha, \beta, \gamma$ can be calculated by:

$$\alpha = 1 - (\beta + \gamma) \tag{15}$$

$$\beta = \frac{yx_3 - x_1 y - x_3 y_1 - y_3 x + x_1 y_3 + x y_1}{-x_2 y_3 + x_2 y_1 + x_1 y_3 + x_3 y_2 - x_3 y_1 - x_1 y_2} \tag{16}$$

$$\gamma = \frac{xy_2 - xy_1 - x_1 y_2 - x_2 y + x_2 y_1 + x_1 y}{-x_2 y_3 + x_2 y_1 + x_1 y_3 + x_3 y_2 - x_3 y_1 - x_1 y_2} \tag{17}$$

Finally, the corresponding point $v'$ of the triangle in the reference mesh can be calculated by:

$$v' = v_1' + \beta(v_2' - v_1') + \gamma(v_3' - v_1') = \alpha v_1' + \beta v_2' + \gamma v_3' \tag{18}$$

where $v_1'$, $v_2'$ and $v_3'$ are the vertices of the corresponding triangle in the reference mesh.

After image warping process, each shape in the training set is warped to the reference shape and sampled. The influence from the global linear changes in pixel intensities is removed.

To reduce the effects that caused by global lighting variations, the example samples are normalized by applying a scaling $a$ and offset $b$:

$$g' = (g'_1, g'_2, g'_3, \ldots, g'_n) = (\frac{g_1 - b}{a}, \frac{g_2 - b}{a}, \frac{g_3 - b}{a}, \ldots, \frac{g_n - b}{a}) \quad (19)$$

where

$$b = \frac{1}{n}\sum_{i=1}^{n} g'_i \, , \; a = \sigma \, , \; \sigma^2 = \frac{1}{n}\sum_{i=1}^{n} (g'_i - b)^2 \quad (20)$$

The establishment of the texture model is identical to the establishment of the shape model which is also analyzed by PCA approach. The mean texture is calculated by:

$$\bar{g} = \frac{1}{L}\sum_{i=1}^{L} g'_i \quad (21)$$

The covariance matrix can thus be given as:

$$\sum_g = \frac{1}{L-1}\sum_{i=1}^{L} (g'_i - \bar{g})(g'_i - \bar{g})^T \quad (22)$$

Calculate the eigenvalue $\lambda_{g,i}$ of $\sum_g$ and the corresponding eigenvector $\eta_{g,i}$:

$$\sum \eta_{g,i} = \lambda_{g,i} \eta_{g,i} \quad (23)$$

Sort all the eigenvalues in descending order:

$$\lambda_{g,i} \geq \lambda_{g,i+1} \, , \; i = 1, 2, \ldots, 2n - 1 \quad (24)$$

The corresponding set of eigenvectors is $\mathrm{H}_g = [\eta_{g,1}, \eta_{g,2}, \ldots, \eta_{g,2n}]$.

To reduce the computational complexity, the PCA method is used to reduce the space dimensions. Choose $t$ largest eigenvalues which satisfy the following condition:

$$\sum_{i=1}^{t} \lambda_{g,i} \geq 0.98 \left( \sum_{i=1}^{2n} \lambda_{g,i} \right) \quad (25)$$

Then any texture instance can be generated by deforming the mean texture by a linear combination of eigenvectors:

$$g' \approx \bar{g} + \Phi_g b_g \quad (26)$$

where $\Phi_g$ is a matrix of dimension $2n \times t$ and contains $t$ eigenvectors corresponding to the largest eigenvalues, $\Phi_g = (\phi_{g,1} | \phi_{g,2} | \ldots | \phi_{g,t})$. $b_g$ is a $t$ dimensional vector and the eigenvectors are mutually orthogonal, so it can be given by:

$$b_g = \Phi_g^{-1}(g' - \bar{g}) = \Phi_g^T (g' - \bar{g}) \quad (27)$$

By varying the elements of $b_g$, new texture instance can be generated using equation (26).

### 2.4 Establish combined model

Since the shape model and texture model have been established, any input image can be represented using the shape parameter vector $b_s$ and texture parameter vector $b_g$. Since there are some correlations between shape and texture variations, the new vector $b$ can be generated by combining $b_s$ and $b_g$:

$$b = \begin{pmatrix} W_s b_s \\ b_g \end{pmatrix} = \begin{pmatrix} W_s \Phi_s^T (\hat{X} - \overline{X}) \\ \Phi_g^T (g' - \overline{g}) \end{pmatrix} \tag{28}$$

where $W_s$ is a diagonal matrix which adjust the weighting between pixel distances and pixel intensities. $W_s$ is calculated by:

$$W_s = rI = \begin{bmatrix} r & \cdots & 0 \\ \vdots & \ddots & \vdots \\ 0 & \cdots & r \end{bmatrix} \tag{29}$$

where $r^2$ is the ratio of the total intensity variation to the total shape variation:

$$r = \frac{\lambda_g}{\lambda_s}, \quad \lambda_g = \sum \lambda_{g,i}, \quad \lambda_s = \sum \lambda_{s,i} \tag{30}$$

Apply PCA on $b$, then

$$b = \Phi_c c \tag{31}$$

where $\Phi_c$ is the eigenvectors of covariance matrix corresponding to $b$:

$$\Phi_c = \begin{pmatrix} \Phi_{c,s} \\ \Phi_{c,g} \end{pmatrix} \tag{32}$$

$c$ is a vector of appearance model parameters controlling both the shape and texture of the models.

Using the linear nature of the model, the combined model including shape $X$ and texture $g$ can be expressed as:

$$X = \overline{X} + \Phi_s W^{-1} \Phi_{c,s} c \tag{33}$$

$$g = \overline{g} + \Phi_g \Phi_{c,g} c \tag{34}$$

Then a new image can be synthesised using equation (33) and (34) for a given $c$.

### 2.5 Fitting AAM to the input image

Fitting a AAMs to an image is considered to be a problem of minimizing the error between the input image and closest model instance [Wang et al., 2007]:

$$\delta I = I_{image} - I_{model} \tag{35}$$

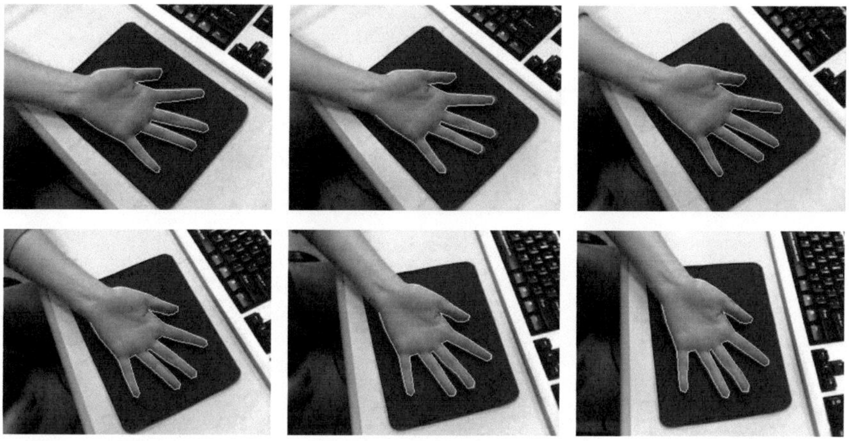

Fig. 3. Results of tracking hand using AAM fitting.

where $I_{image}$ is the texture vector of the input image, and $I_{model}$ is the texture vector of the model instance. The goal is to adjust the appearance model parameters $c$ to minimize $|\delta I|^2$. The simplest way is to construct a linear relationship:

$$\delta c = R\delta I \tag{36}$$

where $R$ can be computed by the following process:

- Suppose $c_0$ is the model parameter of the current image, new model parameter $c$ can be generated by variating $c_0$:

$$c = c_0 + \delta c \tag{37}$$

- Generate new shape model $X$ and normalized texture model $g_m$ according to equation (33) and (34).
- Deform the current image and get the corresponding texture model $g_i$, the difference vector can be written as:

$$\delta g = g_i - g_m \tag{38}$$

$\delta_g$ will change along with the variation of $\delta_c$ and the shape model $X$.
The fitting procedure is shown in Table 2 and the object tracking results are shown in Fig. 3 and Fig. 4. From the tracking results we can see that when the camera moves around the scene, the tracking results are satisfying.

## 3. Factorization algorithm

The flowchart of the factorization algorithm is shown in Fig. 5, and the detailed demonstration will be given in the following sections.

### 3.1 Basic knowledge

The 3D shape of the non-rigid object can be described as a key frame basis set $S_1, S_2, \ldots, S_K$. Each key frame basis $S_i$ is a $3 \times P$ matrix describing $P$ points. The 3D shape of a specific configuration is a linear combination of the basis set:

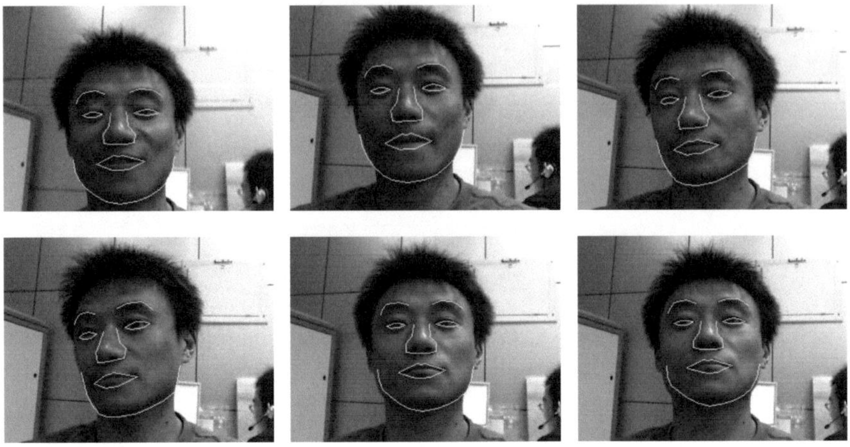

Fig. 4. Results of tracking face using AAM fitting.

Step 1: Generate the normalized texture vector $g_m$.
Step 2: Sample the image $g_i$ below the model shape.
Step 3: Evaluate the error vector $\delta_{g_0} = g_i - g_m$.
Step 4: Evaluate the error $E_0 = |\delta_{g_0}|$.
Step 5: Calculate the pose displacement $\delta_t = R_t \delta_{g_0}$.
Step 6: Calculate the displacement in model parameters $\delta_c = R_c \delta_{g_0}$.
Step 7: Set $i = 1$.
Step 8: Update model parameters $c = c - k_i \delta_c$.
Step 9: Transform the shape to invert the $\delta_t$ transformation.
Step 10: Repeat step 1-4 to form a new error $E_i$.
Step 11: If $E_i > E_0$ set $i = i + 1$ and go to step 8.
Step 12: Accept the new estimate.
where $k = [1.5, 0.5, 0.125, 0.0125, 0.0625]^T$ is the damping vector.

Table 2. The procedure of fitting the input image to the model instance.

$$S = \sum_{i=1}^{K} l_i \cdot S_i \qquad S, S_i \in R^{3 \times P}, l_i \in R \tag{39}$$

where $S = \begin{bmatrix} x_1 & x_2 & \dots & x_P \\ y_1 & y_2 & \dots & y_P \\ z_1 & z_2 & \dots & z_P \end{bmatrix}$.

Under a scaled orthographic projection, the $P$ points of $S$ are projected into 2D image points $(u_i, v_i)$:

$$\begin{bmatrix} u_1 & u_2 & \dots & u_P \\ v_1 & v_2 & \dots & v_P \end{bmatrix} = R\left(\sum_{i=1}^{K} l_i S_i\right) + T \tag{40}$$

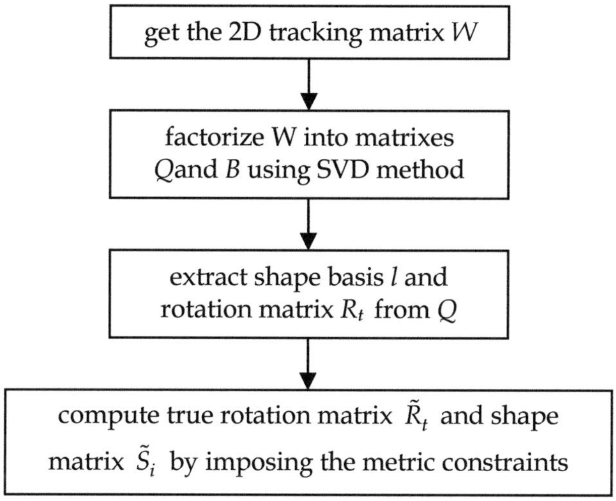


Fig. 5. The flowchart of the factorization algorithm.

$$R = \begin{bmatrix} r_1 & r_2 & r_3 \\ r_4 & r_5 & r_6 \end{bmatrix}, \; T = \begin{bmatrix} t_1 & t_2 & t_3 \end{bmatrix} \tag{41}$$

$R$ contains the first two rows of the 3D camera rotation matrix. $T$ is the camera translation matrix. As mentioned in [Tomasi & Kanade, 1992], we eliminate the camera translation matrix by subtracting the mean of all 2D points, and henceforth can assume that the 3D shape $S$ is centred at the origin.

$$\begin{bmatrix} u_1' & u_2' & \dots & u_P' \\ v_1' & v_2' & \dots & v_P' \end{bmatrix} = \begin{bmatrix} u_1-\bar{u} & u_2-\bar{u} & \dots & u_P-\bar{u} \\ v_1-\bar{v} & v_2-\bar{v} & \dots & v_P-\bar{v} \end{bmatrix} \tag{42}$$

where $\bar{u} = \sum_{i=1}^{P} u_i$, $\bar{v} = \sum_{i=1}^{P} v_i$ .

Therefore, we can rewrite equation (40) as:

$$\begin{bmatrix} u_1' & u_2' & \dots & u_P' \\ v_1' & v_2' & \dots & v_P' \end{bmatrix} = R\left(\sum_{i=1}^{K} l_i S_i\right) \tag{43}$$

Rewrite the linear combination in equation (43) as a matrix-matrix multiplication:

$$\begin{bmatrix} u_1' & u_2' & \dots & u_P' \\ v_1' & v_2' & \dots & v_P' \end{bmatrix} = \begin{bmatrix} l_1 R & l_2 R & \dots & l_K R \end{bmatrix} \cdot \begin{bmatrix} S_1 \\ S_2 \\ \dots \\ S_K \end{bmatrix} \tag{44}$$

The 2D image points in each frame can be obtained using AAM. The tracked 2D points in frame $t$ can be denoted as $(u_{ti}, v_{ti})$. The 2D tracking matrix of $N$ frames can be written as:

$$W = \begin{bmatrix} u'_{11} & u'_{12} & \dots & u'_{1P} \\ v'_{11} & v'_{12} & \dots & v'_{1P} \\ u'_{21} & u'_{22} & \dots & u'_{2P} \\ v'_{21} & v'_{22} & \dots & v'_{2P} \\ \dots & \dots & \dots & \dots \\ u'_{N1} & u'_{N2} & & u'_{NP} \\ v'_{N1} & v'_{N2} & & v'_{NP} \end{bmatrix} \quad (45)$$

Using equation (44) we can rewrite equation (45) as:

$$W = \begin{bmatrix} l_{11}R_1 & l_{12}R_1 & \cdots & l_{1K}R_1 \\ l_{21}R_2 & l_{22}R_2 & \cdots & l_{2K}R_2 \\ \cdots & \cdots & \cdots & \cdots \\ l_{N1}R_N & l_{N2}R_N & \cdots & l_{NK}R_N \end{bmatrix} \cdot \begin{bmatrix} S_1 \\ S_2 \\ \cdots \\ S_K \end{bmatrix} \quad (46)$$

where $R_t$ denotes the camera rotation of frame $t$. $l_{ti}$ denotes the shape parameter $l_i$ of frame $t$.

### 3.2 Solving configuration weights using factorization

Equation (46) shows that the 2D tracking matrix $W$ has rank $3K$, and can be factored into the product of two matrixes: $W = Q \cdot B$, where $Q$ is a $2N \times 3K$ matrix, $B$ is a $3K \times P$ matrix. $Q$ contains the camera rotation matrix $R_t$ and configuration weights $l_{t1}, l_{t2}, \cdots, l_{tK}$ of each frame. $B$ contains the information of shape basis $S_1, S_2, \cdots, S_K$. The factorization can be done using singular value decomposition (SVD) method:

$$W^{2N \times P} = \tilde{U} \cdot \tilde{D} \cdot \tilde{V}^T = \tilde{Q}^{2N \times 3K} \cdot \tilde{B}^{3K \times P} \quad (47)$$

Then the camera rotation matrix $R_t$ and shape basis weights $l_{ti}$of each frame can be extracted from the matrix $\tilde{Q}$:

$$q_t = [l_{t1}R_t \; l_{t2}R_t \cdots l_{tK}R_t] = \begin{bmatrix} l_1r_1 & l_1r_2 & l_1r_3 & \cdots & l_Kr_1 & l_Kr_2 & l_Kr_3 \\ l_1r_4 & l_1r_5 & l_1r_6 & \cdots & l_Kr_4 & l_Kr_5 & l_Kr_6 \end{bmatrix} \quad (48)$$

Transform $q_t$ into a new matrix $\tilde{q}_t$:

$$\tilde{q}_t = \begin{bmatrix} l_1r_1 & l_1r_2 & l_1r_3 & l_1r_4 & l_1r_5 & l_1r_6 \\ l_2r_1 & l_2r_2 & l_2r_3 & l_2r_4 & l_2r_5 & l_2r_6 \\ \cdots & \cdots & \cdots & \cdots & \cdots & \cdots \\ l_Kr_1 & l_Kr_2 & l_Kr_3 & l_Kr_4 & l_Kr_5 & l_Kr_6 \end{bmatrix} = \begin{bmatrix} l_{t1} \\ l_{t2} \\ \vdots \\ l_{tK} \end{bmatrix} \cdot [r_{t1} \quad r_{t2} \quad r_{t3} \quad r_{t4} \quad r_{t5} \quad r_{t6}] \quad (49)$$

here, the $\tilde{q}_t$ can be factored using SVD method.

### 3.3 Solving true rotation matrix and shape basis

As mentioned in [Tomasi & Kanade, 1992], the matrix $\tilde{R}_t$ is a linear transformation of the true rotation matrix $R_t$. Likewise, $\tilde{S}_i$ is a linear transformation of the true shape matrix $S_i$ :

$$R_t = \tilde{R}_t \cdot G \, , \; S_i = G^{-1} \cdot \tilde{S}_i \tag{50}$$

where $G^{3\times 3}$ is found by solving a nonlinear data-fitting problem. In each frame we need to constrain the rotation matrix to be orthonormal. The constraints of frame *t* are:

$$\begin{bmatrix} r_{t1} & r_{t2} & r_{t3} \end{bmatrix} GG^{-1} \begin{bmatrix} r_{t1} & r_{t2} & r_{t3} \end{bmatrix}^T = 1 \tag{51}$$

$$\begin{bmatrix} r_{t4} & r_{t5} & r_{t6} \end{bmatrix} GG^{-1} \begin{bmatrix} r_{t4} & r_{t5} & r_{t6} \end{bmatrix}^T = 1 \tag{52}$$

$$\begin{bmatrix} r_{t1} & r_{t2} & r_{t3} \end{bmatrix} GG^{-1} \begin{bmatrix} r_{t4} & r_{t5} & r_{t6} \end{bmatrix}^T = 0 \tag{53}$$

In summary, given 2D tracking data $W$ , we can get the 3D shape basis $\tilde{S}_i$ , camera rotation matrix $\tilde{R}_t$ and configuration weights $l_{ti}$ of each training frame simultaneously using factorization method.

## 4. Non-rigid registration method

The 2D tracking data can be obtained using the AAM algorithm mentioned in section 2. With the use of the factorization method mentioned in section 3, we can acquire the 3D shape basis. The 3D shape is represented as 3D points in the world coordinates. Given the configuration weights, the 3D shape can be recovered by linear combination of the 3D shape basis. By projecting the 3D points to the 2D image with known camera rotation matrix (suppose the intrinsic camera matrix has been calculated), the estimated 2D points can be acquired. If the error between the 2D tracking data and the estimated 2D points is small enough, we can accept the configuration weights and the rotation matrix. Finally, the virtual object can be overlaid to the real scene using the camera rotation matrix.

The initial configuration weights and camera rotation matrix can not be precise. Optimization of the configuration weights should be done to minimize the error between the 2D tracking points detected by AAM and the estimated 2D points which is projected by the 3D shape points. This is a non-linear optimization problem which can be successfully solved by the optimization methods. Different with [Zhu et al., 2006], we use the Levenberg-Marquardt algorithm. Equation (54) shows the cost function.

$$\sum_j \left\| s_j - s'_j \right\|^2 \to \min = \sum_{j=1}^{N} \left\| s_j - \left( R \sum_{i=1}^{K} l_i S_i \right) \right\|^2 \to \min \tag{54}$$

where $s_j$ is the 2D tracking data $j$ , $s'_j$ is the projected point.

The procedure of non-rigid registration is shown in Table 3.

Step 1: Track the 2D points $s_j$ using AAM.
Step 2: Initialize the configuration weights $l_i$.
Step 3: Initialize the camera rotation matrix $R$.
Step 4: Calculate the 3D shape $S = \sum_{i=1}^{K} l_i S_i$.
Step 5: Project the 3D points $S$ to 2D image: $s'_j = A[R|T] \cdot S$.
Step 6: Evaluate the projection error $E = \sum_{j=1}^{N} \left\| s_j - s'_j \right\|^2$.
Step 7: If $E$ is not small enough, improve $l_i$ and $R$, then repeat step 4-6.
Step 8: Accept the configuration weights $l_i$, and the camera rotation matrix $R$.
Step 9: Overlaid the virtual object to the scene.

Table 3. The procedure of non-rigid registration.

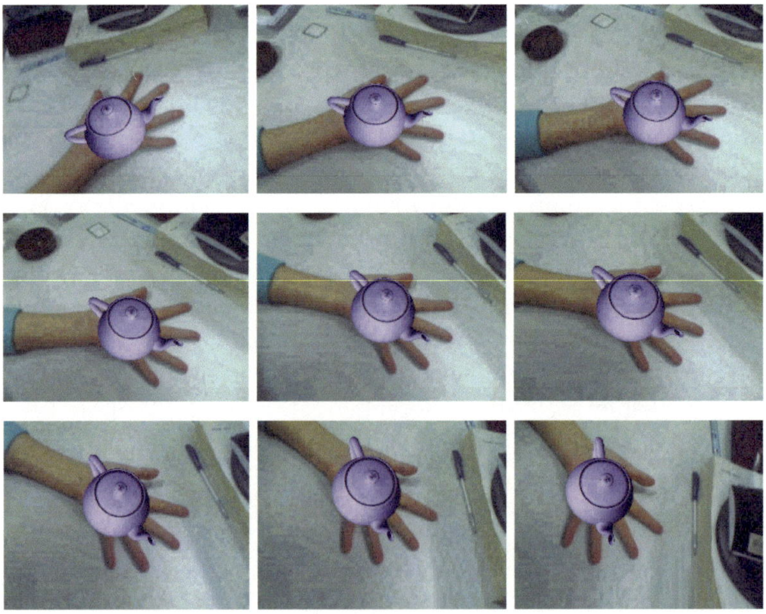

Fig. 6. Examples of augmented images using our method.

Furthermore, we should take the orthonormality of rotation matrix into consideration. The proposed method has been implemented in C using OpenGL and OpenCV on a DELL workstation (CPU 1.7G×2, RAM 1G).
In offline stage, we construct the AAM hand models using 7 training images which are manually labelled with 36 landmarks as shown in Fig. 1. We establish the hand shape basis using 300 training frames which is captured with a CCD camera. In online stage, the 2D points are tracked using AAM algorithm, and then Levenberg-Marquardt algorithm is used to optimize the parameters. Our experiment results are shown in Fig. 6. From the results we can see that the virtual teapot can be overlaid on the hand accurately when the camera moves around the scene.

## 5. Conclusion

In this chapter, a non-rigid registration method for augmented reality applications using AAM and factorization method is proposed. The process is divided into two stages: offline stage and online stage. In the offline stage, the 3D shape basis is constructed. To obtain the shape basis of the object, we firstly factorize the 2D data matrix tracked by the AAM into the product of two matrixes. One matrix contains the camera rotation matrix and the configuration weights, and the other matrix contains the shape basis. Then the rotation matrix and the configuration weights can be separated using SVD method. Finally the orthonormality of the rotation matrix should be the constraints to get the true rotation matrix and configuration weights. In online stage, the 3D pose parameters and the shape coefficients are estimated. The purpose is to minimize the error between the 2D tracking points detected by AAM and the estimated 2D points which is projected by the 3D shape points. The Levenberg-Marquardt method is used to solve this problem. The rotation matrix and the configuration weights are optimized. Some experiments have been conducted to validate that the proposed method is effective and useful for non-rigid registration in augmented reality applications.

## 6. Acknowledgement

This work is supported in part by National Natural Science Foundation of China with project No. 60903095; in part by Postdoctoral Science Foundation of China with project No. 20080440941.

## 7. References

Ahlberg, J. (2001). Using the active appearance algorithm for face and facial feature tracking. *Proceedings of the 2nd International Workshop on Recognition, Analysis, and Tracking of Faces and Gestures in Real-Time Systems*, pp. 68-72, ISBN: 0-7695-1074-4, Vancouver, Canada, July 2001, IEEE Computer Society, Los Alamitos.

Andresen, P. R. & Nielsen, M. (2001). Non-rigid registration by geometry-constrained diffusion. *Medical Image Analysis*, Vol. 5, No. 2, 81-88, ISSN: 1361-8415.

Azuma, R. T. (1997). A survey of augmented reality. *Presence-Teleoperators and Virtual Environments*, Vol. 6, No. 4, 355–385, ISSN: 1054-7460.

Azuma, R. T. (2001). Recent advances in augmented reality. *IEEE Computer Graphics and Applications*, Vol. 21, No. 6, 34–47, ISSN: 0272-1716.

Bartoli, A., von Tunzelmann, E. & Zisserman, A. (2004). Augmenting images of non-rigid scenes using point and curve correspondences. *Proc. IEEE Conf. on Computer Vision and Pattern Recognition*, pp. 699-706, ISBN: 0-7695-2158-4, Washington, DC, June-Junly 2004, IEEE Conputer Society, Los Alamitos.

Bookstein, F. L. (1996). Landmark methods for forms without landmarks: localizing group differences in outline shape. *Proceedings of the IEEE Workshop on Mathematical Methods in Biomedical Image Analysis*, pp. 25–244, ISBN: 0-8186-7367-2, San Francisco, CA, June 1996, IEEE Computer Society, Los Alamitos.

Bregler, C., Hertzmann, A. & Biermann, H. (2000). Recovering non-rigid 3d shape from image streams. *Proceedings of IEEE Conference on Computer Vision and Pattern Recognition*, pp. 690-696, ISSN: 1063-6919, Hilton Head Island, SC, June 2000, IEEE Computer Society, Los Alamitos.

Cootes, T. F., Edwards, G. J. & Taylor, C. J. (1998). Active appearance models. *Lecture Notes in Computer Science*, Vol.1407, 484-498, ISSN: 0302-9743.

Cootes, T. F., Edwards, G. J. & Taylor, C. J. (2001). Active appearance models. *IEEE Transactions on Pattern Analysis and Machine Intelligence*, Vol. 23, No. 6, 681-685, ISSN: 0162-8828.

Cootes, T. F. & Taylor, C. J. (2001). Statistical models of appearance for medical image analysis and computer vision. *Proceedings of the Society of Photo-optical Instrumentation Engineers*, pp. 236-248, ISBN: 0-8194-4008-6, San Diego, CA, February 2001, SPIE-INT Society Engeering, Bellingham.

Duta, N., Jain, A. K. & Dubuisson-Jolly, M.-P. (1999). Learning 2D shape models. *Proceedings of the IEEE Computer Society Conference on Computer Vision and Pattern Recognition*, pp. 8-14, ISSN: 1063-6919, Fort Collins, USA, June 1999, IEEE Computer Society, Los Alamitos.

Guan, T., Li L. J. & Wang, C. (2008a). Registration using multiplanar structures for augmented reality systems. *Journal of Computing and Information Science in Engineering*, Vol. 8, No. 4, 041002-1~041002-6, ISSN: 1530-9827.

Guan, T., Li, L. J. & Wang, C. (2008b). Robust estimation of trifocal tensors using natural features for augmented reality systems. *Computing and Informatics*, Vol. 27, No. 6, 891-911, ISSN: 1335-9150.

Lepetit, V. & Fua, P. (2005). Monocular model-based 3D tracking of rigid objects: a survey. *Foundations and Trends in Computer Graphics and Vision*, Vol. 1, No. 1, 1–89, ISSN: 1572-2740.

Lepetit, V., Lagger, P. & Fua, P. (2005). Randomized trees for real-time keypoint recognition. *Proc. IEEE Conf. on Computer Vision and Pattern Recognition*, pp. 775-781, ISBN: 0-7695-2372-2, San Diego, CA, June 2005, IEEE Computer Society, Los Alamitos.

Li, L. J., Guan, T., Ren, B. et al. (2008). Registration based on Euclidean reconstruction and natural features tracking for augmented reality systems. *Assembly Automation*, Vol. 28, Issue 4, 340-347, ISSN: 0144-5154.

Lowe, D. G. (2004). Distinctive image features from scale-invariant keypoints. *International Journal of Computer Vision*, Vol. 20, No. 2, 91–110, ISSN: 0920-5691.

Markin, E. & Prakash, E. C. (2006). Tracking facial features with occlusions. Journal of Zhejiang University: Science A, Vol. 7, No. 7, 1282-1288, ISSN: 1009-3095.

Pilet, J., Lepetit, V. & Fua, P. (2005). Real-time non-rigid surface detection. *Proc. IEEE Conf. on Computer Vision and Pattern Recognition*, pp. 822-828, ISBN: 0-7695-2372-2, San Diego, CA, June 2005, IEEE Computer Society, Los Alamitos.

Pilet, J., Lepetit, V. & Fua, P. (2007). Fast non-rigid surface detection, registration and realistic augmentation. *International Journal of Computer Vision*, Vol. 76, No. 2, 109-122, ISSN: 0920-5691.

Rosten, E. & Drummond, T. (2005). Fusing points and lines for high performance tracking. *Proceedings of 10th IEEE International Conference on Computer Vision*, pp. 1508-1515, ISBN: 0-7695-2334-X, Beijing, China, October 2005, IEEE Computer Society, Los Alamitos.

Sclaroff, S. & Pentland, A. P. (1995). Modal matching for correspondence and recognition. *IEEE Transactions on Pattern Analysis and Machine Intelligence*, Vol. 17, No. 7, 545–561, ISSN: 0162-8828.

Sung, J. & Kim, D. J. (2004). Extension of AAM with 3D shape model for facial shape tracking. *Proceedings of International Conference on Image Processing*, pp. 3363-3366, ISBN: 0-7803-8554-3, Singapore, October 2004, IEEE, New York.

Tian, Y., Li, Z. Y., Liu, W. et al. (2008). Non-rigid registration using AAM and factorization method for augmented reality applications. *Proceedings of the 2008 12th International Conference on Computer Supported Cooperative Work in Design*, pp. 705-709, ISBN: 978-1-4244-1650-9, Xian, China, April 2008, IEEE, New York.

Tomasi, C. & Kanade, T. (1992). Shape and motion from image streams under orthography: a factorization method. *International Journal of Computer Vision*, Vol. 9, No. 2, 137–154, ISSN: 0920-5691.

Walker, K.N., Cootes, T. F. & Taylor, C. J. (2000). Determining correspondences for statistical models of appearance. *Proceedings of 6th European Conference on Computer Vision*, pp. 829-843, ISBN: 3-540-67685-6, Dublin, Ireland, June 2000, Springer, Berlin.

Wang, S. C., Wang, Y. S., & Chen, X. L. (2007). Weighted active appearance models. *3rd Internatioanl Conference on Intelligent Computing*, pp. 1295-1304, ISBN:978-3-540-74170-1, Qingdao, China, August 2007, Springer, Berlin.

Xiao. J., Baker, S., Matthews, I., & Kanade, T. (2004). Real-time combined 2D+3D active appearance models. *Proceedings of the 2004 IEEE Computer Society Conference on Computer Vision and Pattern Recognition*, pp. 535-542, ISBN: 0-7695-2158-4, Washington, DC, June-July 2004, IEEE Computer Society, Los Alamitos.

Yuan, M. L., Ong, S. K. & Nee, A. Y. C. (2005). Registration based on projective reconstruction technique for augmented reality systems. *IEEE Transactions on Visualization and Computer Graphics*, Vol. 11, No. 3, 254–264, ISSN: 1077-2626.

Yuan, M. L., Ong, S. K. & Nee, A. Y. C. (2006). Registration using natural features for augmented reality systems. *IEEE Transactions on Visualization and Computer Graphics*, Vol. 12, No. 4, 569–580, ISSN: 1077-2626.

Zhu, J. K., Hoi, S. C. H., & Lyu, M. R. (2006). Real-time non-rigid shape recovery via active appearance models for Augmented Reality. *9th European Conference on Computer Vision*, pp. 186-197, ISBN: 3-540-33832-2, Graz, Austria, May 2006, Springer, Berlin.

# 10

# Augmented Reality Applied to Card Games

Hidehiko Okada and Hiroki Arakawa
*Kyoto Sangyo University*
*Japan*

## 1. Introduction

Applications of computer technologies to various entertainments have been researched, known as "entertainment computing" (e.g., kinds of researches have been reported in annual international conferences on this topic, ICEC (Stephane & Jerome, 2009; Scott & Shirley, 2008; Ma et al., 2007)). The aim of our research is to evaluate the effectiveness of augmented reality (AR) user interface for playing card games. Players of a card game need to know rules of the game, so beginners cannot play by themselves until they learn the rules well (or, need help from experienced players). Our idea to solve this problem is a computer system with AR user interface which intuitively guides game plays in the beginners' view. The authors expect that the system enables a beginner to play games even if s/he does not know rules well and learn the rules as s/he plays games with the system (i.e., learn by their game experiences). The authors have been applying our idea to card games and evaluated the effectiveness by experiments with beginner players. In this chapter, the authors report two examples: AR applied to Mate and Bohemian Schneider. These games are selected because the games are relatively minor in Japan (compared with, e.g., poker) and many of us are beginners of the games.

## 2. AR applied to Mate

### 2.1 Game rules

Mate games are played by two players. Twenty cards are used in Mate games: five pieces { A, K, Q, 10 and 7 } of the four suits {♥hearts, ♦diamonds, ♠spades and ♣clubs}. The 20 cards are dealt to the two players, 10 for each. A round includes 10 turns or less. In each turn, a player first opens any card (threat), and then the opponent must open a card that can counter the threat: if the opponent doesn't have any card that can counter the threat, the opponent loses the round. The rules to counter the threat are:

1. if s/he has one or more cards of which the suit is the same as the threat (e.g., ♠), s/he must open a card among them,
2. else if s/he has one or more cards of which the piece is the same as the threat (e.g., K), s/he must open a card among them.

Who opened a card with a higher rank takes initiative in the next turn. Card ranks are as follows.

- Suit ranks (from the highest to the lowest): ♣, ♠, ♥, ♦.
- Piece ranks (from the highest to the lowest): A, 10, K, Q, 7.

If both of the two players opened all the 10 cards, the round is a draw. The winner player of a round gains t * s points where t denotes the number of turns in which the player won the round and s denotes the score of the threat piece with which the player won the round. Piece scores are shown in Table 1. For example, if a player wins a round in the five turns with ♥K, the player gains 20 (=5*4) points. For more details, see a reference book, e.g., (Sackson, 1992).

| Piece | Rank | Score |
|---|---|---|
| A | 1 | 11 |
| K | 3 | 4 |
| Q | 4 | 3 |
| 10 | 2 | 10 |
| 7 | 5 | 7 |

Table 1. Peace ranks and scores in Mate

A Mate beginner will become able to play games by her/himself after s/he learns:

- which card s/he can open to counter the threat,
- which card s/he should open as the threat to win the round, and
- which card s/he should open as the threat to take initiative in the next turn.

Our system should therefore make augmentations appropriately so that a beginner can easily learn these factors.

### 2.2 System configuration

Fig. 1 shows the configuration of our system. Cards opened by players in a game and the deal of a beginner player are continuously captured at a specific frame rate and recognized. CGs for guiding the beginner (e.g., which card in her/his deal is recommended to open) are generated and overlapped to the webcam-captured screen. This system configuration is consistently employed in our card game applications.

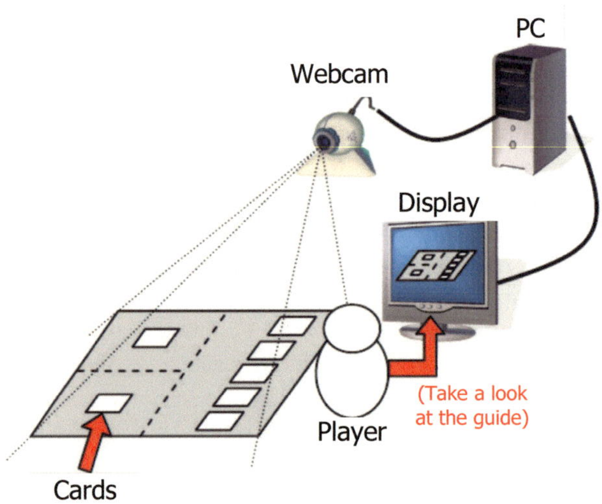


Fig. 1. Configuration of our system

### 2.3 Visual augmentations for beginners

This section illustrates how our system augments the player's view of cards. Fig. 2 shows an example of the webcam screen. Fig. 2(a) is a captured raw screen and Fig. 2(b) is a screen augmented by our software program. The program utilized ARToolkit[1] (Kato & Billinghurst, 1999) for the processes of card recognition and CG augmentation. The authors designed paper cards with bold black frame prints to use each card as an ARToolkit marker.

(a) Raw

(b) Augmented

Fig. 2. Example of webcam screen by our system (the user is to counter the threat)

In this example, the user is to counter the threat opened by the opponent player. The system guides the player to open either of the three ♥s in her/his deal (where the 10 cards in the deal are shown in the lower area of the screen), because the threat card is ♥10. The system augments the webcam screen as follows.

- The threat card is marked with a green frame.
- The recognized suit and piece of the threat card is shown near the card. In the example of Fig. 2(b), the threat card is recognized as ♥10.

[1] http://www.hitl.washington.edu/artoolkit (last accessed: 10/06/2009).

- Cards in the player's deal that can counter the threat are marked as yellow frames. In Fig. 2(b), three cards are marked (♥7, ♥Q and ♥1).
- A card in the player's deal with a higher rank than the threat is marked with a yellow star. The card is a recommended one to open in this turn. In Fig. 2(b), ♥1 is marked with a yellow star because Ace is ranked higher than 10. By countering the ♥10 threat with ♥1, the player can win the current turn and take initiative in the next turn.
- A message for navigating the player which cards are able to open now is briefly shown (in Japanese). In Fig. 2(b), the message shown in the upper-right area (just below the threat card) says "please open a ♥ card because you have ♥s". From the message and the display of the recognized suit & piece of the threat card, the player will learn that s/he can open a card of which the suit is the same as the card the opponent player opened first.

Fig. 3 shows another example of the augmented webcam screen. In this example, the user of the system is to open a card in her/his deal as the threat to the opponent player. In this case, the user can open any card in her/his deal (no constraints for the threat): the system shows this by marking all cards in her/his deal with yellow frames. In addition, the system marks one or more recommended cards with yellow stars: in Fig.3, ♠1 and ♦1 are the recommended ones. In the cases where the user has one or more cards with which the user can win the round (i.e., the opponent cannot counter if the user opens one of the cards as the threat), the system marks them with blinked yellow frames and guides the user with a brief message on the brink-marked cards.

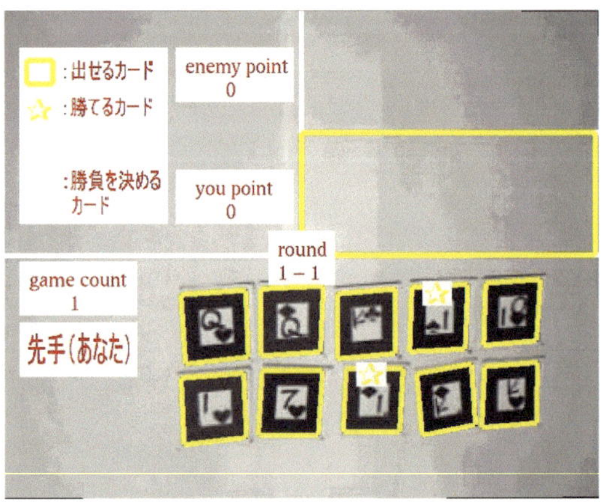


Fig. 3. Example of augmented screen (the user is to open a card as the threat)

Note that the authors do not intend to enable a player to *cheat* by using our system: the system does not tell what the user cannot know even if the user is an experienced. The system neither captures the deal of the opponent player nor shows them to the user.

### 2.4 Evaluation

To evaluate the effectiveness of our idea, the authors had an experiment with Mate beginners. Each beginner played six rounds of Mate games against an experienced player. In the 1st-4th rounds each beginner played with our system, and in the 5th-6th rounds the beginner played without our system. The experienced player always played games without the system. Thus, the ability of our system for (i) guiding a beginner with no rule knowledge

and (ii) helping a beginner learn game rules while playing under the AR guides, can be evaluated by the performances of the beginners in (i) the first four rounds and (ii) the next two rounds respectively.
The experiment took 1.0-1.5 hours per beginner. After the six rounds, each beginner was asked to assess five-scale subjective satisfactions on questionnaire items.
Five university students participated in this experiment where four of them were beginners with no prior knowledge/experience on Mate and the other was an experienced.
The rate of turns in which the beginner opened a higher-ranked card per round ("winning turn rate") is a measure for the system ability. The time per beginners' turn (i.e., how long a beginner took to open a card in a turn: "turn time"), is also a measure. The winning turn rate and the turn time were measured from game logs recorded by our software program.
Table 2 shows the mean winning turn rate and the mean turn time over the four beginners. Even though the beginners knew no Mate rule before the experiments, in the first four rounds they could play games appropriately and win more than a half (64%) of the turns with our system. This result indicates the above-mentioned ability (i) of the system. Besides, even though the beginners played without our system in the last two rounds, they could play games by themselves and win nearly a half (48%) of the turns, i.e., they could play games evenly against the experienced player. In a case where a player opens a card randomly in each turn, the winning turn rate of 50% cannot be expected because of the rule constraints. Thus, the result indicates the above-mentioned ability (ii) of the system.
On the contrary, Table 2 shows that the mean turn time for the rounds without the system was relatively greater than that with the system: the beginners took relatively longer to decide which card to open after they stopped using the system. This result indicates that the beginners did not become familiar enough to make quick decisions within the first four rounds. But, compared with the mean turn time by the experienced player (18.0 sec), it can be said that the beginners didn't take so much time (20.9 sec) even after they stopped using the system. Future work is required to investigate whether the mean turn time in the "testing" rounds becomes shorter as a beginner plays more "learning" rounds.

| | Rate | Time |
|---|---|---|
| 1st-4th rounds with our system | 64% | 13.8 sec |
| 5th-6th rounds without our system | 48% | 20.9 sec |

Table 2. Mean winning turn rate and mean turn time over four beginners

Mean scores of the five-scale subjective ratings are shown in Table 3. The beginners felt our system was useful (mean score of 4.25 for the questionnaire item #4), which supports our idea.

| Questionnaire | Mean score (Best=5, Worst=1) |
|---|---|
| 1. Easy to read screen. | 4.00 |
| 2. Easy to understand meanings of graphical guides. | 4.50 |
| 3. Easy to make decisions (the amount of time required for making decisions is small). | 3.00 |
| 4. Useful. | 4.25 |
| 5. Fun. | 3.25 |

Table 3. Subjective ratings by beginners

## 3. AR applied to Bohemian Schneider

### 3.1 Game rules

Bohemian Schneider is a trick-taking game by two players. Thirty-two cards are used: eight pieces { A, K, Q, J, 10, 9, 8 and 7 } of the four suits {♥, ♦, ♠ and ♣}. First, six cards are dealt to each player respectively and the rest are left as stock. A player (P1) first and the opponent (P2) next opens a card in her/his deal respectively.

- If P2 opens a card of the next rank to the card by P1, P2 wins the turn and gains $x$ points, where $x$ is the score associated to the card with which s/he wins the turn. Card ranks and scores are shown in Table 4. There are two variations: suit must be the same or not. For example, suppose P1 opens ♥10. In the former case, P2 can win with ♥J only. In the latter case, P2 can win with any of {♥J, ♦J, ♠J and ♣J}. The former is the original, but the latter was employed in our application because beginners will play games easier under the latter rule. Thus, for example, if P1 leads with K and P2 follows with Ace then P2 gains 11 points.
- Else, P2 can open any card in her/his deal. P1 wins the turn and gains $x$ points in the same manner.

The winner of the last turn and the other draw a card from the stock respectively (the winner first), and the winner leads the next turn. A game consists of 16 turns. The winner of a game is the player who gains the points more in the 16 turns. For more details, see a reference book, e.g., (Parlett, 2009).

| Piece | Rank | Score |
|---|---|---|
| A | 1 | 11 |
| K | 2 | 4 |
| Q | 3 | 3 |
| J | 4 | 2 |
| 10 | 5 | 10 |
| 9 | 6 | 0 |
| 8 | 7 | 0 |
| 7 | 8 | 0 |

Table 4. Peace ranks and scores in Bohemian Schneider

A beginner of Bohemian Schneider will become able to play games by her/himself after s/he learns:

- the card ranks,
- the card scores,
- a card of the *next* rank is required to win a turn, and
- the winner of the last turn can take initiative in the next turn.

### 3.2 Visual augmentations for beginners

Fig. 5 shows an example of the augmented webcam screen. In this figure, the six cards in the lower area are the deal of the user of our system, and the card in the upper left area (in this case ♠10) is the card opened first by the opponent player. The user is to follow to ♠10 with a card in her/his deal. In the example of Fig.5, our system guides the user to open ♣J (to move ♣J to the upper right area) because J is the only peace to beat 10. The system shows messages in the lower left area: "now it's your turn", "the yellow-marked card is recommended", and "only J can beat 10; open any if no J in your deal," in Japanese. Such messages as the third one in this example will help a user learn the rank relations of card pairs.

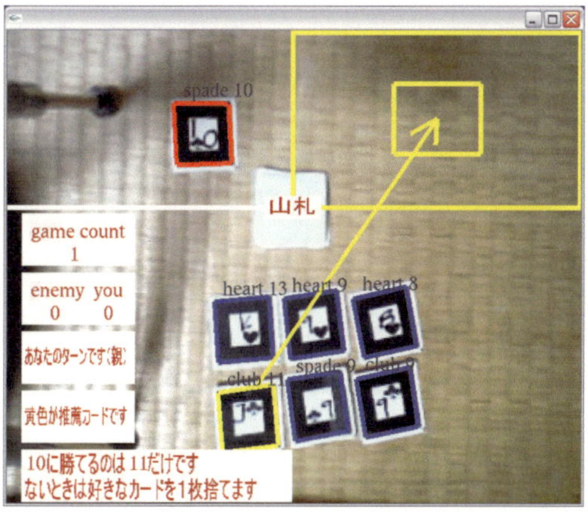


Fig. 5. Example of augmented screen (the user is to open a card second in a turn)

Fig. 6 shows another example in which the user is to open a card first in a turn. In this example, our system guides the user to open ♥A (because the user can win this turn with Ace and thus can take initiative again in the next turn). The system shows messages in the lower left area: "now it's your turn", "the yellow-marked card is recommended", and "you lose this turn if the opponent opens a card of next higher-ranked than yours, else you win." In addition, the card ranks are shown in the lower right area.

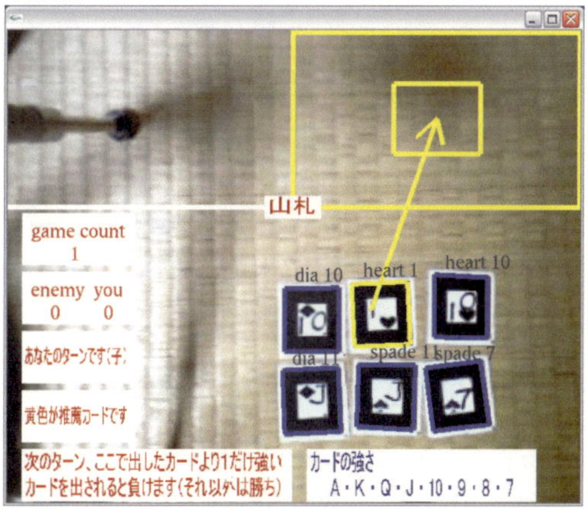


Fig. 6. Example of augmented screen (the user is to open a card first)

Fig. 7 shows another example in which the result of the current turn is displayed after both players opened their cards. In this example, the user first opened ♥A (the card in the upper right area) and the opponent followed with ♥Q (the card in the upper left area). The system shows, in the lower left message area, "you gained 11 points because you won this turn with Ace." The card scores are also displayed in the lower right area, which will help the user learn the scores.

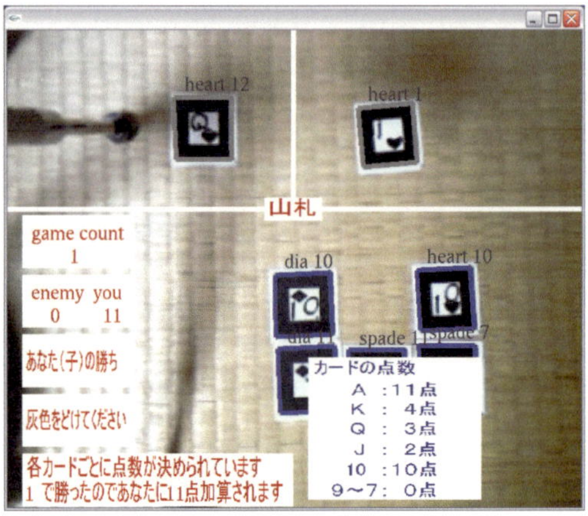


Fig. 7. Example of augmented screen (display of a turn result)

Fig. 8 shows another example in which the system prompts to draw a card from the stock. The stock is located in the center of the screen. The system shows that, in the lower left message area, the winner of the last turn draws first and lead the next turn.

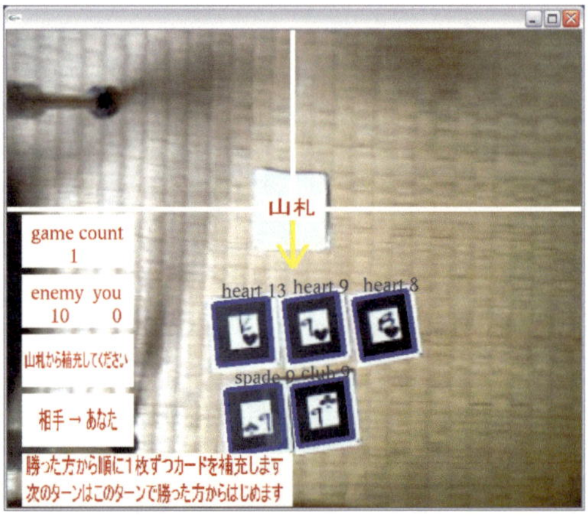


Fig. 8. Example of augmented screen (prompt to draw a card from the stock)

### 3.3 Evaluation

The authors had an experiment with beginners of Bohemian Schneider, in the same manner as the experiment for the Mate application. Each beginner played three rounds of games against an experienced player. In the 1st and 2nd rounds each beginner played with our system, and in the 3rd rounds the beginner played without our system. The experienced player always played games without the system. The ability of our system is evaluated by the performances of the beginners in the first two rounds and the third round respectively.
After the three rounds, each beginner was asked to assess five-scale subjective satisfactions on five questionnaire items.
Five university students participated in this experiment where four of them were beginners with no prior knowledge/experience on Bohemian Schneider and the other was an experienced.
Table 5 shows the mean winning turn rate and the mean turn time over the four beginners.

The beginners could win more than a half (57%) of the 32 turns in the 1st and 2nd rounds, being guided by our system. This indicates the beginners could play games well against the experienced even though they did not know the game rules. However, in the 3rd round, without our system they could win much less than a half (28%) of the 16 turns. This indicates, inconsistently with our expectation, they could not learn the rules enough while they played with our system. The reasons of this result will be that, the amount of "learning" turns was not enough for beginners to learn from their experiences, and improvements in the guidance of our system are required for better learning. The mean turn time for the rounds without the system was greater than that with the system, but the difference was much smaller than that in the Mate experiment. Again, in our future work the authors should investigate whether more "learning" rounds actually contribute to improve beginner performances in "testing" rounds.

| | Rate | Time |
|---|---|---|
| 1st and 2nd rounds with our system | 57% | 6.96 sec |
| 3rd round without our system | 28% | 8.84 sec |

Table 5. Mean winning turn rate and mean turn time over four beginners

Mean scores of the five-scale subjective ratings are shown in Table 6. The beginners felt our system was very useful (mean score of 4.75 for the questionnaire item #4), which again supports our idea.

| Questionnaire | Mean score (Best=5, Worst=1) |
|---|---|
| 1. Easy to read screen. | 3.50 |
| 2. Easy to understand meanings of graphical guides. | 4.25 |
| 3. Easy to make decisions (the amount of time required for making decisions is small). | 4.25 |
| 4. Useful. | 4.75 |
| 5. Fun. | 3.75 |

Table 6. Subjective ratings by beginners

## 4. Conclusion

The authors applied augmented reality (AR) user interface to the card games, Mate and Bohemian Schneider. The applications aim to help beginner players play games by themselves and learn the rules as they play games (i.e., enable experience-based learning). Our system visually augments the player's view of cards so that the player can make decisions on her/his actions (e.g., which card to open at each turn). Effectiveness of our idea was evaluated by experiments with four beginners. Based on the results of the winning turn rate, the turn time and the subjective assessments, it was partially confirmed that our system contributes to help beginners play games and learn rules, but required in our future work are additional experiments with more players and more rounds, more investigations on effective augmentation methods, and applications of our idea to other games.

## 5. References

Kato, H. & Billinghurst, M. (1999). Marker Tracking and HMD Calibration for a Video-Based Augmented Reality Conferencing System. *Proceedings of the 2nd International Workshop on Augmented Reality (IWAR 99)*, pp. 85-94

Ma, L.; Rauterberg, M. & Nakatsu, R. (Eds.) (2007). *Entertainment Computing - ICEC 2007*, Lecture Notes in Computer Science, Vol. 4740, Springer

Parlett, D. (2009). *The Penguin Book of Card Games*, Penguin Group USA

Sackson, S. (1992). *A Gamut of Games*, Dover Publications

Scott, M. S. & Shirley, S. (Eds.) (2008). *Entertainment Computing - ICEC 2008*, Lecture Notes in Computer Science, Vol. 5309, Springer

Stephane, N. & Jerome, D. (Eds.) (2009). *Entertainment Computing - ICEC 2009*, Lecture Notes in Computer Science, Vol. 5709, Springer

# 11

# Visualization Based on Geographic Information in Augmented Reality

Kikuo Asai
*The Open University of Japan*
*Japan*

## 1. Introduction

This chapter is a study on the visualization techniques of geographic information in an augmented reality environment, focusing on its user interface. Augmented reality is a technology that superimposes information over a real scene, enhancing the real world with the scene-linked information. The information is overlaid onto the real scene, dynamically based on the user's viewpoint. When mixed reality is defined as a continuum of environments spread between reality and virtuality (Milgram et al., 1994), augmented reality is ranked within a certain range along the reality-virtuality continuum. An augmented reality environment has the following characteristics: 1) It combines real and virtual worlds; 2) It is interactive in real-time; and 3) Virtual objects are spatially registered in three dimensional (3D) spaces (Azuma, 1997).

In this chapter, however, the term "augmented reality" is used as a 3D user interface that provides a user with an interactive environment. Moreover, a desktop monitor is included as a part of the interactive tabletop environment for presenting the visual scene captured by a video camera, though a head-mounted display (HMD) has typically been used as a display device. Comparison of the user's experiences between the HMD and the licquid crystal display (LCD) monitor showed that the LCD was easier to use than the HMD under the certain conditions (Asai & Kobayashi, 2007). It was because visual instability was caused by unstable images captured by a camera attached to the HMD. The coordinate system between workspace and visual feedback is then inconsistent in the environment using a desktop monitor, which requires user's mental transformation. In terms of interaction techniques, on the other hand, this tabletop environment gives us great merits of visual stability and tangible interaction with information or virtual objects.

There have been various visualization applications based on geographic information using the augmented reality technology. Our aim is here to introduce the basic concept of geographic information visualization using augmented reality, report an example with our lunar surface browsing tools, and show the features of the user interface in the geographic information visualization using map-based augmented reality.

First, the basic concept of geographic information visualization system is introduced by briefly describing general technology and its relevant applications of augmented reality. The geographic information visualization using augmented reality is mainly categorized into two styles: visualizing navigation information using GIS (geographic information system) in the real world and visualizing geographically embedded information using a real map on the desktop environment (Schmalstieg & Reitmayr, 2006). The former is often called as mobile augmented reality, since the location-referenced information is presented by using portable devices. The various commercial-based applications of the mobile augmented reality have appeared in recent years. The latter is called as map-based augmented reality, since the static information on a printed map is enhanced with geographically embedded information superimposed onto the map. The augmented map may give users tangible interactions mediated through combination of physical and virtual objects.

Second, an example with our lunar surface browsing tools is reported. Our systems present information geographically embedded on the lunar surface map, as a user presents sticks with markers that identify the location on the map and the command she tries to control. We have developed three kinds of browsing tools for learning the exploration activities and the lunar surface investigations in the Apollo 17 mission of the National Aeronautics and Space Administration (NASA). The first browsing tool created visualization based on computer graphics. Although tangible interfaces were implemented for manipulating the geographically embedded information on the lunar surface map, the potential of augmented reality was not drawn sufficiently. The second browsing tool created visualization using three interaction techniques based on a real map. The third browsing tool was created for comparison with the above browsing tools, adopting a WIMP (window, icon, menu, pointing) interface.

Third, usability with the browsing tools is discussed on the basis of user studies. Subjective evaluation was done with preference tests in order to investigate the properties of a tangible tabletop environment created by the map-based augmented reality visualization. For the sake of the evaluation, two experiments were designed comparing the map-based augmented reality environments with a WIMP environment. The method and results of the experiments are described, and the interpretations are given taking account of the open-ended comments.

Finally, the above concerns are summarized, and the future direction of the map-based augmented reality visualization is described in the context of the lunar surface browsing tools.

## 2. Geographic information visualization using augmented reality

We here describe design types of geographic information visualization using augmented reality and some applications for viewing the additional information related to the geographic information. The design types are classified by environments dedicated to visualization mainly into two categories; mobile augmented reality visualization and map-based augmented reality visualization.

### 2.1 Mobile augmented reality visualization

The mobile augmented reality provides us everywhere and anytime with a computer-augmented environment that enhances the real world with the location-based information, as shown in Figure 1. A portable device or head-mounted display (HMD) has been used as a display device. A compact video camera, embedded in the portable device or attached to the HMD, captures video images that are used for recognizing the real world and detecting physical objects in the real world. The recent downsizing technology allows the video images to be processed with a CPU in portable devices. Determining the user's position and orientation is necessary to provide the location-based information. The location data is obtained by GPS (global positioning system) and/or geomagnetic sensor (electrical compass) and is transferred to a server through the Internet. The server searches the relevant information based on the location data and provides the user with the relevant information. The relevant information is superimposed onto the scene images at the portable device or HMD.

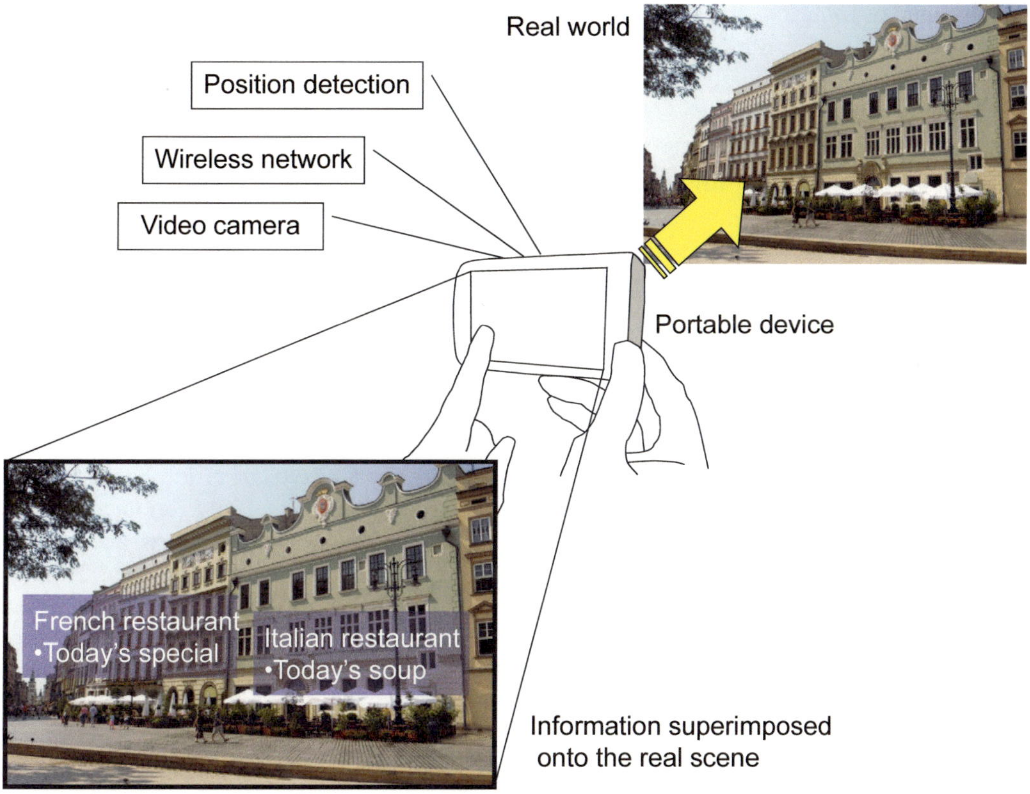


Fig. 1. Mobile augmented reality environment

There have been various systems developed as the mobile augmented reality applications. The Touring Machine was developed as a prototype system that combines augmented reality and mobile computing (Feiner et al., 1997), presenting information about the university campus at an outdoor environment. The prototype system further produced computer-aided navigation such as MARS (Hollerer et al, 1999) and Situated Documentaries (Hollerer et al., 1999). The former provided the user with an interactive multimedia presentation environment between indoors and outdoors, and the latter provided a tour guide by interactive multimedia presentations. These location-aware or location-based computing systems offer services that are related to the user's location (Beadle et al., 1997). The typical service is tour guide and navigation support applications, for example, a mobile edutainment system learning historical facts via a thrilling story, GEIST (Kretschmer et al., 2001), a personalized system touring archaeological sites, ARCHEOGUIDE (Vlahakis et al., 2003), and a tourist guide system supporting collaboration between multiple mobile users in both outdoor city areas as well as indoor areas of buildings, Signpost (Reitmayr & Schmalstieg, 2004).

The BAT system provided a user with an infrastructure of sensor network by using ultrasonic trackers, which offers location-based services throughout a large and populous area (Newman et al., 2001). This created a kind of ubiquitous computing environment inside a building, allowing the user to roam freely within the entire building. Since the system knows the users' locations in the building, it can give the users useful information that they would need at that time and the information about the users' locations can be shared among all the users. The Tinmith-Metro system provided a user with an authoring environment for creating 3D models interactively outdoors (Piekarski & Thomas, 2001). The constructive solid geometry modeler was controlled by using the menu and glove user interface called Tinmith Hand, which supports interaction techniques for manipulating the 3D graphical models. The system was designed to share the 3D models among the users outdoors and indoors in real-time.

Recent portable devices have inspired commercial services of mobile augmented reality applications. The mobile technologies do not just make the handheld devices compact, but also allow the devices to embed various functions such as a video camera, positioning system, e-mail, the Internet, TV, and telephone. Key technology that makes the location-based services successful is position detection of users, including the orientation of the handheld devices or the viewpoints of the users as well as the locations. GPS has mainly been used for determining the position outdoors. The accuracy would be improved by using magnetic sensors (electronic compass) and/or inertial sensors as well as vision-based tracking.

Seamless position detection indoors is an issue addressed for providing the location-based services inside buildings. Current technologies of wireless communications used indoors include infrared communication system, wireless LAN (local area network), IMES (indoor messaging system), and QR code. The infrared communication system offers broadband network services with high security. The wireless LAN is practical because the access points of the wireless LAN currently exist are used for position detection. The positioning information services have already been provided, for example, PlaceEngine by Koozyt and Wi-Fi positioning system by Skyhook Wireless. The IMES is a kind of indoor GPS that is the most promising method from a technical point of view, because the IMES is compatible with the GPS and allows the current GPS receivers to be used with modification of the firmware. The QR code is a two dimensional bar code that is recognized with image processing of the images captured by a camera.

Integrating the above technologies produces various applications. SekaiCamera (tonchidot) is a navigation system using online data by attaching digital tags called AirTag to the real world. The AirTag is a kind of icon overlaid onto the real scene image and has the link information that provides the location information related to the place. OneShotSearch (NEC Magnus Communications) gives the user location-based information about stores, restaurants, and navigation by using a mobile phone with GPS, a magnetic sensor, and a camera. For example, names of restaurants and the direct distances are presented at an order in position closer to the user. When the user selects one of the restaurants, the direction is indicated with an arrow, navigating the user to the restaurant. Real World Perspective Mobile Phone (au One Lab) is an intuitive user interface of obtaining information about humans and objects around the user by presenting a virtual perspective view over the mobile phone. Although it uses simple graphics visualization, adaptive information to the user is presented by estimating the user's status accurately with various sensors for detecting vibration and sound as well as position. SREngine (SREngine) is a kind of search engine to find the spatial information from the scene images captured by a camera. The data of the scene recognition is obtained by only image processing, and the additional sensors such as GPS and wireless LAN are not necessary.

Various portable devices have had positioning system, and have been able to record the data with geographic information. Some digital camera has a function of taking photos with GPS information. The photos would be uploaded on the Internet and shared in the general public. Location-based applications with a new concept will appear in cooperation with CGM (Consumer Generated Media), creating a kind of social network.

### 2.2 Map-based augmented reality visualization

A map-based visualization system is basically a map medium on which geographic data is stored, retrieved, and presented, allowing a user to manage the data linked to location and its spatial features, as shown in Figure 2. The geographic data and the associated attributes are often mapped in one coordinate, and are layered together for the analysis. GIS has been incorporated into various applications such as scientific investigation, resource management, and development planning.

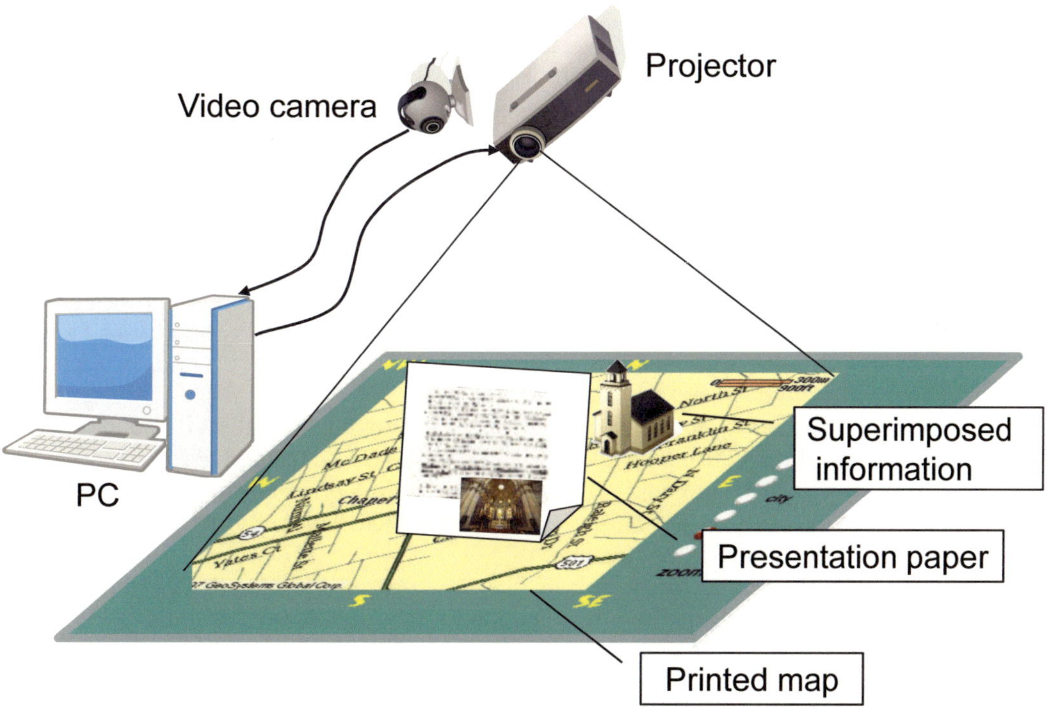


Fig. 2. Map-based augmented reality environment

Although computer-based GIS is an effective tool for visualizing geographic data, printed maps offer high resolution and simple interaction. Because printed maps display high-density information, they support both overview browsing and detailed area investigation. Moreover, the interaction is intuitive due to the direct manipulation; maps printed on a sheet of paper can be freely moved around on a table. However, printed maps do not display information dynamically to match the user's evolving interests.

Interaction discontinuity—the mental switch between the virtual and real worlds—creates problems in interface design when a traditional interface device such as a mouse is used for manipulating 3D objects (Poupyrev et al., 2002). Interaction discontinuity is caused by a spatial gap between the physical and virtual workspaces. One solution to this problem is a computer interface based on physical objects (Wellner, 1993). Augmented reality overlays video images of a real scene with virtual objects, creating a tangible interaction environment in which a user interacts intuitively with the virtual objects by manipulating the corresponding physical objects (Ullmer & Ishii, 1997; Kato et al., 2000; Regenbrecht, 2001).

Augmented reality has been applied to cartography to create a user interface that bridges the gap between the computer-generated information and the everyday experiences of users (Schmalstieg & Reitmayr, 2006). A user of map-based AR can use a printed map to flexibly access geographically embedded information by pointing at the location on the map and superimposing the information onto the map.

The application of augmented maps (Bobrich & Otto, 2002) to cartography applications enables the visualization of 3D digital geographic data overlaid on a printed map using a video see-through HMD. A marker pointer was used as an action trigger to detect the intersections between virtual objects. The pointer is recognized as a marker in the video images of the real scene.

Augmenting maps with information projected from overhead facilitates tangible interaction in a tabletop environment (Reitmayr et al., 2005). A PDA (personal data assistant) device was used as a tangible user interface instead of a marker pointer, enabling intuitive access to information linked to locations on the printed map. The occlusion problem encountered when using multiple maps was overcome by the depth-ordering information computed at the map localization step and the overlays were improved by rendering correct occlusion with other maps. The relevant images to the location on the map are projected at the area inside a square frame.

The Illuminating Clay system (Ishii et al., 2004), a GIS interface for landscape design and analysis, uses a clay model instead of a printed map. It captures the geometry of the clay landscape model in real time with a ceiling-mounted laser scanner and projects the geometry-based information onto the clay model.

A geographic file explorer system was developed to improve retrieval and visualization of landscape data (Favetta & Laurini, 2006). Image and video files of potential interest to a user are retrieved from a large set of geographically embedded documents, and those recorded at the place closest to the one selected on the map are presented. This provides an efficient way to quickly recall the locations of the documents.

Our browsing tools are similar in concept to these map-based visualization systems in that they provide a tangible user interface. Application of our map-based AR tools to the moon explored during the Apollo missions (NASA) is dedicated to creating a learning environment in which users can interactively browse geographically embedded information about the exploration activities and view realistic landscapes of the lunar surface from an egocentric viewpoint.

## 3. Lunar surface exploration and virtual maps

The moon is often used as learning content at science museums to enlighten laymen about astronomy and space science because the moon is the Earth's only satellite and the most familiar object in the sky. It has been extensively explored, particularly during the NASA

Apollo missions, and much scientific data has been collected, including images of the lunar surface and audio recordings of the communication among the astronauts and between the astronauts and the ground commanders.
In this section we briefly describe the Extra-Vehicular Activities (EVA) during the Apollo 17 mission and the geographic information viewers that have existed for navigating the moon.

### 3.1 Apollo 17 mission

The Apollo 17 mission was manned-exploratory mission in a series of the project Apollo. Three astronauts, Eugene Cernan, Ronald Evans, and Harrison Schumitt have directed to the moon, and two out of the three astronauts landed on the moon.
The lunar module (LM) landed in a valley in the Taurus-Littrow region. Three separate lunar surface excursions were conducted during the stay. In the early phase of the first one, the ground-commanded television camera and high-gain antenna on the lunar roving vehicle (LRV) were installed, and video signals around the LM were sent to the Houston space center. The astronauts conducted various scientific experiments during the excursions, spending roughly 22 hours outside the LM and traversing about 35 km in the LRV. They collected nearly 110 kg of rock and soil samples from various areas of stratigraphic interest: light mantle, dark mantle, sub-floor, massifs, and the Sculptured Hills.
The navigation area for the browsing tools is shown in Figure 3. The Apollo 17 preliminary science report (NASA, 1973) contains a huge amount of data, that it is neither easy nor practical for laymen to comprehend in total. For our study, we selected several remarkable experiments and samplings that were performed during the three excursions.
In the first excursion, a deep core sample and a single core tube were taken concurrently using the Apollo lunar surface experiment package. Geological samples, including a rake sample, were collected near the rim of Steno Crater. In the second excursion, geological samples were collected at five stations (the predetermined stopping points) and at eight LRV sampling stops (intermediate points): three between the LM and station 2, one at station 2a, and four between station 3 and the LM. Geological activities in the third excursion included main sampling stops at four stations and several LRV sampling stops between the stations. The Catalog of Apollo 17 Rocks describes each of the 334 individually numbered rock samples.

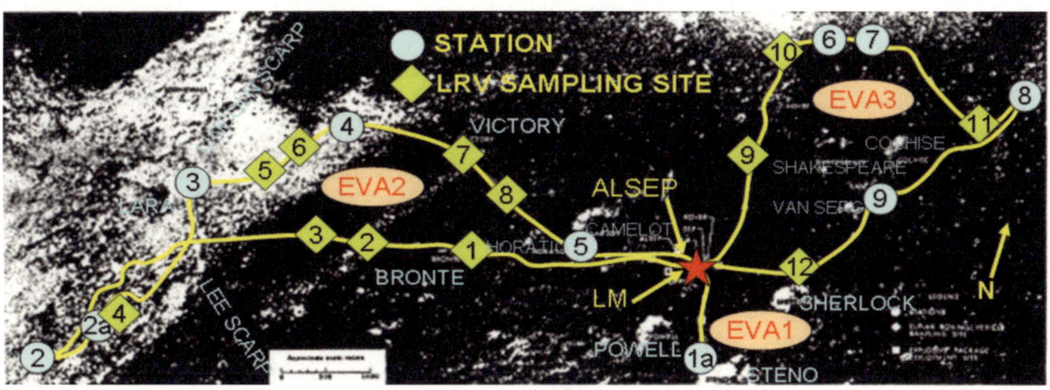


Fig. 3. Navigation area around the Apollo 17 landing site

### 3.2 Geographic information viewers for moon navigation

There have been several navigation tools to visualize the lunar surface exploration data and to display the images of the lunar surface relief. One of these tools is World Wind (NASA), a navigation system developed by NASA to visualize geographical data using zoom-in and zoom-out functions. A person using World Wind can, for example, browse in full 3D the moon terrain mapped by the Clementine spacecraft in 1994 and view details such as craters while navigating the lunar surface. Google Moon (Google) is another navigation tool that enables viewing of each of the Apollo landing sites with a Web browser. It has a simple interface that permits the user to browse geographical data at different scales and with annotations. On July 20, 2009, the 40th anniversary of the Apollo 11 mission, Google also released Moon in Google Earth (Google). The Moon in Google Earth enables users to view high-quality images and landscapes of the lunar surface using the data obtained by spacecrafts.

Other visualization tools, such as VistaPro Renderer (VistaPro) and Kashmir 3D (Sugimoto), enable the creation of realistic 3D landscapes and viewing of geographical relief. By importing lunar geographical data into such tools, a user can generate scenes of the lunar surface that can be viewed from various viewpoints. All these viewers have been developed supposing that users would have a certain level of experiences for personal computers (PCs). At public places, however, such assumption is not often available.

If flexible learning is interactive and individual (Schmid, 1999), then a tangible interface, which tangibly presents information from the user's selected viewpoint, can improve learning flexibility. AR may enhance the learning flexibility by showing the user a miniaturized lunar surface rather than just a framed view. While conventional audiovisual learning systems efficiently present their subject matter, their lack of interaction can lead to boredom. Our lunar surface browsing tools then use the tangible AR interface for the learning flexibility, which offers seamless interaction that bridges the gap between the virtual and real worlds. Our browsing tools create a miniature environment for viewing realistic landscapes of the lunar surface, which enables users to interactively learn about exploration activities of the Apollo 17 mission.

## 4. Browsing tools for learning lunar surface

We have originally developed a lunar surface navigation system at the immersive projection display environment (Kobayashi & Asai, 2003) that gave the user a wide field of view and a strong feeling of "being there." The system was quite large, however, limiting its use outside the laboratory. We then developed two browsing tools as a PC-based learning environment, which would be used for an exhibition at science museums. With these tools users can browse geographically embedded information in the lunar surface areas related to the Apollo 17 mission (NASA). The browsing tools have visualization functions in order to facilitate comprehension of the geographical features around the Apollo 17 landing site.

### 4.1 Computer graphics based visualization

The first version of the lunar surface browsing tool has rendered the lunar surface with computer graphics instead of a paper map (Asai et al., 2006). It kept visual compatibility of the geographic position, because of no registration problem of virtual objects onto the real scene. The browsing tool has provided a tangible user interface by using marker sticks. The user manipulates a virtual space with the sticks whose markers work as control commands when presented in the scene and captured by a camera. Figure 4 (a) shows an overview of the lunar surface browsing tool. Figure 4 (b) shows the markers used for controlling the virtual space and identifying the location where the lunar surface model should be superimposed in the captured scene.

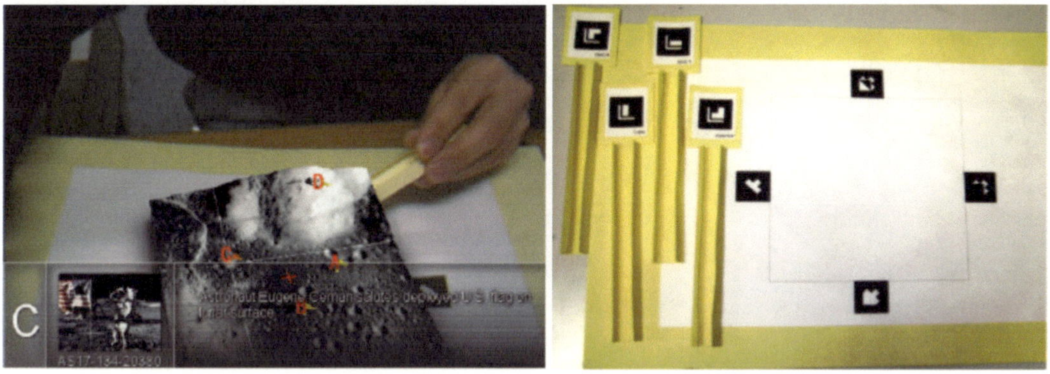


(a)Lunar surface navigation (b) Control command and base markers

Fig. 4. Overview of the first lunar surface browsing tool

#### 4.1.1 Visualization functions

Markers are assigned for the following navigation functions.

1. **Pointer:** By pointing this marker (orange cone in Fig. 5 (a)) at a certain location on the lunar surface, the user can shift the area in view and present the relevant location information.
2. **Area shift:** Pointing with this maker allows the user to navigate to the indicated location. Pressing the space bar on the keyboard centers the pointing place on the view.
3. **Information presentation:** Users point at a label and information pops up on a transparent panel (Fig. 4 (a)). The information—generally images and text or sounds—is relevant to the location on the lunar surface.
4. **Rotation:** The rotation marker changes the viewpoint by rotating the entire area of the lunar surface in view (Fig. 5 (b)).
5. **Zoom:** Users change the scale of the lunar surface map—zooming in and out—by rotating the mouse wheel (Fig. 5 (c)).
6. **Grid:** The grid marker overlays a grid on the lunar surface and presents information about the scale of the area along the edge of the image (Fig. 5 (d)).
7. **Altitude:** Inserting the altitude marker into the video image brings up a color contour for identifying valleys, scarps, and 3D geometrical relief (Fig. 5 (e)).
8. **Rover's path:** Inserting the path marker into the image area reveals the path taken by the rover (Fig. 5 (f)). The viewing area can also be automatically shifted along the rover's path.

The multimedia content embedded along the path taken by the LRV is revealed by manipulating the navigation system, allowing us to learn about the exploratory activities. The audiovisual materials— photos and sounds recorded during the activities—realistically describe the situation on the lunar surface. The voice communication between the astronauts and the space center is particularly effective in evoking a realistic sensation of presence. The shading on the lunar surface model also helps to create a realistic landscape.

(a) Pointer (b) Rotation (c) Zoom

(d) Grid (e) Altitude (f) Path of the LRV

Fig. 5. Visualization functions of the first version

#### 4.1.2 Implementation

This system uses a parameter settings file to designate the text and audiovisual files presented as multimedia content. Topographic data of the Taurus-Littrow region was used for the navigation map. All of the data, text, images, and audio are linked to locations where the astronauts conducted scientific activities. Voice communication between the astronauts can be heard by touching the pointer to a voice label. The data were obtained from NASA's web site for the Apollo missions (NASA).

The PC was equipped with a 2.6 GHz Pentium IV, 512 MB of memory, and an nVidia GeForce FX5700 graphics card with 128 MB of video RAM. Video images were captured with a 640 x 480-pixel web camera. ARToolkit (HITLAB) was used to process images, detect the square markers, and track the positions and orientations of the markers.

### 4.2 Real map based visualization

The second version of the lunar surface browsing tool has used a real map as a medium presenting the lunar surface instead of rendering computer graphics (Asai et al., 2008). A tangible tabletop environment was provided by interacting with a printed map of the lunar surface and marker sticks of the control commands. A camera mounted above the map captures the video images that are processed to recognize the patterns of the markers. Tracking the marker's location enables the user to view information (photos, texts, and sounds) associated with the location on the map. Figure 6 shows an overview of the second lunar surface browsing tool, presenting the geographically embedded information (Fig. 6 (a)) and the tabletop environment with the lunar surface map and markers (Fig. 6 (b)).

The geographically embedded information in Fig. 6 (a) includes an image of the LRV and annotations about the geographic features at station 5 that are revealed by pointing at the label on the map. The annotations are read out as narration at that time, so that people can understand the difficult words. If a voice label on the map is selected, the system plays a recording of the voice communication during the exploration in the Apollo 17 mission. The sort of labels is distinguished with color.

The browsing tool used three interaction techniques; (1) A pointer is used for selecting points of interest on the map by zooming and focusing, enabling reliable selection of points from among many points, (2) A slider is used for designating a range of distance along a path on the map by adjusting the length between two markers, enabling variable viewpoint control, and (3) A local view is simulated at a designated point, enabling dynamic visualization from an egocentric viewpoint.

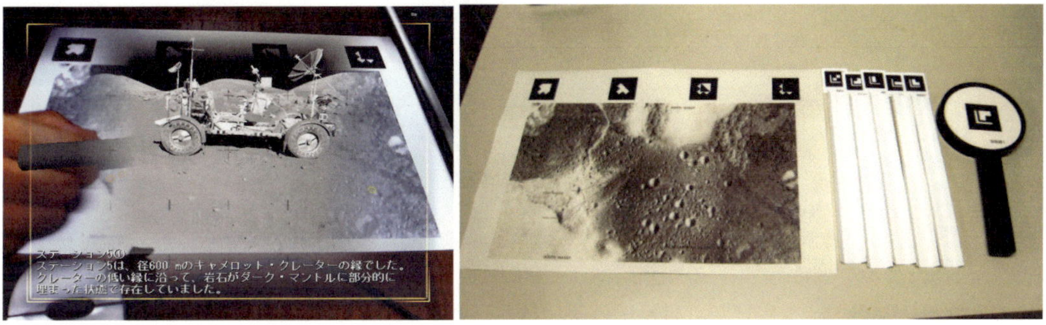

(a) Ggeographically embedded information (b) Lunar surface map and markers

Fig. 6. Overview of the second lunar surface browsing tool

### 4.2.1 Visualization functions

The browsing tool in the second version has several visualization functions controlled with the control command markers.

1. **Lenses** Two lenses are used for accessing the zoom-in views of the lunar surface relief. The user pans one of them over the lunar surface map, reducing and increasing the zoom-in rate by changing the relative size of the lens marker in the video images (Fig. 7 (a)). The other is used as a pointer to retrieve the geographically embedded information by selecting a point of interest on the lunar surface map (Fig. 7 (b)).
2. **EVA data** The geographical data around the EVA are overlaid on the lunar surface map. The data include the LRV's route, the stations (Fig. 7 (c)) where the LRV stopped, and the craters near the route. The user can find their positions, names and sizes.
3. **Contour** Transparent images of the elevation are overlaid on the lunar surface map with contour lines (Fig. 7 (d)) or with a contour color map. The user can find the massifs northeast and southwest.
4. **Grid** Blue grids are overlaid on the lunar surface map for presenting the scale of the EVA area (Fig. 7 (e)). The user can understand the rough extent. The scale size of each grid is set using a parameter file.
5. **LRV track** A miniature of the LRV is presented that moves along the actual LRV's route on the lunar surface map (Fig. 7 (f)). The LRV miniature is quite small on the map. Then, a lens enables the user to see it on a larger scale.
6. **LRV view** The view of the landscape from the LRV's viewpoint is presented at another window in the video images (Fig. 7 (f)). As the LRV moves along the track, the landscapes are animated corresponding to the viewpoints along the route. The window of the LRV view is presented at the size of the LRV view marker.
7. **Slider** The position of the LRV on the map changes with distance between the slider markers (Fig. 7 (f)). The LRV view enables the user to view the landscape animations at the viewpoints along the route designated with the slider.

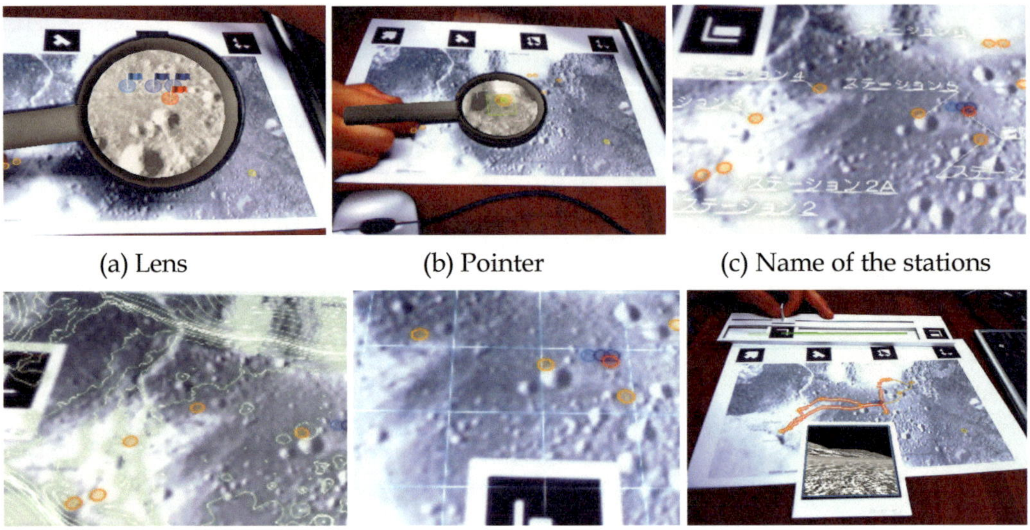


(a) Lens (b) Pointer (c) Name of the stations

(d) Contour lines (e) Grid pattern (f) Local view with the slider

Fig. 7. Visualization functions of the second version

#### 4.2.2 Implementation

This system uses a parameter setting file to designate the text and audiovisual files as the geographically embedded information. A photograph of the Taurus-Littrow region was used as a printed map, and topographic data were used to make the contour lines and contour map, which were obtained by the satellite measurements. All of the documents (including annotations, images, and sounds) are linked to the corresponding locations. The data were obtained from NASA's Web sites for the Apollo missions (NASA).

The software for the browsing tool was installed on the PC equipped with a 2.6-GHz Pentium IV CPU, 512 MB of memory, and an nVidia GeForce FX5700 graphics card with 128 MB of video RAM. Video images were captured with a 640 x 480-pixel web camera. ARToolKit (HITLAB) was used as the image processing library for capturing the video images, detecting the square markers in the images, tracking the positions and orientations of the markers, and recognizing the patterns inside the markers.

### 4.3 WIMP based visualization

GeoMovie Creator (GMC) was originally designed for outdoor education (Hashimoto, 2004). Users can navigate the 3D area on a topographical map that is generated from topographical data from the Geographical Survey Institute (GSI) or from an aerial photo mapped to coordinates from the altitude data. The user can view the geographical landscape and embed additional information, related to the locations in which they are interested, with a WIMP (window, icon, menu, pointing) interface. Personal data files such as photos and videos that contain geographical GPS data are linked on the map. In these ways, students and teachers can create geographic 3D content.

We imported the lunar surface map data and relevant information into GMC, and used the tool as a WIMP interface. Figures 8 (a) and (b) show the graphical user interface and the information presentation, respectively. A red label indicates a location with embedded information. When the label is double-clicked, the information appears in another window. The small 2D map at the bottom right in Figure 8 (a) helps users to locate themselves on the map. The viewpoint is controlled mainly by using the arrow keys on a keyboard in combination with the shift key.

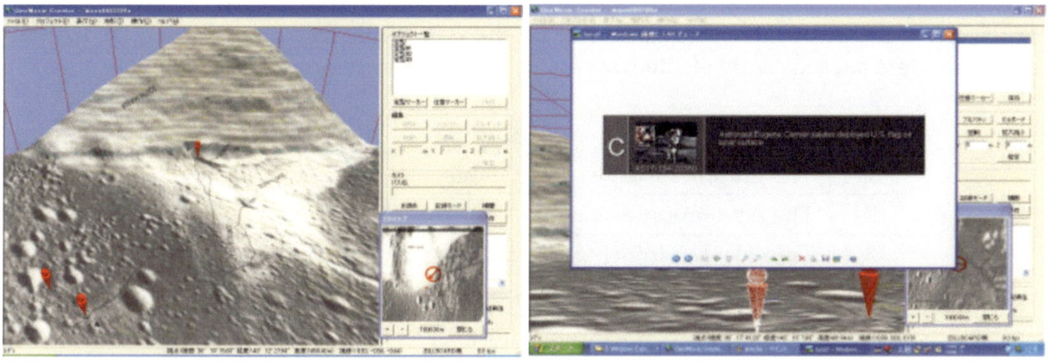

(a) Graphical user interface (b) Information presentation

Fig. 8. Overview of the GeoMovie Creator (GMC)

## 5. User study

We conducted user studies to compare the properties of navigation in a tangible tabletop environment with those of navigation in a WIMP environment. Sujective evaluation was done with preference tests in Experiment I and II.

### 5.1 Experiment I

We evaluated the tabletop environment in comparison to a WIMP environment in order to investigate the usability of the first lunar surface browsing tool. The computer graphics based visualization tool that we developed was used as the tabletop environment. The geographic information viewer, GMC (Hashimoto, 2004), described in the previous section was used as the WIMP environment. Figures 9 (a) and (b) show the aspects of navigation manipulation at the tabletop and WIMP environments, respectively.

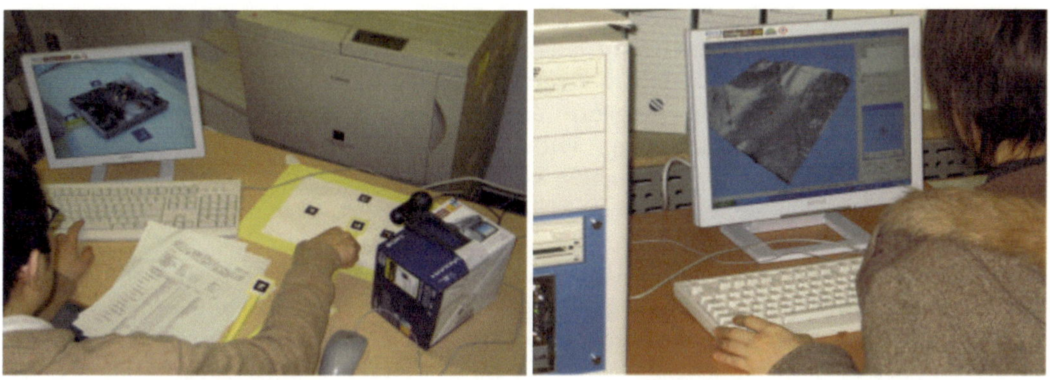

(a) Tabletop environment (b) WIMP environment

Fig. 9. Overview of Experiment I

#### 5.1.1 Method

Thirty undergraduate and graduate students participated in the experiment. They were asked to navigate the virtual environments of the lunar surface and retrieve information about the exploration activities of the Apollo 17 mission. The participants evaluated the usability and manipulability of the tabletop and WIMP environments. Afterwards, each participant was asked to rate the preference for the statements listed in Table 1. Open-ended comments were subsequently elicited.

| No. | Question |
|---|---|
| 1 | The graphics images were stable. |
| 2 | The navigation was easy. |
| 3 | The relevant information was obtained easily. |
| 4 | It is easy to learn how to use the system. |
| 5 | Manipulating it was enjoyable. |
| 6 | The manipulation was intuitive. |
| 7 | Using the system for a long-time is tolerable. |

Table 1. Statements of the preference test in Experiment I

#### 5.1.2 Results

Figure 10 shows the results of the preference test in the Experiment I. The bar indicates the average of the five-step rating given by the participants, and the error bar indicates the standard deviation. The white and black bars correspond to the tabletop and WIMP environments, respectively. A one-way ANOVA (analysis of variance) was performed to identify the effect of the environment for each item of the preference test. A statistically significant difference was observed for Item 1, and a tendency toward significant effects was found for Items 2 and 6. No significant difference was found for the other items.

According to Item 1, the workspace of the tabletop environment was considered inferior to that of the WIMP environment, because the instability was caused by the graphics registration based on the location of the marker in the video image. Unfortunately, the participants tended to rate navigation in the tabletop environment as inferior to that in the WIMP environment, which was more familiar to the participants. However, Item 6 showed that the participants thought navigation manipulation to be more intuitive in the tabletop environment than in the WIMP, which suggests that the augmented reality based system may achieve a better score for navigation once its stability is improved through spatial registration of the lunar surface map with the detected markers. These results were consistent with the open-ended comments. Many participants mentioned that the tabletop environment was enjoyable while the WIMP environment was accurate and stable during viewpoint transitions.

The tabletop environment had some drawbacks. Navigation was mainly accomplished by manipulating control-command markers, but changing the viewpoint needed to manipulate both markers and the keyboard. Moving to another location required pointing the marker at the desired location and pressing the space bar on the keyboard. This combination seemed intuitive, but was not suitable for controlling the viewpoint. Moreover, the camera that captured the real scene was fixed, which invalidated the advantage of augmented reality

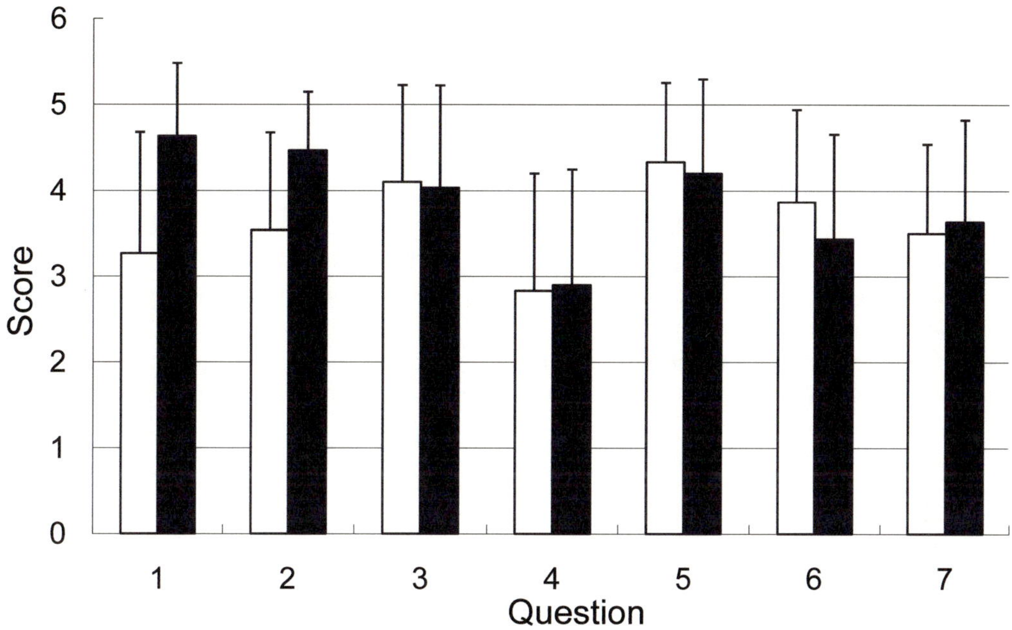


Fig. 10. Results of Experiment I (white: tabletop, black: WIMP)

interfaces in matching the virtual viewpoint to that of the user. Some participants suggested that the augmented reality based environment was exocentric, and the WIMP based one was rather egocentric, which was the opposite of what we expected.

### 5.2 Experiment II

We evaluated the map-based augmented reality environment in comparison to a WIMP environment in order to investigate the usability of the second lunar surface browsing tool (Asai et al., 2008). The real map based visualization system that we developed was used as

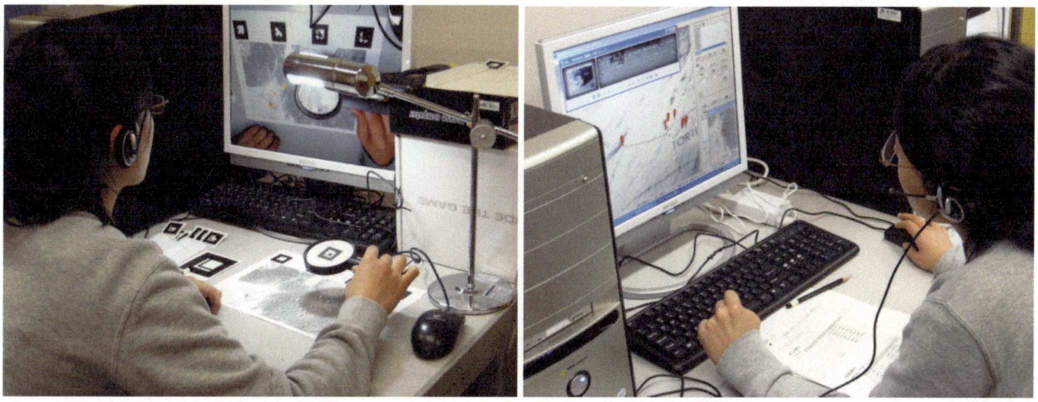

(a) Map-based AR environment (b) WIMP environment

Fig. 11. Overview of Experiment II

the map-based augmented reality environment. The geographic information viewer, GMC (Hashimoto, 2004), was used as the WIMP environment. Figure 11 shows examples of the tool utilization in Experiment II, indicating (a) map-based AR and (b) WIMP environments, respectively.

### 5.2.1 Method

Nineteen undergraduate and graduate students, who were not astronomy majors, participated in the Experiment II. They were instructed to use the system to become familiar with the lunar surface area explored by the Apollo 17 mission and to subsequently evaluate the operation of the browsing tool by answering eight questions in the preference test (Table 2) using a five-point scale.

They were not given any particular task, but they were given as much time as they wanted to use the system. We used an LCD monitor for the display, and the camera was placed next to the monitor on a table.

| No. | Question |
|---|---|
| 1 | Was the system easy to use? |
| 2 | Did the system give you an immersive feeling? |
| 3 | Were you able to look over the entire area explored by the Apollo 17 mission? |
| 4 | Was using the system for a long time tolerable? |
| 5 | Do you think children would be able to use the system? |
| 6 | Do you think people in general would be able to use the system? |
| 7 | Was manipulating the system enjoyable? |
| 8 | Do you think a group of people would be able to use the system? |

Table 2. Questions of the preference test in Experiment II

### 5.2.2 Results

The results of the preference test are plotted in Figure 12. The black and white bars indicate the average scores for the map-based AR and WIMP environments, respectively. The error bars represent the standard deviation. Since the scores for all the questions for both environments were higher than 3, it suggests that both should be suitable for learning about the lunar surface.

A dependent t-test was performed to identify the effect of the environment for each question. A statistically significant difference was found only for questions 1 ($t(18) = -3.77$, $p < 0.05$) and 5 ($t(18) = 2.28$, $p < 0.05$).

The WIMP environment was considered to be easier to use (Q1) probably because it was more familiar. Four participants pointed out in their comments that experience is needed in order to become adept at using the marker sticks for the map-based AR environment. However, as shown by the response to Q5, the map-based AR environment was considered to be better for children. Six open-ended comments pointed out that children would probably enjoy manipulating the marker sticks as well as exploring the lunar surface. The comments were consistent with the score result in Q7, which had tendency that the map-based AR environment was more enjoyable than the WIMP environment.

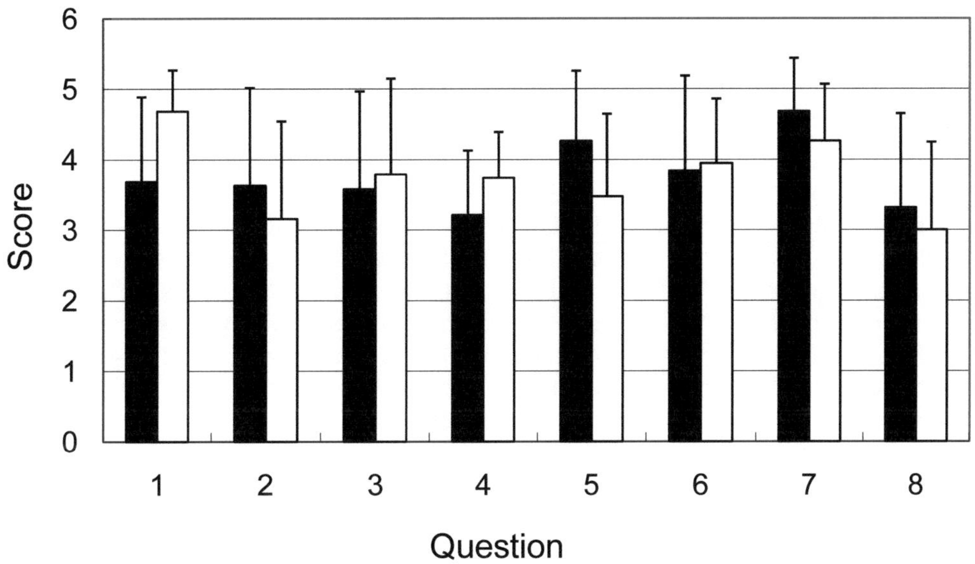


Fig. 12. Results of Experiment II (black: map-based AR, white: WIMP)

The open-ended comments from the participants give us useful suggestions to clear the characteristics of the map-based AR environment. In the positive opinions, five participants commented on the intuitive interaction using the marker sticks, and three commented on a feeling of presence created by the manipulation of the sticks and map. These were interpreted as the benefits of the tangible user interface. In the negative opinions, two participants stated that there were too many marker sticks, and nine stated that the pointing to geographically embedded information was sometimes troublesome due to the density of points within the small map at which the information embedded. Three commented on occasional confusion about the locations of the information on the map. From these comments it would be necessary to make the lens pointing function smoother.

## 6. Conclusion and future direction

We have developed lunar surface browsing tools using a tangible tabletop environment for visualizing geographically embedded information. They enable users to explore the Apollo 17 landing site, to follow the paths taken by the astronauts, and to study the extra-vehicular activity and scientific experiments. Map-based AR enhances the interactivity in geographic visualization, and these browsing tools have capabilities to provide a learning environment that improves the effectiveness of multimedia presentations.

We performed user studies in order to investigate usability of the lunar surface browsing tools, comparing them to a WIMP-based interface. The results showed that the map-based AR interface was enjoyable to use but unstable in the image presentations. The results also suggested that the map-based AR interface would be suitable for learning about the lunar surface and better for children than the WIMP-based interface.

Although the egocentric landscapes were presented in computer graphics in the map-based AR browsing tool, the whole lunar surface was seen flat because of the physical limitation of the map presentation. We expected the evaluation result that the lunar surface presentation with the fine texture would highly contribute to a feeling of presence or immersion. However, this did not work well for presenting the lunar surface relief. The 3D relief was not understandable even by overlaying the contour lines or contour map over the printed map. We are investigating ways to effectively visualize the superimposition of the 3D relief onto the actual map.

An LCD monitor was used as a display device for presenting a real scene of the lunar surface map, and the camera was placed next to the monitor on a table. One of the advantages of augmented reality is, however, viewpoint-based interaction in which virtual objects are presented to match the user's view. This requires attaching a camera to the user's head, which makes the scene view unstable due to the head movement. This issue needs to be addressed for fully turning a map-based AR interface to advantage. Future work also includes a user study to investigate the usability of the browsing tools in practical situations, such as science museum exhibits.

## 7. References

Asai, K. & Kobayashi, H. (2007). User study of augmented reality display interfaces for a lunar surface navigation system, *Proceedings of Human-Computer Interaction International*, 796–800.

Asai, K.; Kobayashi, H., Kondo, T. & Sugimoto, Y. (2008). Subjective evaluation of a lunar surface browsing tool using map-based AR, *Proceedings of International Conference on Computers in Education*, pp.749-753.

Asai, K.; Kondo, T., Kobayashi, H. & Mizuki, A. (2006). Tangible navigation system for learning the lunar surface, *Proceedings of International Conference on Interactive Computer Aided Learning* (CD-ROM).

Asai, K.; Kondo, T., Kobayashi, H. & Mizuki, A. (2008). A geographic surface browsing tool using map-based augmented reality, *Proceedings of International Conference Visualization*, pp.93-98.

Azuma, R. (1997). A survey of augmented reality, *Presence: Teleoperators and Virtual Environments*, vol.6, pp.355–385.

au One Lab, Real World Perspective Mobile Phone, http://kazasu.mobi/

Beadle, H. W. P.; Harper, B., Maguire, G. Q. J. & Judge, J. (1997). Location Aware Mobile Computing, *Proceedings of IEEE/IEE International Conference on Telecommunications*, pp. 1319-1324.

Bobrich, J. & Otto, S. (2002). Augmented maps, *Proceedings of Symposium on Geospatial Theory, Processing, and Applications*, in IAPRS, vol. 34, part 4

Favetta, F. & Laurini, R. (2006). Visualization and exploration of landscape architecture project information, *Proceedings International Conference on Distributed Multimedia Systems*, pp. 153–156

Feiner, S.; MacIntyre, B., Hollerer, T. & Webster, A. (1997). A touring machine: prototyping 3D mobile augmented reality systems for exploring the urban environment, *Proceedings of Internationa Symposium on Wearable Computing*, pp.74–81.

Geographical Survey Institute, Global Map, http://www.gsi.go.jp/ENGLISH/index.html/

Google, Google Moon, http://www.google.com/moon/

Google, Google Earth, http://earth.google.com/

Hashimoto, M. (2004). GeoMovie Creator (GMC): authoring tool for creating 3D educational contents, *Proceedings of Information processing Society of Japan (Japanese)*

HITLAB, University of Washington, ARToolKit, http://www.hitl.washington.edu/artoolkit/

Hollerer, T; Feiner, S., and Pavlik, J. (1999). Situated documentaries: embedding multimedia presentations in the real world, *Proceedings of International Symposium on Wearable Computing*, pp.79-86.

Hollerer, T.; Feiner, S., Terauchi, T., Rashid, G., and Hallaway, D. (1999). Exporing MARS: developing indoor and outdoor user interfaces to a mobile augmented reality system, *Computers & Graphics*, vol.23, pp.779-785.

Ishii, H.; Ratti, C., Piper, B., Wang, Y., Biderman, A. & Ben-Joseph, E. (2004). Bringing clay and sand into digital design - continuous tangible user interfaces, *BT Technology Journal*, vol. 22, no. 4, pp. 287–299.

Kato, H.; Billinghurst, M. Poupyrev, I., Imamoto, K. & Tachibana, K. (2000). Virtual object manipulation on a table-top AR environment, *Proceedings of International Symposium on Augmented Reality*, pp. 111–119.

Kobayashi, H. & Asai, K. (2003). Moon-surface navigation system using immersive projection display, *Proceedings of International Conference on Computers in Education*, pp. 1120–1123

Kretschmer, U.; Coors, V., Spierling, U., Grasbon, D., Schneider, K., Rojas, I. & Malaka, R. (2001). Meeting the spirit of history, *Proceedings of the 2001 conference on Virtual reality, archeology, and cultural heritage*, pp. 141-152.

Milgram, P.; Takemura, H., Utsumi, A. & Kishino, F. (1994). Augmented reality: a class of displays on the reality-virtuality continuum, *Proceedings of Telemanipulator and Telepresence Technplogies*, SPIE, pp.282–292.

NASA. (1973). Apollo 17 Preliminary Science Report, SP-330

NASA, Apollo 17 mission, http://science.ksc.nasa.gov/history/apollo/apollo-17/apollo-17.html

NASA, World Wind and the Moon, http://worldwind.arc.nasa.gov/moon.html

NEC Magnus Communications, Pointing Access Platform, http://necmagnus.jp/GViD/

Newman, J.; Ingram, D. & Hopper, A. (2001). Augmented reality in a wide area sentient environment, *Proceedings of IEEE and ACM International Symposium on Augmented Reality*, pp.77-86.

Piekarski, W. & Thomas, B. H. (2001). Tinmith-Metro: new outdoor techniques for creating city models with an augmented reality wearable computer, *Proceedings of IEEE International Symposium on Wearable Computing*, pp.31-38.

Poupyrev, I.; Tan, D. S., Billinghurst, M., Kato, H., Regenbrecht, H. & Tetsutani, T. (2002). Developing a generic augmented reality interface, *IEEE Computer*, vol. 35, pp. 44–50.

Regenbrecht, H.; Baratoff, G. & Wagner, M. T. (2001). A tangible AR desktop environment, *Computer & Graphics*, vol. 25, pp. 755–763

Reitmayr, G.; Eade, E. & Drummond, T. (2005). Localisation and interaction for augmented maps, *Proceedings of International Symposium on Mixed and Augmented Reality*, pp. 120–129.

Reitmayr, G. & Schmalstieg, D. (2004). Collaborative augmented reality for outdoor navigation and information browsing, *Proceedings of Symposium on Location Based Services and TeleCartography*, pp.53-62.

Schmalstieg, D. & Reitmayr, G. (2006). Augmented reality as a medium for cartography, Multimedia Cartography, 2nd ed. W. Cartwright, M. Peterson, G. Gartner, *Springer-Verlag*, pp. 267–281.

Schmid, C. (1999). Simulation and virtual reality for education on the Web, *Proceedings of EUROMEDIA'99*, pp.181-188.

SREngine, http://www.srengine.com/

Sugimoto, T., Kashmir 3D, http://www.kashmir3d.com/index-e.html

tonchidot, Sekai Camera, http://sekaicamera.com/

VistaPro Renderer, http://www. Monkeybyte.com/

Vlahakis, V.; Ioannidis, N., & Karigiannis, J. (2003). ARCHEOGUIDE: challenges and solutions of a personalized augmented-reality guide for archaeological sites, *IEEE Computer Graphics & Applications*, vol.22, pp.52-60.

Ullmer, B. & Ishii, H. (1997). The metaDESK: models and prototypes for tangible user interfaces, *Proceedings of ACM Symposium on User Interface Software and Technology*, pp. 223–232

Wellner, P. (1993). Interaction with paper on the digital desk, *Communications of the ACM*, vol.36, pp.87-96.

12

# Virtual and Augmented Reality in Finance: State Visibility of Events and Risk

Soha Maad[1], Samir Garbaya[2], JB McCarthy[1], Meurig Beynon[3], Saida Bouakaz[4] and Rajagopal Nagarajan[3]
*[1]Financial Services Innovation Centre, University College Cork UCC, Cork,*
*[2] Arts et Metiers ParisTech, CNRS, LE2I, Institut Image 2 rue T. Dumorey 71100 Chalon-sur-Saone,*
*[3]Department of Computer Science, The University of Warwick,*
*[4]Laboratoire d'InfoRmatique en Image et Sytemes d'Information (LIRIS), Université Claude Bernard Lyon 1,*
*[1]Ireland*
*[2,4]France*
*[3]UK*

## 1. Introduction

The recent financial crisis and its aftermath motivate our re-thinking of the role of Information and Communication Technologies (ICT) as a driver for change in global finance and a critical factor for success and sustainability. We attribute the recent financial crisis that hit the global market, causing a drastic economic slowdown and recession, to a lack of state visibility of risk, inadequate response to events, and a slow dynamic system adaptation to events. There is evidence that ICT is not yet appropriately developed to create business value and business intelligence capable of counteracting devastating events. The aim of this chapter is to assess the potential of Virtual Reality and Augmented Reality (VR / AR) technologies in supporting the dynamics of global financial systems and in addressing the grand challenges posed by unexpected events and crises. We overview, firstly, in this chapter traditional AR/VR uses. Secondly, we describe early attempts to use 3D/ VR / AR technologies in Finance. Thirdly, we consider the case study of mediating the visibility of the financial state and we explore the various dimensions of the problem. Fourthly, we assess the potential of AR / VR technologies in raising the perception of the financial state (including financial risk). We conclude the chapter with a summary and a research agenda to develop technologies capable of increasing the perception of the financial state and risk and counteracting devastating events.

## 2. Traditional use of VR / AR

Virtual Reality and Augmented Reality tools and technologies supply virtual environments that have key characteristics in common with our physical environment. Viewing and interacting with 3D objects is closer to reality than abstract mathematical and 2D representations of the real world. In that respect Virtual and Augmented reality can potentially serve two objectives (Maad et al, 2001): (a) reflecting realism through a closer correspondence with real experience, and (b) extending the power of computer-based technology to better reflect "abstract" experience (interactions concerned with interpretation and manipulation of symbols that have no obvious embodiment e.g. share prices, as contrasted to interaction with physical objects). The main motivation for using VR / AR to achieve objective (a) is cost reduction (e.g. it is cheaper to navigate a virtual environment depicting a physical location such as a theatre, a road, or a market, than to be in the physical location itself), and more scope for flexible interaction (e.g. interacting with a virtual object depicting a car allows more scope for viewing it from different locations and angles). Objective (b) can be better targeted because the available metaphors embrace representations in 3D-space (c.f. visualization of the genome).

VR and AR technologies are currently widely used in the exploration of real physical objects (e.g. car, cube, molecule, etc.) or a physical location (e.g. shop, theatre, house, forest, etc..). In the course of exploration the user is immersed in the virtual scene, and can walkthrough or fly through the scene. The user's body and mind integrate with this scene. This frees the intuition, curiosity and intelligence of the user in exploring the state of the scene. In a real context, agents intervene to change the state of current objects/situations (e.g. heat acts as an agent in expanding metallic objects, a dealer acts as an agent in changing bid/ask quotes and so affects the flow of buyers and sellers). Introducing agency into a VR or an AR scene demands abstractions to distinguish user and non-user actions especially when these go beyond simple manipulation of objects by the user hand, or walking through and flying physical locations (Maad et al, 2001).

## 3. Uses of AR / VR in finance

This section considers three case studies of the use of 3D, VR and AR in Finance. The first case study was developed by the author at Fraunhofer Institute of Media Communication in Germany. It involves the development of a live edutainment financial content MARILYN (Chakaveh, 2005; Maad, 2003a; Maad, 2003b). MARILYN consists of a 3D virtual human avatar presenting in an entertaining, informative, and interactive way multilingual live financial data (news and tickers) taken from various international stock exchanges. The second case study is a virtual reality application in financial trading previously developed by the author at the University of Warwick in UK in collaboration with Laboratoire de Robotique de Paris (Maad et al, 2001). The third case study describes a novel application drawing expertise from two important fields of study, namely digital image processing and augmented reality. The application is developed within the context of the CYBERII project[1] (Maad et al, 2008). It features a human (the user) immersion in a virtual world of financial indicators for exploration and apprehension. This immersion aims at augmenting the user's perception of the financial market activity and at equipping him/her with concrete information for analysis and decision making. The user immersion in a virtual world of financial indicators serves in reflecting realism through a closer correspondence with real world experience, and in extending the power of computer-based technology to better reflect abstract experience.

[1] http://artis.imag.fr/Projects/Cyber-II/

A comparison is drawn to highlight an added value in the shift from the use of 3D to Virtual Reality and Augmented Reality in finance.

### 3.1 Use of 3D / VR in finance

This section describes MARILYN Marilyn (Multimodal Avatar Responsive Live Newscaster) a system for interactive television, where a virtual reality three-dimensional facial avatar responds to the remote control in real time, speaking to the viewer and providing the requested information (Chakaveh, 2005; Maad, 2003a; Maad, 2003b).

Marilyn informs the viewer with a click of a button on daily financial news. The focus is on the provision of choice as well as personalization of information in an entertaining manner. As well as offering live financial data from leading stock exchanges such as New York, London, Frankfurt and Tokyo, multilingual aspects of the information are also catered for.

Traditionally, financial news has been regarded as content-based and rather rigid in format. In contrast, the edutainment aspects of Marilyn can make such a program entertaining as well as informative.

MARILYN consists of a 3D virtual human avatar presenting in an entertaining, informative, and interactive way multilingual live financial data (news and tickers) taken from various international stock exchanges. The use of the 3D virtual character aims at reducing the rigidity of delivering purely structured financial content consisting solely of indicators and charts. The voice replies, facial expressions, and hands and body gestures of the virtual human avatar provide a rather entertaining and informative medium to convey financial knowledge to the target audience. Five stages are adopted in the development of this live edutainment financial content (Maad, 2003a; Maad, 2003b):

- *Stage 1* involves the development of a template for an animated virtual human avatar enriched with facial expressions, voice replies, and hand gestures. The template gives the option to choose a desired virtual human character.
- *Stage 2* involves developing several multilingual templates for live financial news content (tickers, and news) taken from various international stock exchanges.
- *Stage 3* involves establishing a bi-directional communication medium between the virtual human avatar and the financial content.
- *Stage 4* involves establishing an interactive communication medium between the animated virtual human avatar and the target audience.
- *Stage 5* involves checking the compliance of the used technology with the prevailing standards for the target media delivery platform.

The first prototype of the live edutainment financial news content, depicted in Figure 1 above, was developed for an internet platform and was called MARLYN (**M**ultimodal **A**vatar **R**esponsive **LI**ve **N**ews caster). The prototype for the Internet platform consists of:

- ***A facial animation player applet[2] that is MPEG-4 FBA[3] (facial and body animation) compatible:*** The facial animation player decodes an MPEG-4 facial animation content generated from a given source and apply the results to a face model developed using 3D face modelling tools. The MPEG-4 FBA decoding process is based on integer arithmetic and adopts the interpolation from key position method (the same as the morph target approach widely used in computer animation and the MPEG-4 Facial Animation Table (FAT) approach).

---

[2] Developed by Visage Technologies (http://www.visagetechnologies.com/)

[3] ISO/IEC 14496 - MPEG-4 International Standard, Moving Picture Experts Group, www.cselt.it/mpeg

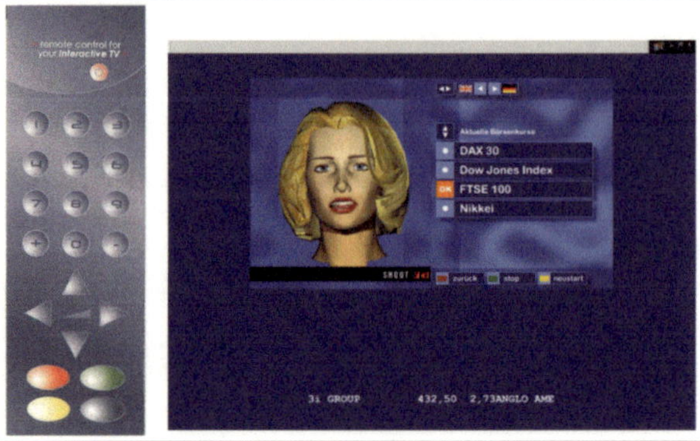


Fig. 1. MARILYN: "Multimodal Avatar Responsive Live News Caster"

- ***A facial and body animation generator tool, Fbagen[4], for dynamic generation of speech and lip sync bit stream files:*** For generating speech bit stream file, the Fbagen tool uses Microsoft SAPI[5] (Speech Application Programming Interface) as an interface for the SVOX[6] text to speech synthesiser (TTS) that uses SVOX voices. Fbagen also uses a lip sync encoder for generating the lip sync files. The lip sync file is encoded as an MPEG-4 FBA bit stream using high-level viseme parameters for lip movement encoding and viseme blend with linear interpolation for co-articulation. The Fbagen tool takes as input a text string and generates the corresponding FBA streams (.fba files) and speech files (.wav files). The generated FBA streams and speech files constitute the facial animation content that is input to the facial animation player.
- ***JAVA programs for extracting live financial contents (news and tickers) by parsing web financial sites:*** The extracted data (put in the form of a *String*) is passed as a command line argument to the Fbagen tool in order to generate the corresponding FBA streams and speech files.
- ***A Flash[7] interface for menu-like interaction with the 3D virtual character:*** The interface provides 2-dimensional navigation of various selection options of the multilingual financial content.
- ***A Flash display of the live financial news content:*** This content is basically the one extracted using the JAVA programs.
- ***A web page framing the whole work:*** This web page consists of 4 frames. These frames are for the applet, the flash interface, the flash financial content display, and the application's header respectively. This web page is preceded by an introductory web page motivating the subsequent content.

The Internet prototype of the live edutainment content is implemented in a client/server architecture. At the server-side, the financial content is extracted and the MPEG4 FBA and speech files are generated. At the client-side, the play-out out of the facial animation, the interaction, and the display of the live financial content takes place, and are framed in a web page.

---

[4] http://www.cybermecha.com/Studio/ca02.pdf
[5] http://www.microsoft.com/speech/
[6] http://www.svox.com
[7] Flash is a Trademark of Macromedia.

The portability of the live edutainment financial content to a mobile Personal Digital Assistant (PDA) platform involves the customisation of the user interaction interface to a mobile device style of interaction, and the in-house development of new versions of the facial animation player and the facial and body animation generator. The new design would ultimately use less system resources and is rather compatible with the uses of high quality voices produced by various text to speech synthesisers (TTS) and speech application programming interfaces (SAPI).

### 3.2 Use of VR in finance

Over recent years it has become increasingly obvious that text-based communication poses significant stumbling blocks to unambiguous communication. Virtual reality showed its benefit for the transfer of information and knowledge through the concept learning from the interaction with immersive 3D environment. Virtual reality and related technologies allows creating virtual environments with key characteristics that represent real world situations. The visualization and interaction with virtual objects is closer to reality than abstract mathematical and 2d representations of complex scenarios. In this respect virtual reality can potentially serve two objectives: (a) reflecting realism through a closer correspondence with real experience, and (b) extending the power of computer-based technology to better reflect "abstract" experience such as interactions concerned with interpretation and manipulation of symbols that does not have obvious embodiment.

The main motivation for using VR in financial trading is to enhance the user perception and cognition about the complexity of the financial market mechanisms and manifestations. The added value of using virtual reality in modeling financial market is its advanced visualization technique and metaphoric representation that mimic real world situations. Immersive multisensory interaction that includes vision, spatialized audio and haptic sensation provides the user with the illusion of being in real financial market. The user is confronted with nested scenarios and has to generate solutions by taking into account multi-criteria affects. He can develop various strategies in virtual environment to support decision making that reduces the risk of making wrong decision in real financial trading conditions. This approach improves learning, allows generating empirically driven decision and gaining experience from a synthetic world close to reality. Being immersed in a virtual environment the user acquires the feeling that he is interacting with real financial trading market. He interacts with the virtual agents and metaphors representing trading operators, he optimizes his actions using the procedure of trial and error. The user can define strategies, he takes actions, and perceives the consequence of his decisions with high degree of visualization that enhances his awareness about the complexity and unpredictable events that could happen in real financial market.

This section describes a virtual reality application in financial trading developed by the author at the University of Warwick in UK in collaboration with Laboratoire de Robotique de Paris (Maad et al, 2001). The virtual reality application, depicted in Figure 2 below, involves a user playing the role of a dealer who sets his/her bid/ask spread to attract buyers and sellers. The presence of the dealer in the rendered virtual reality scene is a simulated presence. As such the virtual reality simulation is fully detached from the real world. The virtual environment is represented to the user through a head mounted display. This peripheral provides the sensation of being immersed in the virtual scene. The actions of the user are communicated to the virtual environment using a 3D interaction tool: a pair of

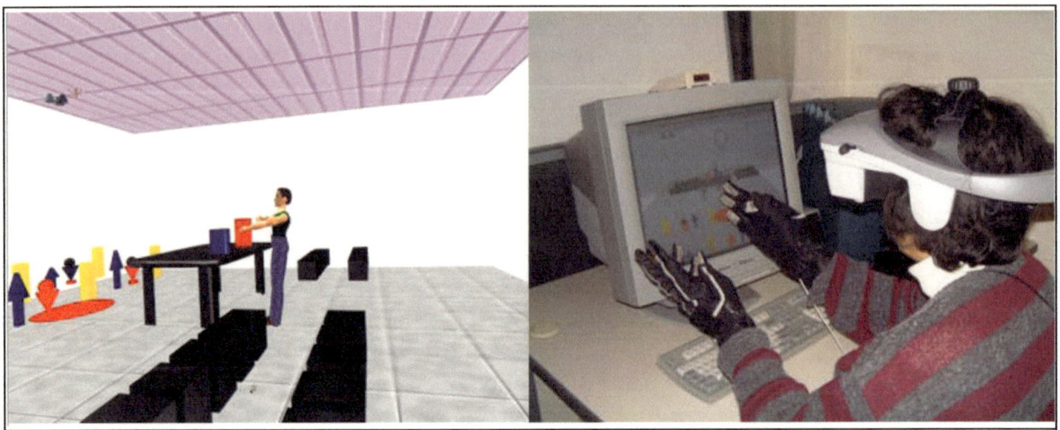

a. The virtual financial environment b. The interaction mode

Fig. 2. The Virtual Reality simulation

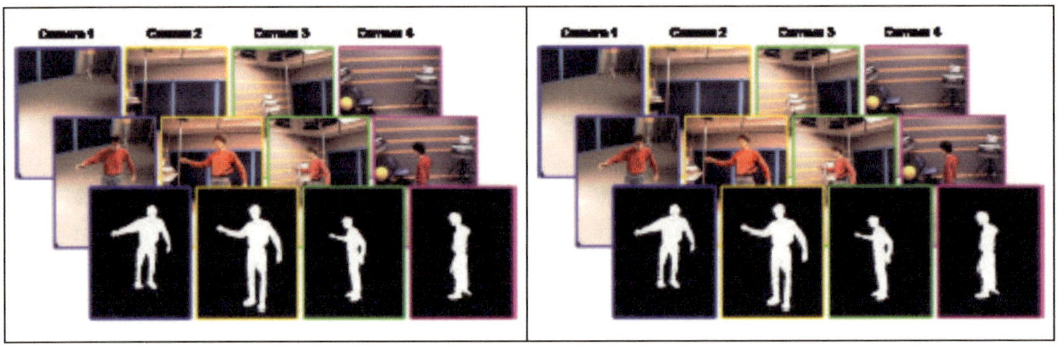

Fig. 3. CYBER II technology: image capturing (left image); image-based reconstruction (right image)

Fig. 4. CYBER II technology: Interaction with: an on/off button (left image); Interaction with a slider active region (right image)

Pinch Gloves. Figure 4 shows a screenshot of the virtual financial environment. The dealer manipulates his bid and ask prices (red and blue cylinders) to attract buyers and sellers (informed and uninformed traders).

Despite the added value of virtual reality approach in financial trading, in terms of the improved user perception of the financial market activities and of the role of the dealer in manipulating the true price of a security, the isolation of the user from the real world and the constrained interaction (the user has to wear a head mounted display and a pair of Pinch Gloves to acquire the feeling of immersion in the virtual world) makes the experience lived by the user (dealer) not sufficiently realistic (Maad et al., 2001).

### 3.3 Use of AR in finance

In this section we overview the CYBERII project (Hasenfratz et al 2004; Hasenfratz et al, 2003) and present the case study of the use of CYBER II technology in Finance (Maad et al, 2008).
The CYBERII project (Hasenfratz et al 2004; Hasenfratz et al, 2003) aims at simulating, in real-time, the presence of a person (e.g. a TV presenter or a teacher) in a virtual environment. Novel paradigms of interaction are proposed within the context of this project. These paradigms involve full body interaction with the virtual world in real time. This goes beyond traditional modes of interaction involving the use of mouse, remote control, pinch Gloves, or human sensor equipments.
The CYBERII project adopts a five steps technique to insert one or several humans in a virtual interaction space. It uses the notion of "Active Regions" to initiate the interaction with the virtual world. Actions are triggered upon body interaction with "Active Regions". This interaction may take the form of touching the "Active Region" and may be technically sensed using image analysis techniques that identify a body presence in the "Active Region". As described in (Hazenfratz et al., 2004; Hazenfratz et al., 2003), the CYBERII project adopts the following five steps:

- Multi-camera image acquisition, from different view points, of real moving bodies (see Figure 3 - left image).
- Reconstruction, modelling, and motion tracking of the acquired bodies and the surrounding environment (see Figure 3 - right image).
- Rendering of the reconstructed bodies and their surrounding.
- The creation of patterns of interaction in the rendered world using "Active Regions" as shown in Figure 2. Examples of "Active Regions" in a virtual interaction space include: the On/Off Button "Active Region" (see Figure 4 - left image) and the moving slider (see Figure 4 - right image).
- Data management and distributed parallel computing to meet the real time and realistic rendering constraints.

The CYBERII project targets various industries including: (1) the TV industry (e.g. virtual sets and online presentations); (2) the game industry (e.g. inserting real persons in the game world); and education and entertainment (e.g. allowing visits and presentation of remote places). The proposed novel paradigm of interaction developed within the scope of the CYBERII project, namely full body interaction with active regions, promises universal accessibility to media content. For instance, physically impaired users may find a greater convenience in full body interaction with a virtual scene instead of interaction with a mouse, a keyboard, or a remote control.
The CYBERII augmented reality financial application, depicted in Figure 5 below, involves the insertion of a user (playing the role of a financial dealer) in a virtual world, and the use of the technique of sliders "Active Regions" to enable the body interaction of the user (dealer) to set his/her bid/ask prices for attracting buyers and sellers (Maad et al, 2008). The

flow of buyers and sellers is abstractly represented by synthetic objects generated in the augmented scene following the user interaction with active regions. Figure 5 shows how the technique of slider "Active Regions" can help the dealer adjust his quotes to attract buyers and sellers. The flow of buyers and sellers is represented by red balls (for sellers flow) and yellow balls (for buyers flow). This flow is trigerred through body interaction with the sliders "Active Regions". This illustrates how the CYBERII concept of full body interaction with a virtual environment and the technique of slider "Active Regions" could be used for greater engagement and unconstrained immersion in a virtual world of financial indicators. The simulation augments the real world with perceptual knowledge about bid-ask spread variation and about the flow of traders (buyers and sellers) as a result of this variation.

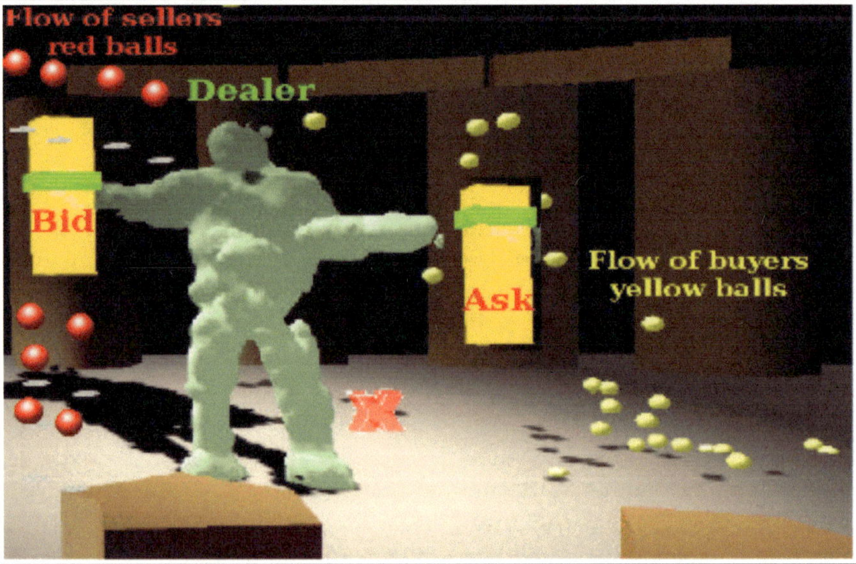


Fig. 5. The CYBERII financial application

### 3.4 Comparative analysis of the use of AR and VR in finance

MARILYN aims at substituting reality (use of 3D avatar instead of real human to present TV programs). The use of augmented reality instead of virtual reality aims at breaking the separation of the financial application from the real world and at augmenting its realism. Further reality augmentation to the rendered scene can be gained by adding, as a background, a synthetic depiction of the activity of the financial market. This is shown in Figure 6 below. Reality augmentation can be also gained by adding a synthesized speech that tells us about the current actions taken by the dealer (the incrusted human), the impact of the dealer's action on the flow of traders (buyers and sellers), as well as on the whole financial market activity.

Many challenges may face the use of the application 3D/AR/VR in finance. These include:

- ***The maturity of the technology:*** Earlier empirical studies conducted in (Maad, 2003a) reveals the limitation of 3D and audio technologies in meeting standards for authoring interactive television content. This is attributed to the lack of realism of the media content authored using the prevalent technologies. For instance in the CYBERII application, we

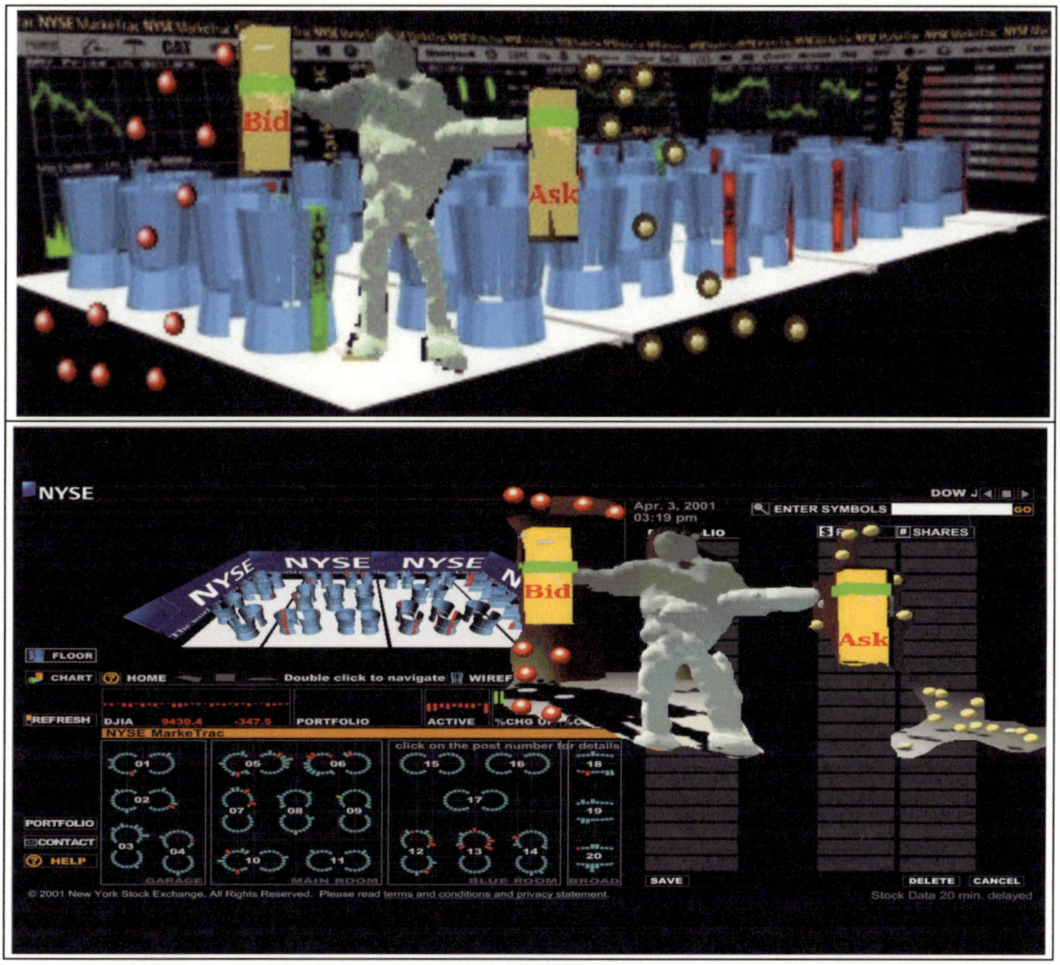


Fig. 6. CYBERII incrustation in a Virtual World of Financial indicators (illustrative example)

can see that the rendered human(s) lack realism as shown in the figures. This may have an impact on the appeal of the current technology to the financial community.

- *The choice of the medium of delivery:* Four potential medium of delivery can be considered, these include: the PC, the Internet, the interactive television (ITV), or other home/office devices. A closer look at the hardware setup of the CYBERII project, described in (Hazenfratz et al., 2004; Hazenfratz et al., 2003) as a networked set of 4 cameras, 4 PC, and one supercomputer, reveals great challenges in the portability and interoperability of the CYBERII technology.
- *Users interest:* The widespread penetration of 3D/AR/VR technologies among the financial community depends on the current demand for applications such as the one described above. If this demand ever exists then it would be limited among a few novice community who fancy new technologies.

In face of these challenges, more research work, beyond the development of the technology, need to be undertaken to justify the usability and utility of 3D/AR/ VR technologies in meeting various industries' needs.

## 4. Financial state visibility case study

The urgent economic problem, linked to the financial crisis, challenges current research and technological development. The scale of the fiscal crisis that undermined the credibility of the financial system motivates the consideration of "Global Financial State Visibility" as a key global challenge that validates research and technological development activities to support the engineering dynamics of automatically adaptable software services along the "global financial supply chain" (Maad et al, 2009). Financial state could be conveyed in various ways:

- perception the state of financial risk
- perception of financial events
- percent of the financial activity
- perception of the financial system and regulatory framework

Our aim is to align the prevalent thinking in terms of mediating the financial state using reports or static models to mediating the financial state using advanced visualisation and interaction technique. Key issues to consider are who will access, manipulate, and govern the financial state. Various entities (policy makers, regulators, auditors, accountants, investors, consumers, suppliers, producers, individuals) need to access /govern / adapt Financial state Visibility depending on service level agreements SLA (see Figure 7 below).

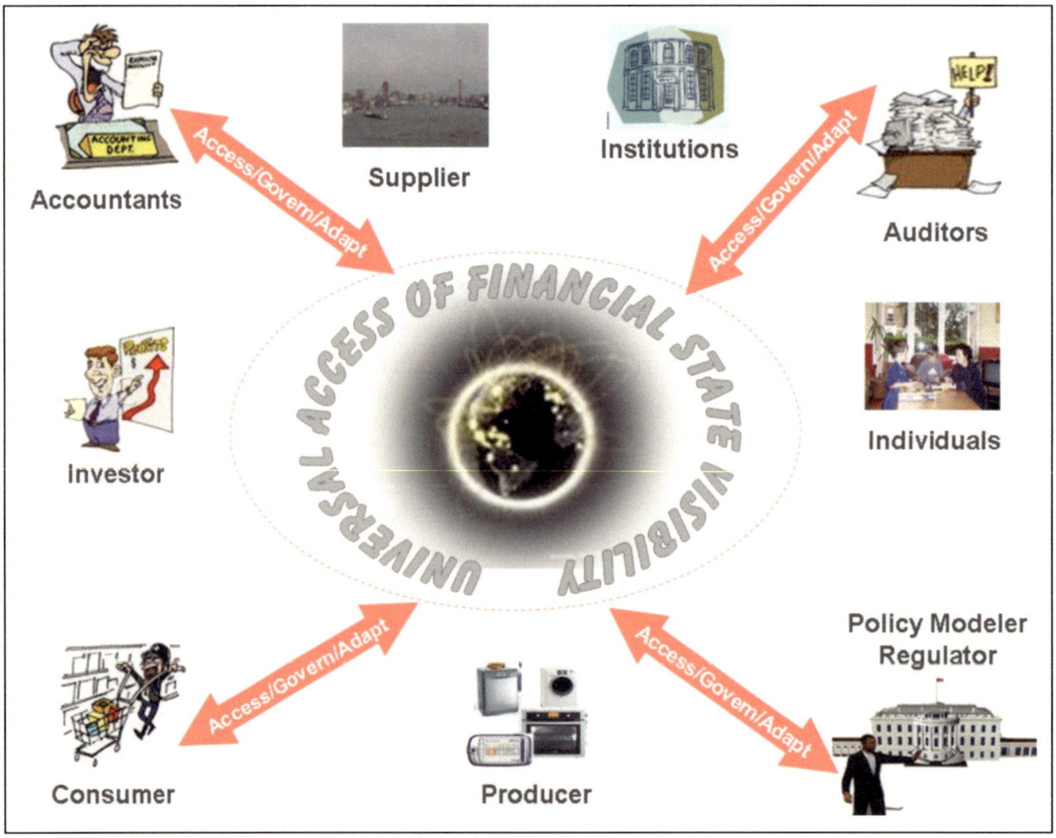


Fig. 7. Actors that need to access /govern / adapt Financial state Visibility

The Financial state visibility challenge has various dimensions:

- *Domain knowledge dimension:* this involves building the financial state knowledge base (the development of techniques to store and manipulate the semantic representation of the financial state by various stakeholders including regulators, investors, and central banks worldwide); and the visual rendering (using techniques such AR/VR) of the financial state knowledge base.
- *Converged ICT and media dimension:* this involves the development of an interoperability layer at the service infrastructure and interface levels to guarantee instant access to financial state via various converged ICT and media devices.
- *Global factors dimension:* financial state knowledge is stored and manipulated in different languages and different structures and formats. This raises geographical cultural, and accessibility technical challenges. Rendering of the financial state needs to adapt to "global context on demand".
- *Governance dimension:* There is an urgent need to support the governance of the financial state with greater perception and manipulation capability tools.

Various financial state visibility services, depicted in Figure 8 below, could be developed taking into account the above considered dimensions. These services can be grouped into various levels and categories:

*Domain Levels Services:*

- Domain Services: Encapsulate/wrap/Render Domain Knowledge aspect
- Technology Convergence services: Accessibility and Interoperability Services
- Global Factors Services: Encapsulate/wrap/render global factors knowledge
- Governance Services: Encapsulate /wrap/render Governance knowledge

*Integration Services Exchange:*

Handle exchange communication between domain level services and integrative framework services

*Integrative Framework Services:*

Integrate functionalities of domain level services

- Integrative Framework Services
- Integration Framework Service Exchange

*Mediators services:*

Mediate Integrative services to various users at various levels according to Service Governance Level Agreement

- Mediator Service Exchange
- Adaptation Service Mediators

The design and engineering of these state visibility services involves: composition, workflow, adaptation at design time and run time consideration, agency interaction, verification and validation. Key issue is the delivery of AR / VR along the chain of services workflow.

Users of the services are conceived at two levels: level 1 end users are developers of internet of things; and level 2 end users are end users of internet of things

Users at both level govern access, discovery, and manipulation of state visibility services according to Governance Service Level Agreements GSLA.

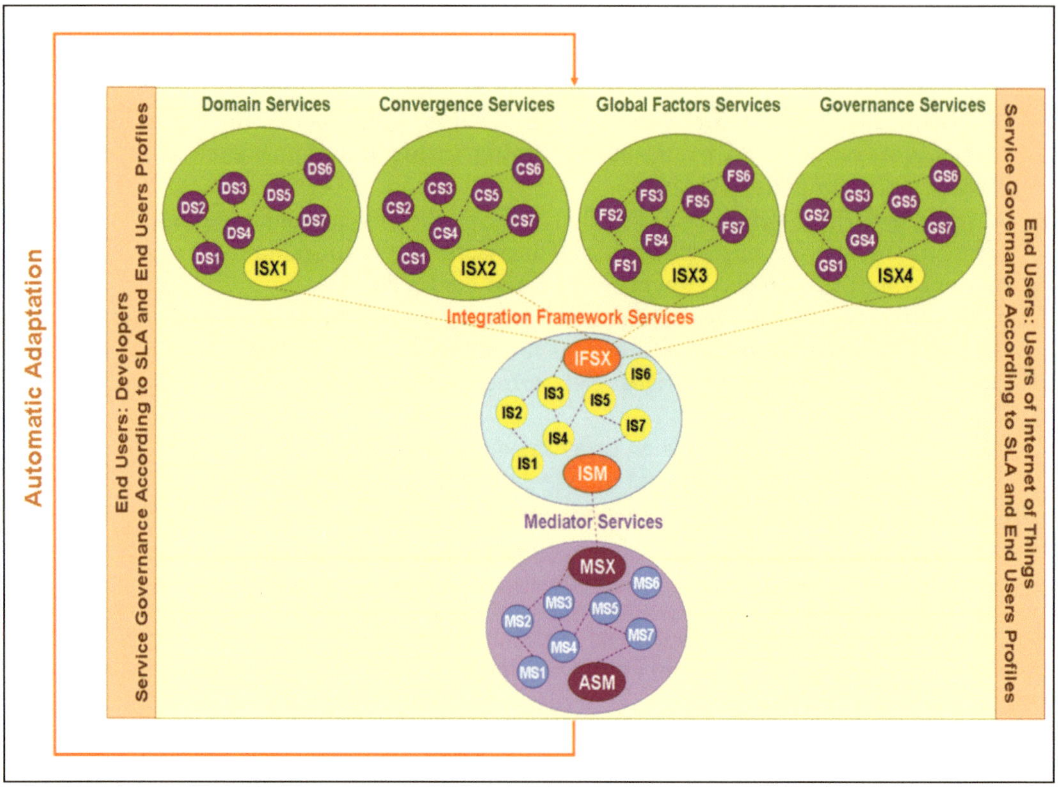


Fig. 8. financial state visibility services

## 5. Use of AR / VR for greater financial state visibility

This section proposes a blend of approaches to mediate financial state visibility as a service using VR / AR technologies.

The 3 applications overviewed in section 3 above highlight a limitation of existing 3D/VR / AR technologies in wide industry penetration. This is mainly attributed to portability and utility of the technology.

We suggest below service oriented software engineering and Empirical Modelling as a blend of approaches for greater portability and usability of 3D / VR/ AR technologies

### 5.1 Service software engineering

Given the need of massive computational power and distributed access by various actors of the financial state, 3D / VR / AR technologies can largely benefit from service oriented computing to mediate, using high end visualization, the financial state and risk to various actors.

According to (Di Nitto et al, 2009), service-oriented computing (SOC) represents one of the most challenging promises to support the development of adaptive distributed systems. Applications can open themselves to the use of services offered by third parties that can be accessed through standard, well defined interfaces. The binding between applications and the corresponding services can be extremely loose in this context, thus making it possible to

compose new services on the fly whenever a new need arises. Around this idea a number of initiatives and standards have grown up, some of them focusing on how such roles need to interact with each other, and some others on how to engineer systems based on such a model and on how to provide foundational support to their development. In particular, so-called service-oriented applications and architectures (SOAs) have captured the interest of industry, which is trying to exploit them as the reference architecture to support Business to Business B2B interaction. According to Forrester Research, the SOA service and market had grown by $U.S. 4.9 billion in 2005, and it is forecasted to have an interesting growth rate until 2010, with a compound annual growth rate of 88 percent between 2004 and 2009.
The SOC road map, figure 9 below extracted from (Di Nitto et al, 2009), separates basic service capabilities provided by a services middleware infrastructure and conventional SOA from more advanced service functionalities that are needed for dynamically composing (integrating) services. The SOC road map highlights the importance of service modeling and service-oriented engineering (i.e., service-oriented analysis, design, and development techniques and methodologies that are crucial elements for the development of meaningful services and business process specifications).

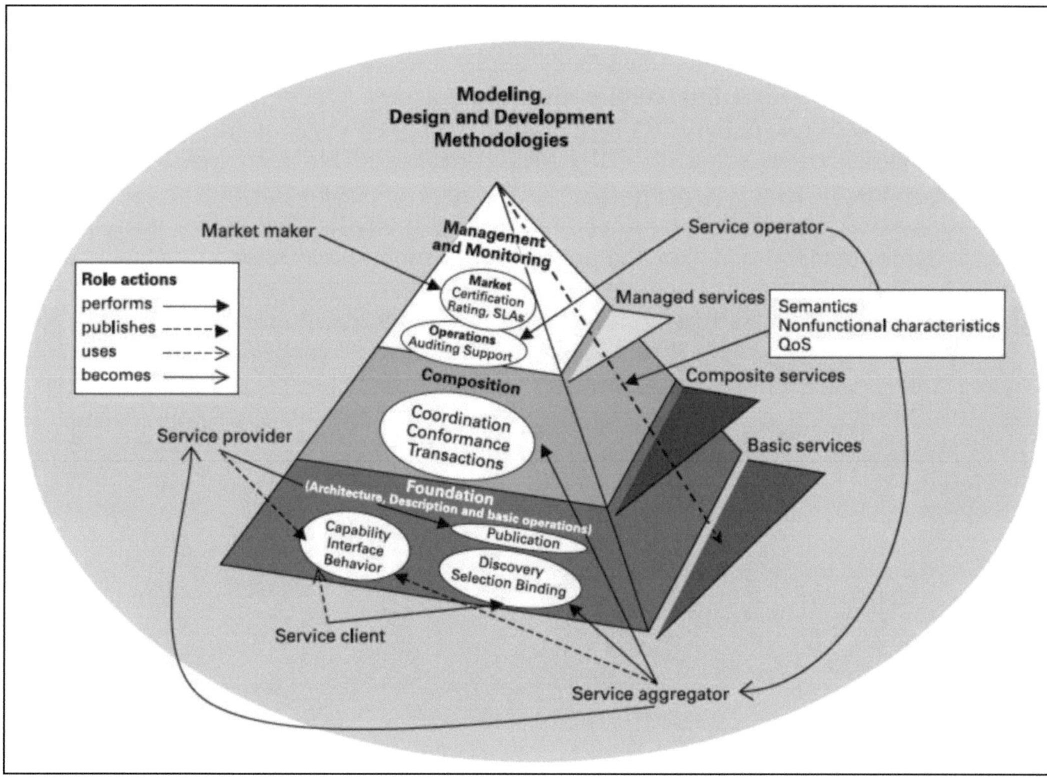


Fig. 9. the Service Oriented Computing roadmap (extracted from (Di Nitto et al, 2009)

## 5.2 Empirical modelling

The challenges faced by the use of 3D/ VR / AR for constructing virtual environments for finance are best revealed by drawing a comparison with its use in computer-aided assembly (Garbaya et al, 2000). This comparison reveals a difference in the objective, considerations, approaches, and user role in constructing visually rich virtual environment for different contexts. The main objective in using 3D/ VR / AR in finance is enhanced cognition of state; in the case of virtual assembly the main objective is to minimise the need for building physical prototypes. The issues to be considered in applying 3D/ VR / AR for financial state visibility and in virtual assembly differ in nature and importance. In virtual assembly, the major concerns are proper 3D picture capturing, conversion, and adding behaviour to objects; in 3D/ VR / AR for financial state visibility, they are geometric abstraction of financial concepts, integration with financial database, and distributed interaction. The steps followed to create a virtual scene for virtual assembly and for financial state are different. A linear, preconceived, set of processes can be followed to develop a scene for virtual assembly. These can be framed in three stages: defining objects to be assembled, preparing the assembly geometry for visualisation, and adding behaviour to visualised objects. Creating a virtual scene depicting financial state is more complicated and cannot be framed adequately in a pre-conceived way. However, a broad outline can be traced to guide the construction process. This involves: identifying entities (both those that admit geometric abstraction and those that have already a well recognised geometric representation) to be included in the virtual scene; choosing an appropriate geometric representation for these entities; adding a situated behaviour and visualisation to entities; identifying the external resources (such as databases, files, data feeds, etc.) to be interfaced to the virtual scene; and framing the role of the user intervention in the simulation. Where human intervention is concerned, the user's role in the 3D/VR/AR scene is more open-ended in a financial context than in an assembly context. In a 3D/ VR / AR scene for assembly the immersion of the user is very important: the user can manipulate virtual objects with his hands. The user's hands, guided by the user's brain, interact directly with virtual objects. This makes virtual reality approach appropriate for modelling the process of assembly task planning (see Figure 10).

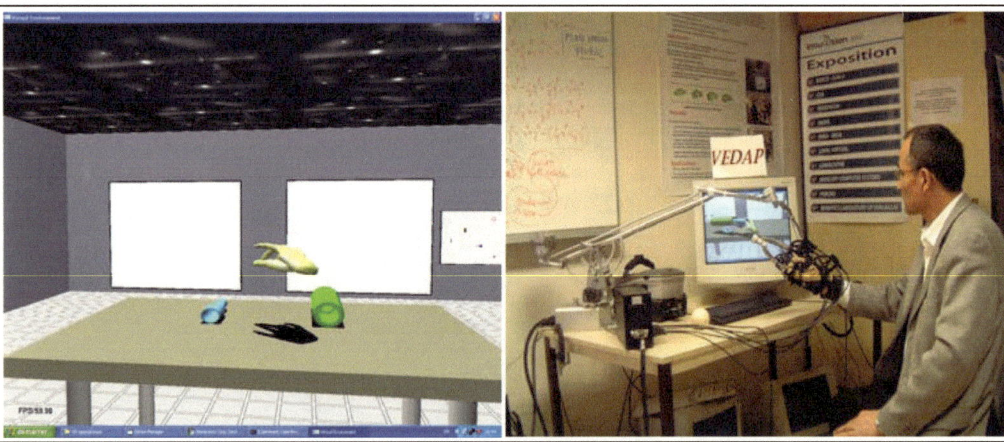


| a. Virtual assembly environment | b. Assembly planning and operation with haptic interface |
|---|---|

Fig. 10. Example of VR modelling for areas such as assembly planning

Construing financial phenomena is a function performed by the human brain. The mental model of the designer can be abstracted in a static diagram, a 2D computer artefact, or a VR / AR scene. Geometric objects in the virtual scene might admit no counterpart in the real world - they are purely geometric metaphors. This makes a virtual scene just one of several possible representations. It also motivates a prior situated analysis exploring possible construals pertaining to the social context. The above comparison highlights the need to support 3D/ VR / AR technologies with principles and techniques to analyse and construe social contexts and to adopt appropriate visualisations for abstract entities (such as financial indicators) that have no real geometric counterpart. Current technologies for Empirical Modelling (Beynon, 1999) can help in construing financial situations and in representing state and the analysis of agency in state change, whilst 3D / VR / AR technologies offer enhanced visualisation and scope for user immersion and experience of state.

## 6. Conclusion

This chapter reflected on the potential of Virtual Reality and Augmented Reality (VR / AR) technologies in supporting the dynamics of global financial systems and in addressing the grand challenges posed by unexpected events and crisis. The chapter briefly overviewed traditional VR/AR uses and described three early attempts to use 3D/ VR / AR technologies in Finance. In light of the recent financial crisis, there is a potential added valued in harnessing the use of VR/AR technologies to convey a greater visibility of the financial state (including visibility of financial risk). Various dimensions of the problem are considered. The chapter suggested a blend of service oriented computing SOC and empirical modelling technologies to support the use of VR / AR technologies in raising the perception of financial state and risk.

There is a very significant distinction between VR modelling for areas such as assembly planning as represented in papers such as (Garbaya et al, 2000), and its application for greater visibility of the financial state and risk. Whilst we can reasonably speak of "using VR to model the reality of the process of assembly planning", the reality of the financial state is an altogether more elusive concept. Where manufacturing assembly deals with objects and actions whose objectivity and real-world authenticity is uncontroversial, financial state visibility is a prime example of an activity in which the impact of technology upon human cognition is prominent, and character of its agencies and observables is accordingly hard to capture in objective terms. Empirical Modelling supplies an appropriate framework within which to address the ontological issues raised by such applications of VR / AR (Beynon, 1999).

This chapter points to the following conclusions:

- 3D/ VR/ AR technologies can help in exploring a particular state in a social context.
- The pre-construction phase of the virtual world can benefit greatly from concepts drawn from the Empirical Modelling literature such as modelling state, state change, and the initiators of state change.
- 3D/ VR / AR technologies needs to be better adapted for the representation of multiple agents acting to change the state and corresponding visualisation.
- The successful application of 3D / VR /AR technologies in modelling social and data intensive environment relies upon integrating these technologies with other programming paradigms and architectures such as service oriented computing and architecture (SOC and SOA).

Future research agenda involves the development of quantitative and qualitative metrics to assess the potential benefits of 3D / VR / AR in modelling a state in a social context. Two dimensions are appropriate: the visibility and the viscosity.

## 7. Acknowledgements

This research is the result of collaboration between partners from Europe. The authors gratefully acknowledge the support for this work obtained from the Image Institute - Arts et Metiers ParisTech.

## 8. References

Maad S, Beynon M, Garbaya S (2001), Realising Virtual Trading: What Price Virtual Reality?, Usability Evaluation and Interface Design: Cognitive Engineering, Intelligent Agents and Virtual Reality, M.J. Smith, G. Salvendy, D. Harris, R.J. Koubek (editors), Lawrence Erlbaum Associates, Mahwah, N.J., ISBN: 0-8058-3607-1, Volume 1, 2001, Part II: Virtual Reality, pp. 1007.

Chakaveh S (2005), Merging Virtual Reality and Television through Interactive Virtual Actors Marilyn - Multimodal Avatar Responsive Live Newscaster, ERCIM News online edition No.62, July 2005, Special theme: Multimedia Informatics, http://www.ercim.org/publication/Ercim_News/enw62/chakaveh.html

Maad S (2003a), MARILYN: A Novel Platform For Intelligent Interactive TV (IITV), Human-Computer Interaction, Theory and Practice (Part 1), Volume 1, Julie A. Jacko and Constantine Stephanidis (editors), LAWRENCE ERLBAUM ASSOCIATES, INC. Publishers, Mahwah, NJ 07430-2262, ISBN: 0-8058-4930-0, year 2003, Section 6. Learning and Edutainment, pp. 1041-1045.

Maad S (2003b), Universal Access For Multimodal ITV Content: Challenges and Prospects, Universal Access. Theoretical Perspectives, Practice, and Experience, N. Carbonell, C. Stephanidis (Editors), Lecture Notes in Computer Science, Springer-Verlag, Heidelberg, Vol. 2615 / 2003, Jan 2003, pp.195-208.

Maad S, Garbaya S, Bouakaz S (2008), From Virtual to Augmented Reality in Finance : A CYBERII Application, Journal of Enterprise Information Management 2008; 21(1):71-80.

Hasenfratz, J. M., Lapierre, M. and Sillion, F. (2004), A Real-Time System for Full Body Interaction, Virtual Environments 2004.

Hasenfratz, J. M., Lapierre, M., Gascuel, J. D. and Boyer, E. (2003), Real-Time Capture, Reconstruction and Insertion into Virtual World of Human Actors VVG-, Vision, Video and Graphics – 2003

Maad S and Coghlan B (2009), The Next Generation Grid: An Infrastructure for Global Business Systems, International Journal for Business Information systems: Business Modelling and Simulations IJBIS (in press).

Di Nitto E., Sassen A.M., Traverso P. and Zwegers A., At Your Service - Service-Oriented Computing from an EU Perspective, The MIT Press 2009)

Beynon, W.M. (1999) "Empirical Modelling and the Foundations of Artificial Intelligence, Computation for Metaphors, Analogy and Agents", Lecture Notes in Artificial Intelligence 1562, Springer, 322-364, 1999.

Garbaya, S. and Coiffet, P. (2000) "Generating Operation Time from Virtual Assembly Environment", in proceedings of the 7th UK VR-SIG Conference, 19th September, 2000, University of Strathclyde, Glasgow, Scotland

13

# Augmented Reality for Multi-disciplinary Collaboration

Rui(Irene) Chen and Xiangyu Wang
*The University of Sydney*
*Australia*

## 1. Introduction

During the past few years, people have started to consider using digital technologies to assist the multi-disciplinary work ( Sonnenwald, 2007; Mentzas & Bafoutsou, 2004; Bos & Zimmerman, 2007). Many design activities involve participants from different disciplines. Cross-disciplines require information sharing. Comprehension also becomes more complicated. Therefore the need of understanding the other disciplines has become more important. However, as the number of specialty areas increases, the languages that define each separate knowledge base become increasingly complicating. Hence, concepts and viewpoints that were once considered as part of a whole become detached. This phenomenon is typical of the development of tertiary education, especially within professional oriented courses, where disciplines and sub-disciplines have grown further away from each other and the ability to communicate with different disciplines has become increasingly scrappy.

Although the combination of different discipline bases within the same school or department has been considered to some extent, many of them do not take the full advantages of the hybrid opportunities that are related to the work within cross-disciplines. Most time institutes or schools educate different disciplines' students separately, therefore, students only can be taught to seek for single-source solutions. Hence, there is a need to establish the knowledge of cross-discipline in education. For example, in a typical construction project, there involves knowledge from several different domains. Architects design the building and coordinate the input of other specialists in the team. Land surveyors survey the property and structural engineers design and specify the structural components of a building including foundations, footings, posts, beams, wall systems, etc. Electrical engineers design the power, lighting and communication requirements of the building. Mechanical engineers design the heating, cooling and ventilation of the building. Hydraulics engineers are in charge of designing the water and sewerage requirements. Quantity surveyors are responsible for the cost estimation of the design. It is apparent that different disciplines need to have a common platform to communicate and collaborate together.

## 2. Needs

It is essential to coordinate a team of specialist consultants, the possible solution to help design and coordinate the cross-discipline work no matter whether it is a small or large

project. Same level of attentions should be paid to each discipline in details. Although usually architects play a valuable mediation role in the built environment, working closely with user groups and clients, builders, trades-people, government bodies, councillors and consultants, balancing their needs and requirements. This mediating role requires architects to have coordination, negotiation and resolution skills (Holm, 2006).
Architects usually need to establish the client's needs, expectations, project requirements and budgets. This usually should be collected to prepare the design brief.
Architects analyses the design brief, the site conditions, features and constraints and then determines the best location and orientation. Architects begin to develop ideas through rough plans, sketches and models. These ideas are brought together into concept design drawings. The most common communication method is to use two-dimensional drawings produced by computer-aided design (CAD) systems to convey design information by means of representing three dimensional buildings and surrounding elements (road, pool, landscape, infrastructure, etc.) and depict their relationship in the project site (Holm, 2006). In addition, the development team need communicate their planning information regarding costs, management hierarchy and feasibility studies in forms of tables and diagrams generated by some spreadsheet software. However, this is often not easily transferred into designs and drawings. It causes the difficulties for each specified discipline to comprehend each other's information due to the fact that their information may be incoherent or are typically viewed in separate working environments. Therefore, there is a need to offer the work platform for knowledge gaining and express the analytical thinking from multi-discipline.

## 3. Collaboration

Hara (2003) summarises collaboration as people working together for a common goal and sharing of knowledge. Similarly, Weiseith, Munkvold, Tvedte, and Larsen (2006) suggest that collaboration takes place when two or more people communicate and cooperate to reach a goal. Effective collaboration requires all involved appropriately and actively working together. There have been studies to identify the factors involved in combining peers. There are certain phases involved in collaboration in design as shown in Fig. 1.
Most time, the first step is to identify information needs no matter which design they are required to implement. Then it moves to the initiation phase which prepares a clear guide about what information to be collected. Then the design phases engage in many different tasks, however, all the disciplines need to actively develop their ideas, through rough plans, sketches and models. Design ideas should be brought together in a later stage and processed to generate proper data for analysis. Since the collaborative work generally involves different specialized knowledge, when they are processed together, there is always a need to be revised. Finally, it can be collated to see if it meets the requirements.
Creamer and Lattuca (Creamer & Lattuca, 2005) underscored the social inquiry aspect of collaboration, suggesting that collaboration promotes people understanding and learning from each other. In describing collaboration as social practice, they emphasise the role of interaction and building relationships. In the context of learning, Oliver, Herrington, and Reeves (Oliver et al., 2007) described collaboration as "interactions that are interdependent and actually promote the kinds of joint contributions of different domain knowledge that enable outcomes to exceed what might normally be achieved by individual activity. Therefore, it is apparent that the lack of mutual understanding of cross-discipline could cause inefficient work, cease the learning esteem and even delay the work progress.

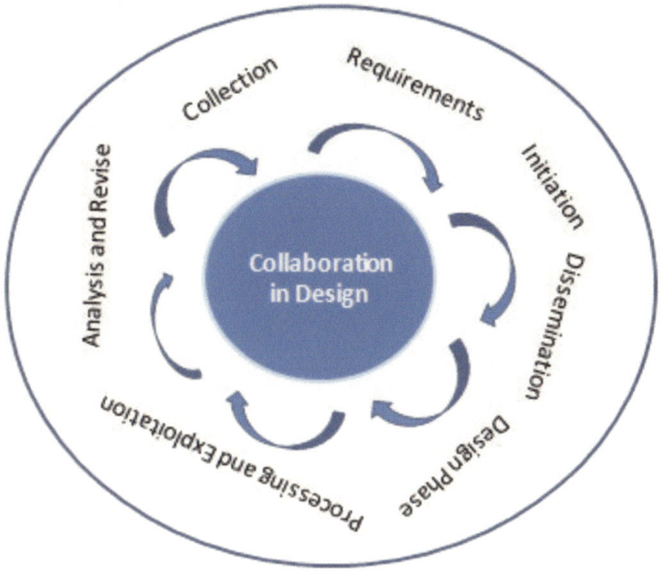


Fig. 1. Phases for collaboration in design

## 4. Related work

The problem of information transfer between different disciplines may result it certain delays of decision-making and also lack in the practicability of the design. Several attempts have been made to eliminate the problems by integrating knowledge from different fields with digital environments that allow multiple disciplines to input their information and also interact with digital information seamlessly and intuitively during the design processes.

The project of FingARtips used Augmented Reality technology that requires users to wear heads-up displays or virtual glasses (Buchmann et al., 2004) (see Fig. 2.(a) (b)) to be able to view digital information that is overlaid onto physical objects in the real world (see Fig.3.(a) (b)). So the setup of urban planning workspace allows the users to see the immersive view of a model.

However, this feature is limited by the number of concurrent users the system can handle at a given time and the cost of equipment for single users may not be feasible for large size of users from different disciplines. Furthermore, another issue is tracking inaccuracy. Only when the glove is reliably tracked, can the system be thoroughly evaluated and put to use.

Another example is MetaDESK called "Tangible Geospace" (Ishii & Ullmer, 2006) which is one of Tangible User Interface system. It has been used in urban design and planning and has been developed for designers who need to collaborate with the other disciplines simultaneously in a single environment. Several physical objects and instruments for interacting with geographical space sit in a translucent holding tray on the metaDESK's surface (Ishii & Ullmer, 2006). Through placing a small physical model (phicon) of Great Dome onto the desk, a two-dimensional map appears underneath on the desk, bound to the Dome object at its location on the map. Simultaneously, the arm-mounted active lens (Ishii & Ullmer, 2006) (Fig. 4. (a)) displays a three-dimensional view of MIT with its buildings in perspective.

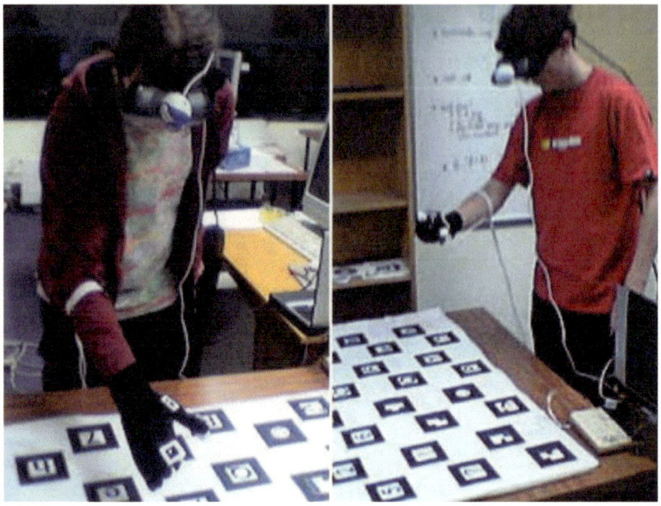

(a) (b)

Fig. 2. (a)(b). The urban planning demonstration setup.

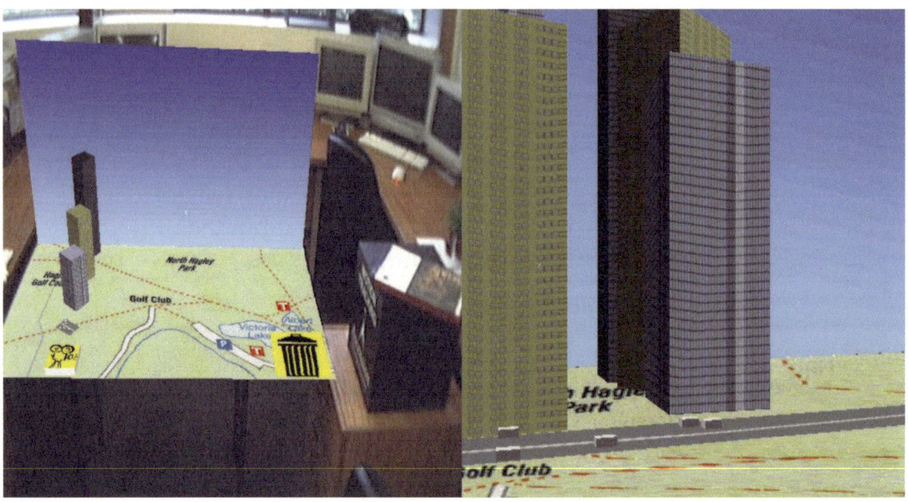

(a) (b)

Fig. 3. (a). The urban planning workspace (b) Immersive view of a model (Buchmann et al., 2004)

As an alternative to the two phicon scaling/rotation interaction, a rotation constraint instrument made of two cylinders mechanically coupled by a sliding bar has been implemented (see Fig.4.(b)). This instrument allows scaling and rotation manipulation of the two geospace control points, while preventing the ambiguous two-phicon rotation by the intrinsic mechanical constraint.

However, this main function is to view existing design and it seems not enough to assist the users from multi-disciplines to make informative design decisions along with engineers and planners.

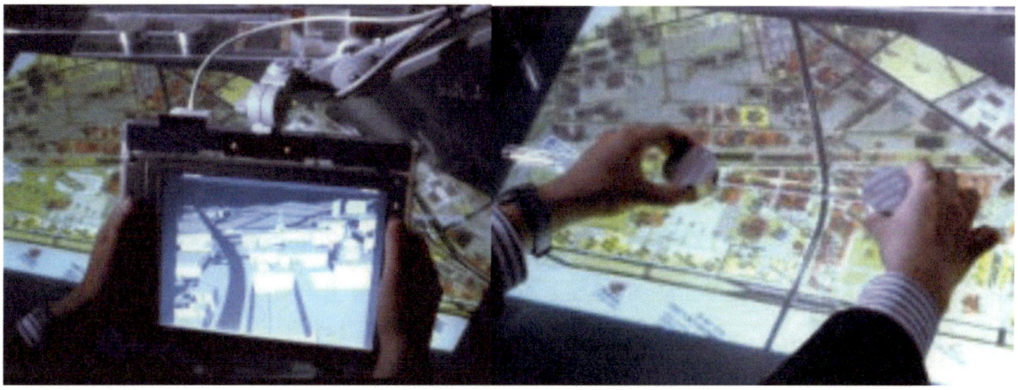

(a) (b)

Fig. 4. (a). Active lens in tangible Geospace (b). Rotation constraint instrument (Ishii & Ullmer, 2006)

## 5. Application framework

In order to ensure dynamic and interactive knowledge among different fields in building design which is an essential prerequisite for effective collaboration, a suitable knowledge base is required for gaining the different information. Therefore, the knowledge base collects from each individual workspace specific to each individual knowledge domain that corresponds to the number of specialists involved, as well as into the shared design workspace (see Fig. 6).

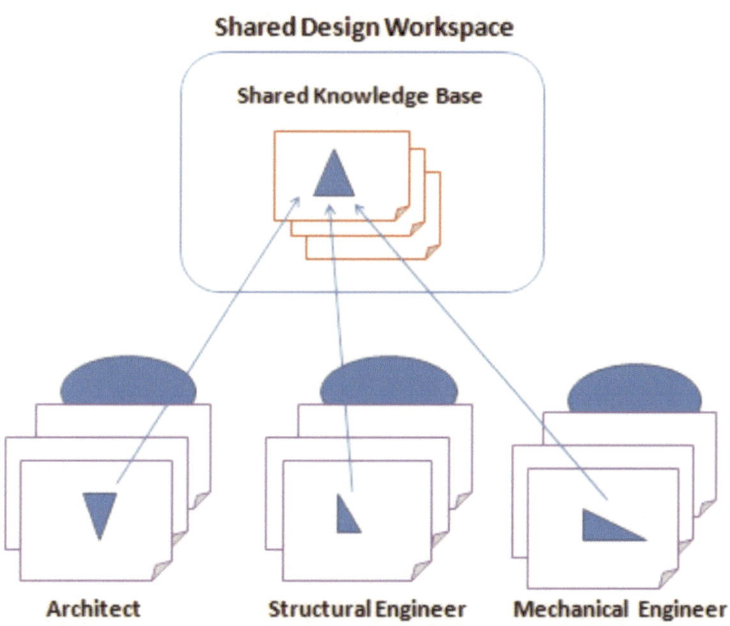


Fig. 6. Private and shared knowledge base

This model presents a distributed structure of independent Design Workspace, each referring to one of the numerous disciplines in design domain. The benefit of this structure is that each of the individual parts are linked directly to a centralized knowledge base so that they can all visualize the integration of the partial solutions.

During the design process individuals are able to create or modify their own personal design with their own specific knowledge and describe it with their own personal or professional languages. This process is none other than merging the knowledge from all the different disciplines into shared workspace.

The database should be developed based on the model of the structure described above. Hence, during the design process each sector can verify their own personal design case using their own specialist knowledge until they have deemed it to be satisfactory. Meanwhile, the updating information will be transferred to the top of knowledge base so updating and combining can be instantly and spontaneously made.

The main application of this framework lies in the interpretation between different disciplines and provides users with immediate feedback with relevant results through an intuitive interface. The process starts when the users from different disciplines enter their primary design with essential data. In some specific part, if users do not know or understand the design from other disciplines, they can directly contact with the other users from those disciplines. Users have their own workspaces which enable them to interact with the physical objects as if they would like to do so with an actual physical of a design project. Information can then be calculated and combined and the outcome can be immediately projected in the corresponding discipline. The Fig.7 has demonstrated the relationships between the different elements in the framework.

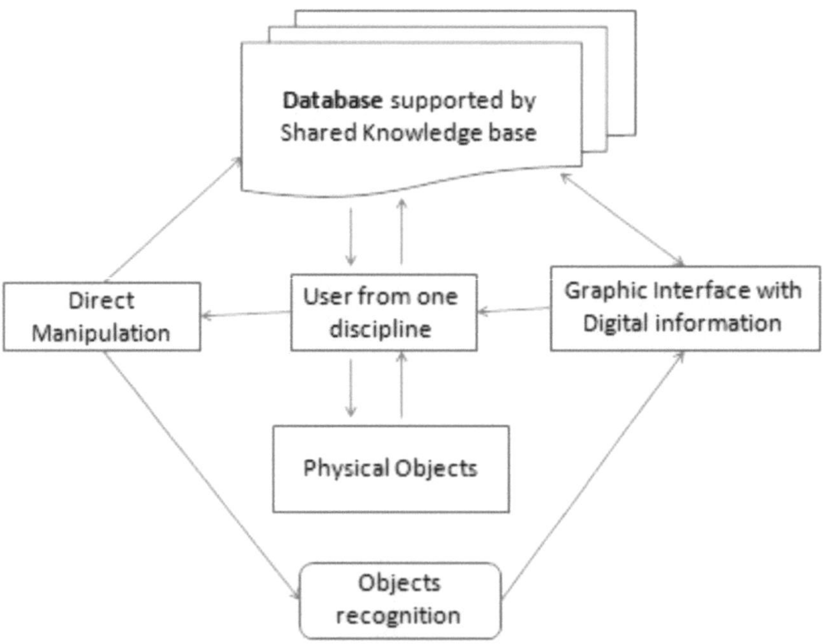


Fig. 7. The relationship between the elements

## 6. Scenario

The scenario based on the framework provides visual aids for interpreting and communicating drawings from architects to engineers. Superintendents/project managers on site usually refer to design drawings and specifications to examine if the work is performed as designed because chances are that workers on site cannot fully understand the design (Dunston & Shin, 2009). Although the architects can be requested to staff on site and check the correctness, it is still unavoidable that miscommunication or misinterpretation can appear quite often. For instance, one architect may try to convey some instructions about a specific task, however, he/she may find it hard to describe in words or 2D sketch. This often fails since during this process, an individual refers to their own mental image of forming and the result of forming an image is different depending on the different tasks and resources. The 2D drawing usually does not contain sufficient information for workers on site to imagine the actual design in actual scale, accurate position and orientation. Some research (Cooper & Podgorny, 1976; Shepard, 1992) indicated that it involves a large amount of time to mentally match a rotated object with an original object as angular difference results in different orientation and also it may require extra mental load to depict the specific position in real world location. Apparently, the mental load experienced in inferring 3D design from 2D drawings increases as a design becomes more complicated. These factors underline the importance of using proposed framework into the design. Since Tangible Augmented Reality systems could help different disciplines of the co-workers to understand

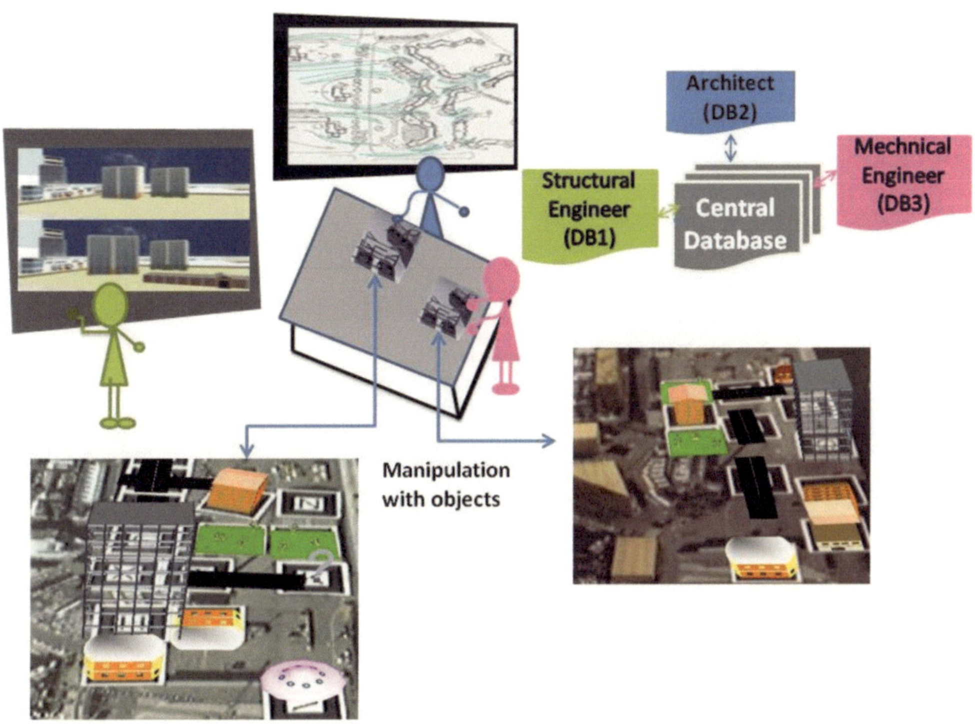


Fig. 8. Scenario demonstration

each other better. Firstly, the Tangible Augmented Reality system could render spatially from the selected portion to display the 3D design model in a real scale. Particularly, the intuitive interfaces are used to couple physical objects with digital information by means of physical input from the users as the demonstration you can see from the Fig.8. The information from different disciplines can be stored in different databases and finally exchanged the information in the central database. The Tangible Augmented Reality systems allow them to get instant feedback from the information being re-updated after the manipulation from the users. Therefore the reflection of the communication from the multi disciplines will not get lost or confused because of the correction or change from various aspects.

With the additional Tangible User Interfaces, the input and output sources can be integrated into the system. The digital information is displayed by overlaying the projector beneath the physical objects (Fisher & Flohr, 2008).

In addition, the database is built based on the structure of a shared knowledge base. Any instant modification or change can be detected and updated to the other user from different disciplines. The re-calculated and updated data can be informed immediately without delay. A conceptual image with calculated 3D design and contextual data can be displayed by Augmented Reality systems (see Fig. 9).

Fig. 9. A conceptual image of AR overlay of 3D design and contextual data (Dunston & Shin, 2009).

During these tasks, all users from different disciplines need to exchange information back and forth until the final compromise is met leading towards an agreeable and premier design. In this way, a common workspace is offered to solve these differences with visual and tactile aids.

## 7. Summary

This chapter presents a framework for multi-disciplinary collaboration. Tangible Augmented Reality has been raised as one of suitable systems for design collaboration. Furthermore, it emphasizes the advantages of Tangible Augmented Reality to illustrate the needs for integrating the Tangible User Interfaces and Augmented Reality Systems.

## 8. References


Bos, N. & Zimmerman, A. (2007). From shared databases to communities of practice: A taxonomy of collaboratories. *Journal of Computer-Mediated Communication, 12*(2), pp. 652–672.

Buchmann, V.; Violich, S.; Billinghurst, M. & Cockburn, A. (2004). FingARtips: gesture - based direct manipulation in Augmented Reality, *Proceedings of the 2nd international conference on Computer graphics and interactive techniques*, 15-18th June, ACM Press, New York, pp. 212-221.

Cooper, L.A. & Podgorny, P. (1976). Mental transformations and visual comparison process: Effects of complexity and similiarity, *Journal of Experimental Psychology: Human Perception and Performance*, 2(4), pp503-514.

Creamer, E. G. & Lattuca, L.R. (Eds.) (2005). *Advancing Faculty Learning Through Interdisciplinary Collaboration: New Directions for Teaching and Learning, No. 102.* New York: Wiley Periodicals.

Dunston, P.S. & Shin, D.H. (2009). "Key areas and issues for augmented reality applications on construction sites", in Wang, X. & Schnabel, M (eds.), Mixed Reality Applications in Architecture, Design, and Construction, Springer-Verlag, pp157-170.

Fischer, J. & Flohr, D. (2008). Selective Stylization for Visually Uniform Tangible AR, *in*B. Mohler and R. van Liere (ed), *EGVE Symposium08*, The Eurographics Association.

Hara, N. (2003). An emerging view of scientific collaboration: Scientists' perspectives on collaboration and factors that impact collaboration. *Journal of the American Society for Information Science and Technology, 54*(10), pp952–965.

Holm, I. (2006). *Ideas and Beliefs in Architecture and Industrial design: How Attitudes, Orientations, and Underlying Assumptions Shape the Built Environment*. Oslo School of Architecture and Design. ISBN 8254701741.

Ishii, H. & Ullmer, B. (2006). Tangible Bits: Towards Seamless Interfaces betweenPeople, Bits and Atoms, *CHI97*, March 22-27, ACM Press.

Mentzas, G. & Bafoutsou, G. (2004). Electronic collaboration, communication and cooperation: A taxonomy and a prototype. In E. Y. Li & T. C. Du (Eds.) *Advances in Electronic Business, Vol. 1, Theme: "Collaborative Commerce"*. (pp. 19-52). Idea Group Publishing.

Oliver, R. ; Herrington, J. & Reeves, T.C.(2007). Representing authentic learning designs: Supporting the development of online communities of learners. *Journal of Learning Design, 2*(2), pp1–21.

Shepard, R.N. (1992). Musing on telepresence and virtual presence, Presence; Telecoperators and Virtual Environments, 1(1), pp 120-126.

Sonnenwald, D. H. (2007). Scientific collaboration. In B. Cronin (Ed.). *Annual Review of Information Science and Technology, Vol 41* (pp. 643–681). Medford, New Jersey: Information Today.

Weiseth, P. E.; Munkvold, B. E.; Tvedte, B. & Larsen, S. (2006). The Wheel of Collaboration Tools: A typology for analysis within a holistic framework. *CSCW '06, Banff, Alberta, Canada.*